Life Worth Living

LIFE WORTH LIVING

SOME PHASES OF AN ENGLISHMAN

C. B. FRY

Introduction by Alan Ross

THE PAVILION LIBRARY

First published in Great Britain 1939

First published in the Pavilion Library in 1986 by
Pavilion Books Limited
196 Shaftesbury Avenue, London WC2H 8JL
in association with Michael Joseph Limited
44 Bedford Square, London WC1B 3DU

British Library Cataloguing in Publication Data
Fry, C. B.
Life worth living.
1. Fry, C. B.   2. Cricket players—
England—Biography
I. Title
796.35'8'0924   GV915.F7/

ISBN 1 85145 026 2
ISBN 1 85145 027 0 paperback

Printed and bound in Great Britain by
Billing & Sons Limited, Worcester

INTRODUCTION

Life Worth Living shows the best of C. B. Fry, because, unlike its garrulous author, it can be picked up and put down when you feel like it. For most of Charles Fry's long life he was a genial, hospitable and cultivated companion, able to talk knowledgeably on a variety of subjects and eccentrically on a number of others. He had a classically trained, inquiring, adventurous mind and he lived a life full of physical and, up to a point, intellectual challenge. He was magnificently built and noble in bearing and as an all-round athlete – at cricket, soccer, athletics and rugby especially – he was without equal in this century and probably in any other.

From *Life Worth Living* you will learn, in generally relaxed and entertaining fashion, all that Fry wished to tell you or could remember about a legendary existence from the early days of the century up to the outbreak of the Second World War. These 'phases of an Englishman', as he subtitled his book, take in such matters as public school and Oxford, cricket for Sussex and England, soccer for the Corinthians, his friendship and travels with Ranji in India and Geneva, hunting and shooting with Maharajahs, the running of the training ship *Mercury*, journalism, a meeting with Hitler, and a visit to Hollywood.

The style is fluent and anecdotal, the tone varying between the modest and self-deprecatory and the faintly hectoring. Fry's head was full of odd notions but he was a genuine enthusiast, a student in the real sense of the term. He could also be opinionated to a degree, high-handed and self-centred.

Grandees do not always wear well in real life, and Fry, a grandee in his heyday if there ever was one – Ranji called him 'Carlo' – was often considerably more wearing to listen to than to read.

There is no one alive now, I imagine, whose cricketing career overlapped with Fry's, though Gubby Allen got his blue at Cambridge the year after Fry, at the age of fifty, played his last first-class match. We have to take his stature therefore on trust and see him through the eyes of others. His performances, however, speak for themselves, especially in the golden summers with Ranji for Sussex. In comparison, though, with the Prince, he seems to have been a manufactured rather than a natural batsman, and as a bowler he was soon outlawed for throwing.

Life Worth Living appeared in 1939, since when two recent books have been published that tell one a great deal more about Fry than he chose to reveal himself: Clive Ellis's biography *C.B.* (1984) and Ronald Morris's *The Captain's Lady* (1985). In addition, there is Denzil Batchelor's *C. B. Fry*, written during Fry's lifetime.

Ellis's admirably sane and balanced account and Morris's extraordinary story of life as a Mercury cadet corroborate each other in essentials. The salient facts seem to be that Fry was little more than an amiable figurehead at *Mercury* during the fifty years that he was nominally in charge and that to all intents and purposes this training school for naval cadets was ruled, in the most austere and tyrannical fashion, by his wife Beatie.

Fry makes only the most fleeting references to his wife in *Life Worth Living*, usually of the order that 'my Madame', as he calls her, bowled to him in the garden or accompanied him to matches in which he was playing. What seems extraordinary about the relationship is that Fry, at the age of twenty-six, one of the most handsome and promising men in England, the possessor of a First in classics at Oxford, a future Test cricketer, with the world apparently at his feet, should have embarked on so strange an arrangement. Beatie Sumner, at the age of fifteen, had fallen in love with a dashing horseman and banker, Charles Hoare, married and twice her age. She eventually ran off with him after the expiration of a court order forbidding their relationship. They lived together for some years and had two children, perhaps even a third (the last officially credited to Fry). Hoare meanwhile had bought the *Mercury*, a renovated China tea-clipper, and turned it into a training ship. It would appear that when the sexual element between the High Anglican Hoare and Beatie waned it was replaced by religious fervour. Hoare was unable or unwilling to get a divorce, and Fry, then teaching at Charterhouse, took up with Beatie, marrying her in 1898. For some years Beatie moved between Fry and Hoare, but after Hoare's death in 1908 Fry moved permanently to the Hamble river and *Mercury*. At the time of their marriage, Beatie was thirty-six, ten years Fry's senior. Her early beauty was now camouflaged under unbecoming masculine clothes and the demeanour of a martinet. However, though their relationship was never judged romantic, she bore Fry two children, the last at the age of forty-eight.

In 1929, Fry experienced a severe nervous breakdown, 'thwarted genius' Beatie put it down to, which lasted nearly five years and reduced him to a pitiable state, often paranoiac and given to periods of wildly irrational behaviour. *Life Worth Living* makes no reference to any of this either, nor indeed to several unsuccessful attempts to become a Liberal Member of Parliament, a career that might well have brought out the worst in him. What Fry nevertheless did write about in *Life Worth Living*, and surprisingly retain through two subsequent editions, was the account of his 1934 meeting with Hitler and his starry-eyed attitude to Nazi morality and intentions. There was something decidedly naïve about much of Fry's thinking, a residue perhaps of that early allegiance to classic ideals that retards many of its adherents, rendering them insensitive to contemporary life. Fry, it seems, devoted to the classics as he was, was otherwise appallingly read, ignorant of nineteenth-century and modern fiction and poetry equally. One of the reasons behind his failure as a politician and often as an after-dinner speaker, was that he failed to do his homework and, despite moments of brilliance, came over rambling, idiosyncratic and unprepared. This was the exact opposite to his approach to the technicalities and techniques of games.

Life Worth Living is the more interesting to read now if we are aware of these omissions from the narrative. The vulnerability and insecurity add extra dimensions to one who had so much ostensibly going for him. No one wrote more evocatively about the glamorous side of Fry than Denzil Batchelor, his friend and one-time secretary: 'It is half-past ten: time for the caravan to start from Brown's Hotel. The Bentley is at the door; Mr Brooks, the chauffeur, is wise-cracking out of the side of his guttapercha mouth. Aboard are writing pads and binoculars and travelling rugs, a copy of Herodotus, a box of Henry Clay cigars and reserve hampers of hock and chicken sandwiches

. . . A monocle glitters. A silver crest passes, high and haughty, above the cities of the plain. C. B. Fry is off to Lord's.'

About the composing of *Life Worth Living* Batchelor observed: 'Charles wrote it, or more often than not, dictated it to me in his dressing gown and bedroom slippers between breakfast and lunch in his flat at Gloucester Place . . . He never re-cast the book, and he hardly re-wrote a sentence . . . The result was an autobiography in the round: more than a picture of its author – a glimpse or a touch of the living man in three dimensions. It gave to the world all he had done, all he had seen, much of what he enjoyed of the fun of the fair.'

Well, not quite all, as it turned out. But enough to be going on with for most people. 'You become a friend,' Batchelor observed, 'though not, I think, an intimate of the man who told the story.' That seems to me reasonable in the circumstances.

Fry, Gubby Allen observed, could be a very awkward man and he rubbed up enough people the wrong way to make enemies. He was never elected to the committee of the MCC, he quarrelled with his editors, publishers and agents, and he spent the greater part of his life in what most of his contemporaries considered to be, in relation to his gifts, a backwater. Yet, the missing dark moments aside, *Life Worth Living* gives off an air of immense well-being, the product of a mind consistently interested in the mechanics of grace – scientific, sporting, intellectual. Not for nothing did Fry know the engine of a car inside out, or all about wireless waves; it was entirely in keeping with his questing intellect that he should have taken lessons in dancing as a means of improving his footwork and at one stage toyed with training racehorses. For someone who turned down a Kingdom he was no snob when it came to rolling up his sleeves and learning a new trade.

Alan Ross, 1986

LIFE WORTH LIVING

SOME PHASES OF AN ENGLISHMAN

BY

C. B. FRY

CONTENTS

CHAPTER I

ORIGINS OF AN ENGLISHMAN

IN common with an easy majority of my countrymen I
have it that my ancestors did not come over with William
the Conqueror; they were here to meet him when he landed.
This claim may have been made by others; but in my case it
happens to be as capable of proof as anything so far away can
be. The proof consists in the certainty that even up to the
middle of the seventeenth century the Weald of Sussex was
so devoid of roads that the people who were there, unless rich
and powerful, had to stay there. Inasmuch as the family from
which I derive are recorded as inhabiting one of the few
clearings in the great Forest of the Ridge in the early Middle
Ages, there is no doubt whatever that they must have been
there as long as you like before. I therefore claim to be a
Weald man of the Forest Ridge of Sussex and of ancient Saxon
stock.

You must know that in olden days the kingdom—not the
county, please—of Sussex consisted of a narrow strip of coast-
land, mostly sea-marsh, with patches of sound and conquerable
soil, the latter selected as landing-places by such adventurers
as Julius Cæsar and William of Falaise, between the long
range of the South Downs and the sea; of these Downs themselves; and north of the Downs of a wilderness of impenetrable
forest 120 miles long by 30 broad, extending inland up to the
North Downs. This forest in Saxon times was called the
Andredsweald, which means the uninhabited woodland.
Along the northern edge of this, more or less parallel with
the South Downs, rose the Forest Ridge which began on the
borders of Hampshire and extended eastwards till it forked
off into Kent and south-eastward down to the Sussex coast
near Hastings—roughly speaking, of course; and it was a rough
country. Round about the times of the Saxon chroniclers and
Doomsday Book it appears that there were only some half-
dozen clearings in all the Weald, and one of these was known

as Ridrefeld, which learned linguists say means "The open country where the horned cattle feed," and which is now called Rotherfield. The district includes Mayfield and Crowborough. You can see all this in the map attached to the Issued Doomsday Book for Sussex.

Now the clearing of Rotherfield was like the other clearings in the Andredsweald in that it lies near the headwaters of one of the slow-flowing Sussex rivers. Sussex is divided into strips of about equal size by five south-running rivers: the Arun, which finds the sea at Littlehampton, the Adur at Shoreham, the Ouse at Seaford, the Cuckmere not far from Beachy Head, and the Rother at Rye. They are not great rivers, but they have had their uses. Other eminent authorities may have other opinions, but I say the history of inland Sussex is that the ancient British inhabitants along the coast-strip used their coracles to push inland as far as they could go northwards up the rivers, and they were the people who started the little clearings near the headwaters of these streams. It was the only way they could penetrate the great Forest; and no doubt when they could go no further in their small boats they followed the streams on foot, as is the habit of those who explore blind woodlands, because if you follow a stream in your adventure you can always find your way back. When the Romans disturbed the aborigines and planted themselves at Chichester and Pevensey and other chosen spots along the coast, I have no doubt that the rightful owners of the soil took refuge up the rivers and along their forest paths; at any rate, there is trace of the Romans in most of the ancient clearings. No doubt the Romans followed them to their lairs. When the Saxons came and occupied the shore (already called Saxon to prevent them adopting it in person) they too pushed up the rivers as far as they were navigable and then followed the tracks up the streams. Hence the Saxon clearings along the Forest Ridge.

What happened to the other clearings is immaterial, but a Saxon "duke," which in those days meant just a military chief of a district, Berthwald by name, was in possession of the district of Rotherfield about a hundred and fifty years before the Conquest. He and his followers were the fathers of the rest of the history of Rotherfield, and if one of his no doubt more honourable retainers was not an ancestor of mine I do not know who was. There is a legend in my family that one of our forefathers was the Saxon soldier who helped his Queen to find the body of King Harold after the Battle of Hastings. (King Harold was not shot in the eye by a high-angle arrow. He was wounded in the groin, and his Queen found him on the field and William allowed her to take him away for burial.) But I cannot vouch for the truth of this except in so far that no legend arises from nothing.

The point of all this is that my family name under the guise of Le Fre comes into documentary evidence at Mayfield and Rotherfield about the time of Henry III and on to the time of Elizabeth, and that its owners must have been hard-working honest folk, because by the time of George I they had succeeded in possessing themselves of a certain amount of land and other substance, so that finally they and their allied family of Burges, sometimes by the lawful process of intermarriage, became possessed of one of the manors and several of the quasi-manor houses thereabouts. These grey stone houses were not great ones, but they were beautiful, and you would have much annoyed any of their possessors unless you called him Squire.

For instance, old Rother House at one time belonged to us; it is gone now, but when it was there the river Rother rose in its cellars. This was not the only river that rose nearby. A main tributary of the Medway and a main tributary of the Ouse have their source within a circle of a couple of miles. Another of our houses was Brook House close by Jarvis Brook. And to show you our antiquity you should note that when they were boring for Crowborough waterworks close by Jarvis Brook they discovered in the blue galt clay the solid footprints of a great bird, now preserved in the British Museum, which resembled those of an ostrich but were three times the size with a stride of seventy inches. That carries you back to ante-diluvian times and the cavemen. Then there was Walshes Manor, which originally belonged to the Fermor family but came into our possession a hundred and fifty years ago and remained ours till the death of my grandfather. Then there was Skipper's Hill near Mayfield, which at one time belonged to my father and I wish it belonged to me, but it does not because my father sold it to Edward Lloyd, the singer, and he sold it to Lord Hood, and he sold it to a Mr. Nicholson. When I was a small boy I saw the ancient manor of Walshes and it seemed a wonderful world—especially as the huge stone farmyard with an enormous black-and-white bull chewing straw was adjacent to the back door. Skipper's Hill I saw during several holidays from school. A squat, rambling super-farmhouse. A small park sloped down to the valley with Crowborough beacon in the distance. A dining-room with a low ceiling and heavy oak beams and an open fireplace nearly as big as the room itself. Behind the great barn abutting on the house there was a clump of tall trees and a pond, the bottom of which consisted of generations of fallen leaves. On the pond was one uncompanionable Muscovy drake. Alongside the clump of trees was a sparse orchard with the finest sea of daffodils in Sussex. After all these generations all that I, the eldest son, now possess in the ancient Saxon clearing is a pew in Rotherfield Church. That is the result of generation after generation of five sons and four daughters. In that part of the world they divide up inheritances.

Skipper's Hill was the excuse of my residential qualification to play cricket for Sussex, but you will agree with me, having read what I have written above, that the accident of my mother being in Surrey when I was born was a very good reason why Surrey should ask me to play in one match and then cast me away to the territory of my forefathers. The truth is that technically I had no qualification for Sussex at all, but equitably I certainly had a right to play for that county because I do not see how anybody can be more Sussex than I am. Skipper's Hill now belongs to Mrs. Nicholson, the widow of the purchaser. This is very interesting because the name of the house was due to it being formerly one of the farm-manorhouses used as a safe-deposit by the smugglers. When my father lived there for a few years the spacious cellars still contained a large consignment of gin of the kind known as square-face. These cellars were at one time connected with a long underground passage to an outlying farm building.

Thus it is discovered that my forefathers were connected with the highly respectable industry of smuggling. Indeed, I suspect that their rural prosperity and reasonable ownership of land were not entirely due to successful farming. In common with most of the squires, farmers, and clergy of Sussex during the seventeenth and eighteenth centuries they were financiers and promoters of fair trade. They seem to have been directly concerned with the better kind of smuggling. This was the illicit export to France and Holland of wool. Indirectly they were behind the tougher but still illicit import of tea, spirits, tobacco, and silk. The successful growth of smuggling in Sussex was due not only to the length of its accessible sea coast all the way from Selsey to Rye, but to the ancient characteristic of this land, the paucity of roads, and the impenetrable woods. In Roman times those best of road-makers succeeded in engineering only two main roads and two subsidiaries. One main road they led from Chichester along the coast to Southampton and then northwards through Winchester. The other, from Pevensey eastwards into Kent, joining up with Watling Street, which runs from Dover to Chester. So the Forest of the Weald withstood any frontal attack even from the Romans. In the time of Charles II there were only four roads mentioned in a Command Survey. Even as late as 1731 the Sussex Itinerary Map of that time shows only three high roads laid down from London to the sea coast. Lateral communications seem to have been mere cattle-tracks. Defoe, writing in 1724, says that a tree felled in the Ashdown Forest had to be drawn "on a tug" by twenty-two oxen, and even then took two or three years to get to Chatham. He also says that he saw an ancient lady of quality being drawn to church by six oxen, "the way being so stiff and deep that no horses could go in it."

The smugglers transported their cargoes up the forest tracks, probably the relics of the ancient Saxon trails up the river valleys. That is why so many of the inland distributing centres were at the head of the rivers, and one of them was at Skipper's Hill at the head of the Ouse and Rother.

The illicit export of wool was lucrative. The inland squires and farmers had sheep land on the flat shore country and on the Downs or else part shares in flocks. There were sometimes 40,000 bales of wool awaiting export at Rye and Hastings and other ports; and it is recorded that in one year there were 140,000 sheep ready for shearing whose fleeces would be in France almost before they were cold. I believe that my respectable forefathers became involved in the liquor trade through owning, as they did, patches of sheep land by the seashore. No one could see any dishonour in exporting wool, and perhaps there was no way of getting paid except in spirituous kind. At any rate, the squires and farmers all over Sussex depended on smuggled imports for many of the articles nowadays regarded as necessaries. In extenuation I call particular attention to the depth to which the local clergy were implicated. For example, there is the story that one vicar had to pretend that he was ill in bed all Sunday because his church was full of kegs. Whence could the Sussex ladies otherwise obtain their silk and lace, and the gentlemen their bandana handkerchiefs? So it was that Huskisson, the statesman, long before the days of Cobden and Bright, told the House of Commons all about Free Trade. "Honourable Members," he said, "are well aware that bandana handkerchiefs are prohibited by law, and yet," he went on, pulling a bright specimen from his pocket (loud laughter), "I have no doubt there is not a gentleman in the House who has not got a bandana handkerchief."

The export smuggling of wool was chiefly a matter between gentry, farmers, and shipmen; wool was not an illicit product stored in bales near seaports; and the ships, though occasionally boarded, were fairly safe at sea, as they mostly made their crossings at night. It was the gangs of land smugglers of liquor and silk who created a perpetual state of warfare with the Revenue Officers in their dangerous job of running their pack-animals up-country. Where, by the way, could they have obtained the quantity of ponies, horses, and donkeys they required for this traffic without the good-will of the land-owners and farmers?

The most famous gang who terrorised the countryside and committed several atrocious murders was known as the Hawkhurst gang. Hawkhurst is a village in Kent, but it is known that most of the operatives were Sussex men. Another famous party was the Alfriston gang. All Sussex went in for smuggling, but the little village of Alfriston, just inland of Cuckmerehaven, near Seaford, made it an industry. This was the gang which worked up the Cuckmere valley and thence via Burwash, where Rudyard Kipling used to live, to the neighbourhood of Mayfield and Rotherfield. Their chief was one Stanton Collins, of whom many a story of audacity not unmixed with humour is told, and who ended his career with a sentence of seven years for sheep stealing. The last of his gang, Bob Hall, aged 94, died in a workhouse at Eastbourne when I was an undergraduate at Oxford. So smuggling in Sussex is not so far away from us.

There was another Sussex industry about which even the honesty of modern times cannot cavil. The man who saw the last iron furnace in Sussex finally extinguished at Ashburnham, near Battle, in 1813, died at Hastings when I was a boy. So neither are the days when the Weald of Sussex was the Black Country of England very far away. All along the fringe of the Forest Ridge, from Blackdown in the west past Horsham and along to Crowborough and then down to the sea at Hastings, were dotted the forges and foundries, generally included in the old annals under the title of iron mills. The cannon with which Drake and Lord Howard of Effingham fought the ponderous galleons of Spain in the Armada were cast in Sussex. So too were the guns which Prince Rupert, Monk, and the Duke of York slogged the Dutch in Stuart times. Almost all the ploughshares and other farm implements were forged in Sussex; the old railings round St. Paul's Cathedral were Sussex iron. There were forges and mills round our old homes in Mayfield and Rotherfield and our big open fireplaces were backed with moulded Sussex irons. I remember well as a boy hearing some names of our farms such as Muddle's Furnace and Ordnance Corner. The conjoined families of Fry and Burges did not include any of the big iron-masters, but sundry of their members were interested in the mills. One can still see traces of the watershoots down from the hammer ponds, formed by damming up a stream on the side of a hill, which used to turn the wheels to actuate the bellows of the furnace and to lift the stamps which broke up the ore.

The Sussex iron industry dates back, it is said, to Roman times. In Tudor days there were royal promulgations dealing with the transport of iron and the mending of Sussex roads for that heavy purpose. It was the felling of the forests for fuel that broke up the impenetrable Weald and perhaps opened up the way for you to Brighton and Eastbourne.

Not the least famous name in the Iron Age of Sussex was St. Dunstan. The most authentic legend about this Archbishop of Canterbury is that he elected by way of asceticism to live in a cave at Mayfield. Some people say he lived in a cell, but the other is the better version. In either case when it was found that his chapel was badly oriented he leant against the wall with his shoulder to put it straight. The story that he was fashioning a gold chalice when the Devil called and he nipped his highness by the nose is incorrect. So too is the yarn that the chalybeate spring at Tunbridge Wells originated from the Devil rushing to a stream there to foment his injured organ. The true story is that St. Dunstan was a blacksmith, and that when the Devil looked in at the window of his forge he was hammering a horseshoe. Pretending not to notice his visitor, he casually took his tongs and returned the horseshoe to his furnace and warmly applied himself to his bellows. Then he suddenly whipped out the red-hot tongs and pinned the Devil by the nose. The Devil did not hurry to Tunbridge Wells. He traversed Sussex southwards in wild convolutions (towards his proper home in France) with the Saint firmly attached. In his final efforts for freedom he ran up to the top of the Downs and flogged a high hill with his tail. He carved out the huge dent now so well known as the Devil's Dyke.

I do not claim either of these athletes as my ancestor.

CHAPTER II

BREAKING IN

K ENT is not Sussex: only next door to it. Nor is suburban Kent quite Kent itself.

To-day the pleasant countryside round about Chislehurst and Orpington is scored with black weals; arterial roads connecting everywhere with everywhere, and especially with London.

Only about twelve miles from Charing Cross; and Charing Cross is the station to which some of the slowest trains in the world were said to run a great many years ago, when I used to watch them from our garden alongside the temptation of the shining rails disappearing into the black mouth of Chislehurst tunnel. We lived in those days just beyond this hole in a sandy hill.

If you went out of our garden gate on the other side from the railway, you found a new sandy road leading down a steep little hill to the lower end of Camden Park. The main road turned right under the railway, away towards Bromley.

If you climbed over the railings and went straight on up the slope of turf you came to Camden House, where the Empress Eugenie lived with her son, the Prince Imperial. I used to see the Empress, a slim little lady, with a sunshade, walking in the gardens. She once came and spoke to our nurse who was wheeling a perambulator, and inclusively to me, on the other side of the fence at the edge of the lawn. I can remember her beautiful violet eyes. She was pale, and walked just as a little boy would expect an Empress to walk. The young Prince Imperial one met any forenoon strolling in the Park. He was a handsome and attractive youth, and always said "Good-morning" with a friendly smile. He often stopped and spoke to me, and nearly always asked, "What are you going to do this afternoon, young man—games?" Years afterwards, when he was killed in Zululand while attached to the British troops, I can remember feeling quite shocked, as if someone I knew very well had died.

Away beyond Camden House was the mysterious wilderness of Chislehurst Common; immense, covered with furze and heather and occasional patches of small birch trees. But this wider world was beyond experience until several years afterwards, when my home had been transferred one station down the line to Orpington. Then I was sent to school at Hornbrook House, facing the big pond in West Chislehurst.

There were two Chislehursts, with a long stretch of common in between: West Chislehurst, on the way to London, and, at the other end, Old Chislehurst, on the road to Sevenoaks. Beyond Old Chislehurst was another stretch of common wooded with birch trees; a bush country full of birds' nests. But five miles further on round my new home at Orpington, among strawberry-fields and hop-gardens, was another sort of country of small rolling hills with hazel hedges and thick hazel copses, where there were fewer birds' nests but innumerable blackbirds and thrushes and sparrows.

Psychologists, why did one so fond of birds so keenly pursue sparrows with a catapult? I suppose that the impulse to stalk small birds sitting on hazel twigs is exactly the same instinct of pursuit which one detected in oneself a quarter of a century later, when sitting in a machan in the jungle waiting for the ghost-like contour of a panther to emerge into the moonlight. But one never shot a song-bird; only sparrows and starlings. There are such a lot of sparrows; and sparrows are not very kind to one another; and starlings are bird vermin. And again, after all, if later on one shoots driven partridges with a double-barrelled gun, need one in early youth be ashamed of shooting sitting sparrows with a bijou catapult? I am not sure.

One makes mistakes and one suffers correction. I was walking along the lane at the bottom of our garden one November afternoon by the gate of a long avenue leading up to the large red house, in the grounds of which the original Mr. Cook invented and cultivated the world-famous Buff Orpingtons. I was looking out for sparrows, when suddenly a little bird flew up from behind the oak fence, and I knocked it over

with a snapshot just as one might shoot a rabbit crossing a
ride. It was a bit of a fluke. The bird fell on the far side of
the fence. As I stepped forward to collect the bird, a quiet
voice just behind me said, "That was a good shot, but you
shouldn't shoot little robins."

There in the road by me stood a tall thin man dressed in
black broadcloth. He wore a wide-brimmed black felt hat
like a clergyman's, and indeed had all the appearance of a
Nonconformist preacher. He had a long, strikingly kind face,
rather like Matthew Arnold, and strangely searching grey
eyes.

"I thought it was a sparrow," I said.

"No. It's a robin."

So I went round through the gate, and a robin it was. But
when I looked over the fence there was no one there. I went
into the road and looked up and down, but there was no one
to be seen; and in the time available there was nowhere for
my sudden stranger to have turned out of sight. What is
more, there had been no one in sight up and down the road
the moment before I shot the bird. Where did he come
from? Where did he go? Who was he? But I never again
shot at a bird without looking.

Dangerous pursuits are learned from unlikely tutors. My
mother's father, Dr. Charles White, a Fellow of Jesus College,
Cambridge, was invited to St. Petersburg as tutor to the
Prince, who afterwards became the Czar Alexander II, and
whose life was ended by a nihilist bomb. When the Prince
grew up, my grandfather came back to England and started
one of the earliest successful private schools near Brighton,
called Hove Lodge. A large, square, whitewashed house with
playgrounds and schoolrooms behind; now unrecognisable in
the extended guise of semi-modern flats. To Hove Lodge I
used to go as a very small boy, in order to get a bad bilious
attack and be dosed with syrup of senna by Dr. Dill, and on
recovery to live on the fringe of some forty boys, who after
my grandfather's death were taught Homer and Vergil by
my uncle Percy White, the novelist. When he shed the boys
and took to writing novels no one of his time was a better
stylist in the English language. He owed his style to Homer

and Vergil, and his complete mastery of French literature. He could write good French prose in English. He was a cricketer, and played for the Gentlemen of Sussex; but he did not teach me cricket: he taught me to shoot with a catapult.

The boys used to make perfect catapult prongs carved out of the tops of cigar-boxes, shaped and polished. The square catapult elastic came from a little shop in Hove Street which purported to sell sweets. The pouch for the shot was made from a strip of dogskin glove, bound on with a finer elastic, and the two ends were similarly bound to the ends of the prongs. The neatest little weapons you ever saw, and instruments of precision. An expert could hit a shilling every time at ten yards' distance. I was an expert. Whenever one of the boys was caught with a catapult the weapon was confiscated, and the iniquity pungently stressed by Percy White. There were always several catapults in the big desk in Percy White's study. Percy White it was who made a target of blotting-paper with one blob in the middle, and taught me to shoot. He strictly enjoined me never to shoot at birds. But how could a student of Fenimore Cooper surrounded by hazel copses at Orpington leave the sparrows alone?

First a shooter, then a trapper. Rake's progress. There was no method of catching wild birds I did not study; but I did let the birds go—even the sparrows and starlings. Dawn of reason. My one unsatisfied ambition was to capture birds with bird-lime. I never could obtain any satisfactory stuff. My best success was achieved by boiling down mistletoe berries into a sort of jelly. I never actually caught a bird with this, but I got several starlings into considerable difficulties with themselves. A lesser effort was when I visited all the grocers' shops and tried to buy bird-lime. The only grocer in Orpington, Mrs. Popplewell, shook her head and denied that she had ever heard of it. So I walked all the long way to St. Mary Cray, and there an astute elderly grocer promptly lifted down a jar, planked some sticky-looking stuff into brown paper, and handed it to me for twopence. When I had marched hopefully home I showed it to our gardener, old Siney, whom I had previously consulted on the subject. Old Siney cackled for a minute into his beard before he told me it was soft soap. If the ready wit of the grocer at St. Mary Cray did not achieve him a fortune he got less than his deserts.

Nevertheless it was not shootin' or limin', but fishin' that most possessed me when small. A colleague of my father at Scotland Yard, a nephew of the great Cambridge scholar Shillito, used to come to stay for week-ends. He gave me a very fat book called *Every Boy's Book*. One section of this was devoted to fishing, and I learned to read for the sake of studying it. I knew the section on chub, dace, and every other kind of freshwater fish by heart, and eventually I persuaded my father to give me a fishing-rod. It was of the elementary kind, of which the top joint fits inside the middle joint and the middle joint inside the butt. It had no fittings for a reel; I had a float and a line wound round a flat spool. One had to tie the line to the top ring.

I fished many times in a pond at Orpington where the river Cray rises just behind Orpington Priory, but I never caught anything. One day, after about ten fruitless afternoons, our governess, a rosy-cheeked girl with smooth black hair, who walked every morning about five miles from Lock's Bottom and was called Alice, casually told me that she had seen boys catch fish in Keston Fishponds. She did not know what they were, but they were fish. Now, Keston Fishponds were over by Hayes Common, some six miles north of our house, but at the first chance I stepped off to Keston Fishponds. I used to walk the colossal distance there and back, and I did it eight times before I came back with a single, very small roach; and I went another five times before I caught a second. But nothing would have stopped me. The excitement of watching a float was an obsession.

One summer holiday we went to stay in North Wales, at Paenmaenmawr, near Conway. I had persuaded my father that we would try to catch trout, so he bought for himself a very whippy hickory fly-rod. He purported to know about trout-fishing, because when he was at our old home at Rotherfield (when I was four), he used to catch trout in the little streams with deep pools which thread the rich meadows between Crowborough and Mayfield. Not with a fly, however, but with a garden worm. He also told a story of how he was once fishing in a mill pool near Mayfield for perch. His float bobbed, and he struck. He missed the fish, but when he lifted his line there was a round object on the hook instead of the bait. This proved to be the eye of the fish impaled like a cherry. So accurate was the emplacement that he thought he would fish with the eye as bait. Ten minutes afterwards his float went down again, and this time he hooked his fish, a perch of half a pound—and it was the perch which had lost its eye. I must have been about seven when he told me that story, and he was the kind of man who could not possibly have invented so good a yarn. Fifty-seven years afterwards I met two ladies named Fenton at Adelaide, who had been in Australia for over fifty years. They had come to meet me at the house of Don Bradman's stockbroker friend at Adelaide. They knew all about the fish story and corroborated it in detail.

However, when we got to Paenmaenmawr I had some trouble in finding out about trout-fishing. It was a weary week before I happened to see a lot of small trout on the slab of a fish-monger's shop. I went in and asked the proprietor where they had come from and where I could catch some like them. He told me that there was a man named Jones at Dwchwlchy, a little place otherwise called the Fairy Glen, and Jones knew all about trout. So we walked over to the Fairy Glen and saw Jones. Jones talked mostly Welsh.

My father arranged for him to come over the next day and take us fishing. He turned up after breakfast with an old creel tied up with string slung over his shoulder, and no apparent rod, and he took us down the line several stations towards Bangor to a place called Aber where a sizeable pellucid stream ran into the Menai Straits. We walked inland several miles till we came to the Aber Falls, climbed up a steep cliff, and there was the stream again, a yard wide, but with fine pools at intervals of about a hundred yards. You could see every brown pebble in the clear water. Then Mr. Jones pro-duced from the pocket in the tail of his drab gamekeeper's coat a bundle of short rod-joints, six in all. These he fitted together. He had made the rod himself out of hazel wood. On the butt was an elementary brass reel whipped on with

string. He had a hemp line such as one fishes with in the sea.
To this he attached about four feet of rather thick gut, and
tied on two flies, a grey spider, and a black gnat.

He then proceeded to show us how to fish. He approached
a pool, bending low, and with rather a short line he fished
upstream with short delicate casts, tripping his flies down
exactly in time with the water. He conjured two or three
little trout out of every pool. When we turned home in the
afternoon he had filled his creel. My father caught nothing,
though he was persuaded to go in front to the best of the
pools. I caught one trout of about a quarter of a pound, the
biggest of the lot. I caught it with a worm, by dropping the
worm over a steep little bank, and I suppose it was the only
time I did not show myself to every trout in reach. When we
got back downstream near the little inn at Aber, having
passed a dozen fishermen who had caught nothing, we saw a
lady fishing in a longish shallow pool. She asked us whether
we had caught anything. She had a beautiful new rod. Jones
showed her the contents of his creel. The lady was so surprised
that she asked him to look at her flies. He did. She had a
new brown leather fly-book full of patterns. Jones took her
rod and said he would try the flies. He stooped along to the
tail of the pool, where the lady had been standing still casting
repeatedly for the last half-hour, and he picked out three
trout in half a dozen casts. He then came back and took my
father's rod, and, beginning half-way up the pool, he picked
out another three trout. He came back to us and said, " 'T' flies
are good."

Mind you, it was a cloudless August evening with a very
bright sun, and the water was as clear as gin. At the inn were
several fishermen, who were amazed at the contents of what
we called our creel. No one else except the lady had caught
a fish, and she had not done it herself.

Of all the fishermen I have seen, in many years, beside all
sorts of rivers in all sorts of country, Jones of the Fairy Glen
was the best. As we went home in the train, he remarked
that we should have got more fish if we had all gone steadily
at the little red worm.

We went often with Jones to the streams in the neighbourhood, the best being at Glen Conway, over by the big river. Jones never failed to fill his creel, and when we went for the little red worms which he brought in a small bag filled with moss, he seemed to pick out a trout every time he cast his worm. He fished with a very short line, and always kept his line taut as he followed the worm downstream towards himself. I saw him pick out trout within a yard of his own boots. He had a wraithlike knack of keeping out of sight of the fish. He was a marvel.

About this time I used to watch net practice exhibited on a tennis lawn by two of the best local cricketers. I could see from a top window in our house. I can remember the peculiar attraction, amounting to a thrill, of the sound of willow against hard leather. Psychologists will note that this thrill released some instinctive impulse in the small boy, who for the life of him could not have restrained himself from running down the garden the first time, and always afterwards, whenever he heard that sound, to watch the game over the thick quickset hedge. I had never had a bat of my own, or a ball, or played cricket; but the appeal was immediate and irresistible. One of the players was Oliver Evans, a relation of the fast bowler who played for Oxford, A. E. Evans. The other was George Allen, the son of Ruskin's publisher, whose house was next to ours along the road leading from Orpington to Green Street Green. Oliver Evans was quite a good bowler, successful in the best club cricket, and young Allen went in first for Orpington. Allen had been at Ardingly School, and was a contemporary of George Brann, with whom I used to go in first afterwards for Sussex. Allen was the only cricketer I ever saw play in white flannel shorts and stockings, but he played forward like Fuller Pilch.

About the twentieth time that my head appeared behind the net over the quickset hedge, Oliver Evans invited me to come round and have a knock. I was soon out through the gate into the road, and round on to the tennis lawn. I batted with a full-sized bat to the underhand bowling of these two swells for nearly ten minutes. I did not move my bat much, but kept the ball out of the wicket. That was how I began, and afterwards these kindly cricketers always asked me to come across for a knock after their practice in the summer evenings.

Naturally I never missed seeing them play when there was a match on the village ground in Orpington, and towards the end of what was my second season, although a very small boy, I was asked to fill up the team one Saturday afternoon when they were short of a man. I went in last, and made 17 not out (not that I moved my bat much except to hit to leg). That was my first cricket match. We drew the game with the last man in.

It was that summer that I discovered I could jump: both high and long—for my size. One day the nurse who looked after my brother and younger sister annoyed me very much by taking me along to see a school treat in a field behind the Vicarage in Orpington. It was a long walk down the dusty road, for the roads there were flint-made, and the grey-white dust used to powder the hedges in summer. You went under the railway, past the station, and came to the long one-streeted village, and half-way along you turned to the right up a cul-de-sac at the end of which was Orpington Church. On the left hand of the Church lane was Orpington Priory, a beautiful old house which now belongs to C. E. Hughes, who was my sub-editor on *Fry's Magazine*. On the right, opposite, was the Vicar's house, and behind it the Vicar's field. Among other entertainments for a pack of noisy village children was a high jump, staged for the boys. The curate who was running the show, being short of entrants, invited me to compete, and I won with ease by about a foot, and went away with half a crown, thereby constituting myself a professional. But I began immediately to take an interest in jumping, and rigged up two posts and a lath, and I soon discovered how much better one can jump off a lawn with bare feet than with shoes. That was the high jump.

Now it happened that there was always at my home a bull-terrier called Joe. There were several Joes. The last and the best had a brown patch over one eye, an underhung jaw and a short tail, and everywhere fought every dog he met. This Joe one day fought a Pomeranian in Orpington Station, and the Pomeranian fell over the platform, but his jaws and Joe's were locked. After a protracted struggle Joe for once let go, and the Pomeranian disappeared up the long straight stretch of rails towards Chislehurst. I remember thinking of these rails years afterwards, when someone tried to make me understand parallel straight lines. Joe came home with me just out of reach, very pleased with himself, but he was badly hurt and died of lockjaw. This loss weighed upon me much, and to please me my father bought a dog from the local rat-catcher. Dan had bowlegs and one wall eye, and tried to bite any postman or policeman who came near him. He was the ratter of the century. He sat as still as a cat and took no notice of the ferret. When a rat bolted he projected himself like a white flash. He attached himself to me, but was rather a nuisance, because he was a great hand at discovering blackbirds' and thrushes' nests near the ground, and he used to eat the entire clutch of eggs like a bowl of soup.

One evening he came with me up our long narrow garden, through the little wicket gate at the top, and up the high bank into the meadow. While I was strolling about looking, in fact, into the Allens' garden at their bees, Dan was hunting in the hedge, and presently came out. I noticed that he was foaming at the mouth. There had been hydrophobia in the neighbourhood, and there was even a report that some of the hounds in the West Kent Kennels near Otford had been infected. This sort of thing acts like lightning in a boy's mind, so I ran half a dozen strides, cleared the sloping top of the bank and the high hedge half-way down it, landed in the soft earth, and was up a Victoria plum-tree before Dan, who was looking at me from the top of the bank, knew what was up. (I was.) He went on champing his mouth, foaming, and wagging his tail, and then came slowly down the steep little path and sat at the bottom of the tree. Presently I saw my father, who had come back from London by the evening train. I shouted to him that Dan was foaming at the mouth. My father, as usual to anything I said, twirled his golden moustaches and shouted, "Nonsense!" but he came up the garden in his black morning coat and London trousers carrying an overcoat and a pudding-basin of water in the other hand. Shielding his legs with the overcoat, he presented the water to Dan, who immediately lapped up the lot. So I came down, though Dan was certainly still foaming. While we were looking at him he turned away, went up the bank, and brought back a large toad which he deposited for our admiration. I then went back to see where I had jumped, and I was astonished at the distance I had cleared from the top of the bank over the intermediate hedge. That is how I found out that I was a long jumper; and it also shows the value of a really ugly dog like Dan.

Dan's predecessor, Joe, who fought the Pomeranian, used to meet me every Saturday at ten minutes past one at the gate at the bottom of our drive. Every Saturday, as sure as the train puffed away down the line towards Chelsfield, Joe was at the gate wagging his entire body. He never went down to the gate at any other time. It is quite useless for any psychologist to tell me that he did not know the day of the week and the time of day.

But I did not always go home by train. One Saturday, having received my weekly sixpence for my railway ticket, I did not wend down towards Chislehurst Station. Being short of catapult elastic, which I knew could be obtained at a toyshop in Old Chislehurst, I decided to walk all the way home and spend my journey-money in refurnishing my armament. So I stepped out the considerable distance through Old Chislehurst, and away across St. Paul's Cray Common all the way to Orpington. Nobody at home took any notice of my being late, but I made the mistake that afternoon of eating a lot of small sweet yellow apples, which grew on a tree in quantities in our little orchard. The consequence was that I had a severe stomach-ache on Sunday, so much so that the doctor was sent for, and further my mother judged me unfit to return to school on Monday, and wrote to the school to say so. And being rather annoyed, she added some animadversion on my having walked home on the Saturday instead of coming by train. As if that had given me the stomach-ache.

When I returned to my school, Hornbrook House, on Tuesday, I was greeted with severe displeasure by Mrs. Humphrey, the Headmaster's wife. At noon I was ordered to attend in the study. There I was severely censured. I was made to understand that if I was not a thief I was the next worse thing. That the lady had suspected there was something wrong with me on the Saturday morning, because she noticed that my left eyelid was drooping, which she averred was always a bad sign in me.

I tried to explain that I honestly thought that if I did not mind the trouble of walking home, there was no harm in my saving the railway fare.

This was a mistake, because I was at once asked what I had done with the money. This was a poser; so I said that I had spent it at the toyshop in Old Chislehurst, which was strictly true.

The lady then asked me what I meant by behaving like this.

I said I did not know.

This was fatal. I was asked what I meant by saying I did not know, and clearly told I was not only next door to a thief, but pitifully untruthful.

I was given two dozen multiplication sums out of school. The point of the episode was that never in the whole of my life have I felt so poignantly the bitterness of injustice. I am not sure whether to this day I have quite forgiven that Roman matron. The humour of it was that nobody ever found out that I had bought catapult elastic.

Two things I am certain of. Nothing on the part of parents or other authorities who purport to have the interests of a boy at heart has a worse effect than to make him feel the pangs of injustice. The other is that it is bad for a boy to be a weekly boarder and come home for week-ends. I have never in my life hated anything as much as going back to Hornbrook House at Chislehurst by the 8.30 train on Monday morning. The reason I was sent to Hornbrook House in order to be educated by Mr. and Mrs. Humphrey was that my mother told my father that I was getting out of control; she never knew where I was from morning till night (due to hazel copses and Keston Fishponds); my father met a man in the train who told him that Hornbrook House was the nearest school to Orpington he knew of. So there I went.

It was one of the old-fashioned dames' schools. "Old

Cribber " was the owner, but the school was run by the magnificent Roman matron, his wife. There were about forty boys, and they ranged from the age of nineteen to the age of nine. There was one assistant master named Caleb William Bowles, and a fugitive young lady who taught French and music. The education was on what we should now call commercial lines—that is to say, there was no Greek, little Latin, and a lot of arithmetic. The house was one of the usual large desirable residences dotted round West Chislehurst Common, with a garden behind. The house faced the main road towards West Chislehurst Pond, on which there were always seven white Aylesbury ducks.

" Old Cribber " came of farming stock; I heard his wife say that as a young man he could lift a sack of corn and load it into a cart as one would pick up a satchel. But he had had some disease of the hip, and was a bent old man with a long white beard and a dome-like forehead. He walked with a limp due to a shortened leg, and carried a thick stick with a heavy brass ferrule. He always wore a broadcloth frock-coat and trousers. His beard covered where his tie ought to have been. He was reputed to have written a monumental work on chemistry, the manuscript of which, about eight inches deep, tied up with pink tape, resided dustily on a shelf in his study. His chief interest in life was his chicken-run at the end of the garden. Twice a day, from the big schoolroom where we spent our indoor life, we used to see him stumping across the middle of the lawn through the opening in the laurels, with a large iron bowl full of bits and pieces from the kitchen. In his spare time he taught the top class arithmetic and geography.

Mrs. Humphrey was a six-footer. She ran all the domestic economy and everything else, including arithmetic in the bottom class. She had very smooth grey hair with a bun at the back, and always wore a white muslin cap with black ribbon inserted round the edge. She is the only woman I have ever really been afraid of. For some reason she did not like me, hated my inability to do long division of money, and always made me feel that I had no ambition in life except to deceive her; whereas in fact I should never have thought of trying anything so foolish. Once, having done all the examples in addition of money, I virtuously wrote out some sums for myself to do. This was fatal, because I put down figures like 23 shillings and 19 pence. There is no law of nature why a boy should not add up any sets of pounds, shillings, and pence that he chooses. But Mrs. Humphrey regarded this virtuous effort at industry as an instance of ineffable deceit; I lost her minimum good opinion for ever.

But the chief thing about that school was the porridge we had for breakfast. After we had been turned out by a small boy who rang an enormous bell round the passages upstairs, had washed in cold water with squares of yellow bar soap, and had scrambled through a torpid first school beginning at half-past seven, "Old Cribber" arrived through the door of the side schoolroom, which was also the dining-room. As he came in the smell of porridge in quantities escorted him. He stumped onto a dais at the end of the room, extracted a tuning-fork from his waistcoat pocket, tapped it on the desk, reproduced the note in a profound voice, and thence found the pitch of the first note of the morning hymn. He sang "do re mi," and if it was "mi" he sang the first note of the hymn and we went on. Three times out of five the hymn was "New every morning is the love." To-day if I hear that Ancient and Modern hymn-tune I immediately smell porridge; and if by chance I smell porridge I hear that tune. I hated porridge; I hated the taste of it, and it gave me boils. Whenever I had a boil Mrs. Humphrey made me feel that it was a personal symbol of original sin. I wish I had dared to tell her it was the porridge.

The day thus begun with porridge was heavy with school work of a similar clotted dulness. For two years I cannot remember having learned anything. The most terrible ordeal was Scripture history, which we had to learn from a black book at week-ends. It was a translation into longer words and more involved sentences of all about Abraham and Isaac. I used to come back on Monday morning from home loathing the name of Abraham.

The top class, to which I never rose, was taught by Caleb William Bowles. He was a bulky, good-looking, fair man with blue eyes and a well-shaped aquiline nose. He was reputed to be a German because, according to his own account, he had fought in the Franco-Prussian War and was entitled to wear the Iron Cross. He certainly knew German, and he taught mathematics and Latin—that is to say, Cæsar—excellently, and he used to pass his candidates regularly in the College of Preceptors' Examination. He spent all his spare time studying fat books on anatomy, and was believed to be ever on the eve of passing medical examinations. I do not think Caleb William Bowles ever became a doctor. About six years afterwards, when my young brother Walter was at a preparatory school called Montrose College at Streatham, Caleb William. Bowles was there, an assistant master still, teaching Cæsar and arithmetic. He ought to have made a good surgeon— according to his own story of how in the Franco-Prussian War he and a squad of his own regiment surrounded a house where a party of French soldiers had surrendered. He, by the order of his sergeant, had stood at the door and bayoneted them to the number of twenty-six as they came out.

The most interesting boys at Hornbrook House were the family of Wilmot. There were about seven of them during my two years at the school. They came from the village of Shoreham, near Sevenoaks, where on the river Darenth their father combined the duties of a country gentleman who hunted with the West Kent and the ownership of a paper mill. He was a unique person, slim, powerful, and alert; he wore a neat square grey-brown beard, surmounted by cheeks like a russet apple, and swift blue eyes. A beautiful rider, and a tyrant technician inside his mill. He used to supply Government Departments with hand-made paper for ledgers; and when orders fell off he went straight to London and interviewed the highest officials, in one case the Right Honourable W. E. Gladstone, at the Treasury. He believed in hand-made paper, he knew it was the best, and meant that it should be used. He had about a dozen sons and daughters, and, as I say, all the sons went to Hornbrook House to begin and finish their education. All of them were intimately knowledgeable about horses, and were always the best-dressed boys in the school. The third son was F. W. Wilmot, now Clerk of the

Course at Lingfield—a very good amateur rider in his time. Being a large family of good clients, none of the Wilmots could do any wrong at Hornbrook House—a privileged clan. They were all of them pretty good at cricket.

But we did not play much cricket because at that kind of school there were no organised games. All I can remember of the cricket was being hit on the thumb on a bumpy pitch on the Common opposite the school. But there was one famous occasion on a Wednesday afternoon, on the West Kent ground near Old Chislehurst, when a scratch game lasted about three minutes. A boy named Charley Ridley, who came from Dunedin in New Zealand, had frizzy hair, and was a good bowler, was captain of one side. Having lost the toss, he began the bowling, but instead of his usual overarm action he shot in a swift daisy-trimmer first ball, which bowled out a boy named Gloag. Gloag refused to go out because it was a sneak, or, alternatively, a trial ball. After argument, Gloag picked up the ball, the only one we had, and put it in his pocket, saying that if he was not allowed to go on neither should we. The altercation pursued Gloag gradually towards the edge of the West Kent ground. He jumped the low iron rail and retired facing us, with a stump in one hand and an open penknife in the other. He then retreated down the long road facing Chislehurst Station. He ran for bursts of about fifty yards, turning at bay, and then repeating his Pyrrhic tactics. He led us miles up the roads towards Bickley, and out beyond into the fields. Finally he stood at bay in a small iron gateway, and we surrounded him as hounds surround a wild boar. A boy named Cardinall Cordey, son of a Norfolk farmer and the cleverest bird's nester I ever knew, crept through a hole in the hedge, came up behind the quarry and pinned his arms. Then we seized the delinquent and conducted him, thoroughly pinioned, across the fields to Bromley. There we hired a four-wheel cab and nine of us travelled home partly inside and partly outside. Nursemaids looked out of windows and pedestrians wanted to know where the yells came from. When we reached Hornbrook House Gloag was hustled upstairs, and the last we saw of him was being locked up in the top-storey bathroom. It was now pretty late in the afternoon, and we were all wondering

what would happen to Gloag. We had seen Mrs. Humphrey
proceeding up the stairs with a thick strap. There was no news
till we were just going to bed. Then we heard a muffled explosion and a noise of a heavy body falling on the floor above.
Gloag had turned on the gas in the bathroom, climbed out of
the window and sat on the window-sill. When Mrs. Humphrey went upstairs to order Gloag to bed, she found the bathroom door barred from the inside. So she lit a candle and
pushed heavily. The door flew open and the escaping gas went
off in a largish flare in her face, and she fell backwards against
a sort of wardrobe, which fell over too. Some of the bigger
boys, including three Wilmots, ran upstairs. Gloag was
dragged in through the window and locked up in a small box-
room. And so to bed. And would you believe it, the next
morning half a dozen of us were found to have scarlatina, and
were sent away to the small sanatorium on the other side of
West Chislehurt pond.

About a month later, when I came back from convalescence,
at tea-time seven peardrops were served out on all our plates,
and I was told that this was a continuation of our reward for
having restored Gloag to school discipline. But all seemed to
have settled down, and by that time Gloag was a rehabilitated
student of Cæsar and arithmetic.

In its way, this was a strange world in which to begin one's
larger life. Most of the boys, and of course all the Wilmots,
were happy enough, but I was not, and the reason was that the
porridge and the heavy suet puddings and the large helpings
of silverside and badly cooked cabbage, though generous
enough and no doubt wholesome, did not at all suit me, and I
cannot ever remember feeling really fit. I am sure, too, the un-
suitable diet made me stupid in school.

All this suddenly ceased. At the end of my second year,
when I was eleven years old, the school was sold to another
kind of headmaster. When I came back after the summer
holidays it was to another and a better world. All the boys
over the age of 14 had been cleared out. We were dressed in
Eton coats and collars instead of any sort of tweeds. A new
big gymnasium had been built, and everything had been
tidied up.

Our new head was H. V. Pears, who had been an assistant master at Uppingham, and was the son of the well-known Dr. Pears, who raised Repton from a Grammar School into one of the famous Public Schools. Our new head started by finding out how much Latin we knew, and I found myself elevated to the top of the school; so Caleb William Bowles must have taught me *some* Cæsar. We forthwith became a modern preparatory school, and were taught Latin and Greek, with an occasional hour of mathematics, and French. We were also given quite different food, and our games were properly organised. School life began to be worth living.

H. V. Pears, a tall fellow with a black moustache, who wore a monocle and always wrote with a heavy silver pencil, had been Captain of Boats at Corpus Christi College, Oxford. He had a gift for appropriate sarcasm, and could teach Latin and Greek. At any rate he taught me rapidly enough, otherwise, having learned little or nothing under the old régime, I should not at the end of a year and a half have won an Open Scholarship at Repton. One of my rivals for prizes was a red-haired, freckled boy named Butters, who was the son of the pastor of the big Wesleyan church, and who once, having a bad cold, began his Sunday letter home, " By dear Bother . . ."

Under the new régime we had plenty of games, and I was captain of cricket and football. We used to play other private schools. In one school match, the professional and groundsman of the West Kent Club was umpiring in proper form in a long white coat. He was a small man, named J. Wells, with a long brown beard and a high brown forehead. He had played for Kent a few times, and was the first man to take four wickets with successive balls in first-class cricket. He was also the father of H. G. Wells, the eminent author of *The Outline of History* and other imaginative works. J. Wells, as I say, was umpiring, and he cannot have been attending at the time I delivered one of my famous leg-hits, because the ball landed square in the middle of the forehead and knocked him out. There was a small red bruise exactly like the caste mark of a Hindu. It was a great shock to me too, because we all thought he was killed; but we carried him down to his little public-

house nearby and he suddenly revived, sat up, drank a glass
of water, and after a few minutes' consideration returned with
us and resumed his umpiring. I made 27 not out, and got
4 wickets; and we won the match. But of course I did not
know that I had nearly slain the grandfather of Mr. Kipps
and Mr. Polly and Mr. Hoopdriver.

Three years ago, passing through Chislehurst, I looked in on
Hornbrook House. It was empty and in charge of a caretaker;
but there in the lobby was the peg on which fifty years ago I
used to hang my cap. The worn grass path still led down
through the laurel bushes to the now deserted chicken-run
where Old Cribber had nurtured his favourites. The house
was now consecrated to National Service as the headquarters of
the local Girl Guides. *Sic transit.* The pond across the road
looked much smaller than of yore. The seven Aylesbury ducks
were still there.

All this time we were still living at Orpington, but there
were no weekly boarders in the new Hornbrook House School,
and I went home only for the holidays. I had given up Fenimore Cooper and taken avidly to Walter Scott; and, *pari passu,*
I did not so frequently harry the hazel copses in pursuit of
sparrows. But I was still an ardent fisherman, and with longer
legs and better tackle I used to catch quite a lot of roach at
Keston Fishponds.

There was a large fish near home I did not catch. He lay at
the outlet of a culvert in the river Cray as it ran under the
road from a pond in Orpington. He was nearly three feet long,
a shadow at the edge of the little wall. I fished for him with
worms and I fished for him with dough and I even tried a ripe
cherry, which *Every Boy's Book* gave as a good bait for barbel.
And how did I know he was not a barbel? One reason why I
did not catch him was that, as occurred to me in after years,
he was a pike, and not, as I hoped, a large trout. But I did
catch some quite good trout in the river Darenth when I went
to stay with the Wilmots at Shoreham. The largest, weighing
just under three pounds, was an adventure. By the paper mill
there was a pool where the sluice opened from the dam above
to divert the water when the mill was not running. It was no
good for fly. One day I was fishing in the swirl by the stakes

which propped up the bank on one side. Nothing happened, so I put down my rod and left my worm to fish for itself while I strolled into the mill to see some paper-making. When I came back in ten minutes I found my line tautly fixed between the stakes. Not having a spare piece of gut, I bared my arm, climbed down to the water and felt as far as I could down the gut. In response to a gentle insistent pull, the line gradually came away, and I lifted out of the water first a small square of wire netting threaded on to the line, and then on the hook a magnificent speckled trout, stone dead. I carried it up to the house in triumph. The young Wilmots said it must be diseased : they would. But their nice sister said it was not; she had it cooked and it was delicious. The fish must have gorged the hook in its holt under the stakes and drowned itself.

This victim was not the only big trout in the Darenth. One day I was fishing for gudgeon off the footbridge across the mill dam. There was a pike in the pool below the mill, and I wanted some gudgeon for bait. I was fishing with fine gut and a very small hook baited with dough. Presently down went my little quill float and I hooked a gudgeon, and was lifting it gently out because these little fish have tender mouths. Just as it cleared the still surface there was a flash of yellow and a big trout jumped clean out of the water, seized the gudgeon, and nearly pulled the rod out of my hand. Down went the monster with a rush, and I tried to play it, but it gave two jerks and broke the thin gut. It was at least a four-pounder. I tried again with purposely attached gudgeon, but the fellow had learned his lesson.

There was some beautiful trout-water lower down the Darenth at Lullingston, belonging to Sir William Hart-Dyke, like the Itchen above Winchester. It looked a perfect dry-fly water, but in those days we did not know the dry-fly. I used to catch trout there by adopting the wet-fly method I had learned in North Wales from Mr. Jones. This nowadays would be considered a feat, but I am sure that Jones would have hooked out even the educated trout of the Itchen and Test with his up-stream sunk flies. He would not have called them nymphs; but he would have made them nymph-like.

At home at Orpington, though one made the best of it, there

was nothing like the variety of adventure available in the hills and valleys of further Kent down at Shoreham, with the West Kent hounds kennelled nearby at Otford and the chalk hills populated by innumerable rabbits. Winter evenings at Orpington could be dull. It was a sleepy village, but now and again we had the excitement of a penny reading. These penny readings, organised by the vicar's wife, could they be reproduced by the B.B.C., would be complete winners. There was a curate who was a great hand at reciting sporting ballads, especially a long description of a race, which ended with the line, "He was glued to the saddle with cobbler's wax." He also sang, but always as an encore, a tenor solo beginning—

"Time was when Love and I were well acquainted,
    I was a pale young curate then."

But there was another and a better tenor whose name was Fox. He was a son of the well-known Fox's brewery near Downe. He was a good-looking young man with a long brown moustache, and always wore immaculate Victorian dress-clothes at the penny readings. His best song was, "When the robin nests again."

The vicar nearly every time gave a reading of Tennyson's "Revenge," "At Flores in the Azores. . . ."

The kind of world in which Chislehurst already figured and Orpington was beginning to figure as a desirable residential neighbourhood seems very long ago when nowadays one is tooling down the arterial road at 60 miles an hour to Canterbury Week. The house we lived in along the road to Green Street Green is still there, but looks about half the size that I remember; whereas the small shrubs round the lawn have grown into tall trees. In that house happened one of the strangest experiences of my life. It was a yellow brick building, originally oblong, looking down the sweep of the long narrow garden; but my father had built on a T-piece at one end, larger than the original house. So it was that from the first landing upstairs a long passage led from the old part down to the new. My bedroom was the first door on the left of the landing, and the passage went away to the right, to the bigger bedrooms belonging to my father and mother.

Three days before the end of one Easter holiday, very early in the morning when it was still dark except for a faint grey light in the window, I woke up with a start, and at once knew that what woke me was the sound of firm, heavy footsteps coming down the long passage towards the door of my bedroom. The footsteps came to my door. The door was pushed open and they crossed by the end of my bed. I saw a tall figure pass behind the striped twill blind, and then there was a dim silhouette against the dim grey light outside. I was not disturbed: it must be my father come to look out of my window into the backyard where the dog was kennelled. He invariably went to see if he heard anything round the house at night, and especially if the dog barked. While I was wondering what had happened, I saw the silhouetted figure gradually fade away, and no one went out of the room.

Then I froze. I remembered that my father was not in the house. He had been unwell a month or two ago, and had gone abroad with a brother for a walking tour. I remained stiffly awake until gradually the morning light came. As soon as I heard the maids going downstairs I got up and dressed. I thoroughly examined the window, of which the top sash was open about a foot as I had left it when I went to bed. The blind hung slightly twisted, but whether it was so overnight I could not remember. I went out of the back door to look at Dan the dog, but he was undisturbed in his kennel and came out wagging his tail.

There is no manner of doubt that I saw what I have described, and that I was fully awake when my door was pushed open. After breakfast I told my mother what had happened. She was not surprised or in the least doubtful about my story. She at once said that anyhow I should be going back to school in a few days, and would I please not tell anybody else, because the cook, Melinda Barber, and the housemaid, Clara Collar, had both given notice. They had several times seen in their bedroom (which was up a secondary stair above my mother's bedroom) a tall woman in a black mackintosh. Melinda was a stout lady, susceptible but not imaginative. Clara was a sharp-faced, matter-of-fact girl, not in the least afraid of mice. As for me, I certainly saw my

father in my room behind the blind. I recognised his footsteps for certain: he had a distinctive tread, and my woodland
habits had made me observant of sounds and sights.

Back to school I went unenlightened; and I never was in
the house again, for when my father came back from abroad
he was advised that the daily train journey to town was bad
for him; and our home was transferred to Streatham Hill.
So my early years in Kent ended in mystery.

CHAPTER III

PRIVACY OF A PUBLIC SCHOOL

EVERYBODY who has never been to one knows what a Public School is like. Everyone who has overcome the handicap of being educated elsewhere can explain why the product of the English Public School has none of the qualities that really count in modern life. But whatever may be the defects of the English Public School, neither England nor any other country has succeeded in inventing a better way of training a boy to become of use to himself and other people. It has been said against the English Public School that there the river of one's life starts in a backwater; a Public School is so much a little world of its own that even its virtues are stagnant.

Life itself in a Public School is anything but stagnant. My salient memory of Repton for the first two years is that there was never any time to get done the things one had to do. There was never time to wash and dress in the morning; never time to beat the clock down to the big schoolroom for prayers; never time for breakfast; never time to prepare one's construe for second school; never time for dinner; never time to change on whole school days for house football, nor on half-holidays for compulsory football; never time for anything, and not even time to have one's sleep out before the house bumpkin with his clanging bell hustled one out of bed into another day. While one was a fag there was never time to light the study fire or wash up the tea-cups. One cleaned many pairs of boots with blacking, but one's own there was never time to clean. In fact, the greatest joy on going home for the holidays was that one could wear shiny black instead of dull green boots. Of course, it was all right when one got a study of one's own and fagged other boys.

If such is my memory, what must be the memory of my brother fag my first term in Number Seven study? He was a fag all his six years at school because he never succeeded in getting into the upper school, although he was a squire in his own right and rode blood hunters with the Meynell in the holidays. He was a nice enough fellow with red hair, and he was squire at Etwall, near Derby. My career at Repton began with a first-rate fight with this squire, which would have done very nearly as well for television as that between Boon and Danahar; and it lasted longer. As nobody counted the points, and as neither of us knocked the other out, it ended in a draw. The *casus belli* was whether, because the squire had been a fag then for three years, and I for only half a day, I should light the study fire every morning. My own view was that it was not my fault that the squire had been a fag for so long, and that we ought to share and share alike. If you have ever tried to light a study fire with a firelighter made of sawdust and glue and with clinker for fuel, you will see the point of it. We fought in the study while the senior boys were still at breakfast. As the squire could not knock me out, we went shares on a friendly basis. We tossed up for the fire that morning and I was unlucky enough to win, because it meant I was the one to wash up. In the vestibule containing one very large bath behind a wooden partition was a row of enamelled basins with a drinking-filter at one end, the tap of which was never turned, and the last on the left of the row of basins, countersunk in the leaden slab, was allotted to washing up tea-things. The outlet was always plugged with tea-leaves.

Study Number Seven was at the end of a long passage upstairs. One had to convey cups and saucers down the stairs on a drawing-board for tray, along the passage out into the yard, which ended in a neck with a heavy swing door. So the very first time I tried my hand I balanced the drawing-board between my chest and the wall while I opened the door. Some idiot came through the other way and all the cups— but none of the saucers—were broken to smithereens on the asphalt. The study had purchased the outfit by subscription the day before. I had to replace the damage out of my slender funds, and was extremely annoyed with Mr. Bound across the village square because he would not sell me cups inde-

pendent of saucers. What was worse, the senior members of
the study condemned me for having too much side, so that I
spent most of my time during preparation hours sitting at
the top of the stairs with a pile of dictionaries, trying to
master the classics, with no desk except the said drawing-
board. Also, though I was not cut off from tea and cocoa
when these were going in the study, I had to drink them out
of a jam-jar.

This ostracism from the study made my first term a severe
experience. It was the winter term, and though, being promoted at once to the Under Sixteen house team, I much
enjoyed the football, my one ambition was to get to the top
of my form. This was not a pious ambition; it was simply
that I hated being beaten at anything, and especially that I
ardently wished to pass out into the next higher form, which
was in the upper school, and thus to cease to be a fag.

My first week I was bottom but one of my form. My second
week I was second from top. I was top every other week of
the term; but I was third after the examinations because I got
very low marks in mathematics. All the same, I was top in
classics, and I do not believe any boy has ever worked harder.

The form I had been first drafted into was above my qualifications. I had never done Latin verses. I had no idea what
they were about. The first week I did one hexameter. The
second week I did twelve. The third I did sixteen, all right.
They were the kind of verses which could only be right or
wrong—true poetry.

The worst of it was that my form-master gave me only
three marks for my third effort. I knew he gave two marks
for each correct verse, and that he had meant to mark me
thirty-two. When we gave in our marks I had the temerity to
say, "Please, sir, I think you've made a mistake."

This was *lèse majesté*, treason, and, worse, impudence. So
he gave me nought and a hundred lines as well. In our Public
Schools there is a certain amount of discipline. So what with
the broken cups and the litigation about the Latin verses, I
started my public-school life badly.

Repton is a one-streeted village in the centre of the famous
hunting country of the Meynell, midway between Derby and

Burton-on-Trent. The river Trent used to flow directly past the rising ground close to the ancient church, the Headmaster's house, and the main school buildings; but long before they were there. The river now flows in a great semicircular bend about a mile away by the village of Willington, where the old turnpike bridge (now but not then gateless) crosses the heavy swift stream. The flat land in between is an expanse of rich pasture, with tall, scraggy thorn hedges dividing the fields. The single street through the long village runs away in the direction of Ashby-de-la-Zouche, passing near to Donnington Park, where we sometimes ran paperchases, but where now the great motor-racing track winds round the rolling turf.

When the cinema people searched for a school with the most typical English surroundings in order to glorify Mr. Chips, they chose Repton, and they also, curiously enough, chose me to come and help produce the old-time cricket and football scenes, but I could not do this because I had to go and watch a Test Match. In truth, I do not think that any of the great schools is more typically English than Repton. For one thing it is situated in the middle of England and under its ancient name of Repandunum was the capital of the Saxon Kingdom of Mercia. Before that it was an important Roman station, and the foundations of the school buildings are upon Roman remains. Quite classical. Part of the ruins of a very early Priory lie along the bank that bounds the cricket field, but part of it is still extant in complete architectural detail. Indeed, until this building was restored with great skill to its original shape as the Repton School War Memorial—certainly one of the finest in England—the Priory was actually used as one of the school-houses. The view of the old Priory through the school arch as one walks towards it along the ancient wall which bounds the playing-fields from the village is one of the fairest instances I know of historic England exhibited in shapely grey stone. The school dates back to the thirteenth century. It became a Grammar School and was endowed by a local magnate named Sir John Porte. It gradually grew into a Public School and was raised to its present eminence by its greatest Headmaster, Dr. Stuart Adolphus Pears.

One of the points that strike me most in looking back on

the six years I spent at this very English Public School, which
for the last eighty years at least has been one of the most
successful not only in scholastic achievement but also in
games and athletics, is that the popular notion of a Public
School as mainly a home of hero-worship in the latter department is a fiction. Repton, when I was a small boy, was
exceptionally strong both in cricket and football, and I can
well remember gazing with distant reverence (when I had
time) at the swells who were in the school elevens; especially
at F. G. J. Ford, the captain of cricket, the most powerful
school batsman I have ever seen, and afterwards in first-class
cricket the hardest hitter. But there is no doubt at all that
the eminent lights of the Upper Sixth and the winners of the
School prizes figured on the whole as more important persons
in public estimation than the successful gamesters. It should
be added that, again contrary to the usual notion, the majority
of the leading members of the cricket and football teams were
in the Sixth Form.

I can remember that much of my available respect (when I
had time for any) was directed towards a very clever boy of
about 15, named Robson, who was high up in the Sixth and
won the School classical prizes, although he was the only
wearer of the speckled straw hat, the mark of the Sixth-
former, who also wore an Eton jacket and Eton collar. He
looked out of place among his tall coevals in the Sixth, such
as Martin Smith, afterwards Bishop of Rochester, and Sir
Montagu Barlow, not to mention the dominating Francis
Ford.

Then, as in most of the Public Schools, we were divided up
into separate houses. There was the Headmaster's house by
the old Trent. There was the Priory inside the school arch.
There were two houses (of which mine was one) in the village
square looking onto the ancient Cross, round which the
country fairs were held. The rest of the houses stood to
attention down the long village street.

All the housemasters did their best for their houses, but
they could not make them first-class hotels. My housemaster,
the Reverend Arthur Flower Emilius Forman, was generous
to a fault, but neither he nor his beautiful wife, a daughter

of the great Dr. Pears, succeeded in rescuing us from the daily
discomfort and turmoil which all Public Schools until recent
years seemed to have inherited from *Tom Brown's Schooldays*. We lived in studies about the size of a hen-coop; two
or three Upper School boys and two or three fags in each.
That is to say, the fags lived chiefly in the passages and such
stray corners as the so-called reading-room, where there were
no books, no chairs, and not even any newspapers. They also
inhabited the so-called changing-rooms, which were otherwise
filled with damp jerseys and misshapen boots.

We depended for anything in the way of service upon one
frightened boy in a pink-striped cotton coat, called the house-
bumpkin. He was supposed to supply coal and fire-lighters to
the studies and to clean the boots. He did go away with the
wet boots overnight in a big wicker basket, but he never came
back with them; they had to be retrieved by the fags in the
morning. There was one very big bath inside its wooden
partition, but nobody could get a hot bath except once a week
according to schedule. The water came from a well and was
pumped by hand by a big wheel with two handles, nominally
by the bumpkin, actually by a couple of fags. The big bath
was filled overnight (throb, throb, went the wheel as one was
trying to learn one's repetition just before bedtime), and one
rushed down, if one had time, for a cold dip in the morning.
After football one either did or did not mop off the Midland
mud in one of the lavatory basins.

It was a marvel how the whole school, with the exception
of some half-dozen boys who were cut off by the Headmaster
in full academicals on the steps of the Big School, succeeded
in arriving for prayers in the dark on a winter's morning
often through mud and rain and sometimes through snow.
Some of the houses were at least half a mile away. Not
surprisingly, the boys from the Priory, next door to the Big
Schoolroom, always won the Challenge Cup for fewest
boys late—the Challenge Cup was a clock. After first school
we hurried back to our houses and scuttled through a breakfast of thick bread and butter, porridge (if it did not give you
boils), and, if one could afford them, hard-boiled eggs privately
introduced in one's pocket.

Then came the forenoon in the form-rooms, and we hurried back to the heavy mid-day meal of roast beef or mutton and suet pudding or baked rice. The mid-day meal did not take long, else one was late for games. On whole schooldays after another three hours in school came tea; like breakfast without porridge. Beyond preparation, which meant the lower school doing their work in the dining-hall and the upper school in their studies, nothing else happened except supper, which scarcely anybody attended and which consisted of bread and cheese. Everybody except a few unpopular fags made some sort of supper with cocoa, toast, or Genoa cake in the studies. The whole life was rather like that of soldiers on active service indoors.

But incredible as it may appear, we all succeeded in enjoying ourselves, thinking well of our way of life, and maintaining an energetic fitness which I hope is still achieved under the rationalised and enlightened régime of modernised Repton. There is no doubt that our school life was hardy. Indeed, I should say that hardiness was one of the main features of Repton in those days. The results were good. There was no dearth of scholarships won by Reptonians at Oxford and Cambridge, and in games, for our numbers, just over 300, we were as successful as any Public School.

At that time the ancient castle of the classics was unassailed. Repton was essentially then a classical school, and any clever boy could travel up to the Sixth Form without bothering about anything else. For instance, I was top of every form from the Remove upwards into the Sixth, without having to trouble about any mathematics worth the name, without being able to ask intelligibly for a cup of coffee in French, and without obtaining any knowledge of the English language other than that, and it is no mean amount, which happens to be derived from doing Latin and Greek prose and Latin and Greek verse. Six years, in fact, of solid and undiluted Latin and Greek.

It is easy enough to contest the value of dead languages on the ground that in the same time a clever boy with the same effort should be able to learn and talk half a dozen modern languages, and to combine this accomplishment with a workable knowledge of the main elements of several sciences, together with genuine competence in his mother tongue. On the other hand, the majority of the remarkable men in the Home and Indian Civil Services, in the Law and other learned professions, and furthermore in statesmanship of the Victorian and Edwardian periods, were products of the old-fashioned classical education. There is no evidence that the more modern generation educated on more modern lines is in any degree whatever or in any respect superior. There is, too, the curious corroboration from Germany, where some forty years ago it was discovered that boys who had spent most of their education in classical studies, when they turned over to science and " realist " pursuits, in quite a short time overtook those educated from the beginning in the other kind of way.

Anyhow, in my time at school, though there was a Modern Side, which except for its few clever boys at the top was the refuge of incompetents, a successful school career meant successful excavations in the classical quarries. If a new boy had been taught mathematics well and was clever at them, he started not very far from the top mathematics Division, and in those airy heights he could become good at the subject, but the ordinary boy went away to his one mathematical hour a day with no alacrity, and learned very little from the Classical Masters, who were equally undesirous of teaching him figures.

I spent my first term in the bottom mathematical Division. The master who taught us also took the bottom form in classics. He emerged from a side door into a small ancient classroom attached to the Priory, told us to do the odd-numbered sums on page 80 in the arithmetic book, and then went away. We all discussed and some of us did some of the sums during the next fifty minutes. He then returned, told us to exchange papers, and read out the answers, which we marked with a big R or a big W, but at the end of the term we knew exactly as much as we did at the beginning. The top half-dozen were moved up. At the end of two years, having progressed upwards about three divisions in mathematics, I had nevertheless gone upwards through all the classical Forms into the Sixth. I could have made a fair show at a scholarship paper in classics at Oxford or Cambridge, but I could not have done a compound interest sum or a quadratic equation if a fortune had depended on it. Then in accordance with the convention I went to see the Headmaster and asked him whether I could read Thucydides in my study, which meant could I, for the rest of my schooldays, dispense with mathematics.

As for French, the Forms attended one hour a week with Monsieur Guillemant, B. ès L. Him we respected; he had perfect manners, a white pointed beard, and a formidable scar across his forehead, reputed to have been acquired in youth in a desperate duel at the University of Paris. He used to give us dictation which we corrected, but we learned no French. M. Guillemant also taught us drawing out of doors in the summer; we sat on camp-stools and drew our versions of trees and birds and anything in sight.

As for English, it consisted in having to write once a week what was called a theme on some set subject, such as "Courage" or "It's never too late to mend." The theme was done on Saturday evening, and on Saturday evening none of the volumes of the Encyclopædia Britannica could be found in the Library. If you were too late to get the volume containing Alexander, you got the one containing Julius Cæsar, or, failing him, Zenobia. The idea was that any subject of a theme could somehow be attached to a big name. We elaborated our pages of foolscap, and saw them again marked, but otherwise untouched, about a week later. We never knew how much English we perpetrated; but spelling mistakes were marked with a cross.

In the Sixth Form we did an essay about once a month for the Headmaster, and some of the elect wrote good ones; but little or no notice was taken of them. As I say, if we learned to write English at all it was from writing Latin prose.

Now I offer you a peculiar paradox. Anybody who by some mischance has ever heard of me will certainly put me down as a devotee of cricket, football, and suchlike pursuits. But when I look back on my Public-School days, they seem to have been filled with little else but strenuous endeavours to defeat my friends and associates at Latin and Greek. I did get into the school football eleven as right back at the age of 16, and a very strong team it was, as indeed were all the Repton football teams of my time, capable of putting up a good show against some of the professional teams (not reserve teams, either) of the Midlands, including Derby County. I remember too that we played a draw against Cambridge, when F. G. J. Ford was captain and kept goal for the University. And we were only just beaten by a strong team of Corinthians in the time of Tinsley Lindley, the great England centre-forward. There have been few stronger school Association football teams than those of my time at Repton. But in those days we played no school matches such as are now played against Shrewsbury, Malvern, and Charterhouse.

It was due to a fine game which we won against the Casuals in my first year that I was invited to go on the next Christmas tour with the famous London club, and played for them against the great professional teams of the north of England and the south of Scotland, and also in the F.A. Cup at the age of 16. Thus began my career in first-class football, which lasted for another sixteen years, and which included a final of the English Cup. The Casuals' cup-team was pretty strong in those days, because the Corinthians did not then enter for the Cup, and it mustered the pick of the amateur talent except such as was bespoke by the Old Carthusians, Old Westminsters, and Old Etonians. An interesting and first-rate member of the Repton team was Walter Buckmaster, the great polo player, an excellent half-back who kicked over his head like a ballet-dancer with the full length of a vertical leg.

Both the Palairets, L. C. H. and R. C. N., afterwards so well known in first-class cricket, were in the football team, and they were fine forwards. R. C. N. Palairet was brilliant.

The cricket elevens at Repton in which I played were perhaps not as strong as in the previous years, when the famous family of Ford were the dominating figures. Dominating figures are just what they were. Francis Ford, who was captain my first summer term, was the last and greatest of them. When I got into the team three years later, again at the age of 16, L. C. H. Palairet was captain. He is still well remembered in the cricket world as perhaps the most perfect example of pure style in batsmanship. He was a beautiful batsman at school, even then possessing the perfect off-drive which is still unforgotten. What is more, he was for a schoolboy a very powerful bat, and was even then capable of making plenty of runs in first-class cricket. He and his brother, R. C. N., had been given fine coaching by their father, who used to engage such bowlers as Attewell of Nottinghamshire to coach them in the Easter holidays. A fine chance. L. C. H., by the way, was a first-rate school bowler, medium right-hand, and headed the averages. R. C. N. at school was not as powerful a batsman as his brother, but he was very nearly as good, and he was a better player on a wet wicket, because of his sound back play. There is no doubt that if he had not broken his knee-cap at football up at Oxford he would have rivalled his elder brother's success for Somersetshire. Both the Palairets were peculiarly graceful and had a natural sense of style. They were both in the Sixth Form at the same time as I was, and Lionel once won the School prize for Greek Verse.

The question is much discussed whether or not coaching at school is advantageous. We certainly had a high standard of cricket at Repton, but we certainly had little or no coaching. We had a fat old professional with a husky voice, named Scothern, who used to bowl innocuous slow-medium stuff at the nets. He was a good practice bowler because he was accurate, but all he did in the way of coaching was to roll up half a dozen good-length balls on the off-stump, and then pull up the stump from which he delivered the ball, advance his left foot as though to test whether the turf would hold his weight, make a slow push with the stump, and utter the cabalistic words, " Come forward at 'er, sir." He was the kind of bowler who invariably ought to be either played back or driven hard. I remember I used to drive the ball straight back at him with a good thump, and he used to skip out of the way with uncongenial agility. That made him say, " Come forward at 'er, sir," all the more. But if one obeyed him in the feeling and tentative manner he suggested one was liable to play outside his occasional off-break. He knew just exactly nothing about the art of batsmanship.

One of the masters, whom we called Pat, and otherwise Mr. Exham, occasionally came to the nets and offered a few sarcasms in general terms. He was the master who under-marked my early hexameters, but was a good cricketer, reputed to have been twelfth man for Cambridge along with several others of his year, and he sometimes turned out for Derbyshire. He was a good judge of cricket, was Pat, and he told a friend of mine (who of course told me) that he did not see how I was ever going to get any runs against first-class bowling. What he meant was that, although I might be successful in punching school bowlers, what was required against first-class bowlers was the conventional off-drive applied with respectful skill. My housemaster, who was reputed to have been twelfth man for Oxford, and was certainly a fine hitter and a useful fastish underhand bowler, also occasionally had a net himself, and afterwards gave us some advice about not being afraid to hurt the ball. We admired him because he used to break the tiles on the pavilion roof with his on-drive. He always played cricket in a deer-stalker hat. He was not unlike a darker, clerical W. G., except that the black curly beard was clipped to the pattern of an admiral's and not let loose in the manner of Moses. He was once, on an Old Rep-tonian tour, mistaken for W. G. by a porter at Nottingham station.

I evolved such cricket as I achieved from watching Lionel Palairet play, and from my own inner nature. Mostly the latter, because I was a driver with a full swing, and not a modulated lunger in the stylish manner of Palairet. I made about as many runs as he did, and was several times top of the batting averages, so the yarn that I had a miserable talent for batting until I met Ranjitsinhji in the Sussex eleven is probably due to my being a fast bowler as well.

The two Palairets at school were both of them technically better bats than I was, chiefly because I had the fault of tugging too much at my drives, as it were trying to get too much force into them, or in a mistaken effort to get body-weight into them. I had not yet learnt that in batting one

ought to think quickness and not force. Then again, one's
mind was diverted from the proper way of applying a wooden
club to a ball by a strange conventional formalism, the gist
of which was that one should concentrate upon a purely
artificial stroke called "playing forward." The idea was that
if you could play forward correctly you were a batsman; otherwise not. Nobody ever told us, and we only found out more
or less subconsciously by trial and error that the essential and
difficult point about learning to bat is to watch the ball and
deliver the stroke at the ball itself, and not at a point in space
where you hope the ball will presently be. There was a sort
of suppressed major premise about batsmanship, that if the
mechanism of one's forward stroke was correct, somehow or
another this would ensure that the bat found the ball; whereas
it is much better to play forward incorrectly with one's eye on
the ball than correctly with one's eye somewhere else. Then,
of course, nobody ever suggested to us that from a good
bowler one receives just as many balls which ought to be
played back as ought to be played forward. Still less was it
ever suggested to us that so-called correctness in batting consists in nothing whatever but a natural swing combined with
movement of the feet in order to obtain a position of
mechanical advantage, and with a poise of the body that
allows the swing to operate instead of preventing it. In short,
the sort of way we tried to bat tended to be the conventional
system of getting into a difficulty and then trying to get out
of it when the ball arrived at a point in space where the bat
ought to meet it.

The wonder is that such a lot of good cricketers were
evolved from a world so clouded with misconceptions. Somehow, quite a number of my contemporaries built up a successful body of skill upon entirely erroneous first principles, or
none at all. Perhaps it was because there were generally no
first principles that we did get somewhere by trial and error.
My memory is that quite good results were evolved in batting
out of a mistaken formalism, and that bowlers arrived entirely
by the light of nature.

But in my school days the peculiar term the "hook" had
not been invented. If one hit a hall in an unexpected direction

to the on-side, intentionally or otherwise, one apologised to the bowler. Being by nature a rebel, I used to heave a short ball round to the on-boundary on slow wickets, even if it was straight, but I did not call the stroke a hook until years afterwards. An advantage was that the opposing captain never by any chance put a fieldsman there; he expected you to drive on the off-side like a gentleman, even if his bowlers presented stuff which, by the exercise of a modicum of agility, one could turn into long-hops to leg.

Now I come to think of it, it is all very well talking like this, but our cricket at Repton was very good, and I doubt whether any other Public School over a period of years about that time produced stronger elevens.

One interesting point that occurs to me is that cricket talent for the most part was discovered in the inter-house matches. That is where in particular young talent was unearthed. A boy of 16 would be in the fourth game one summer, come to the front in the house-matches, and get into the school eleven next year. These matches were played under the kind of high pressure one encountered later in Test Matches; and high pressure brings out latent ability.

There was a curious feature connected with inter-house matches at Repton in my time; the House which had the School captain always won the cricket cup, no matter whether his team was the best or not. My last year as captain, my house knocked out in the semi-final an eleven which was twice as strong as ourselves, and which contained nearly half the school team. Then in the final, half-way through the match, a boy in our house in his last term gave what was called a "leaving-grub." That meant a considerable supper, with salmon, roast beef, and steak and kidney pies in the big study. I was carving the beef at one end, so I missed the steak and kidney pie, but nearly everybody else ate it, with the result that the whole of our team except myself and two others were laid out with ptomaine poisoning. The next day our opponents were due to open their second innings in the afternoon. We went on to the field with eight substitutes. I bowled one end. Our only other first eleven man, R. B. Hope, bowled the other, and the third survival (afterwards Lord Moncrieff, but then called "The Goozer") had to keep wicket, which he did with every part of his body, including his forehead. The end of it was that we had 120 to make in the last innings, with only three men available. I was missed in the slips when I had made 10 by Tom Horton, afterwards captain of Northamptonshire, but after that I made 90 not out. Hope stayed in for a few overs, and Moncrieff succeeded in sitting on his splice at the other end while I made the runs. He batted too with nearly every part of his body, including the back of his neck, for the wicket was very fiery and bumpy, and we had the first eleven fast bowler against us. Nothing but the convention that the captain's house always won could have pulled us through. I rather fancy this was the best innings I ever played at Repton, except perhaps an innings of 25 on a sticky wicket against the Derbyshire Friars and the bowling of F. R. Spofforth, then not much past his prime.

Spofforth played pretty regularly for Derbyshire. He was the Midland representative of the Star Tea Company, of which he was a Director. He must have been nearly as good at trading tea as he was at bowling; he died worth seventy thousand, which shows that even an Australian cricketer ought not to be condemned to the limitations of the game. One could not deal with Spofforth on a sticky wicket by playing forward and hoping for the best. Under the stress of the occasion, and not by enlightened forethought, I found myself either playing right back within about eighteen inches of my wicket, or thumping him in the air over his head. The speciality of Spofforth's bowling was that it was impossible to tell from his delivery whether the ball was coming fast, medium, or slow, and he graduated his off-break so that whether the ball pitched two inches or two feet outside the off-stump, it would hit the wicket. It was on this occasion that I formed the useful guiding principle that even a Demon on an evil wicket can only bowl one ball at a time, and that if you really look at the ball you have a good chance of playing it.

The two Palairets were great friends of mine at school, in spite of the extreme rivalry in everything to do with games between their house and mine. Both of them were exceptionally fine-looking. Lionel, the elder, was tall and shapely, with rather curly black hair, large blue eyes, and features which had they been smaller would have been rated Greek according to the statues. It was not only in cricket that he was graceful. He had a natural grace in everything he did, including his handwriting. Dick Palairet was slighter, with brown hair and a neater face. He was very alert, and had a pair of eyebrows such as are the origin of the term "supercilious."

Dick and I sat side by side in the backwaters of mathematics, which was really all wrong, because both of us, had we recognised it, were quite good at the subject. In the last term before we both retired to Thucydides in our studies, we received an unexpected promotion and arrived together at the first mathematical hour of the term, and sat down side by side. The master, whom we called "Ducky," floated up to his desk and started the lesson by ordering Dick to sit in one far corner of the room and me in another. After this disposal, he went to the blackboard and read out a piece of algebra as he wrote it up, beginning with "$x + y + z$—see—see—see?" Dick Palairet, in perfect good faith, wrote down "$x + y + z$" and then the three letters c, c, c. After a pause Dick held up his hand indicating inability to understand.

"Ducky" told him to bring up his paper. "What is this nonsense, Palairet?" he demanded. "This is impudence. Take a hundred lines!"

Under some misapprehension of telepathic collusion he then made me bring up my paper; but I had got it right. "Ducky," I believe, was surprised that if Dick Palairet was involved in any nonsense, I was not in it too. We soon found out that "Ducky" never wrote anything up on the blackboard without enquiring "See—see—see?" but I am afraid neither Dick nor I ever saw much.

Both Lionel and Dick Palairet were first-rate at athletics as well as at football and cricket. Lionel was one of the best long-distance runners the School ever had. He won the steeplechase and all the longer distances, except the quarter-mile, in which he was second, and he got his blue at Oxford for the Three Miles. He was beaten in the School quarter by a boy named Bailey, who was Head of the School. This was a most remarkable fellow. He was easily the cleverest boy I came across either at Repton or anywhere else, and had never before run in a race and never ran again.

Dick Palairet and I were fairly even competitors in all the short distance races. He could beat me at the 220 yards, but I could beat him at the 100, unless the turf was wet. He was a wet-wicket runner. I had the advantage of always winning the high jump, long jump, and the hurdles, so I won the Athletic Cup twice to his once. Afterwards at Oxford he never reproduced his school form on the cinder-track, even before his broken knee-cap stopped his running. Our athletic sports were held on the cricket field at Repton, and if the weather happened to be wet, the going on the heavy turf was not good. In the high jump I managed to do 5 feet 5 inches off the gravel in the school yard when I was under 15, and my 21 feet in the senior long jump was a record until H. M. Abrahams, afterwards an Olympic winner, obliterated it.

My housemaster, Mr. Forman, was the only coach I ever had in athletics, and that on only one occasion. One afternoon he happened to be crossing the School paddock when I was practising the long jump on the rough turf into an elementary pit. He stopped for a few minutes, told me I did not jump high enough, took off his black mackintosh and made a heap of it between the take-off and the pit. The mackintosh frightened me into jumping much higher. That was the only piece of coaching I ever remember receiving in athletics in the whole of my career. It is rather interesting that up at Oxford when I jumped over 23 feet and did a world's record in the long jump, I used to be well over 5 feet in the air in a human ball at the peak of my parabola. No doubt I saw a ghostly mackintosh and remembered Mr. Forman's vibrant voice. Nowadays, they have invented a new technique, called the hitch-kick, with which performers such as Jesse Owens cover some 26 feet. At the peak of his jump Jesse Owens is by no means a black ball in the air. He figures rather like an angel sprinting up into the clouds, with his legs repeating his previous strides along the level. In fact, rather like running up Jacob's ladder. The new records put the old ones in the shade; all the same I would rather bank on the old method if there were a broad ditch in front of me and an angry bull behind.

Considering the Public Schools were always emporia of Greek and Latin culture, I wonder why they concentrated on everything concerning the greater ball games which had little or no connection with the classical tradition. They gave no attention at all to detail or technique of athletics proper—running and jumping and dancing, in which the ancients achieved the highest standard of art the world has yet seen. We know, and those of us who do not know could easily find out by going to the British Museum, that the ancient Greek training in all forms of pure athletics was to the last degree scientific and artistic. Their physical education began with the children when quite small, and was pursued throughout with minute attention to the basic qualities of movement.

Nowadays, the standard of knowledge and technique, developed first in America and afterwards on the Continent, especially in connection with the training of competitors in Olympic Games, has been adopted in the Oxford and Cambridge University Athletic Clubs, and has greatly raised the whole standard of performance. The main points of style in running and jumping are known and practised; and though in the 'eighties and 'nineties we used to see good results from purely natural runners and jumpers, there was nothing like the general standard of style now attained.

At the Public Schools, with a wealth of magnificent material available to work upon, nothing was ever done to teach boys what to aim at in improving themselves in athletics; and this was a pity, because a knowledge of how to move effectively has a great influence on the whole being. When one remembers the enormous attention given in the Public Schools to success in the major games, it is very strange that no thought is ever given to the principles of good movement, which necessarily are the basis of success in all physical activity.

The strangest thing of all is that nobody ever thinks that it is worth while to learn even to walk well. We all do much more walking than anything else, and the way we walk has a great influence on our physical and mental attitude. There must be a feeling that because it is natural for everybody to walk, it is also natural for everybody to walk well. This shows itself up as an enormous error the moment one investigates—take up your stand for half an hour at the end of the Strand. Surely it is wonderful that in the Public Schools, the homes of devotion to success in games, one detects no standard at all in the way youth walks about and carries itself. You have only to watch the boys at any Public School sloping about on their everyday occasions to see nearly every fault of carriage and movement. Why it is that there is no effort made at improvement in this respect remains a paradox. Here we have the pick of the youth of the country gangling about with its hands in its pockets, its head hanging forward, and its shoulders either hunched or bottled; it wears its hair too long and often dishevelled; and you may even detect it trying to salute a Master with one hand in its pocket and the other searching negligently for the brim of its straw hat.

One of the consequences of this convention of carelessness is the peculiar self-consciousness of the average Public School boy, and his inability to come into a room without an air of discomfort. This goes along with the funny attitude of mind in the Public Schools to what they are pleased to regard as "side." The result is an apologetic gaucherie, a kind of communal symbolism in refutation of any possible accusation of "side." It will be a great day when the average product of the English Public Schools, besides being on the whole the most valuable product of education in Europe, can make its appearance on any public occasion, say an afternoon tea-party, without betraying marked self-consciousness.

On the other hand, although I spent six years of my life at a typical English Public School, and was an assistant master at another, I have never been able to discover any correspondence of my own experiences with the portrayal of this world in the best-known novels dealing with Public School life. The little old men and elaborate introverts who inhabit their pages appear to me impure fiction.

No doubt *Tom Brown's Schooldays* represents Rugby as it really was in the experience of the author, and also in fact, but then it deals with normal boys in a normal world of active youth. I am still waiting for a school story which represents, for example, Sherborne, St. Paul's, Harrow, or Eton, as they really are, instead of as they might be were the fellows who inhabit them for the most part budding Swinburnes.

The only criticism of the English Public Schools which holds is that with all their quality and with all the remarkable advantages of their buildings and traditions they are not better than they are. The Royal Naval College, Dartmouth, shows up the average Public School badly in respect of behaviour and bearing. One reason is that the Masters at Public Schools are not officers who carry out the duties of officers; they accept the equivalent of commands from below. The boys impose their standards. Another difference is that the traditions of the Public Schools have been evolved from succeeding generations of mere boys with callow likes and dislikes, whereas the Royal Naval College embodies the surviving traditions of a great fighting Service. If the merits of Dartmouth could be grafted on to the merits of Eton, then——

The notion that the English Public School turns out every boy from the same mould and obliterates individuality is bunkum.

CHAPTER IV

JUDGMENT OF PARIS

PARIS in the virtuous 'nineties figured in the minds of nearly everyone in England who knew nothing about it as the city of light, of ladies, of fashions, and of night revels. None of us younger ones regarded Paris as other than a world of gay adventures, the more so the less likely we were to go there, and the less likely we were, even if we did, to dare such adventures in a language which we had never taken any trouble to learn at school.

Nevertheless, my German tutor for the Indian Civil Service examination, who for some reason or other was the only schoolmaster who ever succeeded in teaching me any French, strongly advocated that I should spend one Christmas holiday in Paris. So he took me there, and I learnt a lot.

He was a heavy man with side-whiskers, thick lips, and a square, rosy face; but he was a good coach. He advised me strongly to speak no German to him in public there, because the language even then was not popular in Paris. What he was doing there I never found out, but I used to take him German exercises three times a week, and in six months he taught me enough to get 75 per cent. marks in the examination. This was a good performance on his part for the time being, but I soon forgot it all. He lived himself in rooms just off the Boulevard St. Germain, but he planted me out. At Repton School he lived in a thatched cottage near the school, and was a family man.

There were no thatched cottages in Paris of the 'nineties, and he planted me in an aerial apartment at the very top of a huge block, Numéro 3, Rue de Bassano, a street which radiates downhill from the Arc de Triomphe. There I dwelt with M. le Comte de Beauregard and the Comtesse.

M. de Beauregard was an advanced and entire Republican.

He dropped the "de" and he dropped the "Comte." If he said once to me he said a score of times, "Jeune homme, faites vous ouvrier. Le futur, c'est chez les ouvriers," which was pretty good for a thorough aristocrat of that time of day. All the same, he always spoke in a tone of delicate respect of M. le Prince de Luisignac, who inhabited a magnificent suite some four stories lower down the staircase.

He spent his life, did M. Beauregard, sitting in the salon of the *appartement*, the chief furniture of which was an enormous charcoal stove always invisibly glowing inside itself. The other rooms were four bedrooms, one large for himself and Madame, three very little ones—one for Pauline, one for me, and one for another guest *en pension*, a young American lady called Miss Sproull, in Paris to study singing at the Conservatoire.

Monsieur sat all day in his armchair in a greatcoat, smoking a large, ancient pipe with a bowl that admitted about as much tobacco as an opium pipe admits opium. Madame always referred to it as "mon ennemi." He was a burly, handsome old man with exquisite manners (if you leave out the pipe), and a pointed white beard of the old régime; not an imperial, but pointed.

Madame was thin, small, and authoritative. She had been and now and then reappeared *chez elle* as an accomplished soprano; quite good she must have been before her voice had become faded and in parts uncertain. An artist, however, in her way.

Pauline, the maid *à tout faire*, was even thinner, with a pale hawk-like face and flat carroty hair; a marvel at marketing and cooking. She bought very little, perhaps a fraction of a chicken, but she converted it into delicious food. It is no fairy-tale that she would return with two drumsticks, some carrots and haricot beans, and a few mysterious paper bags, and somehow succeed in converting them into a better dinner than I have often paid a pound for in London. The cold at the time was intense, but I never saw Pauline in a hat or a coat. She had a scanty black shawl with which she was as skilful as with her hands. She, too, was most certainly an artist. She was treated with exquisite politeness by Monsieur, who no doubt regarded her as a domestic *ouvrière*. She never said a word, whereas Madame said a great deal, by way of a perpetual running commentary on everything and nothing, but she said it with the peculiar aptness of the French language.

Miss Sproull, who went away very early in the morning and came back just in time for dinner, was a serious young lady, and, as Madame was always saying for some reason, "*très peu de coquette.*" She was very nice, and thoroughly disapproved of the rare occasions when Madame decided to open the piano and sing as from "Carmen."

Such was the environment.

M. Beauregard accepted for no reason at all a certain responsibility about my education. He gave me some not very good advice about the best way to learn French, with a delicacy of expression which went perfectly with his lucid and philosophic attitude towards life. Failing that, he advised me to spend as much time as I could in the Latin Quarter, attending lectures at the Sorbonne and the Collège de France, pointing out that nowhere in the world could one hear better French spoken than by listening to the eminent lecturers.

As the vast gay life of the resplendent city was quite beyond me, and as I really wanted to learn the language, I used to descend the lofty stair of the block every morning before nine o'clock, and walk all the way down the Champs Elysées through the Place de la Concorde and the Place de Notre Dame across the Pont St. Michel, take a cup of chocolate at the Café St. Michel, and then seek out the best available "*conférence.*" I should not have known that "*conférence*" meant a lecture had not M. Beauregard so informed me.

The best lecturer undoubtedly was M. Leroy Beaulieu, whose subject was Political Economy. He lectured in a large amphitheatre in the Collège de France, to me, about a dozen workmen in blue smocks, and some half-dozen very senior-looking students who were taking down his lectures in order to have them duplicated to sell to the younger students who ought to have been there. The workmen were there because it was bitterly cold. The lakes in the Bois were frozen several feet deep, and populated by skaters in tight black breeches and gaiters, and one could scarcely do up a button in the open because one's fingers were so frozen with the cold.

It was not until I spent those arctic weeks in Paris that I realised how scanty were our opportunities of skating in England. Indeed, I had reached the age of nineteen with a tale behind me of scarcely a dozen hours on the ice. Yet how fascinating was the scene on the lake in the Bois, where the gentlemen and ladies of the *Cercle* anticipated with much more formality and perhaps better taste the future glories of St. Moritz and Mürren.

Nearly all the gentlemen wore the uniform of the club— tightly fitting tunics of military cut in very dark grey or black, with tightly fitting breeches and gaiters to match. The ladies were dressed with the perfection characteristic of their nation, in floatingly dependent skirts, some of them, and to my mind the best, accordion pleated. Both gentlemen and ladies wore cossack caps of fur or astrakhan. The members of the club skated beautifully, and I doubt whether the generality of first-rate performers of latter days can waltz any better. There was a complete absence of hurly-burly skating, and even the casual skaters exhibited a certain reverence for what they were doing as one of the fine arts.

It struck me at the time how strange it was that we in England did not in those days learn to skate whenever our temperate climate permitted the exercise. Indeed, one's admiration of the skaters in the Bois was tinged with a quite poignant jealousy of their accomplished skill.

There were no oranges on the ice, but round the banks of the lake there were innumerable braziers where one could buy the best of roasted chestnuts. It was a delightful scene. The French do not take their pleasures sadly, and they never make a noise about them.

Talking of oranges, equality, and fraternity, I remember once afterwards, while exercising myself innocently well before noon on the ice-rink at Mürren, being boarded by an indignant girl in a yellow skirt who peremptorily ordered me to "get off her centre." I apologised, and said that it was the last place I wished to be, but looking down I noticed that there was an orange, and apologised further and more adequately, recognising that any orange on the ice must be a private orange. None of this could have happened on the ice in the Bois among French people.

As I was saying, the cold in Paris helped to fill the lecture-rooms, though perhaps the workmen may have attended on the principle that M. Beauregard was right, and they must prepare for their future. Or perhaps the French sense of style, which prevents the appearance of a single bad paragraph in the French papers, attracted them to M. Leroy Beaulieu, whose diction, form, and matter were equally perfect. I used to listen to him in rapt admiration, and I never heard the French language so perfectly exploited till many years after, at Geneva, I listened to M. Henri Bergson when he was pleading on behalf of the appropriation of funds for Intellectual Co-operation.

There were other excellent lecturers, whose names I forget, but they none of them lectured in quite as warm a theatre with quite such big stoves, and they attracted fewer of the *ouvriers*. Incredible as it may appear, the essence of all the time I spent in Paris consisted in these lectures, and this simply because they were so beautifully given that they fascinated me.

But all the life I saw in the Latin Quarter was fascinating, because, even to the superficial extent to which I tasted, there was a certain sparkle and a perpetually interested *joie de vivre* about it. One never seemed to overhear conversation that was other than witty and intellectual in the sense that it seemed important under a kind of light touch of treatment. After all, one is more educated by simply living in a medium than by any other means. That is why I said that I learnt a lot in Paris.

There was a whole world of life, intensely interesting even within the confines of the one café which I frequented, the Café St. Michel, where one might easily see sitting at their accustomed tables such characters as Emile Zola, Anatole France, Paul Verlaine, Clemenceau, and his friend Claude Monet. It was quite remarkable how distinguished was the appearance as they sat at their tables of any number of un-known frequenters, and the veriest student who came in with his wide black felt hat came in with an air as of a junior but entirely equal member of this world of clever conversation and polite cynicism. One thing about a Frenchman is he can read a newspaper (partly because it is conveniently attached by the left-hand edge to a split stick) with an air of appreciation and enlightened criticism.

It was while sitting over a tall glass of black coffee and croisson one midday that I suddenly heard a sound like the sea, and hurried out to be involved in what looked like the beginning of a revolution. You must know that two evenings before Madame Beauregard had taken a hand in the education of both Miss Sproull and myself by arranging that we should take her to the Théâtre Français, where it was advertised that a play would be given called "Thermidor." We did not see "Thermidor" because before the curtain went up the elder Coquelin stepped in front of it and told us that he was desolated to inform the very distinguished audience that it was not possible to present "Thermidor," which had been interdicted by the Government. It appeared that the play exhibited certain incidents and aspects of the French Revolution in a way which the Government, as the direct descendants of the revolutionary régime, felt was not permissible. Another play was presented, but was received by what we should call the pit with a deluge of what the Australians would call barracking, and what the Parisians call "tapage." Indeed, there was a very impolite uproar.

The consequence was that a paper called Le Radical printed next day a biting article attributing this disgraceful conduct, not to the large and distinguished audience who had received the Government fiat with becoming consideration, but to a pack of students who had somehow found enough to pay for entrance, if indeed they had not come in without paying. But not indeed students; rather the riff-raff of the Latin Quarter who soiled the good name of students by an idle and furtive life under that title.

The students of the Latin Quarter, real or pretended, took this article in very bad part. It was an insult. Having done an immense amount of talking in every café of the Quarter, they assembled in the late evening by some telepathic con-

spiracy, they invaded the offices of *Le Radical*, broke the
windows, distributed the type into the street, and went away
with huge bundles of the offending journal, with which they
made bonfires in the Luxembourg Gardens. One party made
their bonfire in the band kiosk, which suffered.

Unfortunately, I had gone home far away up the Champs
Elysées to magnificently sedate residential Paris before these
stirring events were afoot. The sound of the sea which involved me in a kind of Severn Bore of excited humanity
flowing down the Boulevard St. Michel was the sound of
innumerable feet marching with what the students call the
"*pas de gymnase*"—that is, marking time, but nevertheless
progressing. Emerging from the front of the café just to see,
I was involved in the sweep of the tide. Somehow or other
I soon found myself in the front ranks of the demonstration.
There was no going back, so with about a score of others I
became the flotsam that percolated through the cordon of
gendarmes drawn across the Pont St. Michel to prevent
the revolution crossing the Seine into the valuable part of
Paris.

After a few boisterous moments, there we were, we others,
on the far side of the cordon. Nobody bothered any more
about us, so we stood there gesticulating and every one of us
except me making speeches, while the foremost figures of the
demonstrating phalanx in front of the gendarmes were being
arrested, punched, and having their heads broken. Blood in
small quantities was flowing freely, and the French language
was being strained to its most expressive limits.

This could not last, so a tall cadaverous student beside me
unfurled a long black streamer, attached it to the end of his
cane, shouted some martial command, and we all fell in in
single file behind him and marched away to the Place de
Notre Dame, round which we continued to march for half an
hour. The black streamer declared in large letters, "*Vengeons
nous!*" But the only revenge we got was a lot of exercise for
our legs at the expense of the pavement of the Place de Notre
Dame.

On this side of the Seine all was normal. On the other side
there were gesticulating crowds and immense excitements. In

due course we marched back to the Pont St. Michel, but the gendarmes had been reinforced, and the rear rank facing our way addressed us as *messieurs*, but refused to let us pass into the Quarter. A veritable *ils ne passeront pas.* We marched away to an adjacent bridge, but every bridge was blocked by a heavy cordon, and we were stranded. What happened to my comrades I do not know, but as it was evident that this afternoon no one would be allowed to cross the bridges, I passed away up the Champs Elysées to the *appartement* in the Rue de Bassano, where M. Beauregard was alone with his pipe in his greatcoat and his armchair. I detailed to him, in French infinitely more voluble than I had previously compassed, the events of the day. He shrugged his shoulders, gave me a delightful exposition of the psychology of the Latin Quarter, explained that what had appeared to me a tremendous demonstration really amounted to nothing at all, but nevertheless might well develop into a revolution. He said that behind these students there was doubtless a deep-seated annoyance among the workmen of Paris, and would I please remember that " *le futur, c'est chez les ouvriers.*"

The next morning, having been assured by M. Beauregard that probably it would be safe, I walked as usual into the Latin Quarter, took my cup of chocolate in the Café St. Michel, and there was nothing whatever happening. The whole storm appeared to have blown over. All the same, for about three days afterwards there was an immense amount of conversation, louder than usual, but much too quick for me to understand properly, in all the cafés that I visited in search of events. *Le Radical* must have succeeded in re-collecting its type, because everybody was reading it, and it contained plenty of finely written sarcasm and vituperation on the subject.

That was not the only time Madame Beauregard arranged that Miss Sproull and I should take her to the theatre. We went to hear her favourite opera, "Carmen." This, however, did not end in a riot; it ended in Madame giving us her own version of the airs when we got home. She was annoyed with me because I thought well of a singer who had played the part of Carmen, she being young and attractive, whereas

Madame had no opinion of Carmen, but thought well of another lady, who played the part of the high-born dame. It was the part of the high-born dame which Madame herself was conversant with and could sing.

Madame instituted another expedition, but this was not to a theatre. She had formed the idea, and repeatedly stressed it, that Miss Sproull did not take proper advantage of Parisian life. Miss Sproull ought to see the sights. So Madame commanded me to take her to see over the unequalled cathedral of Notre Dame de Paris. We both ought to see it, and especially we ought to see the elevated parapet from which suicides took their headers.

Docile as always in a strange city, I took Miss Sproull on the expedition one afternoon. We escaped all the guides except one, who positively showed us the church in all detail, not forgetting the dramatic parapet. To reach this, one ascends a narrow spiral stone staircase. With insular politeness, I stood aside to allow my American lady to ascend. She ascended six steps and then descended in a hurry, and insisted that I should go first. It is true that I saw the white hem of her petticoat and the merest hint of an ankle. It is true that the spiral stair was very steep, but in the days of Victorian skirts the lady had nothing to fear. Being a shy youth, I was nevertheless much astonished. I began to understand what Madame had meant by " *très peu de coquette.*"

What was happening all this time to my German guardian and tutor I do not know. He must have been very busy about something, because he was perpetually re-arranging the hours for me to attend upon him with a packet of German prose in my pocket. All I know is that he read the journals with assiduity, because there was always a pile of them in his room on our small side-table beside a carafe of water and a bowl of sugar. He used to drink several glasses of water with several lumps of sugar during our sessions, and was otherwise, for all I knew, a much more abstemious man than he looked, although on the few occasions when he took me out to lunch he advised me of the virtues of *un bock.*

What impressed me almost more than anything, with the exception of the display of jewels in the shop windows of the

Rue de Rivoli, was the possibility in Paris of leading a most amusing life in the free and fraternal world of the boulevards, whatever might be your means. How different in London, where anything in the shape of a restaurant signified extravagance. Then how very attractive the complete absence of snobbery. In that gay world, gay in the Gallic sense of lightness of touch and easy conduct between all men, no one was ever rude and dictatorial to a waiter or domineering to the services even of the driver of a *fiacre*. The habit, too, as it were, of accepting everyone and presenting onself in turn in the third person, has a peculiar efficacy in promoting liberty, equality, and fraternity.

Then, too, how pleasant to be able to enter into conversation with one's chance neighbour at a café table without being formally introduced. Whether Paris was the best place in France to go to learn French may be disputed, but without doubt even a few weeks there on one's own when relieved from *tourisme* in the quality of a temporary resident is a valuable education.

When, thirty years afterwards, I went to Geneva to the Assembly of the League of Nations on the Indian Delegation, I found that I had an enormous advantage over most of the English there, in a sympathetic understanding of the way of thought, not only of the French, but of the other Latin representatives. Not that at that distance of time I had preserved a great glibness in conversational French, but I did remember how to understand it very well, and to apprehend the angle of thought. What is more, one never again was a victim of that peculiar stiffness which is perhaps the chief cause of misunderstanding between the English and Continentals. So to that extent M. Beauregard and Madame and the Café St. Michel did me a good turn.

In those days there was no Metro railway in Paris, nor any other easy way of getting about except by walking, and it is astonishing in Paris how far everywhere is from everywhere else, especially railway stations, and how extremely hard are the *trottoirs*. Besides, one had to be very careful in crossing the street. Once I stepped off an island, just a right foot forward, at the bottom of the Champs Elysées, and a gorgeous carriage and pair containing a lady in magnificent furs, with a swiftness incredible before the days of *autos de luxe*, swished its near front wheel precisely over the welt of the toe of my boot.

A young Frenchman in the best pattern of fashion, who was beside me, politely said: " English, is it not? Monsieur would do well to note that in Paris one is excessively fined if one permits oneself to be run over. Terrible to lose, in the same moment, a toe and several *billets de banc*."

On the other hand, the dangers on the pavement were far less than at home, because everyone looked where he was going, and all mutually steered a considerate passage. Why one should remember these small differences at this distance of time is another proof of how educative Paris could be. The more so as in those quite insular days of the 'nineties it was the custom to be amazed at what we regarded as the idiosyncrasies of the Frenchman. Really, we were rather on the edge of being barbarians, especially we of Public School age, or scarcely more.

How strange that a young Englishman, who really wanted to learn French because an examination including that subject (with marks to be obtained) was looming in the near future, should be sent to Paris with a German tutor! And still more strange that this German tutor should teach him more French (for examination purposes) in five weeks than he had learned in five years at a great English Public School. Not that it is necessary for an Englishman to learn French (except for examination purposes), but a reasonable facility in reading the language is certainly an aid to culture.

Nor is it out of place to wonder why it was that we Public School boys could not bring ourselves to take our French masters seriously, or anything they tried to teach us. I believe the explanation was that we objected to any form of external politeness, however convinced we were of our own internal possession of that virtue. No doubt that is all changed now.

I expect you have heard the story of the new French master at Eton to whom the Headmaster gave a little fatherly advice, to the effect that the average English boy could scarcely be said to understand the less abrupt methods of a French gentle-

man, and that it was well to impress one's pupils from the
start that one would not stand any nonsense from them. So
the French master, accepting the advice with a courteous
inclination, opened his first lesson with the following ulti-
matum: "Now, you boys, attention! If you do not behave
as it become, I box your eye!"

Of course, one of our insular difficulties in learning French
is that in this language you can say what you have in mind
only in one precise way; whereas in English you can do it in
several ways.

I ought to have said when talking of Saxon origins that a
forefather of mine on my mother's side was one Bailly, Mayor
of Paris in the French Revolution.

CHAPTER V

OXFORD: A CLASSIC PERIOD

OXFORD is not the home of lost causes. Oxford is the castle that still defends causes that deserve to win.

An ancient people may fancy that it has modernised itself and grown up to date, but its roots are in its distant past. It depends for its quality to an unrealised extent upon tradition. The specific homes of tradition are sacredly valuable.

There is a difference between the idea of a University as a centre of culture where from the life and doctrine the humanities may be imbibed, digested, and assimilated, and the idea of a University which is just a higher high school attended by students whose objects are solely careerist and utilitarian. Oxford and Cambridge were intended to be a preparation for life, and any and every career, whereas the conception of the more modern Universities is immediate equipment for a job of work. Read Cardinal Newman on the subject.

Whether modern time is long enough for the former conception is a question. But hurry does not always mean progress. Time at its worst is fairly long, and a young man is not very old at 20.

In one of the early years after the War I happened to be at a banquet in the hall of one of the old City Companies. A venerable, spacious, and historic hall, with an atmosphere of ancient stability. I asked E. V. Lucas, "I wonder how the Germans thought they were going to beat this?"

E. V. replied, "That is a thought."

My own entry to this world was in the nature of a happy accident. Accident was indeed the hall-mark of my educational career. I was intended for Aldenham School, but found myself at Repton, because I was sent there for practice, and got a scholarship by mistake.

From that day onwards, the attention of my parents being

otherwise occupied, I found for myself for the rest of my life.

After spending six years at Repton, I made another mistake about a scholarship. One very cold morning in 1890, after first school, the Headmaster, Dean Furneaux, proposed to me that I should try for a scholarship at Trinity, Oxford. I was not intended for any University, but for the Indian Civil Service, and neither I nor anybody else knew what would happen to me if I did not pass for the Indian Civil. I regarded the proposition as meaning that a Reptonian sixth-former ought to get an Oxford scholarship for the honour of the school.

The examination was held in the great Hall of Wadham. The story is that Wadham College was built as a memorial to Nicholas by Dorothy. I know what Dorothy was like, because Lord Birkenhead had a unique portrait of her in his house at Charlton, near Banbury, which hung beside an equally venerable oil-painting of the arms of his earldom, with the motto, "Faber meæ fortunæ." This, for the sake of Cantabs, means, "Smith of my fortune." The mellow widow of the Somersetshire squire is said to have come up to Oxford with a party of stonemasons. The result is that gem of Jacobean simplicity Wadham College, built with enthusiasm, grey Cumnor stone, and the advice of no architect.

It was only on entering the beautiful arch surmounted with the figures in stone of Nicholas Wadham, Armiger, and Dorothy his wife that I discovered that the examination was jointly on behalf of Trinity and Wadham Colleges. Even then I did not know I was a competitor for a scholarship at Wadham. Nor at the time did I know that somewhere among the swiftly writing youth along the dark oak tables was the future Lord Chancellor of England, F. E. Smith.

Lord Birkenhead, in one of his autobiographies, has given an imaginative account of this examination, so fateful in his own career. What actually happened was that I just missed being selected for a scholarship at Trinity, being beaten by Dr. Alington, the present Dean of Durham and ex-Headmaster of Eton, and by Cecil Lubbock, who was the head boy of Eton and is now one of the Directors of the Bank of England. How the examiners co-ordinated themselves I do not know, but Trinity gave me their Senior Exhibition, and Wadham made me their Senior Scholar, thereby endowing me with the eternal fame of beating F. E. Smith, who was placed fourth on the list.

Lord Birkenhead has described how with a beating heart he stepped out boldly from his lodging in Wadham College and steeled himself to go to the porch and look at the list of results on the College notice-board. He suggests that he was delighted to see his name there on the list among the selected scholars of Wadham. My belief is that he was extremely annoyed at not being first.

Note that this was an examination in pure classics, with an English essay as a corroborative side issue. A legend has grown up in the light of the great career of F. E. Smith in politics and the Law that he was a brilliant classical scholar who carried all before him during his academic days. The truth is he was a fair classical scholar for his age when he entered Oxford, pretty good at Latin and weaker at Greek, and that he won his fourth place in the scholarship list at Wadham because he was first-rate at an English essay. Afterwards he did not get a first class in classics. He got a second; and instead of reading Greats as he was earnestly advised by the Warden, he took Law, and just scraped a first more by native ingenuity than by acquired knowledge.

Where he really came to the front was by staying up a fifth year, working hard and winning the great Law scholarship, the Vinerian, in which he beat Sir William Holdsworth, the authority on Constitutional Law, already a B.C.L. That is what started him on his way to fame. In classical subjects he was not particularly good at composition, and in translating from Latin or Greek he was inclined to improve upon Cicero, Vergil, Thucydides, or Sophocles by ingenious and often pretentious improvisation. From what I know of him, he would with great confidence have composed a speech for Cicero in the style of Tacitus, had the historian been a master of the Latin tongue. However, in all he did he exhibited an ingenuity which would have been highly appreciated in a less ancient University.

I, for my part, did not go round to look at the list at all, and I never discovered that I was Senior Scholar of Wadham College for entry in the October term of 1891 until my Headmaster told me so after I had gone back to school. Perhaps I lacked Lord Birkenhead's courage.

Having eluded the Indian Civil (purely for want of mathematics), I remembered my scholarship at Wadham College. So I just did nothing till next October, when I packed a small trunk and went up to Oxford. I had no allowance from home, I had about £3 in my pocket, and my £80 scholarship of course I should never touch, as it would be absorbed in College fees. But the porter at the College gates knew nothing of this, and indicated that my oak-panelled rooms were on the middle stair on the right-hand side of the front quad, easily the most expensive rooms in College, and redolent of ancient wealth.

And so to dinner at the bottom of the Scholars' table in the great baronial hall, with its tall narrow stained-glass windows and venerable portraits of celebrities. At the scholars' table sat my four unknown colleagues. Opposite me sat one of them, of whom I immediately took notice. I knew his name was Smith. I saw that his hair was rather untidy, being of the kind that stands upright unless prevented. He had a long lean brown face and an impudent nose, but very remarkable eyes. They were the colour of a peat pool on Dartmoor, full of light, and fringed by luxuriant silky eye-lashes.

The moment he opened his mouth he betrayed a Lancashire accent that would rival Gracie Fields. The first indication of his being an uncommon intelligence was that, discovering with characteristic promptness that no sort of provincial accent was an advantage at Oxford, this perceptive youth entirely cured himself in about six weeks, and indeed developed a tendency to preciosity.

After Hall, we four scholars of the year forgathered, of course in my rooms, for coffee. But we found we were not four, but five. A tall Scots youth, with sloping shoulders and an advanced tawny moustache, obviously older than we were, drifted in and announced that his name was McVey, that he was "vurra deeply read in philosophy," was a pupil of " Sammy" Butcher, the famous professor of Greek at Edinburgh University—of which he, McVey, was a B.A.—and that he was Junior Scholar of the year before, but had persuaded the Warden of Wadham to allow him to finish his course at Edinburgh. So here he was at Oxford, a year after his time.

F. E. Smith elicited that his Christian name was Tom, and ever afterwards referred to him as Tam. Nettled, I am sure, by the suggestion that we others were less deeply read in philosophy, he pursued all sorts of lines of enquiry, especially as to whether McVey had left a tow-headed lassie behind in the North. Indeed, he never ceased pulling the leg of this accomplished Scot for the remaining four years of our Oxford life.

McVey was a genuine character, and succeeded in discovering all sorts of stray scholarships (such as those of the Gold-smiths' Company), which could be obtained by anyone able to represent himself as in complete indigence. He never told us anything about these opportunities; otherwise Smith and I would both have been after them fast enough.

F. E. did have a small allowance from home, but nothing like enough, and for all his subsequent legal and political eminence, I do not think he knew any more than I did how he was going to finance himself at Oxford. In point of fact, he had the advantage over me that he did not become immediately involved in the more expensive side of University life which goes along with gaining Blues and their concomitant social obligations. In those days one really needed £250 a year at Oxford to be comfortable. It could be done on £200, but few, if any, of the comparatively leisured gentlemen commoners whose company I frequented had allowances of less than £400 a year. I am told that the modern rate of comfort means £300 a year, and that two-thirds of the University have some sort of subsidies from various educational sources. It would seem that I coincided with the last years when the holders of scholarships were only a small percentage and Oxford was still the cultural resort of the well-to-do gentleman commoner. At that period, for youthful eminence at Oxford, one had to be either a Blue or a Craven scholar; a rowing Blue for choice. Nowadays I am told you will be famous only if you are a politician, though a few years ago skill in writing free verse would fit you for glory.

The F. E. Smith of those days, apart from his more serious occupations, exercised his rare gift of wit and humour, not only at the Union but in practical directions. He had a talent amounting to genius for landing his friends in situations he regarded as humorous. In fact, my career at Oxford not only began but ended under one of these ministrations.

The first Sunday of my first term our party of new scholars of the college all had breakfast together in the Oxford manner —in my rooms, of course. In those days breakfast on Sunday was as described by the lady novelist. It began about ten o'clock and took the form of a considerable lunch, and included nearly everything in the old-fashioned breakfast régime, and we still drank Oxford ale out of tankards in quite the old style. Formal dress was not worn. We most of us appeared in flannel trousers, pumps—meaning the evening shoes of those days, with bows—and Norfolk jackets.

So in this guise, after breakfast, we all went out into the quad on our way to another man's rooms. As we were passing by the wide stone steps leading up to the archway beyond which were the buttery and dining-hall, F. E. pointed out various aspects of Nicholas Wadham and Dorothy, his wife, and we halted round him to be amused. Then, in continuation of his not too flattering interpretation of Dame Dorothy, he told me, guessing intuitively that I was the sort of youth who could be dared, that I could not climb up on to the capital and kiss the lady. I climbed successfully while an admiring semicircle offered advice below. The last few feet required my full attention, but I surmounted them and turned round in triumph, with my arm round Dorothy's cold waist. My friends had vanished, except their heads protruding from the windows on the nearest stair. Below stood the Sub-Warden, the Reverend Patrick Arkwright Henderson, who was lame and a Scot, and had a small brown pointed beard and humorous blue eyes. He stood there looking up with an expressionless face, leaning on his stick.

"Mr. Fry, Mr. Fry," he said, "come down please, Mr. Fry, Mr. Fry." As always happens in such adventures, it took me quite a long time to come down where I had much more quickly climbed.

"Mr. Fry, Mr. Fry," said the Sub-Warden in a gentle reproving voice, "you have not long been a member of this University, but would you, Mr. Fry, wish a member of any other College to see you, on Sunday morning, in flannels and slippers, climbing up the face of the College on an amatory adventure?"

To this I could find no appropriate answer; the more so that my mind was occupied by the grinning faces at the windows and future means of revenge.

When I called on the Sub-Warden at nine a.m. on Monday, he said, "Mr. Fry, Mr. Fry, while your spirit of enterprise put to proper purposes may be regarded as admirable, I should be glad if you do not exercise it in this way again. Please do not kiss the wife of the Founder again in public. And, anyhow, why kiss a stone lady, Mr. Fry, Mr. Fry?"

You would suppose that this would have been a lesson to me, but four years afterwards it happened that F. E. and I and several other out-college men came out together from the entertainment called "After-Common Room" at Magdalen, and F. E., as a sort of natural sidepoint in the delivery of his considered opinion about the quality of various wines, turned to me and told me I could not jump and catch hold of the bracket arm of the first lamp-post in High Street, haul myself up, turn out the gas, and then light it again with a match from a box in my right waistcoat pocket. He offered the details without hesitation. I felt my right waistcoat pocket, and there was a matchbox, so I immediately essayed the not difficult feat. Just as I was relighting the gas-burner and looking down in triumph I found that the party had disappeared round the corner of Long Wall, and I was being inspected by a policeman.

The policeman said, "I know who you are, sir. Come down."

I wanted to light the gas, but the policeman would not allow this. So I came down and tried to explain. I even explained that I was sorry to put the officer to this trouble, and proposed to compensate him, but he only shook his head and kept repeating, "Very sorry, sir, very sorry."

The consequence was that in a week's time I had to appear in the Mayor's Court. The Mayor was Mr. Cooper, the inventor of the celebrated Oxford Marmalade. I had to wait about an hour while several sordid cases were dealt with. Then the policeman with what I regarded as a considerable amount of cumulative detail bore witness to my delinquency.

Of course I had nothing to say to rebut the charge. I had put out a street lamp, and my only defence was that I was about to light it again when prevented by the officer. The Mayor shook his head and consulted the Clerk of the Court. At this point up jumped a little man in a white tie and gown, and presented a claim that my case be transferred to the Vice-Chancellor's Court under a statute of Queen Elizabeth.

Mr. Cooper again consulted his clerk. He beamed upon me and said that he found that he had no course except to assent to my transfer to the Vice-Chancellor's Court, and he hoped that the Vice-Chancellor would take as lenient a view as he had proposed to do, namely, a fine of eighteen pence.

The sequel was that I had to appear about a fortnight later in the Vice-Chancellor's Court, which caused me to stay up ten days over the end of term. Mine was the only case before the Court. The policeman this time gave an account of the affair from which you would judge that I had done positively nothing at all. He had merely found me climbing up a lamp-post. He further testified that I was entirely sober and quite well-behaved.

The Vice-Chancellor then asked me whether I was not Senior Scholar of my college, whether I had not taken first-class honours in Classical Moderations, whether I had not been Captain of the University Cricket Club, Captain of the University Football Club, and President of the University Athletic Club.

I admitted all this, rather hoping that the items were intended as endorsing the high opinion of me that the policeman now appeared to entertain. But no, the Vice-Chancellor, after consulting his clerk, fined me £2 7s. 6d., or in default offered me a fortnight's imprisonment. This annoyed me very much, and I was severely tempted to subject the Vice-Chancellor's Court to the absurdity of the second alternative, but my only friend in Court, Gilbert Scott, the hurdler, and in later life, I believe, Chairman of the Stock Exchange, dissuaded me in an emphatic whisper. He also produced enough to pay the fine, in case I was relying on the eighteen-penny judgment.

I had other memorable days. There was my short-lived attachment to the stage. My last year, when I had to take rooms out of college, I shared digs at 15, Long Wall, near their college, with two Magdalen men, "Teddy" Armistead and Copley Hewitt. Armistead's father was Vicar of Hawarden and a friend of Gladstone; Copley Hewitt's was Sir Thomas Hewitt, Chairman of the Ocean Accident Assurance Association. Sir Thomas was also boss of the taxes of the City of London, and my friend Copley was somehow appointed his assistant, and somehow afterwards succeeded to the eminent position, and is still in enjoyment of that office.

Copley is a remarkable man. He came from Charterhouse, and got his Blue at outside left in the soccer eleven. He was nicknamed "Mason" because he so resembled a hairdresser at Charterhouse of that name. He has been High Sheriff of Kent, and is a Commissioner of Boy Scouts of international reputation. He also owns one of the most notable country houses in England, the Friary at Aylesford, which is to this day a complete medieval ecclesiastical establishment with *dortoirs*, refectory, and all other appurtenances.

Once when I was stopping there he took me over to lunch with the Commander-in-Chief at Chatham, Evans of the *Broke*. Among the large party at lunch that Sunday was Admiral Gordon Campbell, V.C. Admiral Campbell asked me where I was stopping.

At the Friary; and did not he know it, wonderful place?

He said no: whom did it belong to?

I said, "That man over there. He's head of all the taxes of the City of London."

"Please introduce me," said the Admiral. "I have an idea I want to put to him."

So I beckoned Hewitt over, and the Q-boat hero explained to him that the taxi-ranks of London are all wrong, and ought to be arranged in quite another way.

Then Hewitt, who has palatial offices at Gresham College, near the Guildhall, explained that he is down in the telephone book under the heading "King's Taxes"; and that a man once rang him up and ordered a taxi. When Hewitt expostulated, the man said, "But aren't you Mr. King, and don't you let out taxis?" So the Admiral's retreat was covered.

But that is not the story I was going to tell. Hewitt, Armistead and I were roped in by "Tim" Snagge of New College, now Sir Harold Snagge, Chairman of Napiers, to act for the O.U.D.S. in "The Merchant of Venice." I was the Prince of Morocco, and had a lot to learn. Hewitt had about ten lines, but most of them were cut out by the Censor. (So he says.) "Teddy" Armistead had one line, namely, "Madam, I go with all convenient speed." Armistead, at a rehearsal, had a black-out, and could not remember his line. He spent at least three-quarters of an hour after breakfast for the next month studying his part. He is now in the Church.

I was all right until the first night, when on discovering that I had made a mistake about the casket, I said my lines beginning, "Oh, Hell, what have we here?" with such emphasis and effect that the next night the entire University turned up to hear C. B. say, "Oh, Hell." Not being able to trust my countenance, I had to leave out the swear words for the rest of the run and say, "What—have—we—here?" very slowly. Nevertheless, "The Merchant of Venice" was a great success. The chief parts were well filled; and "Tim" Snagge was a fine stage manager.

During my time the O.U.D.S. numbered among its members the younger Henry Irving and Nigel Playfair, not to mention Michael Furze, the present Bishop of St. Albans, who was heroic as Hercules in Aristophanes' "Frogs."

One feels one has become a man as soon as one leaves school behind and becomes a freshman. The sense of liberty is stimulating in the direction of leisure. It is a sensation to leave a world where every moment of one's activity is charted out for one, and enter a world where one can cut a lecture with impunity. Nothing more impressed me with my new liberty as an undergraduate than an early acquaintance with Max Beerbohm.

Max lived in elegant rooms in an old house in a corner of Merton Street. He was exquisitely dressed. He wore just the kind of bow tie that no undergraduate could engineer with his fingers. What year he was in, I forget; probably his sixth. He was probably writing a book. Anyway, he asked me to breakfast and immediately endowed my new world with a sense of literature and art and the science of life. Owing to my early successes in the athletic world, the editor of the *New Review*, I believe W. E. Henley, the poet, commissioned Max to do an interview with me. So I invited Max to breakfast— so he wrote. Actually he came round to my rooms at tea-time (possibly round about his own breakfast hour) and we talked.

In the interview, he arrived while I was still splashing noisily in a cold bath. I came out to meet him with a Turkish towel and vociferous apologies. All that did not matter, but he had the originality to make me coin the phrase, "Golf is glorified croquet." Such a phrase was beyond me at that age, and I had never played golf, and Max had never mentioned the subject; but he thereby succeeded in earning me a wide unpopularity.

It was through Max Beerbohm that another character from the big outer world drifted into my Oxford. This was Will Rothenstein, now Sir William, and nearly as great an artist then as he is now. Will Rothenstein came up to make a book of pen-drawings of Oxford characters, and appears to have been advised by Max to start with me. Perhaps this was the greatest feat I compassed as a freshman. When Will Rothenstein asked me to collect specimens for him, I was of course delighted and I did collect for him at lunch a variety of the best rowing, cricket, football, and Athletic Blues. He showed his gratitude by saying in his reminiscences that I was perhaps the greatest brain of my time at Oxford.

Naturally, I wanted him to draw me in cricket flannels, but he insisted on representing me in football rig. I objected that the result looked like a coal-heaver; but it was a good drawing.

Another sideline of Oxford life was the Union; and therewith the Wadham College Debating Society, which exhibited a strong contingent of the oratorical ability of the whole of Oxford. In addition to F. E. Smith, there were John Simon and Adair Roche, now a Lord Justice of Appeal, and Francis Hirst, and Charles Lowe, afterwards an Indian Provincial Governor, and Lister, another distinguished Indian Civilian. Nor did I entirely withhold my voice. The distinguishing feature of the Wadham Debating Society was that rarely did we get beyond Question Time.

Although I was not myself a member of the Union, in spite of earnest suggestions from F. E. that I ought to join and speak and presently stand for office, I came across a good many of the very able Union speakers of the time. According to the historians, F. E. himself might be supposed to have been unique, and indeed he was the speaker who attracted the largest audiences. He was the most entertaining and witty speaker in the popular sense. But the real orator of the day was Hilaire Belloc, and he was the speaker I myself went to hear from the Strangers' Gallery.

John Simon, of course, was admirable. In spite of his most distinguished career at the Bar and in politics, indeed, perhaps because of it, he has accumulated in addition to many friends a certain number of invidious critics. I have quite often seen it represented that in his undergraduate days, in contrast to the popularity and bonhomie of Lord Birkenhead, his was a cold, calculating, and unsympathetic character. The truth is that neither of them at Oxford, except in the Union, was very well known. Nowadays, success in the Union renders an undergraduate a celebrity; but it was not so then.

John Simon was a far better scholar and a far better philosopher and historian than F. E. He took brilliant firsts in Moderations and in Greats. He was not cold, calculating, and unsympathetic. He was a quiet, genial, and popular member of the College, who had a reputation for unselfishly devoting himself to college interests. He played college games and was a standby in college clubs and societies. He was a year junior to F. E. and myself. What I noticed about him was a curious iron-like certainty in his dealing with any pursuit, coupled with an imperturbable suavity. He had no enemies then, and plenty of friends. He was a fresh-faced, healthy, industrious product of a Scottish school; and wore red stockings at football. He had curly brown hair and was typically English, in spite of his acumen.

People are always asking me which of the two in their Oxford days, Lord Birkenhead or Sir John Simon, seemed to me the superior brain. Were I, however, asked whom I should place as the ablest man of my time at Oxford, in my college, judged on ordinary undergraduate contacts and not in the light of the backward illumination from their subsequent careers, I should not name either Birkenhead or Simon, but Alexander Adair Roche, now Lord Roche, a Lord Justice of Appeal.

Lord Roche was a scholar of Wadham, a year senior to F. E. and myself and two years senior to Sir John Simon. He took two brilliant firsts for pure classics and for ancient history and philosophy. He was a first-rate speaker, both forcible and witty, and would have been one of the leading lights of the Union had he devoted himself to this activity as did F. E. and John Simon. Between him and John Simon in the matter of scholarship there was little to choose; both were first-raters. But Roche, in this respect, was easily superior to F. E. How the great Lord Birkenhead would have figured in this competition had he worked as hard at the classics as the other two, I do not know, because he did not do it. What F. E. could do was this: if he knew a shred about a question, he could write an answer imposing enough to render the existing authorities on the subject obsolete.

Roche had a genial, grown-up comprehensive mind and a talent for lucidity which appeared to me equal to John Simon's. He was very well read. He had a gift for extracting the essence of a subject and presenting it in clear relief. He told excellent stories; and we used to chaff him that no matter whether the story was about an Irishman, a Frenchman, or a Greek, he always began it with, "Say, stranger . . ." He himself was an Irishman who came from Norfolk. He had the Irishman's love of a horse. He has always been a keen rider to hounds. He still hunts with the Heythrop and neighbouring packs from his home in Oxfordshire.

To those who devoted themselves to it the Union was an absorbing pursuit. I saw little of it, but I remember in par-

ticular two debates, one on the Franco-Prussian War, in which
Belloc, who had served his time as an artillery driver in the
French Army, took the French side, and one Zedlitz, of
Trinity, the German. It was a brilliant debate, in which F. E.
intervened without disclosing on which side he was.

The other was a debate in which Sir Wilfrid Lawson,
M.P., the temperance advocate, came down to speak and
was attacked by F. E. in the most impudent speech I have
ever heard, and about the wittiest. The point was that Sir
Wilfrid had inherited an exquisite cellar of wine from his
father, and made a public show of its destruction. F. E.'s
animadversion on the iniquity of this sacrilege was as superb
as it was devastating.

In retrospect one is inclined to minimise the severer body
of one's Oxford life. But it could be severe enough—at any
rate for a Scholar of his College who had to earn his own
living concurrently, and was involved in playing cricket and
football both for his University and for the College, and
also in representing the University in track athletics. One
spends one's first year and a half in being supposed to be
working for Classical Moderations, a matter purely of Latin
and Greek scholarship, with Logic appended if your tutor
can persuade you to take this subject. Now it happened
that I possessed what a supercilious Don would estimate as
a good sixth-form facility in Latin and Greek composition,
especially in writing Latin and Greek verse; and being even
then very fond of the ancient classics, I had read a lot of them
and was fairly competent in translating at sight. Looking
back, I can see that without being up to the standard of
University prizes in classics, I was pretty well furnished for
my age. According to one's standard as regards knowledge
of the classics in later years—the standard applied by the
critical Don—all that perhaps does not amount to very much.
But for me it amounted to achieving a first class in Classical
Moderations on about two months' work at the special
books.

So far from being lazy, I was a hard worker and genuinely
fond of the classics, but what impeded me from going further than I did—and this is worth the attention of people

who are critical about the so-called sporting side of under-graduate life—was not that I was engaged in representing the University in cricket, Association football, and for one year in Rugby football, too, and also in track athletics, but that my vacations, instead of being available for reading (and it is during the vacations that one can really read), were occupied in tutorships and in modest efforts at saleable literature in order to meet my University expenses.

Remember that actual term-time at Oxford or Cambridge takes up only twenty-four weeks of the year. The actual time expended on games and athletics by a man who is a Blue is not more than that expended by a man who simply represents his College and is probably not heard of in the outside world, whereas the Blue has the limelight focussed on him. There are plenty of men who play every sort of game for their Colleges and yet gain first-class honours in all their examinations. For example, in my third year, when I was President of the Athletic Club, every one of our first strings against Cambridge was a Scholar of his College, and one of them, G. S. Robertson, our hammer-thrower, was a University prize man, being a Winchester Scholar of New College of eminent ability.

My experience of my college tutors in those days was that they did not really hunt one enough. They told you what you ought to do, and hoped that you would do it, but they did not keep their eyes on your progress from week to week, nor check up on you. After all, an undergraduate is rather young, and needs something more than intermittent tutorial advice. My classical tutor, Herbert Richards, was a scholar of European reputation, a great authority on classical texts, especially of Aristotle. You can find his name—"emendavit H. Richards"—in many of the voluminous German commentaries. He was also, by the way, uncle of Grant Richards, the publisher. He used to lecture in College on Thucydides and Vergil; and he contrived to arrange his lectures at awkward times, including Saturday mornings.

His foresight in putting on his own in-college lecture from twelve to one on Saturday ingeniously spiked the guns of F. E. and myself. F. E. was always wanting to get away by a morning train on Saturday on some adventure or other, chiefly to do with making speeches on provincial political platforms. As for me, whenever the University were playing a football match in town or in the Midlands, I wanted to get away, too; a freshman hoping to get his Blue does not much fancy refusing an invitation to play for the Varsity. The result was that, not in collaboration, we both of us risked cutting " Dick's " lecture on our several errands.

"Dick" did not, as we both hoped, fail to notice our absence; we were called to account and gated. This was most inconvenient. But it happened I had discovered that there was a builder's yard in Hollywell Street which led through to a pile of ladders stacked against the very high wall at the back of the College. Purely as an experiment one evening I had found that you could push a long ladder upwards on to the top of the wall, where it balanced, and if gently conducted from the outside it would slide sweetly down and take the ground among the bushes in the quad. This secret I communicated to F. E. For the rest of our period in College, and particularly during our period of gating, we found it quite easy to return to College without going through the big gate under the eye of the porter who kept the book of entry. The only difficulty was to replace the ladder in the builder's yard. This was done by the reverse process of pushing the ladder up to balance on the top of the wall, but as there were no other ladders on the quad side, it was more or less a gymnastic feat, because one had to perch half-way up a not too solid plane tree.

My own adventures in this line of escape do not compare with F. E.'s. There was the famous occasion when he could not get leave to go to the Coming-of-Age Ball of the Duke of Marlborough, and took French leave, was stranded at Blenheim and rode back on a horse which he borrowed from a brake belonging to another party. I was not there, but if F. E. really did this he must have entered College over the back wall.

After our first term F. E. and I had rooms on the same stair opposite one another, and we always had breakfast together. After breakfast he very often used me as a try-out for his speeches at the Union. His method was to write out the beginning of his speech to the extent of a page and a half, and also the peroration to about the same amount. For the rest, he relied on enlightened improvisation. He used to read his preamble and peroration to me, treating me as a *vile corpus*, and invited my comments, but I do not remember that he paid the slightest attention to them.

It was on one of these occasions that he invited my assistance in escaping undetected for the week-end, because he wanted to go and stay with Lord Beauchamp at Madresfield Court, Malvern. He could not, he said, get leave, and was going to risk it. Would I, he asked, ruffle his bed, wash in his basin, and otherwise deceive his scout into supposing that he had not left his rooms? This behest, of course, I faithfully performed. On Monday I was the laughing-stock of the College, because F. E. had never left Oxford; he had merely transferred his habitation to a room in the back quad which for the time being was untenanted. A fair proportion of the University knew all about it by nightfall.

About the only person in College upon whom F. E. failed to exercise his peculiar talent with success was our common tutor, Herbert Richards. In fact, he is the only man I remember F. E. to have been afraid of. He feared his tongue, and that, from F. E., was a high compliment. I used to take Herbert Richards my Greek and Latin compositions. He would read them through, make occasional corrections with a slim gold pencil, and that was all. He offered no comment or constructive criticism. I remember taking him a copy of Latin verses of which I was rather proud at the time. He suggested in pencil the change of one epithet, and I am not sure it was an improvement, but actually never said a word except to give me the next piece to do. He had a habit of sniffing, but one could not be sure whether by way of praise or blame.

Then there was a Fellow of the College named Stone, who was reputed by tradition to be a great Vergilian scholar. We saw his grey beard disappearing down corridors once in a while. He was not a tutor. He wrote no books on his subject.

He was a Fellow. No doubt he was an amiable and genial character, but I never discovered that he contributed anything to the life of the community except his intra-mural reputation.

The Warden of Wadham was Thorley. He suffered from poor health and wore dark glasses and a large woollen scarf, but we saw nothing of him.

The Don who took the most interest in the men and life of the College was Joseph Wells, a distinguished authority on Greek and Roman history. His lectures on these subjects were famous throughout the University, and if you could get hold of the manuscript notes from which he lectured, you saved yourself the trouble of reading through many heavy volumes. He had a neat, concise, and selective mind, and was a remarkable teacher. He succeeded Thorley as Warden, and did a great deal for the College.

He made a habit of entertaining undergraduates in selected parties, especially freshmen. One morning four shy freshmen went to breakfast with him in the Senior Common Room, and Joey Wells was late. He came in on the party, washing his hands politely, and remarked, "Good-morning, gentlemen. We have had a little sun this morning."

One of the nervous freshmen was betrayed into saying, "Oh! May we congratulate you, Mr. Wells? I hope mother and child are doing well." Joey Wells was at the time a noted bachelor. At least, F. E. Smith told this story, and it consequently became history.

Remember, all this was over forty years ago. The modern Dons and tutors at Oxford are for the most part younger men, and the whole system of supervision of the work of undergraduates has, at least in my College, been vastly improved in efficiency. Even in my time Wadham was notably successful in the schools. Relatively to numbers, for Wadham was a small college, we rivalled Balliol and New College in successes in the examination-room, which suggests that Herbert Richards achieved more than one would suppose with his sniff. Now I come to review him at a distance, I can see that he was a great man.

He did not, however, approve of games and athletics. Or,

rather, for him they did not exist. In my first term I won the long jump in the freshmen's sports with a jump of nearly 23 feet, a distance in those days approaching a record. The following term, on the day of the University sports, on the results of which Blues were awarded, Mr. Richards invited McVey to go for a walk. These invitations were issued in turn to the Scholars, and were regarded with dread.

When McVey started on his walk he tried to persuade "Dick" to take the Iffley Road running-ground in the ambit, and look in there because I was expected to win the long jump and perhaps beat the record. "Dick" said with several sniffs, "I am afraid, Mr. McVey, that would not interest me." So I did not have the support of Tam McVey in my effort. All the same, I did win the long jump with a world's record which stood for many years—i.e., 23 feet 6½ inches. McVey made much mention of this characteristic piece of obstinacy.

The standard of track athletics at Oxford and Cambridge was high in those days, but there was not the technical knowledge and specialised training we see to-day.

Oxford and Cambridge athletics were about the only instance of team athletics. That was why so many Varsity athletes dropped the pursuit after going down. Athletic sports meetings, whether in London or the provinces, brought out the individual champions, but they were simply competitions on an individualistic basis. There was no social side and none of the comradeship which makes University track athletics so delightful.

Track athletics from the point of view of a social sport has in recent years been entirely changed owing to the institution of the Achilles Club. One prime mover in this effort was Bevill Rudd, the Oxford and Olympic runner, a Rhodes scholar from South Africa, who later on was private secretary to Lord Birkenhead. This club provides a continuation of team athletics for Oxford and Cambridge men after coming down, so that there still remains for them a world of their own where they can continue their athletics without being condemned to mere individual pot-hunting. Further, the existence of the Achilles Club, and its connection with the Olympic championships and the great athletic clubs of

America and the Continent, has had a striking influence in sending up the standard of technique at Oxford and Cambridge. The Milocarion Club is a parallel club for members of the Royal Navy, Army, and Air Force.

I myself, though up to record standard in the long jump, and capable if properly trained of running the 100 yards in ten seconds, never competed in track athletics of any kind after leaving Oxford. This was a pity, because I should probably have improved during the next four years. The standard performances in every kind of track athletics has in recent years gone up amazingly. No one has settled the question whether the individual men are superior or whether the improvement is due to improved technique and more specialised training.

The best long jump from toe mark to heel I made was 24 feet 2 inches, but I took off 9 inches before the board. In those days the taking-off board in the long jump was fixed with the breadth of the board vertical and the upper edge flush with the track. There was a sheer drop into a little trench about 5 inches deep on the far side of the take-off; so if one overstepped by a couple of inches one took a severe header into the pit. Nowadays the whitewashed taking-off board, which is twice as broad as it was, is flush with the surface on both sides, so that a jumper, though his jump does not count if he oversteps the mark, has nothing to fear in the way of an accident. But even allowing for this, I think that the modern method of long-jumping called the hitch-kick is technically superior. The new method amounts to a run into the air rather than a pure jump such as one would use to clear a ditch if chased by a bull.

Really the most interesting thing about my sudden leap into notoriety at Oxford was that before I discovered I could do it, thereby surprising myself, we had four other long-jumpers who could clear, like me, about 21 feet. One of them was W. J. Oakley, the famous international Association full-back; another was G. J. Mordaunt, the cricketer, who played for Kent and the Gentlemen; and a third H. M. Taberer, who played cricket for Essex and was afterwards Native Commissioner in Matabeleland. The fourth I forget; but the point is that, immediately I succeeded in jumping over 23 feet, all of them took to jumping over 22 feet. As the long jump in the Oxford and Cambridge Sports in those days was often won with a jump of under 21 feet, this little bit of athletic history might engage the interest of the psychologists. It must be remembered in considering modern achievements that there has been much improvement in the condition of running tracks and appurtenances.

Another point which interests me in retrospect is that although I was first string for Oxford in the long jump and 100 yards and won them both, the event I really fancied myself at was the 120 yards hurdles. My first two years we had several very good hurdlers, and I was not allowed to develop my ambition. Afterwards I was wanted for the long jump and the sprint, and could not take on the third event. Why is it that one always wants to do something else?

I did once run against Godfrey Shaw, the amateur champion hurdler of the time. He beat me, but to mitigate my defeat told me that he was sure that if I took up hurdling seriously I might win the championship. A pleasant thought across nearly fifty years.

The track athletes of my day were fine fellows, but I have no hesitation in saying that the rowing men in the Varsity boat in my time were the finest-looking lot in any of the athletic departments in the University. They included two splendid specimens in W. A. L. Fletcher and R. P. P. Rowe, the latter of whom I bracket as one of the two finest physical specimens I have ever seen. The other was S. M. J. Woods, the Cambridge fast bowler.

In my time Association football at Oxford was decidedly strong. We had, all four years, teams fit to play an ordinary League side level without quite being able to beat them. In fact, the calibre of our teams was such that had they been translated into professionalism and put among the League clubs, we should certainly have taken a good place. In my view, year in, year out, the Varsity teams both at Oxford and Cambridge are underrated in public estimation, but perhaps that is not surprising inasmuch as no matter how good the

Association eleven is, the Rugby fifteen of the same time always ranks far higher in the eyes both of gown and town.

I played four years in the Association team, but I was a more important footballer from the Varsity point of view as a near-Blue in Rugby than as a Blue and International at Association.

The three star men of the strong Oxford soccer teams in which I played were G. O. Smith, the centre-forward, W. J. Oakley, the left back, and G. B. Raikes, the goalkeeper, all of whom played for England against Scotland. Another international was the present Sir E. Farquhar Buzzard, Regius Professor of Medicine and also Physician to the King.

Buzzard (who was called "The Bird") was an Old Carthusian, and even in those days had an excellent bedside manner, in the sense that he not only looked wise, but was accepted by his friends and associates as a repository of wisdom. One of those fellows with a weighty manner and a knack of chipping in at the end of a conversation with a final and conclusive opinion. I cannot remember that he did anything in particular in examinations, but he inhabited the science laboratory up by the Parks. I met him a few weeks ago at Oxford, and the Regius Professor is scarcely distinguishable from the undergraduate I knew nearly fifty years ago. He was never young, and he is not now old.

I did not remind him that he once let me in for a very precarious situation. A year or two after I came down, my sister suddenly said to me, "Charlie, whatever is this? Mollie Dawson says she saw you without any clothes on in Regent Street!" My sister had and has dimples, and I thought she was being amusing. Not at all. She maintained that her friend had seen a picture of me in the nude in a book illustration in a Regent Street shop window.

Then I remembered. "The Bird" had persuaded me one Sunday afternoon to go up to the science laboratory to be photographed for scientific purposes in all sorts of poses for the purpose of portraying muscular structure. The result evidently was that I became anonymously immortalised in the pages of a book on anatomy for art students, in various statuesque attitudes. The book is to this day the principal textbook on the subject, but I claim no credit for its merits. I only hope I am still as much like what I was then as is my betrayer.

Buzzard was a strong player at left half-back. I hope he is as good a Regius Professor as he was a footballer.

The year I was captain of soccer we had a wonderful season and lost only one match. Unfortunately, that was the match against Cambridge, for which we were odds-on favourites. We lost partly because Cambridge were strengthened just for that match by several fourth-year men, notably the inside forward G. P. Dewhurst, but mainly because when we got to Queen's Club we found the ground frozen like iron and really unfit for play, and it had happened that there was a thaw at Oxford the day before, and all our men had arrived with long knobs on their boots, whereas it was still freezing at Cambridge, and their team turned up with shallow bars of felt.

Just before the match the referee put it to the Cambridge captain and myself as to whether we were ready to proceed on a ground unfit for play. The Cambridge captain was doubtful but willing, and I thought that we could not lose the match. But I also had in mind that Oakley and I were first strings in hurdles and long jump in the University sports within a fortnight, and, as President of the Athletics Club, I feared a postponement might interfere with our activities. So I made the mistake of agreeing to play; and probably the best side that ever represented Oxford at Association football got beaten, and, what is more, on the play of the day, on its merits. It was more like ice hockey.

In the cricket world at Oxford I started with the uncommon advantage of being a known man. It happened that L. C. H. Palairet, who was captain of cricket, had been captain at Repton and had given me my school colours. I had batted with him the other end in many school matches and had also been one of his main bowlers. Then again, in the summer before, I had played for the Surrey first eleven in one match. I was picked to play in the Freshmen's match, scored a century, and went straight into the Oxford eleven. Better still, I scored another century in an early out-match against Somerset, which was a feat of sorts, because the Somerset bowling, otherwise fairly strong, included the redoubtable S. M. J. Woods, then in the prime of his career as one of the best fast bowlers of all time. What is more, he was a complete artist with consummate skill in disguising his change of pace without varying his action.

It would be absurd for me to endeavour to escape, in the light of after years, a certain notoriety as a cricketer. About six years afterwards, when I began making two thousand runs a year and being top of the English averages and that sort of thing, the people who wrote about cricket started a legend that I was not much use as a bat at Oxford, and anyhow had no style, but was a useful fast bowler.

In corroboration of *soi-dit* bowling ability, no one has ever succeeded in disabusing me of my memory that on two occasions for Oxford *v.* M.C.C. I did the hat-trick. And at Lord's! And the names! The first series was A. E. Stoddart, A. E. Gibson, and W. C. Hedley; the second, T. C. O'Brien, C. W. Wright, and A. H. Heath. Two great and four good batsmen. Further, the first time I played for the Gentlemen at Lord's it was as the fast bowler of the side. Again, in a Gentlemen *v.* Players match at the Oval—then of nearly the same repute as the match at Lord's—I once got 8 wickets in the game as well as about 100 runs. I am, you see, trying to prove that I was quite a useful bowler without being the inferior batsman of subsequent legends. The critics, however, always added that I was no batsman until I came under the influence of Ranji.

I played in every match in my first year, and enjoyed the distinction of helping to win a remarkable game against Cambridge at Lord's. This was the match in which G. J. V. Weigall of Cambridge did more to win the match for Oxford than anyone on our side. Cambridge had a magnificent team, captained by F. S. Jackson, so strong in batting that A. O. Jones and D. L. A. Jephson, both afterwards county captains, were the last two on the list. They had E. C. Streatfield, an all-rounder of England class, C. M. Wells and A. J. L. Hill, both of whom played for the Gentlemen, and the rest were of almost equal calibre.

On paper we were not in the betting. But Gerry Weigall ran out F. S. Jackson when well set, A. J. L. Hill before he got going, and C. M. Wells when he was becoming dangerous. Gerry then went on to score an imperturbable 63.

In our first innings we lost 2 wickets for 0. When I joined Malcolm Jardine (the father of our modern Douglas) the board read 0—2—0. Jardine and I then put on about 100 together before I was bowled by Jackson for 44.

Jardine went on to score 140. He was a beautiful player, with a perfect back-stroke and a perfect cut and neat late off-drive. Had he afterwards played county cricket I think he would have played for England. He was a superb fielder at mid-off. There was a dramatic moment in the Varsity match when he was in the nineties. E. C. Streatfeild, bowling round the wicket, planted a ball on his foot. The umpire gave Jardine the benefit. Jardine was afterwards the leader of the Bombay Bar, and he told me that when he was leaving India for good the Viceroy, Lord Chelmsford, on saying good-bye, added, "You know, Malcolm, you were out that time."

Well, our left-hand hitter, V. T. Hill, who afterwards played for Somerset, flogged up a magnificent century. We topped the Cambridge score and won easily.

Cambridge, however, had their revenge next year. Our batting failed, and I was top scorer with only 35. This was the match Kumar Shri Ranjitsinhji played for Cambridge. He did not make a score, but fielded marvellously at short slip.

The next year I was captain, and I and F. A. Phillips, an old Rossall boy, made most of the runs, of which I contributed precisely 100 not out. It was touch and go for three figures, because when I was 84 our last man, the Winchester wicket-keeper, R. P. Lewis, came in white in the face. He was a beautiful wicket-keeper and a hopeful if incapable bat. I was the other end when he took guard, and he then walked down the wicket and whispered hoarsely, "Charles, I won't get out." He did not get out that over. He kept his bat plugged in his block-hole and scarcely moved it to meet the balls he did not leave alone. I knew the next over was my only chance, so I gambled and carted four straight balls to the square-leg boundary. The first ball of the next over Lewis lifted his bat from the block-hole and was bowled all over his wicket. We won easily, as R. C. N. Palairet and H. K. Foster quite brilliantly knocked off the runs required in the second innings.

My last year I split my finger against the M.C.C. just before the Inter-Varsity match, and ought not to have played, except that I could bowl. I could scarcely hold my bat, and scored a well-deserved 0 and 1. That year G. J. Mordaunt of Wellington was captain. He was a beautiful bat, but was not successful at Lord's.

During my four years at Oxford we had good but not outstanding bowlers, except the medium-pace left-hander G. F. H. Berkeley, who played my first two years and was one of the best amateur left-handers I ever saw, much admired by Ranjitsinhji, who was caught at the wicket off him in the Inter-Varsity match. Were I a bowler, I would rather have praise from Ranjitsinhji than from any other batsman.

Two members of the Oxford elevens of my time whose names have since become familiar in the cricket world, not only as players but also as pavilion magnates, were H. D. G. Leveson-Gower and P. F. Warner. The former is the perpetual President of the Surrey County Cricket Club, after being captain of the Surrey eleven for some years; the latter has been the Standing Chairman of the England Selection Committee until quite recently, after captaining Middlesex for many years, and also being captain of two successful England teams in Australia. He has achieved the honour of knighthood for services to cricket. This reminds me of W. G., who, according to a wholly unfounded witticism, was the only man who ever became a Doctor of Medicine on account of successful operations on the cricket field. One also recalls that W. G. always referred to Leveson-Gower as Snipe, whereas his otherwise invariable nickname was Shrimp.

Shrimp Leveson-Gower came up to Oxford when I was already in the eleven. We had heard of him owing to his remarkable success as a boy in the Winchester team. I happened to meet the Winchester professional the year before, and asked him what sort of a cricketer his young prodigy was.

"Don't know about progidy, sir, but Mr. Leveson-Gower is a champion."

"What do you mean—champion?"

"Well, sir, all I can tell you is, he is another W. G."

I expected to meet a six-footer with at least the beginnings of a beard. Instead of that, a scanty little figure appeared, with a stooping stance at the wicket and a notable talent for amiability. The Shrimp was otherwise quite unlike W. G., except that for his size he hit the ball astonishingly hard. He could hit all round the wicket, but his characteristic strokes were a slithery little cut, off the middle of the blade between first and second slip, done with a minute fish-tail flicker of the bat; and an off-drive which went past cover point when you expected it to go past mid-off. He could always be trusted for runs at a pinch; which is a good character, because, as I heard W. G. once say, "There's lots of 'em can make runs, but there's not so many can make 'em when they're wanted." The Shrimp afterwards earned a tall reputation as a captain.

I first saw Sir Pelham Warner in a match on the famous Close at Rugby between the Old Reptonians and a men's team, mostly Old Rubeians, in which he was the only boy. He looked about 13, but was no doubt older. It was a mud wicket. He went in first and carried his bat for 50 out of a small total. This in spite of the fact that I was bowling at him all the time, and our umpire gave half the opposing batsmen out for l.b.w.

Sir Pelham was the apple of Tom Emmett's eye. Tom Emmett had been the most famous fast left-hand bowler of the old Yorkshire eleven, and was a severe coach. Sir Pelham tells me that Tom's method was to fire down two wides outside the off stump, then a wide to leg, then a snorter which pitched on the off stump and knocked the leg stump flying, and then to say, "Young Mr. Warner, a cricket ball is meant to be hit." Nevertheless, Sir Pelham was an imperturbably accomplished school batsman and made a lot of runs.

The second time I saw him playing was in a selected schools' eleven at Richmond, of which Clive Wigram of Winchester (now Lord Wigram) was captain. Young Sir Pelham went in first as usual, with Percy Latham of Malvern, afterwards captain of Cambridge the year I was captain of Oxford. I was in first wicket and sat padded in the pavilion the whole of the afternoon, because young Sir Pelham and his partner omitted to get out.

Sir Pelham's long and enthusiastic career in first-class cricket is not at the moment in question. At Oxford he was equally enthusiastic, but was chiefly an off-side player with an excellent drive along the ground, whereas he afterwards developed into an on-side player with an ability in defence which was the despair of the Yorkshire bowlers. At the moment I cannot remember any match between Sussex and Middlesex in which he did not make a century. At Oxford he studied Law, and devoted any spare time he had to cricket. In what intervals of time he obtained his meticulous knowledge of the facts which most of us have to look up in Wisden remains a mystery. Even in his Oxford days there were few more reliable batsmen in England to open an innings. He always took a great interest in the welfare of his brother cricketers, and was even then an optimist.

H. K. Foster, the eldest of the famous family, in my last year at Oxford scored one of the genuinely brilliant centuries in the history of the Inter-Varsity match. He had a peculiar turf-singeing off-drive, of the type rarely found except in a racquet player. Afterwards in county cricket he developed many more strokes all round the wicket. And the reason of this was that under the tutelage of Alfred Shaw he altered his stance from the rigid Public School position to the easier type exemplified by Arthur Shrewsbury, Ranjitsinhji, Trumper, and Walter Hammond. In later times he always reminded me of Henry Chaplin, the famous sporting squire of Blankeney. He was a selector along with me when I was captain of England; an excellent and resolute judge of cricket. He had, and quite rightly, a great opinion of the Foster family as batsmen.

The most successful Foster was R. E. I was in with him

while he made his two centuries in Gentlemen *v.* Players at Lord's. But he was after my time at Oxford.

Memories of Oxford to one who has been in the cricket eleven must always largely flutter over the Parks.

There is no lovelier cricket ground.

CHAPTER VI

ROUND THE CAPE

THERE was a cricket enthusiast of a Scot who, starting as a railway porter, promoted himself to be the Spiers and Ponds of the Cape. There was a peer who, instead of making speeches in the House of Lords, devoted himself primarily to Yorkshire cricket and secondarily to taking teams abroad. There was an England bowler of the best who was sent to the Cape for his health. There was the temporarily dispossessed Heir Apparent of an Indian State who had become a fantastic success as a batsman, and who with Rajput love of honour and glory desired to see Sussex champion county. There was a recent addition to the Sussex county eleven in whom the Rajput Heir Apparent saw possibilities. That is how I came to be in South Africa in the year of the Jameson Raid.

That is to say, a cricket team was collected at the instance of Douglas Logan of Matjesfontein, managed and captained by Lord Hawke, aided by George Lohmann of Surrey, and modestly adorned by myself on the recommendation of Ranjitsinhji.

As a producer Ranji was right because the experience turned me from an ordinary good University cricketer into a candidate for the Gentlemen's Eleven, and for England. The legend that I was a bad bat who learned to become better simply through watching Ranji is erroneous. What promoted me was the education of this tour in South Africa in a strong team with complete liberty to devote myself to the game.

Lord Hawke may or may not have been a good captain. The authorities differ on this; personally, I think he was a very good captain off the field. He was certainly a superfine manager of a cricket tour. What is more, he was a batsman whose excellence has been underrated because on the Yorkshire side he used to put himself in low on the list when often few runs were required. He was a diplomat and a social success. He was also a good runner. He won races at Eton and even once beat Macaulay, the famous half-miler. This I did not know at the Cape in 1895, so I lost a fiver in backing Audley Miller, the Wiltshire captain, to beat him over a hundred yards. Charles Wright of Nottingham pocketed the fiver. Martin Hawke was a lovable man, although the story of his being a great captain was a myth.

Lord Hawke's team of 1895-6 in South Africa was the strongest he ever captained. Included in it were Sir Timothy O'Brien, ranked by both Ranjitsinhji and W. G. Grace as amongst the best half-dozen batsmen of the period; H. T. Hewett of Somerset, one of the greatest left-handed hitters of all time; Tom Hayward, the great Surrey player, for many years England's number one batsman; A. J. L. Hill of Cambridge and Hampshire, another batsman of the highest order, and quite one of the best stylists of those days; the famous C. W. Wright, who for long held the record for the highest aggregate of runs in the Oxford and Cambridge match; that tremendous all-round cricketer, S. M. J. Woods; and another fine all-rounder who never achieved the fame he deserved, H. R. Bromley Davenport, who would certainly be in the England team to-day as a fastish left-hand bowler. That is a good bunch. In addition we had George Lohmann, still the best medium-paced right-hand bowler in the world; E. J. Tyler of Somerset, a slow left-hand bowler about as good as Hedley Verity, but kept out of the England eleven by such units as Briggs and Peel. We had Butt, the Sussex wicket-keeper, sharing that position in our team with C. W. Wright; Audley Miller, captain of Wiltshire, and Christopher Heseltine, the Hampshire fast bowler.

Lord Hawke, Sir Timothy, and "Colonel" Hewett travelled to Cape Town in a Union Castle mail boat, R.M.S. *Moor;* the rest of us in the Intermediate liner *Goth.* We had lovely weather, and it was a superb voyage. My education was much advanced by sharing a cabin with Sammy Woods, whose only rival in the cricket world at telling stories was C. W. Wright. The most vivid incident of the voyage was when Charles Wright, being on the entertainment committee, failed to persuade a lady to play the piano at a concert, and dodged round the corner of the deck to retort in a very audible voice, "Well, you ain't no bloody water-spaniel, you ain't!" Charles Wright was friendly with another lady who was a cabin-companion of the recalcitrant, and had told Charles that she never had a bath. His polite phrase was not original. It was derived from a story about W. G. Grace in his first visit to Australia. The English team had gone to play an up-country match, and W. G. and his company were welcomed by the hotel proprietor of a quadrangle of iron shanties, who said, "Pleased to meet you, Dr. Grace, but we can't do you here like they do in the cities. Not much in the way of bloody bathrooms and such-like."

"That don't matter," squeaked W. G. "We Graces ain't no bloody water-spaniels."

W. G. always tried to put people at their ease. Charles Wright, on the other hand, expected everybody to be as impervious to barbed words as he was himself.

We arrived at Cape Town just before Christmas, 1895. Cape Town was in those days, and probably still is (since towns south of the equator do not change much in character), more attractive at first sight than any other city I have seen, and rivals Colombo in immediate fascination. It would remind one of the French Riviera, and in a way of Monte Carlo, if the hills of the Riviera, parallel to the coast, were all lumped into one lion-shaped mass like Table Mountain. On the blazing blue day when we arrived, there was no table-cloth of cloud. Christmas Day we spent climbing the mountain, but we did not climb far. We stopped to bathe in a cove, but not much because the water was icy cold, and we fled out faster than we ran in. Most surprising, because in the great heat of the afternoon no water has ever looked more attractive.

The glory of Cape Town is the garden suburbs, which are really gardens without artifice. They are strung along the railway, which runs round inland of the mountain and then on in a southerly direction to Simon's Bay, the British Naval Station on the other side of the Peninsula. All of them have flowery names, such as Wynberg and Rondebosch. Newlands, where the cricket ground of the Western Province club is situated, is one of them. We practised on the Newlands ground, a delightful spot with an unpretentious pavilion on the edge of a pinewood which flanked the side furthest from the mountain. One could see the lower slopes in the near distance covered with a lighter green which looked like scrub oak. In all the suburbs there are long wide red roads with avenues of tall gum-trees and frequent villas. The occasional old white Dutch houses with gables the shape of an ace of clubs, very thick walls and wide, shady stoeps, had gardens splashed with tall bushes of fuchsia and bougainvillea. No one would believe that all the flowering shrubs as well as the trees (except the acacia and thorn bushes) had been imported. They look indigenous enough.

In those days the Newlands ground was of turf, of the kind called buffalo grass, and the wicket was matting. The modern ground has a marl-made wicket of the Australian kind, with an outfield of couch grass that looks like velvet.

We played a match after a week's practice, and then were invited to lunch with Cecil Rhodes at Groet Schur. I had met Rhodes at Oxford at breakfast with a don at Oriel College, and was looking forward to seeing him again in the land which he had made almost synonymous with his own name. But Cecil Rhodes was not at Groet Schur to welcome us. In his place was Captain Porter, the harbour-master of Cape Town, a little man, weather-beaten and clean-shaven, who could not be other than a sailor. He apologised for the absence of Mr. Rhodes, and we had a wonderful lunch in the large wainscoted dining-room, cool and almost dark behind the thick white walls of a house built on the old Dutch plan. Plenty of "the widow."

After lunch we went out to see the grounds, and the zoo on the side of the mountain, where all sorts of South African fauna were enclosed in paddocks resembling Whipsnade. In one paddock was a truculent solitary wildebeeste. Sammy Woods and I and H. H. Francis (a midget, who had played for Gloucestershire but did not belong to our team) approached the compound. The creature has the hairy head of the gnu and the body of an antelope; a packet of slate-coloured hostility. It stamped its foot and advanced. Francis climbed on the oak gate of the compound, sat on the top, and drummed his heels to tease the beast, which promptly charged the gate like a horizontal bomb. Francis was unseated, and would have fallen on the gnu had I not caught him in the slips by his coat-tail. He hung suspended thereby. Sammy Woods grasped him by the seat of his trousers and lightly recovered him, laughing as only Sammy Woods could laugh. By that time it was late in the afternoon, and we drove down to the station in Cape carts. On the way home the newsboys were selling " ticky-slips "—that is to say, stop-press news on small bits of paper at threepence apiece. The ticky was the least coin then known in South Africa, a land of millionaires on the gold standard. Then we knew why Cecil Rhodes had been adrift. It was the news of the Jameson Raid. We heard afterwards that Rhodes was in his palatial office in Cape Town consoling himself with "the widow."

The Raid raised a hubbub in Cape Town, and we were delayed there for ten days. Everyone in the hotels and clubs was considering the situation precisely as Cecil Rhodes did; for nobody at the Cape in those days considered any situation—even the sale of a small block of shares—except in the light of at least a half-bottle of pop. My memories of Cape Town reveal a canopy of dark blue, the moon shining down between the gum-trees, and the pop of champagne corks.

Presently it was deemed useful to send us to Johannesburg as an antidote to the inflamed melancholy of that distant city, then in the throes of not knowing what to do after the failure of the Jameson Raid. We entrained late one evening for the thousand miles journey to the Rand. We traversed the northern part of Cape Colony in the dark, wound up the zig-zag of the Hex River Pass into the Karoo desert, and arrived early in the morning at Matjesfontein for breakfast. One did not obtain food on the train in those days; one stopped at convenient stations where Mr. Logan had planted refreshment-rooms, and one never missed getting for breakfast porridge so hot that one could not master it before the train was due out.

The Karoo desert looked like a boundless flat dust-heap. If an occasional sudden hill appeared in the distance so clear was the atmosphere that one could see even several miles away the veins on the rock. At midday, near the borders of the Orange Free State, an acre or two of locusts included the railway line in their visitation. The rails were so lubricated with their squashed bodies that the wheels would not grip. The engine staff had to sprinkle spadefuls of earth.

When the train ran into the Transvaal frontier station a line of burghers with bandoliers and loaded rifles ranged themselves in extended order on both sides. We had to turn out for inspection and douane. A careful process; we had to pay duty even on our cricket bats. Inadvertently I admitted that mine cost a guinea each. I had to pay out half-a-crown from my slender resources on each of them. Charles Wright gave in the cost of his—which were identical with mine—at five shillings each, and he paid *pro rata*.

Sir Timothy O'Brien had some aristocratically Irish objection to something done to his luggage, and he caused trouble, diplomatically smoothed away in the end by Lord Hawke. But the crisis was when a Customs official glimpsed what he thought was a revolver in the trouser pocket of H. T. Hewett. The "Colonel," obstinate and imperturbable, refused to be searched. He just said "No," and looked so threatening that the official fetched some more officials. Then followed an altercation, noisily on the part of the officials, silently insistent in the negative on the part of the "Colonel." Armed burghers added themselves to the group, and they, too, talked. In a word, the most vehement altercation, with the "Colonel" in the middle as obstinate as a cornered grizzly. Again Lord Hawke had to exercise his diplomatic talent. In the end the "Colonel" succeeded in entraining with the rest of us, with his cylindrical tooth-brush bottle from his dressing-case still in his trouser pocket, unexamined.

A few miles outside Johannesburg we heard a noise like the salvo of a battleship. As soon as we arrived in the station we found that three trucks of dynamite had blown up in a siding, and made a hole big enough to contain an ocean liner. The Malay district of the town was wrecked. The casualties were terrible. One native was killed by the head of a donkey which was blown two hundred yards.

At the hotel we found the water-supply cut off by the commandos stationed in the neighbourhood. We had to wash in soda-water at two shillings a bottle. The price of beer was five shillings a bottle. Not until the Reformer Abe Bailey had bought himself out of prison for £20,000 did we succeed in getting a bath. The other main prisoners, George Farrer, Lionel Phillips, Frank Rhodes, and Percy Fitzpatrick, had to be condemned to death by hanging before they signed cheques in favour of Oom Paul for £25,000. The prisoners were out of luck all round. Lord Hawke, Tim O'Brien, and Charles Wright went to dine with them in prison to cheer them up and took £98 off them at poker. If Abe Bailey had not already repatriated himself, twice the money would have gone the other way.

Our first few days in Johannesburg were unfamiliar. The Boer Field Artillery were emplaced on coigns of vantage overlooking the town from the near hills. One afternoon as we were walking back to the hotel a strong contingent of mounted burghers, with their neat ·303 carbines across their thighs at the ready, like hunting whips, cantered through the town. Their bearded faces and flapping felt hats were just as in the pictures of the first Boer War in the *Illustrated London News*, when there were no half-tone blocks but only line drawings. They looked formidable and truculent. They had a jaunty air of "We are the people of the land who can shoot. What is all this riff-raff of money-grubbers and street-bred adventurers?" The town was nervous. Scores of mining officials and bank managers were mixed up in the abortive adventure. Many of them were on the lists for trial.

Meanwhile the Wanderers' ground, where we were to play, had been turned into a hospital, and after several days we were sent on, of all places, to Pretoria, where Paul Kruger was sitting in a saturnine triumph. The whole of Jameson's troops, who had been cornered at Krugersdorp in a narrow defile, were in prison.

Some of us, including as usual Sammy Woods and myself, rode out to the scene of the disaster. They gave Sammy

Woods a known buck-jumper to ride, but forgot that Sammy was an Australian. Sammy was hurt, but not from falling off. He said, " I suppose you think that this blighter can buck. Let me tell you he's only a pig-rooter." We saw the marks of the machine-gun bullets on the rocks, and a number of dead mules. The burghers had trapped the raiders and plastered them from behind two converging ridges. Jameson's men had had no chance except to surrender as quickly as they could twist a pocket-handkerchief. We never knew what the casualties were, except that Charles Coventry had a bullet through his back which missed his spine by a fraction of an inch. He was in hospital, and all the nurses in South Africa were volunteering to attend him.

The Raid would have got through had not someone forgotten to cut a telephone wire. The mistake gave Oom Paul eight hours' start. It was a stirring time, and the lounges and bars of Johannesburg, then a town which ended on all sides in unfinished roads but had a centre of gaiety, were full of stories of various degrees of inconsistency. The main story I gathered was that the host of adventurous young men in Johannesburg had promised to sally out, meet Jameson's troop of raiders, and proceed to capture Pretoria by a *coup d'état*. We heard that hundreds of rifles had been smuggled in by rail in piano-crates. Whether the belligerents were as capable of acting as they were of talking, I very much doubt. At any rate, Paul Kruger had waited until the tortoise had put out its head; so the tail of the tortoise never came into active collaboration. What with the explosion of the dynamite and of the projected *coup d'état*, Johannesburg was not at all its brilliant self. Mining, finance, and the world of saloons were subdued to a semitone. People were even rather careful what they said. The rumour was that it was an accident of garrulous indiscretion late one evening in a billiard-room that had betrayed to one of Oom Paul's agents the plan of the Jameson Raid. Curiously enough, the supposed delinquent was a man very well known in English first-class cricket, who a few years before had joined the numerous band of Savile Row younger sons in the adventurous mining city.

The story of the Raid has been told many times, together with its repercussions in England; but at the time and at the place one had the impression that the gay world, where a young man could be a successful financier one day and a waiter the next, had talked itself into an ill-judged adventure. There was much more behind it than this—big financial interests had found themselves perpetually stalled and milked; and even a casual visitor would not miss, if he was an Englishman, the uncomfortable feeling that he was regarded by the burghers as one of an inferior race. Ten minutes in a wayside saloon where young Boers were present gave one the feeling of being sized up at the small rating of a compatriot of the roineks defeated at Majuba Hill. But when, owing to the impossibility of our cricket team functioning as a diversion at Johannesburg, we were moved on to Pretoria, we played against an eleven in which Dutch names were predominant without any feeling alien to the pleasant rivalry of an English cricket field.

Pretoria was a quiet and sedate town lying among round downs, reminding one of Sussex. In the centre was a large square of hard red earth, where one could imagine ox-wagons in laager, with fine solid Government buildings dotted round it. There was a pleasant club, with a pleasant membership of young barristers and officials of the Kruger régime. A clear mountain stream ran through the garden with big pools such as one sees in North Wales, and I saw the flash of fish under the banks, which I hoped were trout.

Did we see Paul Kruger? We did. We called on him. Lord Hawke was persuaded to arrange this. So in small sections we were invited to call at his villa at seven o'clock in the morning. Wanting to have a good look at the notorious old man, I attached myself to two sections. He was not disappointing. He was exactly as one had seen him portrayed in newspapers and periodicals, with his broadcloth frock-coat, big head sunk in his shoulders on a short neck, long biblical face, quick cunning eyes, in a frame of patriarchal beard. He did not stand up. He sat in a chair with Tante Kruger standing behind him, a watchful, buxom old lady, with her hands crossed under her bosom like a reproachful landlady. All the time he smoked Boer tobacco in a large crooked calabash. We sat round the big parlour on wooden chairs and were served with mug-like cups of sweet coffee. A young Dutch barrister introduced and explained us. Lord Hawke on the first occasion, and Sammy Woods on the second, offered some polite phrases. Lord Hawke said that he hoped the President would find our visit of interest to the President's capital, and that the people of the town would come to see the cricket match and enjoy it.

I believe that Oom Paul understood English, but he did not betray it. The interpreter translated, I expect adequately —he was a bright young man. Oom Paul grunted and said three words which I do not think the interpreter translated quite literally. He said that the President was very pleased. The President did not look at all pleased. I believe what he said was, "No good here."

On the second occasion Sammy Woods introduced our side of the interview by saying, "Well, Mr. Kruger, we hope we find you well. We have come all this way to see you." Although the tone of his voice was cordial, he looked, did Sammy, for the first and only time in his life, as if he thought he had made a mistake and was not quite sure how he would be taken. This time Oom Paul grunted and made no reply.

It was a silent interview, lasting like the first about half an hour, relieved only by the sweet coffee. When we went out through the wide stoep up the little path and out of the wicket gate, which many people have seen just as we saw it in the film "Rhodes of Africa," Sammy Woods remarked that the old blighter was not very hearty. We certainly got as little out of Oom Paul as did the Reform Committee of Johannesburg; but, on the other hand, he got much less out of us. Oom Paul was a one. All the stories about him were true. The best of them, perhaps, relates to when he was invited to open a synagogue and accepted on condition that he should not have to make a speech. But he did. He said, "I declare this synagogue open in the name of the Lord Jesus Christ."

Myself, I got this much out of Kruger that I was able recently at John Drinkwater's house to give Oscar Homolka, who was playing Oom Paul in "Rhodes of Africa," some few

hints about the old President; how he sat, how he shot his
cold blue glances without turning his head, and other details.
Homolka portrayed the old man to the life. I cannot say the
same of the characterisation in the film of Cecil Rhodes himself. Walter Huston is a brilliant actor, but he was not Cecil
Rhodes.

From disturbed Johannesburg and placid Pretoria we left
on our long train journey down to Natal. Not far down the
line some large corrugated iron sheds were pointed out to us,
where we were told the prisoners of the Jameson Raid were
in safe keeping. Eventually we ran down past the foot of un-
forgettable Majuba Hill, and early in the morning tried to
eat our breakfast of superheated porridge in the railway
station at Ladysmith. And so across the Tugela river, not
knowing how historic our surroundings would presently be,
to Pietermaritzburg.

At a small wayside station a few miles outside Maritzburg
an old Zulu, with crinkled grey hair and an immense slim
wiry body about 7 feet tall, loped on to the deserted platform.
He was a local policeman, and the original of Umslopagaas
in *King Solomon's Mines*. His long thin arms even then
appeared well able to wield the fabulous battle-axe called
The Woodpecker, with which Rider Haggard's heroic Zulu
gently bored holes in the skulls of his enemies. The train
went on before I could escape to interview this striking figure.
I would not like to have met him at close quarters with no
room to run away; even with space those long sinewy legs
boded ill for escape.

Pietermaritzburg across the years, which have included
quite some time spent in India, resides in my memory as very
much like a cantonment town in the Punjab, if you take
away half the temperature and add more greenery. It was a
British Army station with a cavalry depôt of the 7th Hussars.
Among the officers was Prince Alexis of Teck, Queen Mary's
brother; and also that English equivalent of Umslopagaas,
R. M. Poore, afterwards a great batsman, who one year
topped the averages in England, a noted performer in the
Naval and Military Tournament, and the best back in the
Army at polo. There was a certain amount of clash between

the hospitality of the 7th Hussars and of the local Reception Committee. One evening when we were dining with the soldiers we ought to have been at a smoking concert arranged for our special entertainment. But when we did arrive at the smoking concert very late Sammy Woods obliterated all misunderstanding by his enormous success on the platform. Had Sammy Woods devoted himself to the music-hall stage he would have made a fortune; he could beat Albert Chevalier to the tune of " My Old Dutch," and was unrivalled with :

> " It really is a very pretty garden,
> And 'Ampstead from the 'ousetops can be seen.
> With a pair of opera glasses
> You can see to 'Ackney Marshes
> If it wasn't for the 'ouses in between."

He also had a remarkable song of which the refrain was :

> " Wear a flannel next your chest,
> And when you go to rest
> Keep a night-light always burning by your bed, bed, bed."

Sammy was a magnificent figure, like the statue of the Athlete at Rome, with an engaging baritone voice and a battery of facial expression, but when once he stepped on to the platform the question was whether he would ever come off it. I have never seen a less self-conscious performer nor one who so enjoyed his own interminable repertoire.

The most important event on paper here was the cricket match, but not the most exciting. Still, the cricket match was enhanced by the Mayor, who offered a medal for the highest score. Charles Wright was top scorer in the first innings and stood champagne to everybody that night. Subsequently Sir Timothy O'Brien made a century and thought he was top scorer, and also stood champagne. In the end I myself made 153 and won the medal, but I did not receive it for over a year, when the conscientious Mayor had the kindness to send me a gilt trophy of crossed bats and pendent shield, care of The Honourable Sussex County Cricket Club, Hove, Brighton, England. There was not time before the train went for me to stand champagne, and in any case it would have been on tick—like the medal.

But the great event was a polo match between the very high-class mounted four of the Hussars and six of us on foot.

That is to say, a mixture of polo and hockey; and—would you believe it?—Lord Hawke's Footmen won the game. Our team consisted of Bromley Davenport, Heseltine, Hill, Miller, Sammy Woods, and myself; and I have never been so hot in my life. The notable feature was the skill with which the Hussars avoided knocking anybody down, especially as the ponies wanted to exercise their habit of riding us off the ball. Afterwards, in Johannesburg, we made the mistake of challenging the local polo club, and that time we were badly beaten, because the Johannesburgers, including the popular sportsman named Bettelheim, who played back with a beard, were unable to translate their intentions into the movements of their ponies. I have never been knocked down so often, even in the final of the Association Football Cup. What is more, the polo ground at Johannesburg is very hard red earth.

Nothing much happened at Durban except that we saw the bowling of C. B. Llewellyn, a boy left-hander who afterwards qualified for Hampshire and was chosen as a reserve for England in a Test Match, and that Tom Hayward was so attractive to mosquitoes that he was indistinguishable from a beefsteak for at least a fortnight. Somehow, Durban reminds me of Bombay, only at Durban one never went anywhere in those days except in a rickshaw pulled by a running Zulu boy in white cotton pants and a festoon of ostrich feathers.

Durban, fine city as it is, with its beautiful residential quarter of Berea, we were not sorry to leave. We took ship hoping to be cool again, but it was so hot at night that we slept on deck. So we presently arrived at the port of East London, about half-way between Durban and Cape Town. It was a formidable landing. We were lowered from the ship in a big basket into a tub, and the tub made for an opening in the coast which seemed to be obscured by a recurrent wave of prodigious size. This was the bar. We crossed the bar by an accurate piece of timing on the part of our skipper, who lay off until the right moment and then shot his cockleshell of a tub through a corner of the wave just as it subsided, and we found ourselves inland of a wall of water which quite obscured the ship from view.

When I say "we," I should say all of us except George Lohmann. George had been there before. Hours before we reached East London, George casually let it drop that he would be unable to land there, but would travel in the ship on to Cape Town and join us later. Nothing would induce him to renew his previous acquaintance with the bar where, on some occasion, I suppose, the skipper had mistimed his spurt. When we were safely inside we were more sympathetic with George than when we left him on the ship.

So we went on to King William's Town, and thence, leaving civilisation behind us, by Cape cart across the veldt to Grahamstown, a journey of two days. On the first day, which began by being a typical South African day of cloudless blue and transparent sunshine, just when we arrived at a deep spruit the light of the sun went out in a grey pall of clouds. Crash after crash of thunder foretold the end of the world. The sky was a fountain of fire with perpetual flashes of lightning, and the rain came down like a waterfall. The horses refused to budge. They swung round with their tails to the slant of the deluge, and there we sat. I never thought we should see another day; my only consolation was that if I was blotted out in a flash of fire, so would the whole of the party be. Why this subconscious jet of comradeship should have been a consolation only a modern psycho-analyst can explain. The watery, fiery chaos subsided as suddenly as it had arisen. Then on the brow of the spruit, from a scrap of scrub you would not think would hide a hare, emerged a six-foot Kaffir in a greatcoat, with his boots slung round his neck by the laces. He approached us with a stick over his shoulder, from which dangled a dead snake. It was a specimen of the dreaded black M'amba, and he sold it to Christopher Heseltine, who collected such things, for one shilling. He disappeared through the thorn bushes, having saved himself the trouble of tramping to the nearest township to collect the Government reward. But he would not have tramped; he would have sloped along with the rhythmic lope of the Kaffir.

The drivers whipped up their horses and we pursued a silent journey to the half-way house at Breakfast Vlei. Here was an arrangement of one-storied corrugated iron buildings:

farmstead and hotel in one. The next morning after breakfast Sammy Woods, A. J. L. Hill, and I went for a walk to see the ostriches in their vast compounds bounded by interminable wire fences. We saw a statuesque black cock ostrich sitting down about a hundred yards inside the wire, and Sammy Woods proposed that I should go and pull out one of its luxuriant white tail-feathers. I stepped through the wire and advanced just to see what would happen. When I had gone thirty yards the ostrich stood up and twisted its head round without moving its neck, and looked at me precisely over its tail. I began walking. The bird began walking. I began stepping out. The bird began stepping out. I began running. The bird began running. I ran very fast, and I do not believe any Derby winner ever ran as fast as the ostrich. No chance of climbing the fence, so I took a header clean through a square in the wire, and the imperturbable bird, whose inscrutable face expressed no animosity, kicked the fence hard enough to rattle it for thirty yards on either side. I should say the bird's leg missed the soles of my boots by less than a hundredth of an inch. I have twice been chased by a bull and once by a stallion, but none of them have got as near me as the ostrich. The bird, by intent a murderer, stood a few yards off, looking at us in quiet surprise, and even put his head through when Sammy pretended to offer him a bun. At least, what Sammy said was, "Have a bun, old fellow!" I was not at all amused. I had a very sore pair of hands and a jolted shoulder. In case it may help any other adventurer, I add that at the hotel a farm employee with local knowledge told me that I would have been all right if I had simply lain face downwards and wrapped my arms round the back of my neck, because the ostrich could not have kicked me, but could only have jumped on me. Have you ever examined the toes of an ostrich?

A troop of baboons on the side of the hill had been watching the adventure. The moment it was over we turned to look at them, and they fled for their lives.

So in due course we continued our journey with no further adventures to Grahamstown, where there is a famous school and a small cricket ground. On this ground, with twenty-two in the field, the only way of scoring is to play tip and run, and Sam Woods and I actually ran several times to short slip without accident.

From Grahamstown we travelled round inland by Cradock to Port Elizabeth, which is further along the coast between East London and Cape Town. It is a highly civilised and comfortable town with a grass cricket ground, the only other in those days besides Newlands. Everybody bought ostrich feathers in long tin cylinders, for Port Elizabeth was the centre of the old prosperous trade in these luxuries.

Our exit from Port Elizabeth was only one degree less formidable than our entry to East London. Had George Lohmann been with us he would have refused this time to leave the land. We went out to the ship in another tub of a tender and a very large swell, and we circled round the ship a dozen times before we were lifted on deck in a huge wicker basket. Everybody was seasick except Sammy Woods and myself, and Charles Wright said things that even I had never heard before.

By sea and land we presently arrived at Bloemfontein, the capital of the Orange Free State. There Sammy Woods and I made an expedition over the rolling grass plains in the direction of Basutoland. I rode a wonderful roan Basuto pony which ate nothing but grass and could go all day at that delightful pace known in the Cape as the triple—something between a slow canter and an amble. All the Boer farmers teach their ponies to go at this gait, and they cover enormous distances in a day. We stopped at a farm one day with nothing but the sky and grass in sight, the kind of spot which I figure to myself (never having been there) resembles a hacienda in the pampas of the Argentine. One afternoon we crept, walked, ran, and progressed in every other invisible manner after a herd of springbok, which refused to do more than just move out of range. The springbok won the day, and, for all I know, their descendants are grazing there still.

A less arduous and more exciting pursuit of springbok belongs to our visit soon after to Kimberley, where we stayed at the hotel of Barney Barnato's sister. Kimberley was then a scattered township of corrugated iron roofs blistering in the sun under a brazen sky. The cricket ground was grey grit, flanked on two sides by hedges of cactus; a modification of the surrounding blue ground and heaps of blue dirt piled up from the diamond mines to crumble before being sifted for the precious stones. It was a little world of grey-blue glare, but, as everywhere in South Africa, the mornings were the quintessence of clear, cool freshness.

On one such morning Woods, Heseltine, Hill, and I were taken a long way across the colourless flats in Cape carts by a sporting assistant manager from De Beers. We were met by two young farmers, who left the horses and carts in charge of some Basuto boys. We walked several miles over a scrub country which looked flat but was really a series of long slopes and rises. On the way we put up a covey of partridges, and the man from De Beers shot one on the wing with a single bullet from his ·303 rifle, which had an ivory bead foresight. The rifle was a Lee-Metford, a sporting carbine with a Martini-Henry breech of the kind much used by the burghers; a handier weapon than the ·450 Martini-Henry.

Presently we came to a small round hill, where our conductors found traces of buck, so we were spread out in line at intervals of about a hundred yards to walk through the bush just as one walks up partridges in England, in the hope of putting up small bush buck or duyker on the way to where it was expected we should find the springbok on the open plain. I was playing outside left forward, and, as happens in undulating bush country, I got separated from my inside man. After a bit I heard rifle shots, miles away, it seemed, on my right, and as I did not know where the bullets were going, especially as Sammy Woods was over there, I thought well to sit down behind a very large ant-hill and on the other side of it. I had not been there ten minutes before I saw strings of springbok converging from all points of the compass in my direction. One of them I judged would pass close to me, so I lay down and watched it narrowly. Soon I could see the string would pass by a grey rock which I calculated was 180 yards away, and when I stepped it out afterwards I found it was 168 paces. I had a ·450 Martini-Henry carbine, which has a much less flat trajectory than a ·303. So I put up the 200-yard sight and registered the intention of shooting low. Sure enough the string of springbok passed close to the rock, and I drew a careful bead on the leader of the file and allowed six yards ahead when I pulled. The consequence was that I knocked over the fifth buck in the string. Which shows that my range was as accurate as my pull-off was erroneous.

So there I was with a dead springbok in the middle of an empty veldt; no one in sight or hearing. One rifle shot I heard, and it sounded somewhere on the distant horizon. I had no knife to gralloch the buck, so there I was. But I stayed there as the best chance of being found. I was found quickly enough by a single vulture which dropped out of the blue from nowhere, and within a quarter of an hour there was a circle of seventeen vultures squatting in a ring round myself and the buck. They annoyed me so much that I had a pot at one, but he only ruffled his feathers and hopped a yard or two.

After about an hour, as much from nowhere as the first vulture, A. J. L. Hill suddenly appeared. He had a sheath-knife, which he drew in a determined manner. He sketched a line round the stomach of the buck, and then said, "We had better wait," and sheathed his knife again. He was no bad judge, for, again from nowhere, one of the young farmers drove up in a sort of tax-cart. He appeared to know everything that had happened and that I had shot a buck. I think he spotted the situation by seeing the vultures collecting on the wing and by hearing my shot. He soon did the gralloching, and the vultures, approaching within five yards, took the proceedings for granted. Nobody else secured a buck, which shows the value of an ant-hill.

Two mornings afterwards the Kimberley Hounds held a meet for our benefit. Horses were brought to the hotel soon after sunrise to mount the whole team. I was late and inherited the only steed left. He was a tall, scraggy, flea-bitten grey pony. The man who brought him advised me to take the one spur which he had in his pocket, as otherwise the animal might be lazy. He certainly looked as if he might. He was furnished with a venerable saddle and a light snaffle-bit with a venerable single rein.

So off I went after the party, which contained half a dozen members of famous hunts at home. Some three miles beyond the outskirts of the town hounds were invited in an informal way to scatter through the sparse thorn-scrub. They were an irregular sort of pack of about ten couple, but all of them more or less like foxhounds. They were keen enough and pushed about well. Presently a sandy-looking fellow gave tongue excitedly and went off like a greyhound, and the remainder went after him as if he himself were the quarry. There was certainly some scent, though the ground, except for a dusty sparkling dew on occasional patches of grass and on the sparse bushes, was as dry as the ashes in a grate, and about the same colour. Perhaps the leading hound was coursing some small animal by sight through the scrub, which, though only a foot or two in height, was enough to hide a buck of the duyker species, which is not much bigger than a hare and gallops very flat with head low and little horns laid back. Nobody saw what hounds were after, but they went at a rare pace dead straight across country. The country consisted of loose shale-like stones and small antheaps, and would be regarded at home as execrable riding. As so often on the veldt, the ground extending to the horizon looked like a flat plain, but was really a series of rises and falls like a solid sea, where a long ground swell had congealed into a kind of friable cement. Hounds ran fast enough for anything, but the horsemen, mounted on their unfamiliar steeds, some of them good-looking enough but not too fond of athletics, proceeded with caution. All except me on my flea-bitten weed.

The moment hounds began running this bag of bones cocked his ears and went off like Blue Peter. He was as sure-footed as a mule, and treated the flying stones as nothing. Very soon he outdistanced his superior-looking rivals, all but a thoroughbred brown ridden by our friend from De Beers, which could canter faster than the rest could gallop. In a couple of miles hounds suddenly threw up at a wire fence, and one by one they came back to look at the De Beers man and me. The De Beers man said it must have been a buck, and we neither of us could assist hounds. The remainder of the hunt gradually collected at a careful pace, and there was much technical discussion about the character of the going among the followers of the Quorn, V.W.H., and Bramham Moor.

My animal subsided into his original inattention, and we drew many more square miles of scrub without finding again. When the sun began to climb, the experts were unanimous that there would be no more scent, and we turned our heads homewards. The moment we did so my flea-bitten adventurer lost all interest in hounds and the other horsemen and wanted to set off home at a gallop. It was with difficulty that I could restrain him into behaving as if I knew all about how to ride home with proper and companionable discretion. But there was no doubt that the animal knew all about hunting on the plains of Kimberley, and I guarantee that, had we gone out again, he would have fallen to the lot, not of the last, but of the first man out of bed. He was a Basuto pony, and must have scuttled about in his native hills ridden by some brave with his knees as high as a modern jockey, and only his bare big toe inside rusty stirrups. Anyhow, he could go, and I remember him with affection and admiration.

The diamond mines at Kimberley, before Cecil Rhodes and his friends succeeded in amalgamating all the separate enterprises, consisted of an enormous hole in the earth like the crater of an extinct volcano. That is what it had been ages ago. Hence the deposits of transparent carbon. We were shown all over the modern mines, which are scientifically bored, and through inordinately deep shafts and transverse tunnels, whence the blue clay was elevated, just as one can see done in one of our coal-mines in the Black Country or Durham. We handled pailfuls of diamonds classified in size and quality and spread out on wooden tables in the sorting-sheds. One or two of our plutocrats bought some stones, and we were all of us given packets of garnets. One of these, set in a gold stud, still occasionally adorns my shirt-front. Whenever I light on it in search of a collar stud I remember that flea-bitten grey.

On the way down to Cape Town we stopped for some days at Matjesfontein, the headquarters of Douglas Logan, the financier and inaugurator of the tour. At Matjesfontein were the whitewashed buildings and the large refreshment room, the prototype of Logan's far-flung catering business; and nearby a large square of gritty ground flanked on the side farthest from the station by Logan's house and a line of a few small houses. At each end of the square was a wire fence with two empty pillars of concrete like park gates, leading to the open grey Karoo. There was a stable half-way along the row of houses, with a rather frail green gate. The houses were all glistening white. Mark these details!

Douglas Logan was a stocky Scotsman with a long rectangular face and a pugnacious yellow moustache—a blend of genial hospitality, business-like energy, and latent pugnacity. His connection with cricket had arisen from a kind act in inviting George Lohmann to be his guest when he discovered that George had been sent to the Cape in the hope of scotching incipient tuberculosis. The laird of Matjesfontein could not let us leave South Africa without entertaining us in his little city of the desert.

The first day we spent there was organised for cricket, but Logan could not collect his team; and, as there was not much to do, Heseltine and Hill, always on the lookout for shikar, wanted to go shooting. Logan said that they might find some wild ostriches away over the Karoo. As there was a third horse, I volunteered to join the party.

Accordingly, we, mounted respectively on a roan pony, a tall grey horse, and a taller chestnut, spent a long day finding no ostriches. Hill's pony ran away while we were stalking an alleged bustard on foot. A Cape boy took my chestnut to catch the pony, and they, too, disappeared for ever. Then a mounted policeman arrived and arrested the three of us for shooting without licences. The policeman marched us home, where Douglas Logan in his capacity of magistrate fined us £10 apiece. This was all a hoax, but the consequences were nearly fatal to me.

That evening at dinner-time Lord Hawke's brother arrived by train from Cape Town. He was a captain in the Lincolnshire Regiment, and weighed 18 stone. The story of the shooting stirred this sportsman, and he wanted to go shooting next day. As there were only three horses, and my chestnut alone was capable of carrying 18 stone, I had to drop out of the party. Just as they were starting I met a friend of Logan's coming out of the station, who volunteered his horse, as he had to wait for the evening train. He was a road surveyor who had ridden in early in the morning. We went through the green gate and he saddled his nag for me. He told me it had a very light mouth. It was an unfriendly-looking dun standing over at the knees. I tripled off after the party, who were down in front of our cottage at the end of the square.

Hill said, "Haven't you got a gun? Why not go back and borrow Logan's rifle?" So I turned and tripled back towards the house.

When we were passing the stable yard my animal swerved like lightning and tried to dash through the gate, which was swinging open. Crash went the gate. Round and round the yard we pelted half a dozen times. By good luck the stable door was shut. Out of the gate again with another crash, straight for the station wall. It looked for a moment as if we should charge it head-on at breakneck speed. A swerve to the left down the square, straight at the wire fence. Another swerve to the left within a yard or two of the fence, and out between the concrete pillars. I had no chance of holding the mad animal. I thought he was going down the road which ran more or less parallel with the railway, but he cut out straight as a dart inside the road beside the line.

The going was far worse than at Kimberley. How the fellow kept his feet among the scattering stones was a miracle. When we had gone a mile or so at the rate of knots, I saw ahead an arch under the railway, and remembered with the instantaneous perception one has at such times that a very deep spruit ran under the railway at right angles. I had noticed it coming down in the train. I saw ahead a precipitous plunge in the chasm, which was much too wide to jump. So, disengaging my feet from the stirrups, I hunched forward and, picking a clear piece of ground, executed a jump forward out of the saddle and landed on my left foot and right hand. I rolled over once and then stood up and watched the disappearing beast, which stopped with all four toes jammed into

the ground on the brink of the chasm. I wondered whether
he would have done that with me on his back. He turned
left, trotted with a high action and head in air till he found
the road, and away he went into the far distance to the
surveyor's camp. I turned round to walk home, but could
not put my right foot to the ground. I saw a rescue party
coming in my direction, so I sat down and was carried home.
The young surveyor was one of the party. All he had to say
was that the horse had a very light mouth.

This was the nearest shave I ever had for my life, and I
still admire my acrobatic feat—at a distance.

My right ankle was bound up. There was general astonish-
ment that I was still alive. The sight of me going full tilt at
the wire fence had been too much for Tom Hayward, who
had bolted indoors as I passed and locked himself up in his
bedroom.

The next day we went to Cape Town by train, and my
injury was diagnosed as a broken fibula. I must have done
this going through the gate, because I landed on my other
foot in my circus act. That finished my cricket, and I could
not play in the final Test Match at Cape Town, but my leg
was completely reconstituted in plaster of Paris during the
voyage home.

I should add, of course, that among other activities of the
tour were seventeen cricket matches, including three Test
Matches. Although the England team won all three, there is
no doubt that this tour was the beginning of the subsequent
eminence of South African cricket. Our opponents had one
of the finest all-round cricketers in the history of the game in
J. H. Sinclair, of Johannesburg. He was a very tall, powerful,
freckled fellow with a great reach as a batsman; he could play
an orthodox stylish game, but was really a hitter, and when
in the vein he was one of the longest drivers I have ever seen.
He was a lively right-hand medium-pace bowler of the Hugh
Trumble type.

Then there was E. A. Halliwell, the wicket-keeper, who
certainly ranks in the half-dozen best of his craft. None has
been cleverer at taking the ball on the leg side.

Two good bats were Tancred and Tom Routledge, the latter

a tough cricketer with a reputation as a wrestler and a notable drive past cover point. He looked like a Rugby forward, but had a large pair of oyster-grey eyes fringed by long dark eyelashes like a girl's.

R. M. Poore, of the 7th Hussars, who is down in Wisden for that year as Lieutenant, but who is never remembered except as Major, was included in the South African side. He was a great batsman with two strokes—an off drive played with a long stride and a steady thrust which sent the ball variously between mid-off and cover point, and a sabre-like cut which he used with great precision against fast bowling. He stood at his full lean height, and always appeared to dominate the bowling while he was in. He was not, however, successful in the three Test Matches.

Except for a left-hander, J. Middleton, and Sinclair, and the slow bowler, G. Rowe, the South African attack was not strong. Although we played on nothing but matting wickets, there was none of the leg-break bowling that afterwards rendered South African teams so formidable.

We won the first Test at Port Elizabeth by 288 runs, and the two others each by an innings. At Port Elizabeth George Lohmann got 7 wickets for 38 and 8 wickets for 7 runs. He bowled as well as ever in his life; but with his high rotary action his best-length ball on matting frequently went over the top of the wicket. In this match we scored 185 and 226. I was top scorer in the second innings with 53. After the match Sammy remarked to me, with his engaging grin, "Charles, I shouldn't be surprised if you and I don't make more runs than all these good bats put together." As I had made more runs than anybody else already and was beginning to see no reason why I should ever get out, I thought this was very clever of Sammy.

In the second Test at Johannesburg, Tom Hayward made 122 and also ran me out. The other scores were 65 by A. J. L. Hill, 64 by myself, 71 by Charles Wright, and 84 by H. R. Bromley Davenport. Sammy made only 32—serve him right. Our total was 482. South Africa could muster only 151 and 134. George Lohmann got 9 wickets for 28 in the first innings and 3 for 43 in the second. Our only other bowler to succeed

was Heseltine, who took 5 for 38 in the second innings with
his windmill action and flyaway swifts.

In the third match South Africa scored 115 and 117 against
our total of 265, which was entirely due to a beautiful innings
of 124 by A. J. L. Hill. Brownie Hill was one of the three
best bats in the Cambridge team of 1892 captained by F. S.
Jackson. He was one of the most accomplished cricketers of
my time, and did not get his due in big cricket.

George Lohmann reaped his usual crop of wickets, this
time 7 for 42 runs in the first innings; but in the second
innings Sammy Woods and A. J. L. Hill did the damage.
Thus we won all three representative games.

The South Africans by no means did themselves justice,
being up against a lot of big names without having had any
opportunity of discovering in a tour in England that bowlers
with big names can be played and batsmen with big names
can be evicted. I remember Sammy Woods saying at the end
of the tour, "These young fellows will be as good as the
Australians before many years are out." As Sammy was an
Australian born, this was a good deal to say. For once he was
not far wrong.

Tom Hayward made most runs in the tour, as was proper—
822 for an average of 31. My quotum was 750 for 34 apiece,
which topped the averages. Sir Timothy O'Brien, without
doubt a very great batsman, did not present his true form.

As for our bowling, George Lohmann was in a class by
himself. He took 157 wickets for an average of 6. H. R.
Bromley Davenport, in his fastish left-hand style, took 45
wickets for 10 apiece. A. J. L. Hill and I took 37 apiece, he
with an average of 9, I with one of 12.

George Lohmann was perhaps the greatest medium-pace
bowler England has ever had. He had a lovely rhythmic
action, and to my mind ranks with F. R. Spofforth, the Australian, as a consummate artist in disguised variation of pace.
His slow yorker would be successful even against our modern
batsmen. He was a handsome fellow with an Anglo-Saxon
complexion, browned to the colour of a cup of tea with cream
in it. He had a pale gold Anglo-Saxon moustache, but his
eyes were of a lambent brown such as one sees among the

Meridionals. He is one of the famous slip-fielders in the history of the game, and had he chosen he could have been a fine bat, but he did not care for making runs, as it spoiled his sense of touch. " If I make forty," he said, " the ball feels like a lump of dough instead of like the notes of a piano."

He was a truly great figure in the great cricket of his time. He died at Matjesfontein a few years afterwards, in spite of the kindly care of J. D. Logan and the crystal air of the Karoo.

Everyone who has ever been to the Cape wants to return. The space and the crystal air are recalls to delight.

CHAPTER VII

MOTORIN', HUNTIN', FISHIN', SHOOTIN'

NOBODY nowadays believes that motoring was ever an adventure. Of course, even to-day, and even with Belisha Beacons, the records show that it is still a bit of an adventure for the pedestrian. There are still motor accidents as between car and car, but nobody thinks that one of them will happen to himself. In short, modern motoring is nearly as safe as flying.

I can assure you, however, that in the early days there was a genuine spice of romance about the craft. True, this was not universally recognised; I remember once offering to write an article on the subject for the *Strand Magazine*, but the editor, Greenhough Smith, tabooed it on the ground that there was no sport in driving an engine down a high-road.

But there was.

For instance, I was there when Charlie Rolls and John Scott Montagu, afterwards Lord Montagu of Beaulieu, were the leading conductors of a primeval rally of cars at Bournemouth, when each car was required by law to be preceded by a man on foot with a red flag. The law had at the time chiefly in mind traction engines. Indeed, in the eyes of the law a motor-car was a traction engine. I say I was there, and I say it was an amazing sight.

Perhaps, too, the law had horses in mind. The curious fact is that in the early days every possible horse stood on its hind legs and tried to run away when it met a motor, whereas a few years afterwards the majority of horses appeared to have acquired a pre-natal familiarity with the monster.

I certainly saw the first aeroplane that lifted itself from the ground in Europe on the occasion of this feat—namely, Santos Dumont's box-kite contraption in Paris. I also certainly travelled in one of the earliest motor-cars capable of a journey. I have several times seen the annual Old Crocks' race from London to Brighton, but I have never seen quite so venerable a vehicle as the Daimler car in which I blooded myself in petrol by uneasy stages between London and Portsmouth. This car had a minute iron box with a square front where the bonnet ought to be. I cannot recall the radiator, but I can recall the "allumage." The charge in the cylinders, when sufficiently compressed by the pistons, was ignited fitfully by the red-hot ends of two thickish bars. The bars projected externally for the process of heating, which was done by a powerful furnace of methylated spirit. The body of the car, for four passengers besides the driver, was a cross between an Irish jaunting-car and a waggonette, broader at the base than at the apex on which one sat. There was a pyramidal feeling about the coach.

Nevertheless, on a pouring wet day we succeeded in travelling from London to Portsmouth. Some half-dozen times we stopped and attended to the methylated spirit. We had an occasional trouble with the petrol-feed. As an entirely blank mind about what was happening inside and underneath I found the excursion to the last degree exciting; like a new large-scale mechanical conjuring-trick. If a dozen rabbits had bolted out from the back axle I should not have been surprised. I wonder if there was a back axle.

However, all went reasonably well until we had passed through Petersfield and were nearly to the top of the steep chalk cutting over the downs at Butser Hill. Suddenly the machine emitted one primeval cough, and stopped dead. The chauffeur began a piecemeal overhaul of the car. He confessed he did not know quite what had happened, nor where to look for the fault. Meanwhile it went on raining, so we left him, since we could not help him, and took refuge in a shepherd's cottage. The shepherd had a good heart: hot tea and generous chunks of bread and butter.

At the end of an hour the driver came to report that all was well; it was only the petrol tap which had turned itself off, but he had nearly pulled the car to pieces before he discovered this. That, for future motorists, was a lesson worth learning. The rest of the journey was uneventful.

After such an experience at an average speed of some fifteen miles an hour, it was, of course, impossible not to hope to own a motor-car. So, not so very long afterwards, what with the rapid progress of motoring, when they were no longer called "horseless cars," we obtained quite a cultivated vehicle in the shape of a small Clement Talbot. The reason for this selection was that a friend of mine knew the Earl of Shrewsbury, and we went to see him about it. Being concerned with the firm that produced it, he was quite sure that a Clement Talbot was quite the best car on the market, so we bought it. Note, please, that in those days one was surprised at oneself for writing out a cheque worth half a year's income for a vehicle one was not at all sure would go. No "never-never" system in those days. But this little yellow car, with its pointed nose and low-tension ignition, proved to be a positive wonder.

In those days of county cricket one never saw one's garden or home from the beginning of May till the end of August. One played against Lancashire at Old Trafford and against Yorkshire, say, at Harrogate, but not once did Madame or I travel by train; and we were never late for a match. It is true that on one occasion, after Sussex had defeated Leicestershire at Leicester, we were a little lucky to arrive at Bath in order to defeat Somerset. Ranjitsinhji, the Sussex captain, never expected to see us on the ground in any match. He was for once mistaken. Quite late one bleak windy evening we ran out of petrol (having carefully inspected the tap to see it was not turned off) somewhere among the moorland hills about seven miles from Bath. We did not know where we were, but my Madame said we were in the Duke of Beaufort's hunting country, and she was probably right, because she used to hunt with the Duke's hounds as a girl. At the moment we did not know we were only seven miles from Bath. We did not know where the next petrol could be obtained. So we pushed the car up a short hill, and then took seat for a ride down the incline. Would you believe it, we ran in comfort, except for two short pushes, without any petrol all the way to the hotel by the bridge in Bath. In the dark, too.

To-day this appears just nothing. We felt rather like a

Transatlantic flier when he lands safely in the States. Or perhaps as he used to feel a couple of years ago. In a word, it felt like a successful adventure.

Now the modern motorist should note that in those days every motor trip of any distance over twenty miles did seem like a bit of an adventure. One talked of going motoring (not driving) rather as one might talk of riding in the Grand National. If one did one's distance without a puncture, one talked about it for several days. We did so in particular; because the leather clutch of our wonderful little car was so fierce in spite of perpetual attention that there was little rubber left on our tyres after a couple of days. Otherwise, as I say, she was a wonder; and she never went wrong, except once, when we entered Derby with everything under the bonnet, except the cylinders, red-hot. We thought nothing of this: we just stopped to cool down.

Once, when I was down on Exmoor hunting with the stag-hounds, my Madame drove the Talbot all about the country-side without any brakes—down Parracombe Hill, for instance, which is like a precipice; and also down the hill into Clovelly. She ran over a sheep, which so flattened itself on the road that it was not touched. Our chauffeur, one Willis, who was never allowed to drive, spent a fortnight completely white in the face. My Madame did not know much about the inside of the engine, but she was a superb driver. She believed in driving on the engine and using her low gears.

Lord Shrewsbury was right. The proof was that the regularity of our appearance at first-class cricket matches earned the car so great a reputation that, after we had driven her all over England for two years, a lady who frequented the Sussex county ground at Hove chased us round for a fortnight with a cheque for exactly what we had originally given for her. So, after much hesitation, we parted with the Clement Talbot. In those days a car known to be able to go had a value—at whatever hand.

By this time we knew something about motoring. We knew Charles Jarrott, the celebrated ex-racing driver, who, as the firm of Jarrott and Letts, specialised in high-class French de Dietrich cars, made by the great firm in Lorraine which produced the French railway engines. The firm prided itself on the perfection of its metal. This car, with its heavy chain-drive and slow-moving tappets, we bought in 1905, and she carried her marque, the blue cross of Lorraine, with unmitigated reliability up to the end of the Great War. The only time she ever stopped on the road was for a broken tappet-spring.

Meanwhile, we concurrently had several other cars. One of them was a Humber. This car itself was a slight adventure. The advertising manager on *Fry's Magazine* thought it would be good to run a competition with a Humber as a prize. The prize was for the best and shortest description of the most desirable quality in a car. We received a quantity of replies. The settlement cost me many days of laborious sorting. Finally, I decided in favour of " First speed, second speed, third speed." The winner entered under a pseudonym. He was discovered to be the well-known war correspondent, Sir Perry Robinson. Lord Riddell, one of our directors, who in particular liked directing *Fry's Mazagine*, which I also liked directing myself, was very much annoyed because Sir Perry had been one of our contributors, and according to Lord Riddell ought to have been ruled out. I did not see this, and Sir Perry got the car. But he did not want it, and sold it to a friend of mine. After a year or so my friend no longer wanted it, so we took it over. What Lord Riddell would have said if he had known this would not have been publishable, even in the *News of the World*.

This car, too, had an adventure. We were going up a steep little hill near Southampton, called Mousehole. Near the top we stopped the car, because a horse in a trap was playing up. The brakes failed, and the car began running down the hill backwards, gathering speed. The aforesaid Willis tried to guide it, but we cannoned into the trap and broke one of its shafts. The horse climbed the hedge. We went on. There was a T-bend at the bottom, but by luck and management Willis got the car safely round on to the flat. My son Stephen, aged five, then said to the white-faced Willis, " Please do it again." Stephen afterwards proved a good officer in the Royal Navy in the War, and was recently Director of Broadcasting in Palestine. So you see they know their man.

How many years various motor-cars, driven by my Madame, took me about England to county cricket matches I cannot remember. And do we, any of us, I wonder, remember how very little we knew of England before motor-cars?

But where this means of transport did me the best turn was in the matter of hunting. It is true that in those days no one had thought of tooling a couple of horses in a van along with him behind his car; but for oneself, one could always get there and get back with ease.

In the eyes of the élite, Hampshire does not figure as a hunting country in the sense allotted to the Midlands and some parts of the West of England. North of the Winchester to Petersfield line there is a lot of down and downlike land, generally open, where anyone can ride about without encountering obstacles. It is for the most part a cold scenting country, especially in many of the big woods, and still more so in the beech hangers, where the dry crinkled leaves among the straight tree-trunks often carry scarcely any scent at all. But in pre-war days it was a very good poor man's country; and the Hampshire Hunt in the north and the Hambledon Hounds in the south used to provide plenty of fun.

When I began hunting, Captain Bill Standish, of Marwell Hall, was master of the Hambledon West. He was a genial, generous, and explosive sportsman, devoted to hound-work, and severely critical of any followers of the more ardent type, whom he constantly advised, if they wanted to ride, to go somewhere else. All the same, he was a first-rate master, and showed excellent sport.

One evening, when riding home with Bill Standish, he asked me into Marwell Hall for a drink. We entered the tall, ecclesiastical grey stone manor house into the high hall with its blazing fire of logs. Standish indicated decanters and syphons standing on an enormous heavy oak chest. My syphon had a hair-trigger, and I splashed, with apologies, the black oak lid of the chest. "You have squirted," said he, "the last resting-place of the lady of the Mistletoe Bough." This, then, was the authentic oak chest of the old ballad, where the bride hid herself for fun and for eternity. There are other chests on the market, but this is *the* one.

A year or two ago I saw Marwell Hall again in its timbered seclusion about five miles from Winchester. The big lake called Fisher's Pond, near the Southampton road, has been turned into a tea-garden and quasi lido. The old hall, with its tall narrow windows, was deserted and empty. I prised open a window and walked round the bare rooms where I had remembered the pleasant hospitality of a genial country gentleman. The echoes of my feet on the bare boards were a melancholy punctuation of a period that is past. I believe that the hall is now inhabited by a new owner; but Bill Standish and his hounds and his atmosphere of the England of the Squires are gone.

Bill Standish used to regard me, together with Admiral Sir Geoffrey Blake (then a Lieutenant) and Captain Percy Long of Southwick, as a thruster, requiring a close eye.

One reason why I used to get into so much trouble was that my best horse was a very visible flea-bitten grey, which the Captain used to treat as a species of landmark. One day, just behind Marwell Hall, in a lane, the Captain held half a dozen of us up when we knew perfectly well the hounds were running on the far side of the Marwell coverts beyond some rising ground. Along the skyline in front of us someone was seen galloping on a grey horse. "There's that fellow Fry again," shouted the Captain. "I shall go up to Lord's next season and wave my arms behind the bowler when he's batting. How will he like that?" He then went on to lecture on the iniquity of not attending to what hounds were doing. He never found out that I was sitting within five yards of him, or that the delinquent was a lady of much experience and consummate obedience. In fact, his wife.

That flea-bitten grey of mine was the best horse I ever had. He was a grand shape, up to any weight, and had belonged to Mr. Fernie, the famous M.F.H. in the Midlands. I saw him first in a hiring stable in Southampton, and I was told that in the intervals of being jobbed out to go with the New Forest hounds, he was driven in a cab in the town. He was, however, such a gallant and spirited fellow that I doubt whether he would have submitted to that. He had become a bit of a puller, and I expect that is why Mr. Fernie sold him;

I do not think that otherwise such a remarkable performer would have been allowed to go.

The first time I saw him out hunting with the Hambledon, I had hired him to mount Sir Frank Newnes, who was staying with me. After that I got hold of him myself whenever I could. You could not miss his quality.

The next summer I was down hunting with the Devon and Somerset from Dulverton. They had sent two horses for me to South Moulton for a meet at Yarde Down, and I was specially asked to change in the early afternoon because my first horse was not too hard. We had a long run and I found myself somewhere near the Doone Valley, without anybody in sight. With no prospect of finding my second horse, I was on the point of starting home in the supposed direction of South Moulton when I saw a man on a grey horse coming over the heather. I rode up to him for information, and discovered he was riding my old flea-bitten grey. He said he too wanted to go to South Moulton, as he had lost the man for whom he was bringing out the grey; but he himself had come from a hunting stable at Lynton, on the north coast, by the sea. So I persuaded him to take my horse back to South Moulton, which was southwards, and let me ride the grey, which I would deliver there in the evening. I found hounds again—that is to say, they found me—and goodness knows where we ran to.

On the edge of nightfall I was again lost, for no one who does not know Exmoor well can keep in touch with hounds, and one has to speculate as to where to go to pick them up after they have wound through a maze of combes and blind stony valleys where it is impossible to ride. One has to keep to the high ground in the hopes of being on the right side of the hole.

Anyhow, I was lost. The flea-bitten grey was not lost. He gave an indicative snatch or two at the bit, and started off at a purposeful gait. He was going home, so I thought I had better go with him. We came to a bubbling moorland stream, where he selected a convenient pebbly pool, knelt down, and served himself with a good drink. He then stood up, shook his head, and set out on a bee-line across the moor. Eventually, quite late in the dark, we arrived at Lynton, where he lived. I immediately bought him off his proprietor for £35, and presently got back by a circuitous coach and railway route to Dulverton via Barnstaple. I must have gone about a hundred miles that day. But it was a good day.

That flea-bitten grey carried me magnificently for six years with the Hambledon and elsewhere. I had to cure him of a sore back due to high withers and bad saddling. He did pull a bit on dull days, but he was always at the top of the hunt in a run, could last all day in heavy going, and could jump anything. The only time we crashed, over some awkward timber with a bad take-off, I lost hold of the reins, but he stood still like a charger for me to remount. He had a roach-back and tremendous quarters. He was the best £35 worth of anything I ever bought.

I had some other pretty good horses over the years, but never one to equal the grey. I used to get horses from Deacon of Swindon, and sometimes kept a horse there to go out with the V.W.H. when Butt Miller was Master. It was grand going on the grass country round Swindon, though the turf was often very heavy. Butt Miller rode the best horses of the old-fashioned short-legged type I ever saw. He gave great sport. But though this was a far better country, I do not think I got more fun than with the humbler Hambledon. Half the fun of hunting is taking the ups and downs of the day along with one's pals, and knowing enough of the lie of the land to take a line of one's own.

I had a few days with the Blankney in Lincolnshire when Sir Robert Filmer was Master. Reggie Spooner, the cricketer, who was such an ornament of the England team when I was captain, was agent to Lord Londesborough at Blankney, and used to persuade the Master to give me a mount from the hunt stables. A very fine hunting country, though rather heavy going, except when one gets away on the Belvoir side, which is a delight.

If I say any more about fox-hunting, except that on the hither side of the hounds there is nothing more captivating as a pursuit, I shall be taken for a hunting man, which I was not, except for about ten years. No sport that does not involve the companionship of a horse can be as good as one that does.

That is why polo is probably the best game; but I cannot go beyond probabilities as I never played. One good point about the Australians is that they are genuinely fond of horses.

Whether post-war hunting is as much fun as in former days I do not know. But I do know that after the War, when I went out a few times, so many familiar figures were no longer there that it did not seem worth while any more.

Shooting is a different matter. No doubt the grouse moors in Yorkshire and Scotland are much the same as they always were, and no doubt in the all too few instances where country life of the old type survives, pheasants fly as high when properly put over the guns and driven partridges still swerve over the hedges in the old way. Nevertheless, there is a large area of agriculture in the neighbourhood of Cambridge, where I spent many a day with Ranjitsinhji in his hospitable and hard-worked parties, which is now covered by the aerodromes and aerial appurtenances of Duxford. However, Cambridge-shire is a large county, and no doubt still produces whizzing partridges when properly driven. But I doubt if anybody now extant in that region is as clever at arranging for them to be driven as was Ranji. He was himself a beautiful shot, and I never saw a quicker, but he spent more time in providing that his guests got the shooting, and in outwitting partridges and pheasants, than he did in occupying positions of vantage himself.

Few people know the story of how he came to lose that marvellous right eye of his. You know that he lost his eye during the War, and ever afterwards carried a glass right eye and wore spectacles. But the spectacles were not to help him to see with his remaining left eye, with which, to the end of his life, he saw with more accurate precision than most people with two. With one eye he was all but as good a shot as before.

He served two years in France on the staff of General Will-cocks. He came across for a fortnight's leave. He went out shooting near Gillingham in Yorkshire, of which village his old tutor at Cambridge was the Vicar. A local sportsman fol-lowed a bird with his gun and shot down the line. Ranji had in the butt with him one of the Vicar's daughters, who had been his friend since his undergraduate days at Cambridge.

Ranji, with his instantaneous quickness, jumped in front of the lady and covered his face with his right arm. One little shot came through under the crook of his elbow. No one ever made less fuss about a major accident. Two years in France in the Great War, and to lose an eye near a peaceful Yorkshire village!

All the guns who came out with Ranji from Cambridge were not as expert as he was himself, but they were good fellows. When Ranji was an undergraduate at Cambridge he lived in his rooms in Bridge Street not only in term time but in vacation, and he made many friends among the people of the town, especially at the Cambridge Liberal Club, where he used to defeat most of them at billiards with breaks of 100 and over. After he became famous, and everybody began to call him the Indian Prince, a lot of other friends accrued, but Ranji never gave up his earlier friends in Cambridge, and it was chiefly these who came out when I used to shoot with him.

One of them I remember in particular, Harry Stearn, the photographer in Bridge Street, who used to take the college groups. He was a keen sportsman with a gun, and always had at least fifty pounds in notes in his pocket. That was no reason why he once blew a hole through a fir tree about a yard above my head, shooting at the hen pheasant which got up in front of me in a narrow drive cut across a belt when he was walking up with beaters. I gave him the shooting volume in the " Fur and Feather " series, with certain passages marked. Ranji told me that Harry Stearn took this as a great compliment, and put the book on his drawing-room table, but never opened it.

Then there were the cricketing friends, notably W. L. Murdoch, the Australian and Sussex captain, and W. W. Read of Surrey, regarded by many as for some years the next bat in England to W. G. Billy Murdoch had, in Australia, been a noted pigeon shot, and retained his heavily choked india-rubber-padded hammer-gun. After lunch sometimes he used to carry this weapon at the slope, with the muzzle downwards, full cock. When we made representations, he used to say, "Don't Billy-old-boy me! If you don't die till I shoot you, you'll live a month of Sundays." The only time a choleric stranger, to wit, a colonel, tried to take his gun from him, Billy snapped open the breech, and there were no cartridges in it. Billy was perfectly safe, and in the mornings shot very well.

Billy Murdoch was a thorough Australian of the best sort. Medium height, but rather round all over, with a round black moustache, round black eyes, and a round tanned face. At cricket he always thought he was going to make a century. At least he did not think he was not going to, no matter whether he had a month of minute scores behind him. The most sanguine, dark-complexioned man of my era.

The great W. W., a burly, heavy-shouldered ex-school-master, with an oblong brown face and quick, rather cunning brown eyes, was on the other hand a careful sportsman who much objected to casual practice in the shooting-field. He was a good shot, but mistrusted some of Ranji's other guests. In particular there was a nice old gentleman who used to turn up with two comparatively young sons. He was a successful London builder, and had taken to walking turnips rather late in life. He had some good shooting of his own in Hertford-shire, where Ranji and I used often to shoot with him. When he coincided, however, with W. W. Read at Cambridge, W. W. was always looking for trees and haystacks to hide behind, because he maintained that "Grandad was for ever following round with his gun."

One day the old man shot at a driven partridge, but quite high, more or less down the line. One vagrant pellet hit a son in his cloth cap, and the boy yelled out, "Who's shot me? Who's shot me?"

W. W. put his head out from behind a haystack and in a shrill voice shouted, "Daddy did it, sonny!" and then bobbed in again. All the same, nothing amiss ever actually happened at one of Ranji's parties, and we had wonderful fun.

In addition to his shoot near Duxford and at Papworth Hall, financier E. T. Hooley's place, and elsewhere around Cambridge, Ranji had a very good small shoot at Methwold, in Norfolk. It was in the middle of some big shoots and next door to Duleep Singh's domain. The partridges were the biggest I ever saw, and after Christmas flew like bullets, especially in the snow. In the middle of Ranji's shoot there was a square wood of no great size with a lot of oak trees in it, and Ranji used to raise about 200 pheasants there, but we used to shoot a hundred in it regularly once a fortnight throughout the season. One sometimes saw a raisin or two in the rides in this wood, but Ranji said the pheasants came after the acorns. Ranji's keeper there was a handsome young man called Bradman, who was a distant relation of the great Don. I doubt whether there was ever a better small shoot than this. We used to come overnight from Cambridge to stay at an inn at the village of Brandon.

One 30th of September, when we were over for an early day after partridges in the roots, I went to one of the barns belonging to the inn to look for a bicycle. What I found was a heap of pheasant feathers large enough to fill a cart. Someone had been anticipating. Some of them, I expect, belonged to Prince Duleep Singh. He, by the way, was a grandson of that fine warrior the Lion of Punjab, who with his Sikhs beat us several times in pitched battles before we finally conquered his country. After the peace his eldest son was given a princely pension. So the grandson lived in Norfolk and married Lady Victoria Coventry. His domain was beautifully laid out for shooting.

The best shot and most knowledgeable man about game who came shooting with Ranji was Charlie Rush, who was nearly 7 feet tall, and at the time had a farm near Babraham, but was afterwards agent to Lord Ellesmere and lived at Newmarket. He was a friend of Arthur Sadler, the trainer, and knew a lot about running horses. He used to have long arguments with Harry Stearn about the relative intelligence of town and country. He was one of the most expert large buyers of cattle in England.

I never shot at Babraham, but the extended array of small copses on hillocks, ensuring that the birds flew high over the guns, made it one of the most sporting pheasant shoots in England. It had, however, no stand for pheasants equal to a steep valley with woods on each side and a ride running along the bottom at Killick Percy, in Yorkshire, where the shooting belonged at one time to Admiral Walker of Beverley Hall.

The Admiral was a small, lion-like sailor, who studied Aristotle's *Ethics* every day, and was always telling his son, "You know, Philip, Aristotle says that the body is only a horse for the soul to ride on." He worked his shooting parties with ship's discipline, and we were rather afraid of him. No one was allowed to smoke at Beverley except in the butler's pantry, and then only when the household had been invited by the Admiral to retire, with brass candlesticks, which we formally lit in the hall.

The Admiral once lent me his best two-piece greenheart dry-fly rod to go and fish for trout in the famous Driffield Beck near Malton. He lent it with express misgivings at the last moment. While kneeling down on the edge of the beck, trying a long cast to a fish under the far bank, there was a sudden jerk on the line behind me just as I was returning the fly. The rod was bent nearly double, and the reel went round with a scream. When I whipped round, a semicircle of red heifers were stampeding away fanwise, and my fly was in the pole of one of them. The whole length of the reel line was run out as I chivvied after the heifer. I ran twice round a large field in waders, and fortunately the little hook detached itself. I never told the Admiral.

The trout in Driffield Beck were large, and took some catching. It was there that I learned to manipulate the dry fly up to a certain point of proficiency, which stood me in good stead on the Itchen and the Test in years to come. With the right kind of stiffish rod and a heavy reel-line properly greased, my view is that anyone fairly adept in the use of the wet fly on clear Welsh and Scotch rivers, where one has to fish upstream, can very soon adapt himself to the supposedly intricate culture of the dry fly. Anyway, when I went to live in Hampshire, from the first and before I had read the dozen fat volumes on the subject, I used to catch as many trout in these classic streams as I ever did after years of study and practice.

These two lovely chalk streams are not now what they used to be, because the tar-washings from the roads not only ruin the fish in parts, but also damage the hatch of fly. At least, so I think. But a day in the Hampshire water meadows on the banks of the Itchen or Test in June, when the blue irises are in bloom and the fresh summer green endows the fields and the hedges, is no whit less delectable than the descriptions in the books.

The best book about all this, and about fly-fishing, is that written by Lord Grey of Fallodon, one of the few properly so-called classics that have been written about sport. I used to see Lord Grey fishing in the Itchen near Itchen Abbas, above Winchester. He was a masterly fisherman as well as a genuine naturalist. He could talk about a speckled trout, not with objective knowledge only, but as though he himself were inside its scales, and he treated a missel-thrush in conversation as though he were speaking from within its feathers.

Dry-fly fishing has a long list of celebrated executants, some of whom I used to see by the Hampshire rivers. Some of them obtained great reputations for practice by the simple process of evolving a great deal of theory. The gayest story of all is that of the two brothers who between them, under an assumed name, wrote several classics on various aspects of dry-fly fishing, one of which was concerned with how to make an ideal dry-fly stream. Not exactly make the stream itself, but render it ideally dry-fly fishable. Their book was much studied. Presently they themselves took a long lease of a south-country river, and set about practising their theories upon it. Their stretch of water was already pretty good, else they would not have started upon it. When they had thoroughly dealt with it as to sub-aqueous horticulture and so on, and had carefully stocked it on eugenic principles, its appearance was much improved; the number of sizeable fish swimming in it increased. But for some obscure reason not included in their theory, all the trout universally and with one accord refused to feed off floating flies, natural or artificial.

I must say that some of the earlier heroes of the dry fly were fine fishermen, notably one Marryatt, who lived in the Close at Salisbury and had an excellent little floating fly named after himself. But the good fishermen were pretty much of a muchness. Of those I saw intimately, I do not think that any were more expert than two cricketers. One was E. M. Sprot, for some time captain of Hampshire, and the other was, as no doubt you have guessed, none other than Ranjitsinhji.

Ranji was by no means an early convert. From youth upwards in England he had been a devotee of bait-fishing, especially for roach. He inhabited the rivers round Cambridge, and was most obstinate when I tried to convince him of the superiority of fly-fishing.

Once, when Sussex were playing Somerset at Taunton, he heard that perch could be caught in a mill-pool close by. He asked Tyler, the Somerset left-hand bowler, about this. Tyler and some pals, egged on by Sammy Woods, the Somerset captain, persuaded Ranji that it was no good except at night, so Ranji agreed to fish all night. Billy Murdoch, our captain, heard of this and absolutely forbade it. Ranji assumed obedience, went to bed early, and displayed his shoes outside the bedroom door. Billy Murdoch reported to us that Ranji had gone to bed after all. But he had not. He crept out privily and spent the night in catching perch. The next day the Somerset team, who were in the know, entertained high hopes of dismissing him at a moderate cost. They were disappointed. He made a facile 280 not out.

It is not generally known that all the time that Ranjitsinhji was making his phenomenal scores and achieving an unrivalled reputation as a batsman he used to suffer badly from asthma, which prevented him from sleeping at night. As often as not during the cricket season he did not go to sleep till five or six o'clock in the morning. He was a martyr to asthma during A. E. Stoddart's tour in Australia, and yet was highly successful with the bat. He nearly died of asthma in India not long before he became ruler of his State.

As I say, he was for years an obstinate float-fisher. Once when he came to stay with me in Hampshire, and I had obtained leave on an excellent stretch of grayling water, he insisted on going instead to fish for roach in the Stour at Christchurch. He caught a sackful.

In the end I did convert him. I gave him the best fly-rod obtainable, which he preserved as a document for several years. At last, when we were up in Yorkshire for a cricket match, I got him to come and fish for trout in the river Rye.

He pretended not to think much of it, though he caught some trout, but from that moment he became an addict. After he had lost his eye out shooting he transferred all his affections to the new game. We had some wonderful times together. After the War he took to salmon fishing, and first rented and then bought one of the finest resorts for salmon and sea-trout in the British Isles. This was Ballynahinch Castle in Connemara. The Ballynahinch river runs into the sea at Roundstone on the west coast not far from Clifden, on the far side of Galway, from a chain of loughs, of which four are large ones. A group of blue hills called the Pins of Connemara stand up in the near distance. The short four or five miles of river run through stony, peaty ground. Some of the best pools are flat water, and for good fishing wind is needed. In August both the loughs and the river used to offer about the best sea-trout fishing in the British Isles. When the salmon were running, from the middle of June to the end of July, the salmon fishing of its kind was superb. There is a spot between the upper and lower Ballynahinch loughs called Sna Beg, about some fifty yards of slow stream connecting the two pieces of water, where salmon are catchable more frequently than anywhere I have known. The so-called butts, which are the moving and troubled water where the stream runs in at the head of the loughs, especially Derry Clare butt, were always great chances. One way and another it used to be a fisherman's paradise.

The summer salmon there do not run large—from 6 to 12 pounds—but they run with more energy than any Scotch salmon of twice the size. There is a pool just above the bridge at Roundstone into which the tide floods. This was Ranji's favourite resort. He was most successful there, and once said to me, "Carlos, those fish down by the bridge are positively violent." He was a perfect dab at circumventing difficult fish. He would spend hours and hours—nay, days—trying to outwit fish at spots where they used to lie, but where no one else could catch them, just as in India he would sit up in a *machan* every night for a fortnight to bag an unventuresome panther.

I once caught sixty salmon in three weeks in the upper waters. No one ever knew quite how many Ranji caught, because his fish were not always entered in the record book. Neither, for the matter of that, were mine. Some of Ranji's Indian servants were nimble-minded sportsmen, and used to get up very early in the morning to exploit the spots where fish were believed to be from overnight statistics. The largest fish Ranji caught was 28 pounds, and I got one of 29 pounds in the Colonel's Pool just below the Castle. My big fish led me a rare dance several hundred yards downstream. We had no gaff with us, but an ordinary large landing-net. When at last I manœuvred him alongside, old John, my ghillie, could get only half of him into the net, so he cleverly looped the tail and hoicked him out. The moment he had the monster clear of the water he embraced him like a baby and ran inland twenty yards up a steep bank for safety.

One of the charms of the salmon fishing at Ballynahinch in the river was that one could fish with a small single-handed rod and light tackle; and in June and July one used a small fly, number 7 or 8 hook. I used only three patterns: one, the Connemara Black; two, the Irish Thunder and Lightning; and three, the Grey Monkey. Ranji was very successful with quite small flies of the size normally allotted to salmon trout, and he used, except in rough weather, quite a light dry-fly rod.

It was in the Ballynahinch river that Mr. A. H. E. Wood, afterwards of Cairnton on Deeside, first exploited his method of fishing for salmon with a greased line. I tried this, but did no good with it. I also tried dry-fly fishing for salmon, but did no good with that. It was a work of art to persuade the fish in the flat pools when there was no wind. I found that a single small fly, with the finest undrawn gut, was the best lure.

Ballynahinch Castle is a large gabled house of the type of the Scotch shooting-lodge. It was about the only large house in the district not gutted during the Irish rebellion. The first year we were there the stone bridges over the river above and below the Castle had been blown up and were trestled over with wooden planks. But we never found the inhabitants other than perfectly delightful people. My old ghillie, John Malia, who lived in a small white farm cottage and had three

sons in the army and seven in America, was the sort of gentleman who could easily have figured in diplomatic society.
What is more, he always had a tin of worms in his coat-tail
pocket, together with a cast and hook weighted with a few
inches of lead wire in case a blazing sun and no wind rendered
the salmon otherwise indisposed. It was the delight of his
life if he could persuade me, at the end of a blank day, " just
to give the worm a chance."

In our early days in Ireland we were told that if two of the
locals met one another walking along a lonely road they
politely said good-day and then each of them walked backwards as if retiring from one another's royal presence, until
out of pistol shot; but I think this was a yarn. However, the
days of trouble were barely past, and we never really knew
quite how welcome we were in Ireland.

I got up half a dozen of the best whisky from Galway by
train, and ran myself down in one of the Ford cars to call on
the senior priest of the district by way of courtesy, and I left
the half-dozen with him in case there were any invalids in his
flock who might benefit by it. After Ranji heard of this he
arranged an even wider distribution of the creature. Moreover, there was never any difficulty about any of the ghillies
or servants getting to Mass on Sunday morning in a Ford car.
Whether or no, we never had any difficulty about the services
of anybody on any day, including Saints' days or Sundays,
after early morning Mass.

One August, with the water low under a blazing sun, after
the run of salmon had been over for several weeks, the Maharajah of Alwar insisted on accepting a long-standing invitation
to come and try for some fish. He had had a Scotch river of
his own, and knew all about it. For some obscure and no
doubt symbolic reason, he arrived with half a dozen secretaries
and a dozen A.D.C.s and as many split-cane fishing-rods of
various lengths. About noon next day he had all his rods
mounted and marched his party, with Ranji and myself in
unarmed attendance, to the nearest pool. He then insisted on
beating the pool with a bait made of a heart-shaped piece of
red leather. He assured us that he did not believe there was a
salmon in the river at all. To prove this he placed half his

retainers at the head of the pool and half at the tail, got a
boat up from lower down the river, and thrashed the pool
with the oars. None of his men saw a salmon bolt up or down
stream, so the Maharajah claimed that his case was proved.
The next day he visited another pool, where the water ran
fast. Into this he walked without waders nearly up to his
armpits, and exhibited perfect skill in casting. But he had
no luck.

He pretended that he considered Irish rivers compared very
badly with his own in Scotland. Why he did all this we never
discovered, and even Ranji could not explain it.

I have fished for salmon in the Orchy and the Dee and the
Spey and in several of the west coast rivers of Scotland. In-
deed, I have fished pretty well all over Scotland and Wales.
I have fished for sea-trout in the Outer Hebrides. I have
caught large trout in the Himalayan streams of Kashmir, and
I have caught the electric rainbow trout of New Zealand.
With the exception of the positive fairyland of New Zealand
streams, I have never had such sport with rod and line as in
Connemara.

On one of our summer visits to Ireland, Ranjitsinhji and I
were the guests of the Government under Mr. Cosgrave's
régime in Dublin, together with a remarkable gathering of
representative notabilities for the Tailtean Games, an attempt
at reviving the tribal Olympic games of Ireland. We had a
great banquet. There were many speeches, among others one
by Tim Healy. Among other things, Tim Healy said: "We
have many distinguished guests here to-night. Among them,
if I may make a distinction, none is more welcome than His
Highness the Maharajah Jamsahib of Nawanagar. He is a
distinguished cricketer, and he is even a distinguished ruler
of an Indian State. His Highness has paid us a great compliment by his presence here to-night, and even by his presence
in Ireland at all. His Highness occupies a throne in the far
purple East. His Highness might have gone to fish in the
Indus; he might have gone to fish in the Ganges, the Brahma-
putra, the Narbudda, the Jumna, the Cavary, the Irawaddy,
the Sutlej, the Chambal, and in many another great river of
India whose name I cannot adequately pronounce. His High-

ness did nothing of the kind. His Highness came to Ireland to fish in the river of—Ballynahinch."

I sat at this banquet between G. K. Chesterton and Sir John Lavery. Chesterton made a speech which he began by saying that he was not there to throw his weight about. Many Irishmen made speeches. Most of them began in an eloquently complimentary tone, but most of them half-way through paused suddenly, assumed a new air of gravity, and continued in the Irish language, giving the history of the woes of Ireland from the time of Brian Boru. At least, that is what Chesterton told me.

Right at the end Mr. Cosgrave's brother-in-law came round to me and said that everybody had forgotten to provide for a speech about the Games, and would I please say a word. So I said a few words. I then made a sudden pause, and delivered about thirty lines from the "Frogs" of Aristophanes in undeniable Greek, which I remembered from a speech-day at school. I once repeated the stunt at a dinner I gave to the South Africans after they had sung me a complimentary ballad in Zulu. Clifford Bax, who was there at the time, interpreted my Greek as a delicate compliment to Xenophon Balaskas.

Just as I sat down after my effort at Dublin, an Irish waiter uncorked a bottle of champagne with a resounding pop, and was heard to remark, "That's what we want here. We want over here in our Government classical scholars like His Highness and C. B."

Irish waiters know everything, including Greek. So does Senator Gogarty, who was one of the guests.

CHAPTER VIII

THE STREET CALLED FLEET

THERE are writers who enter the craft on purpose and because they see in it a sphere for the exercise of the talents with which they credit themselves. There are those who drift into journalism because they have failed in other less exacting activities. The common saying is that the failures in other branches of journalism are gradually relegated to sport.

Starting as a schoolmaster, I favoured journalism as a subsidiary activity; because by accident, when an assistant master at Charterhouse, I discovered that I could earn by journalism three times the income for the expenditure of a tenth of the time.

The enormity of my conduct in being the first cricketer and footballer to write about sport under my own name is disguised by the fact that everybody nowadays is doing it. I am not sure that my move was a wise one, but I retain across the years a feeling that if I had not liked writing of things I knew about I should not have done it.

The first time I was ever paid properly was for an article contributed to the *Windsor Magazine*; some character sketches of cricketers, including Prince Ranjitsinhji and the famous Australian captain, W. L. Murdoch. I still consider these quite decent of their kind. The article certainly induced other publications to invite me to write. A young, sensitive, and not unenterprising mind was thus infected with the firm conviction of a literary capacity likely to minister to such important ambitions as playing cricket all the summer. That is how I became involved in contributing to the *Athletic News*, the *Daily Express*, the *Daily Chronicle*, *Lloyd's News*, the one-time successful boy's magazine *The Captain*, the *Strand Magazine*, and, finally, in conducting a magazine.

The *Athletic News* was a Manchester paper which reported the events of all popular games at full length. The front page and part of the second page consisted of paragraphs. Then there were special articles by experts. I pretended to be an expert. Nevertheless the best feature in the *Athletic News* was the paragraphs, and their value was that they were mainly about people and were written by other people who had something to say. The delusion that a paragraph ought to be about nothing and can be written anyhow by anybody may have existed during the lifetime of the *Athletic News*, but it was far less prevalent than nowadays. As, however, I wrote articles, I was relieved of any necessity except putting words on paper one after another. The editor of the *Athletic News*, very famous in the Association Football world as J. J. Bentley, President of the League, always put my articles in without diminution or correction.

J. J. Bentley was so occupied with League business and with going about, and with being genial, and with looking wise (the necessary characteristic of a League official), and with writing articles himself, that he had no time to use a blue pencil. I regarded him as a good editor.

But presently either he or his proprietors found J. J.'s official duties too heavy, and he retired in favour of the smallest man who ever edited a newspaper, the well-known J. A. H. Catton. Now J. A. H. Catton was another amenable editor. The only time I ever fell out with him was when I telegraphed my weekly article from Loch Boisdale in the Outer Hebrides, where I had gone to catch sea-trout. It was not the telegraphing that he really objected to, but the fact that I forgot to send a newspaper slip entitling me to press rates from the postmaster at Loch Boisdale. The consequence was that my 1,200 words cost the *Athletic News* plenty of money. Now I come to think of it, I am not sure that this episode did not terminate my connection with the *Athletic News*.

I transferred my activities to the less exigent world of monthly magazines—a world which gives one much more time to think, and much more trouble in finding something to write about. The great firm of George Newnes had just started a boys' magazine called *The Captain*. The idea emanated from the brain of R. S. Warren Bell, a master at a private school with a talent for writing school stories as well as school reports. Himself the editor, he persuaded me to figure under the title of Athletic Editor; a lapse on the part of a man otherwise endowed with a sense of humour. He also engaged as another contributor none other than P. G. Wodehouse, but he did not cite P. G. on his front cover as Humorous Editor. He simply published P. G.'s stories, which were a great success, even before the time of Jeeves.

For my part, I consider that I wrote a lot of good articles for *The Captain* about how to do things; but though these were all right in their way, what I made my hit with was "Answers to Correspondents." I sometimes re-read the intelligent questions, real as well as imaginary, and the inspired answers with genuine appreciation.

The Captain was, I suppose, the most successful boys' magazine that has ever appeared, and it lasted for many years; but it never persuaded advertisers that it was read by parents. Advertisers did not believe that boys are likely to buy such articles as soap and whisky. I have always thought that the disbelief of advertisers in the capacity of boys to absorb soap was the snag which eventually tripped up the career of *The Captain*.

It is possible, however, that *The Captain* would still be in existence in a big way had my one and only decision which was at all in the nature of editorial been affirmative instead of negative. One day Sir George Newnes asked me to come to his room, and told me that he wanted my opinion on a proposition put to him by a clever American. This was Thompson Seton. Sir George outlined Thompson Seton's organisation of camping clubs in America, called the "Thompson Seton Indians." The clubs had a code of conduct embodied in maxims; they had the whole outfit of physical and moral procedure with which we are now familiar as the Boy Scout Movement.

It was arranged that I should see Thompson Seton himself. This original man described most attractively his system 'of clubs. He had fixed on me as the fellow to promote a parallel movement in England. What I thought and said was that in America, with real mountains and forests and space, the idea must succeed, as indeed it had succeeded. But in England, with our limitations, it would be artificial. Could you have Tom Sawyer and Huckleberry Finn in Surrey?

Thompson Seton's idea was that with a magazine like *The Captain* behind such a movement there was no reason why the American success should not be translated into English. As the Scout movement in England is really nothing but Thompson Seton's idea supplemented by the ingenuity of Lord Baden-Powell, quite evidently my decision that the thing would not work in England was mistaken. But I do not think that I was at all the person to carry it out. I disbelieved then and disbelieve now in any form of training for boys (the principle underlying Thompson Seton's movement) unless that training contains a real foundation of discipline. I thought at the time that such large existing organisations as the Church Lads' Brigade were a superior form of boy-training for England. Discipline of simple goodwill has great value provided it is built upon the rock of the discipline of necessity, and not barely on the shifting sands of itself. However, my only decision in the capacity of Athletic Editor of *The Captain* appears to have saved me from being under some other name the first Scoutmaster in England. Not the least of my athletic feats.

Sir George Newnes, who made as few mistakes as any magnate of the publishing world about new ventures, always maintained that a good magazine for boys ought to succeed. He was a notable man. He had two characteristics of greatness. He not only just thought about and round about whatever he happened to have in mind; he thought it right out. This capacity to think a subject right out is rare. Robert Blatchford has it. I regard Robert Blatchford as one of the finest friends I ever made, and as the greatest literary journalist of my time. Whenever I have a birthday I send him a greetings telegram wishing him many happy returns of it.

Another feature of Sir George Newnes's mind was an instinctive knack of simplifying: a knack of not seeing any part of a question at issue that did not matter. He was a shortish and burly figure, but alert. He stroked a square brown beard gently upwards and then stated his conclusions with concise precision. He had vivid blue eyes and a solid sense of humour. In addition, he was really original; he hit upon lines which an army of copyists afterwards developed. Everybody knows that in inventing *Tit-Bits* he invented a host of other weekly papers. In the *Strand Magazine* he invented the sixpenny illustrated magazine. The first editor, Greenhough Smith, told me that Sir George's main idea was that people would like a story magazine if they found an illustration at every opening. But the great success of the *Strand* actually arose from its being half the price of the usual magazine and from the sudden appearance of Sherlock Holmes.

Sir George was an excellent organiser; adroit and unruffled. He was good-tempered, sanguine, and pleasant to deal with. What he objected to most was objections. When he wanted to start something new the whole interior of Southampton Street came forward with different kinds of objection, each according to his department; and the Advertising Department always discovered more objections than any other department. But Sir George would say, "Yes, Mr. So-and-so, what you say would be very much to the point if we were not going to publish this paper. But we are. Now, consider the advantages."

Sir George liked starting something new. He was by temperament a projector and a promoter. He liked to settle the essential aim and character of a publication, to find someone who he believed would carry out the idea, and to leave the rest to him. He never interfered in the details of a publication when once it had been launched.

This side of the great man I can vouch for. One day Eustace Miles, who was a champion at real tennis and a protagonist of vegetarianism, came to persuade me to persuade Sir George to start a magazine about Physical Culture and Health. At that time Sandow had made the British Isles what would now be called "muscle-minded." As, like Eustace Miles, I had many rebellious ideas on the subject, I thought it worth while to put the idea before Sir George.

Sir George listened with his habitual patience, and then said, "No, no, Mr. Fry, no, no. We mustn't go in for the propaganda of a cult. But, Mr. Fry, what we will do is to start a magazine of sport with you as editor." He then proceeded to discuss the kind of magazine we should make, as though the whole question had been under full consideration for months.

I listened with my habitual patience, and then suggested to Sir George, "But what about Eustace Miles?"

"Oh," said Sir George, "Mr. Miles, I am sure, is a very clever man, but he is a propagandist, so I am afraid we must shed him."

That is how *C. B. Fry's Magazine* came into being. Sir George Newnes sat me down in an office chair with an assistant editor and an office boy and left the whole thing entirely to me. I had to find out all about the complicated question of paper, and how to buy it in quantities which appeared to me gargantuan. I had to find out all about printers and printers' estimates. I had to find out how to concoct the editorial side. And I had to write a lot of it myself.

When Sir George discussed the project with me I told him that no doubt he realised that I was completely blank as to how a magazine was produced. Sir George at once regarded this as an objection, and as such not to be countenanced. He explained that a monthly magazine is the easiest production imaginable. I should sit in a comfortable chair, with my mind at ease, and select some seven or eight excellent articles sent in for consideration by clever young men such as barristers waiting for briefs.

"You will say to yourself, Mr. Fry," he continued, as he moved his hand from one letter to another lying on the desk, "you will say to yourself, 'This month I will have this one, but not that one. That one will keep till next month.'"

Such may have been Sir George's experience when he watched Greenhough Smith engaged on the first number of the *Strand Magazine*. It was not mine.

My experience was that contributed articles could not be counted on to supply more than one or two fill-ups a month. The gist of the magazine from start to finish emanated from the heads of the people in the office, and, to the best of my memory, chiefly from the head of the heads—namely, mine.

The way a magazine is produced is by the editorial having ideas and knowing where to find the man inside or outside the office to execute them.

My first assistant editor was none other than the late A. Wallis Myers, C.B.E., the distinguished authority on lawn tennis, who had been a young man on the staff of the *Westminster Gazette* and knew something about the inside of a newspaper office, but he did not know any more than I did about magazines. The office boy was too young to know anything, but he is now on the editorial staff of the *Strand*. Afterwards an assistant was provided for Mr. Myers in the person of Mr. Gentry, now in charge of the book department of Cassell's. In fact, everyone connected with the magazine, except myself, has gone up and up and up. I have always felt that my real *métier* was that of a producer.

Soon after the projection of the magazine, having discovered that Sir George's contribution to the effort amounted to approval, and that I was to be thrown entirely on my own resources, it occurred to me to go and see T. P. O'Connor. Not long before this he had started *T.P.'s Weekly*, with his usual success. I did not know him : I just thought he would be a good adviser, so I went to see him without further ado. He was as genial as his name, and his advice amounted to this, that one ought never to start a publication without knowing exactly what one was going to put into it. This, of course, is precisely what is wrong in the case of nearly every new venture of the kind. Sir George Newnes identified me with sport, by which he meant the popular interests of cricket, football, and athletics. I identified myself rather with the world where field games occur as an incident, but a world of a much more general kind. Hence it was that the first number of the magazine was very different from what Sir George expected, but when he saw it (and he did not see it until it was printed and bound) he decided that he liked it because it was different from anything else of the sort that had previously appeared.

I can best explain the point by the fact that I decided myself to provide an article on Physical Energy, the great equestrian statue which was in process of being made by G. F. Watts. I went down to see him at his country home near

Compton, on the southern slope of the Hog's Back, and he was kind enough to tell me all sorts of things. He was a frail old man with a small white beard. He wore a black velvet skull-cap suggestive of Florence and Old Masters. He had a gentle mind that dwelt on the symbolic expression of the kind of abstract ideas which touch human nature. The statue itself, modelled in clay, was in a big hole in the ground at a small foundry in the purlieus of Kensington. I went to see it there. As happens to all equestrian statues, all sorts of people criticised the horse. Some affirmed that no horse could possibly have arranged itself on its hind legs in the position chosen by Watts. To me at the time, under the gentle influence of Watts's presence, the statue appeared a magnificent expression of the idea of Physical Energy, and I wrote so at considerable length.

I may say that mine was the only item in the first number about which Sir George Newnes had any doubts. He smoothed his brown beard and kept repeating through it, "But, Mr. Fry, why Physical Energy? Why Physical Energy?" Like many other friends of mine who ought to have known better, he could not see any subject properly subscribed to my name except cricket or football.

Nevertheless, the first number of the magazine sold well enough to redeem my error of being myself instead of what I was supposed to be.

Well, *Fry's Magazine* continued a successful existence from 1904 till the year before the War. Its last year was on an independent basis. I and Lord Riddell, who had recently become Managing Director of George Newnes, Ltd., could not agree about the conduct of the publication. He wanted to run it. So did I. And I saw it first. So the magazine went away as a separate concern. When the War came the concern came to the conclusion that it had better stop until the War was over, and when the War was over it decided not to start again. Production expenses, especially for paper and printing—the greater part of costing—had gone up, and the future of an advertising revenue was problematic in the new world. As it happens, in succeeding years the field of advertising appropriate to such a magazine has much increased, so probably had we restarted the magazine it would by now have become prosperous.

During the early days of the magazine occurred the adventure of Diabolo. I am afraid that I was the inventor of the name. One day when I was sitting in the office in Burleigh Street—the office where Sir George originally started *Tit-Bits* and the *Strand Magazine*—the door opened to admit a very shiny top hat founded on a dark, neatly bearded face. Their owner invited himself in. He pretended in English of the French type that he had something very interesting to show me.

This was Monsieur Georges Phillipart, who had somehow eluded both my assistant editor and the office boy. He was the only entrant who ever did elude the office boy. Besides his top hat, he was superbly dressed in morning coat, dark striped trousers and patent leather boots. He placed a little black bag on the table, opened it with slow ceremony, and produced an elephantine edition of the article afterwards known as a Diabolo. Just two tin cones soldered together at their apices. He also produced two batons joined with a string, and proceeded to show me that the novel projectile could be made to spin on the string by careful dandling. He then sat down and invited me to advise him how to make all this into a game; he understood I was a prominent sportsman.

Desiring to maintain this reputation in the eyes of so distinguished a foreigner, my swift mind, like the wild boar in Vergil, divided itself this way and that, and I immediately advised him to go back to Paris and have the thing manufactured about an eighth of the size, and of celluloid, with a rubber tire round its rim to prevent accidents. This was an inspiration due to my remembering that table tennis had become a rage when the celluloid ball replaced the miniature rubber ball previously used.

M. Phillipart was much interested, very much obliged, and bowed himself out, this time under the careful eye of the office boy. He returned a month later with the small celluloid double cone which eventually achieved international vogue. By this time what he wanted was a name, and the formulation of a game on the lines of lawn tennis. The first name that occurred to me, instantaneously of course, was "Trajecto." No sooner had I written the word down than my eye caught a small statue of the Discobolus on the mantelpiece. Then I remembered that the Greek equivalent of the Latin verb was "Diaballein." So I wrote the word "Diabolo" on a small piece of blotting paper and handed it to M. Phillipart.

One glance at the name and M. Phillipart disappeared without further compliments like a well-dressed black flash. He returned in the afternoon, this time eloquent with compliments, to tell me that he had registered the name.

As the last generation will remember, "Diabolo" spread like a prairie fire, but not in the guise of a serious game. So my book on the subject, which appears to have been translated into nearly every European language, remains a neglected classic. In fact, "Diabolo" is the only first-class game to which I have devoted serious attention that has not more or less turned up trumps. What is more, nobody will ever know that I invented that historic name. Nor that the name involved M. Phillipart and his Paris firm in a law suit. He lost his case because the other side produced a sailor who gave evidence on oath that years ago the game had been played under that very name on a ship in the middle of the Pacific. A good yarn, but it really made no difference; imitative manufacturers could anyway produce double cones with complete legality, and it was not their fault if everybody called the attractive little gyroscopes diabolos with a small "d."

Moreover, M. Phillipart got home in every European country except, I believe, Luxembourg and Russia.

When M. Phillipart was finally ready with "Diabolo" he invaded England. He brought a French journalist and the French journalist's wife and daughter. The daughter was called La Petite. La Petite, aged about twelve, had two pigtails, and was a conjurer of the most surprisingly expert in the new game. M. Phillipart had businesslike ideas about what he called good advertising. He kept the journalist busy. The latter was a slim man, extremely well dressed in the tweed tail-coat of the period, a military moustache which stood out at right angles, and a bowler hat which he wore at a tilt. M. Phillipart, with the assistance of the journalist's wife, kept this sportsman industriously at work writing articles, which he sent to every editor in London. An astonishing number of those articles was published, as I know very well, because I had to translate them into English, to the enlargement of my French vocabulary.

Among other efforts, M. Phillipart instituted a demonstration of the game in the grounds of the Earl's Court Exhibition, when La Petite figured to much applause. I was raked in at the last moment, most unwillingly, in the rôle of an umpire. Another instance, I suspect, of M. Phillipart's talent for good advertising.

Whatever the merits of "Diabolo" as a game, it led me into an interesting visit to Paris. M. Phillipart knew Santos Dumont, who just about that time was constructing small flying-ships and elementary aeroplanes. I saw his aeroplane, of the box-kite type, lift off the ground and fly two hundred yards. This was at the time when the Wright brothers had constructed an aeroplane in America which had flown for several hours. In Paris their achievement was accepted as a fact, but not so in England. When I came back I wrote an up-to-date article on the conquest of the air, which I believe was the first article published in England treating this subject seriously. Nobody took the slightest notice of it. Lord Riddell referred to the new machines as "aerophones" and disbelieved in them.

In the fledgeling days of flying, when no one except the brothers Wright, of Dayton in America, had credited themselves with maintaining a machine in the air, the obstacle in the way of progress was that it was only with the machine in the air that practical research about flying could be made. The dilemma was that you could not experiment except when the machine was actually flying, and you could not fly until you had perfected the machine by experiment. That was the case put to me by a clever Belgian scientist named Dr. Tacquin.

He was an acquaintance of my father in Brussels, and wanted me to go in with him for aeronautics, on the ground that this was the thing of the future, and that I ought to give up cricket for so important a project; because, as he put it, " one had only to snap a small tendon and one's cricket career was finished." The notion that cricket was a more dangerous game than flying was not intended to be humorous.

Before I could join up with him the versatile Dr. Tacquin had side-tracked his project of aerial experiment with aeroplanes running on long wires stretched between balloons in favour of a previous scheme of his to develop the Sus district of Morocco.

Dr. Tacquin was an experienced explorer, and had spent much time in the country south of the mountains which run eastwards from Mount Atlas and the Atlantic and form the southern barrier of Mediterranean Morocco. On the Atlantic coast of the Sus district, on the southern side of the mountains, there were, he said, three natural harbours, one of which was Agadir. Such trade as there was among the scattered inhabitants and wandering Moors was done by way of seasonal fairs in selected spots. The Sultan of Morocco, in collaboration with various foreign interests, and also with the interests of merchants in the northern ports, had instituted that the ports on the Sus coast should be closed; and he maintained that he could not control any operations in the Sus. This ensured that any trade went up northward over the mountains to the benefit of the Sultan and of the merchants in the northern ports.

Dr. Tacquin's view was that the inhabitants of the Sus would benefit by being able to export dates and other products directly from Agadir and another port called Massa. He believed that the confidence of the Sheiks of the Sus and their followers could be obtained by peaceful graduation. What he projected was the formation of a fishing company to exploit the rich banks off the Sus coast. Four steamers with wells could carry fish to European ports, and fish-canning factories could be established on the coast. In connexion with these factories, a convenient trade could be developed with the natives, and a system of import and export established.

But he had in mind two further developments. He had discovered that there were a number of mineral workings, including gold, along the coastline, where it appeared that the

Romans had obtained metals. In addition, there was a river called the Dra, which resembled a little Nile, and which, with proper barraging, could be induced to irrigate considerable tracts of country where wheat and perhaps cotton could be grown. He had a further idea that a successful sporting club could be developed for the pursuit of big game, such as leopards and perhaps even the fabulous lion of the Atlas. Apparently, too, there was the prospect of cork forests on the hill-slopes to the north of the Sus district, and also of esparto grass, which is valuable for the manufacture of paper. All this, being within four or five days' steaming from England, seemed to offer interesting possibilities.

Dr. Tacquin duly got up his Belgian and French syndicate. They secured a small sailing-ship, a schooner, the *Moonstone*, and as he was anxious to sail under the British flag he asked me to come in as ship's husband, for registration. Being advised that this was all right, I became to that extent involved in what developed into the famous Agadir incident and nearly into a European war.

What happened was this. Dr. Tacquin sailed in the *Moonstone* to Agadir and began tentative operations. Presently a series of articles appeared in the London Press calling attention to the danger of adventurous commercial operations in the Sus district. The political difficulties involved for the Moroccan Government and possible international complications were stressed at length and in plausible detail.

The fact was that the German Consul in Morocco, having heard of Dr. Tacquin's movements, had got busy. He persuaded the Sultan's Government to send urgent representations to the British Foreign Office. The main point was that, as Morocco was a French sphere of influence—in return for an arrangement between the French and British Governments that the British should have freedom of influence in Egypt— any attempt by the British to develop the Sus district, which the Moroccan authorities specially desired should not be developed, would end in troublesome complications. What this had to do with German interests did not clearly appear; but the German Consul evidently thought so. So far as I could see, the fact that the Sultan could not guarantee the lives and immunity of Dr. Tacquin's party in the Sus involved no danger at all except to Dr. Tacquin. The German Consul, however, was successful in pressing his view of French political interests, and Dr. Tacquin was told by the British authorities that he must come away. A British gunboat, strangely enough commanded by an officer who was a friend of mine, was despatched to see about the matter and call upon a few sheiks.

There, you would suppose, the matter would be concluded. Not at all. When Dr. Tacquin and the *Moonstone* were safely out of the way, a much more pretentious but otherwise similar expedition was made to Agadir, nominally by the Mannesmann Brothers, of Frankfurt. One of the firm arrived at Agadir and toured about the Sus with considerable pomp. Dr. Tacquin had intended to develop relations with the sheiks slowly and patiently. His German rival went about it with undisguised immediacy. The sheiks developed differences of opinion among themselves as to the desirability of his presence and intentions. The result was that the Kaiser sent his powerful gunboat to Agadir to give the German prospector moral support. The result of that was severe complications. The French became energetically perturbed. Germany became energetically annoyed. Diplomatic relations became acute. In effect, Germany threatened war, and secured the fall of the French Minister, M. Delcassé.

War was avoided at the cost of a severe diplomatic rebuff to France. The settlement was at last effected by the Algeciras Conference of 1906, in which Britain was concerned in a final straightening out of the Moroccan tangle.

All this goes to show how easily a stray private Englishman, whose father happens to know an adventurous and energetic scientist, may in a minor degree very nearly involve his country in a European war. The only point where I came into the later developments was when the Franco-Belgian syndicate wanted to sell the *Moonstone*, and could not do so without the consent of the ship's husband.

Dr. Tacquin and Santos Dumont were not the only interesting people I met on the Continent. Georges Clemenceau was some sort of a relation to Mme. Phillipart, and I saw him. I have been told that Cousin Georges always drank coffee through a straw, but he did not. I wish I had known at the time that he was going to be so great a figure in history. I also met Colonel Picquart, the brilliant soldier who figured so prominently in the Dreyfus case, and, indeed, was the brain that unravelled the impossibility of Dreyfus being guilty of betraying military secrets to Germany.

Back to London. . . . A visitor of an unusual type to enter the offices in Burleigh Street in early days was E. V. Lucas. He did not enter unheralded like M. Phillipart. He was meticulously introduced by the office boy to the assistant editor, and by the assistant editor he was passed into the oak-panelled sanctum.

When I was projecting the first number it occurred to me to get J. M. Barrie to write an article on cricket. What I wanted was something about cricket by someone who was sure to be original and certainly could write. Barrie invited me to call at his bird's-nest of a house in Lancaster Gate overlooking Kensington Gardens—or, rather, looking into Kensington Gardens half-way up the railings. There I had interviewed this minute man in his minute study. That is to say, he had interviewed me. He spent the best part of an hour extracting from me in detail how the more prominent players of the day made their runs or got their wickets. Especially he wanted to know whether Bobby Abel really did play with a cross-bat and whether I thought that Lockwood threw. I said "No" to both these libels. On the precise object of my visit all I got out of him was that I had far better ask his friend Lucas. I noted his Scottish skill in avoiding a direct refusal.

From Shakespeare onwards successful poets, dramatists, and other artists have been peculiarly interested in cricket. This trend of the first-class literary mind is about the finest tribute to the merit of the game. What is it in cricket that so fascinates novelists, poets, and dramatists? Myself, I believe that there is a certain mystery in how a man becomes a famous batsman or bowler, which is hidden even from the performers themselves, and has a curious appeal to premier imaginations. Cricketers themselves have no imagination—at least, no first-class cricketers. Otherwise they would be so nervous sitting in the pavilion at Lord's that they would never make any runs or take any wickets.

I do not claim that all cricketers, even first-class cricketers, are running examples of this interpretation. But unless it is correct, how comes it that one never meets any man distinguished in literature and music, art, or the drama who does not appear to be much more interested in cricket than in anything else? For instance, I mention at random from my own acquaintance George Meredith, who wanted to know whether I believed in the whip stroke or the long swing; Andrew Lang, who wrote a better essay on cricket than he wrote on any other subject; Sir James Barrie, who did not mind a bit when my half-bred Scottish terrier Jane Brindle fixed him in the Achilles tendon; she was such a wonderful fielder and knew at a glance where each stroke was going and could retrieve a cricket ball by scent from the middle of the cabbage patch over the wall. And the reason she bit Barrie's Achilles tendon was because he was standing too near to my Madame when she was bowling to me on the lawn. Then there is that beau Clifford Bax, who introduced his brother, Sir Arnold, to me as " a very useful bowler," and who is prouder of having hit a six at Lord's than of *Socrates* or *The Rose without a Thorn*; John Galsworthy, John Drinkwater, Conan Doyle, A. E. W. Mason, Francis Thompson, Sir Hugh Walpole, Alec Waugh, A. J. Cummings, John Strachey, Ben Travers—to mention just a few of all colours of literary performance and cricketing promise. And there is every known actor under the ægis of Aubrey Smith, who does not count because he was a cricketer first. When I went to interview G. F. Watts about Physical Energy, he halved my precious hour in interviewing me about cricket. He had drawn a wonderful set of illustrations for the famous textbook *Felix on the Bat*, the originals of which are hung in the writing-room at Lord's; his picture of an Apollo-like young man doing the obsolete draw in a pair of dancing-pumps is superb.

The result, however, of my meeting with Barrie was that I wrote to E. V. Lucas, and he wrote back in a letter which went down the page to a point, the point being his signature at the bottom of the inverted triangle. Well, Lucas arrived, and I believe the only reason he came was that he wanted to look at me close to; just then I was making a lot of runs. I found him much more difficult to deal with than Barrie. I began by telling him that I hoped to get people who could really write to write about cricket in my magazine. He countered by explaining indirectly what a bad writer I was myself. I explained that the bother was that nobody who had any real knowledge of the game ever had any ability to write. He said that Albert Knight, at that time the best batsman in the Leicestershire county side, was the best writer on cricket. I told him at once that I did not consider that Knight could write half as well as I could. But I did not know that Lucas was at that time collaborating with Knight to produce a book called *The Complete Cricketer*, which, when it did come out, proved to be the best book on cricket I have ever read. It is not very well known. Years afterwards—in fact, about three years ago—Lucas told me that I was the only writer on cricket that he could ever read with any satisfaction. So I asked him, " What about Albert Knight?" He said, " Yes, but Knight wanted a lot of editing." I said that so did I, but no editor knew how to do it.

From the moment Lucas entered my office all those years ago we became close friends. He was not expansive. He was a repressed sentimentalist with a tongue which intended to be kind but could not help being caustic. He had a fastidious good taste which prevented him from being otherwise than sceptical about the merits of nearly everything except the county of Sussex and Charles Lamb. He was a Sussex man by birth, a nephew of the famous Verrall, the scholar who edited Æschylus. The V in E. V. stands for Verrall. He was no relation of the Lucas family of Horsham who sized largely in the annals of Sussex cricket. He began life at the age of 15 as an assistant in a small bookshop. He began his literary career by proposing to the editor of *The Argus*, the local Sussex evening paper, to report cricket matches in a new and better way. Later he was one of the bright minds—bright in the ancient and not the modern sense—who produced the " By the Way " column in *The Globe*, the turnover article on the front page of that pink paper. It has never been success-fully imitated. Harold Begbie and Sir William Beach Thomas were his associates. Harold Begbie was afterwards another great friend of mine; but Lucas and Begbie seem to have been always politely at daggers drawn. Lucas said that Begbie always put in everything that ought to be left out. Begbie said that Lucas always left out everything that ought to be put in. Begbie wrote a verse:

> "Lucas had a little Lamb—
> And this is all we know;
> That everywhere that Lucas went
> C. Lamb was sure to go."

Lucas, though otherwise a good judge of poetry, never forgave this verse.

I may mention with regard to John Drinkwater, another great friend of mine, that Lucas said that he, John Drink-water, could not write verse, whereas John Drinkwater said that he, Lucas, could not write prose. All the same they both admired each other very much. Lucas once went the length of characterising Drinkwater's prose as " upright."

E. V. Lucas wrote about cricket in my magazine some of the delightful excursions which subsequently developed into the best book ever written on cricket of olden times—*The Hambledon Men*, a book which is in the library of everyone who likes to read about the game. I was very fond indeed of Lucas, and once gave him a gold matchbox inscribed " E. V. L. Be thou my good."

Another and a frequent visitor at most unexpected moments to the office in Burleigh Street was Will Crooks, the most genuine Labour man the House of Commons has ever con-tained and failed to spoil. He was short of stature; and wore an overcoat in August. His head was large and enveloped in a black beard. He had a voice of a peculiar deep resonance. I do not know to this day why he first dropped into the office, except that he too may have wanted to look at me closely instead of from the shilling seats at the Oval. He must have been a cricket fan, but I never remember him saying a word about the game. He was the kindest-hearted man it is possible to imagine, and wholly devoted to the well-being of the poor.

He once succeeded in persuading my wife to go down to
Poplar and to drink several tots of peppermint at public-
houses in back streets, she being a most hostile teetotaller.
Will Crooks was an orator, and he could not even call attention to a chicken running across the road without being impressive.

Another caller, but one who knew what he wanted, was
none other than Hilaire Belloc. He succeeded in entering by
a small side door which communicated from the street to a
cubby-hole inhabited by the office boy.

Hilaire Belloc came to say that he was going to Morocco on
a walking tour, and was going to write a book about it; and
would not *Fry's Magazine* publish it serially? The proposition
astonished me. I explained that Belloc's writing would in a
certain sense be too good for us, we being by intention a
popular magazine; that is to say, ought he not to propose his
serial rights to a magazine like Blackwood's?

No: Belloc did not see that at all. Anyhow, could he tell
me what it would be like, this Moroccan adventure of his?

Belloc said that it would be rather like his *Path to Rome*.
Now it happened, incredible as this afterwards appeared to me,
that I had never read Belloc's *Path to Rome*. I was taken
aback because, knowing that Belloc was a Roman Catholic, I
had supposed that the *Path to Rome* was the history, past,
present, and future, of the Roman Catholic Church.

So I said that, of course, I knew the famous book intimately
by repute, but would Belloc believe it, I had actually never
read the work?

I read it going down in the train. I have read it many times
since. I sent Belloc a telegram the moment I reached home,
saying we would gladly accept his offer. But we never got the
prize. Within the next fortnight Belloc went down with
typhoid, and he did not—at any rate, then—go to Morocco.
The only writing we published by this uniquely admirable
and delightful author was a *chef d'œuvre* in the shape of an
article on "Marching." I regard Belloc as the aptest writer of
modern times. What is more, he is the only writer, of those
who wrote during the Great War about what was happening
in France, who succeeded in explaining to me what was hap-

pening. Lucidity is a gift as fine as it is rare. Perfect prose is rarely written by anyone who cannot think in French.

Another interesting caller emanated from the enterprise of A. Wallis Myers, my assistant. A fertile journalist, he invented an original feature under the title of "Outdoor Men and Women." Paragraphs and pictures. If you discovered that George Meredith went in for croquet, in he went for croquet. If you discovered that W. G. went in for whist, in he went for whist. Myers discovered that the authoress of *Bootle's Baby*, a best-seller about a baby planted on a Major and adopted by a regimental mess, went in for gardening; so in she went for gardening. Hence a letter from her husband, pointing out that the paragraph was incomplete, and that he would like to come and see me about it. He came in a frock-coat and top-hat, with a formidable, silver-mounted ebony walking-stick. In a formal sense he was the best-dressed man who ever entered our portals, with the exception of M. Philli-part. He sat down on the opposite side of my large desk with his walking-stick across his knees. After compliments, I found that the defect of our paragraph consisted in no mention of a preparation for the hair invented by the authoress of *Bootle's Baby*. I explained that we had never heard that the lady went in for hair-restoring, and if we had there would be some difficulty with the Advertising Department. This did not convince my caller that the paragraph was other than incomplete: a term he reiterated. So I called on the lady and explained the misfortune of the omission; but I was unable to convince her of the impropriety of combining a paragraph on her devotion to gardening with her ingenuity in inventing a new preparation to make the hair grow. The interview concluded by her remarking, with a smile altogether in character with the authoress of *Bootle's Baby*, how curious it was that the only other journalist with whom she had ever had a quarrel (this word smoothed by the smile) was also a sportsman. I replied with what I intended to be an equally qualifying smile that all the sportsmen I knew had kept their hair.

The military character of the hero of *Bootle's Baby* reminds me that it was through my connection with the magazine that I met Field-Marshal Lord Roberts. It will be remembered that

Lord Roberts failed to persuade the country that National Service was imperative. No one listened to his prophetic phrase, "Germany will strike when Germany's hour has struck." He then tried his best to encourage the formation of Rifle Clubs. One of his assistants wrote to ask us to publish a series of articles in support of this campaign, and we did so. One morning a secretary rang me up to ask if I would have lunch with Lord Roberts at his house in Portland Place. When I arrived at Portland Place I was welcomed by a young officer in a morning-coat and with the general appearance of a formal occasion. Lord Roberts had asked me to arrive half an hour before lunch. When Lord Roberts came into the small drawing-room where I was waiting, he too was wearing formal morning-dress. After we had talked for a quarter of an hour he rang the bell and sent the servant to find Captain So-and-so. When Captain So-and-so came he told him to entertain me for a few minutes, and then excused himself. He returned in five minutes dressed in a light tweed suit. I had come up from home without knowing that I was going to lunch with the most famous soldier of the day. Lord Roberts had the remarkable kindness to relieve me of any embarrassment.

I often met Lord Roberts afterwards, and heard him make several speeches. He was one of the most effective speakers I ever heard. He had a way of being explicit without wasting a word, and of imbuing what he said with all possible force without any effort at emphasis. He remains in my mind as one of the absolutely first-rate brains of my experience. He had in a marked degree the power of simplication which is the surest sign. Two others who affect my memory in the same way, very different both from one another and from Lord Roberts, were Lord Haldane and Lord Balfour. I do not say that Lord Balfour particularly aimed at simplicity in his exposition of a subject—for instance, " A Defence of Philosophic Doubt "—but he had a notable power of thinking simply first whatever he said afterwards.

Whether anybody can think simply when he is editing a magazine I doubt, I philosophically doubt. Activities are switched into so many divergent directions. For instance, I remember one day being asked whether we should accept the

serial rights of "Sanders of the River," before anybody had
ever heard of Edgar Wallace. I am pleased to say that I said
yes in the middle of trying to invent a scheme for a colour
picture by Charles Crombie. Whether it was the unseen influence of Edgar Wallace or not, what I did invent was a
series of pictures of old-time golf, cycling—that is to say,
velocipeding—and other sports, a style of picture which was
afterwards magnified on the hoardings by a famous whisky
firm. You see, when the sub-editor came in with the typescript
of " Sanders of the River," the advertising manager was trying
to persuade me to have colour pictures of various kinds of
sport to assist him in canvassing. It is not easy to come by an
attractive three-colour cover in terms of, say, modern cycling.
So I solved the difficulty by a dive into olden times.

Strange it is that successful devices in the publishing world
are often the result of pressure on the spur of the moment,
and of insistence, backed by no constructive suggestion of
its own, of the Advertising Department. Your advertising
manager meets one man in the train who finds fault with one
item in last month's issue, and you are then invaded with
the proposition that the whole of the issue was rotten and
universally condemned by all the hundreds of thousands who,
according to the advertising manager when he is outside the
office, form a fraction of our readers. The Advertising Department of a magazine, in my experience, regards itself as the
entire business side of the institution. It refers to itself always
in such terms with the implication, sometimes tacit, sometimes
very explicit, that the Editorial never knows what it is doing
and is always in error and contributes nothing towards the
production of any revenue. The Editorial is a fanciful world
quite divorced from reality, and wholly unable to see the
advantage of publishing a score of pages of no particular
interest in order to catch the attention of one advertiser who
may possibly buy a single quarter of a page. The Advertising
Department is always blowing in with complaints that it
receives no attention from the Editorial. Nevertheless I spent
a good deal of my editorial time in inventing ideas, verbal and
pictorial, for the advertising manager to take round to his
clients with a view to persuading them to buy space in return

for his brilliant ideas. The procedure was not unsuccessful; and quite a number of the ideas originating in Burleigh Street enjoyed a vogue in the pages of other periodicals and on the hoardings of urban and rural districts.

We had our assistant editors. One was C. E. Hughes, a polished writer, who did not know much about sport, but was otherwise highly accomplished. He was a contributor to *Punch*, and could sketch admirably. He drew on a piece of blotting-paper a portrait of Will Crooks which I still preserve framed and glazed. He it was whom I saw one day scribble the notorious lines which achieved celebrity in America, and are still unforgotten:

> " Algy met a bear.
> The bear was bulgy,
> The bulge was Algy."

How did he succeed in thinking of this gem on the spur of the moment in order to fill up a blank eighth of a page?

But I do not think that for effective originality that *jeu d'esprit* really equalled the achievement of another assistant editor of mine, the poet Ralph Hodgson, who appears in anthologies as the author of *Time, You Old Gipsy Man* and *The Bull*. Confronted one late afternoon by precisely the same task which Hughes so glibly overcame, he inserted a small half-tone block of a rabbit, more or less in the air, with the astonishing underline " An evening nibble." There was no evidence that the rabbit was eating or to be eaten, nor was there any hint of evening. Nevertheless this small item was a major success.

Another but previous assistant was Bertram Askey, who afterwards did very well as a writer of fiction. He wrote several serial stories about a character named Smiler Bunn, and after that he never looked back, except that at one time he combined the earning of a large income from literature with running a large brickworks.

My last assistant editor was another clever fellow, W. Burton Baldry, nowadays so well known in the City of London.

I began writing signed articles in the *Daily Express* from the beginning of the career of that not unknown newspaper when it was started by Sir Arthur Pearson. He started the

Daily Express in accordance with his principle that where there was room for one successful periodical there was always room for another, if introduced by Arthur Pearson. This was a guiding principle among future newspaper magnates in those days. Lord Northcliffe was originally on the staff of *Tit-Bits*. He decided that he could do the same thing on his own, and founded his great career by starting a rival to *Tit-Bits*, with a yellow cover instead of a green one, entitled *Answers*. Arthur Pearson was also on the staff of *Tit-Bits*, and he decided that he could reply successfully to *Answers*, so he started *Pearson's Weekly*. Arthur Pearson replied to the *Strand Magazine* with *Pearson's Magazine*; Alfred Harmsworth replied to *Pearson's Magazine* with the *London Magazine*. After Alfred Harmsworth had scored an enormous success with the *Daily Mail*, Arthur Pearson saw an opening for the *Daily Express*. I believe that Lord Northcliffe's original conception of the *Daily Mail* was a very neat half-penny *Times*. Arthur Pearson's idea was a bright paper with the principal news on the front page, also at a halfpenny.

Northcliffe once told me one of his guiding principles was that people should always be able to find the same sort of news in the same place on the same page. He had a powerful mind which expanded rapidly in consonance with the scope of a successful daily paper. He had the gift of foresight. To mention a small instance: once when I was lunching with him at Sutton Place he suddenly said, "Are you going on writing about games? What you ought to do is to take up a regular campaign on physical fitness. You know more about it than anyone else, and you have the prestige of your success in games."

Arthur Pearson's principles were that what anyone else did could be duplicated, and that a popular paper should be popular and very paragraphic. In the *Daily Express* office in Tudor Street every editorial room was placarded with "Paragraph! Paragraph! Paragraph!" The consequence was that when anybody like myself sent in an article of a continuous nature on a subject such as "The Decline and Fall of British Football," one saw it next day split into a couple of dozen short paragraphs measured out as it were by the inches of a rule of thumb. The paragraphic principle is good, but if the writer has forgotten to write in paragraphs the result of purely spatial distribution may be quite startling. Nevertheless, the new kind of sports journalism which we began in the *Daily Express* was a success, judged by the perhaps negligible standard of increased circulation.

What better standard of merit, however, can there be than an increased circulation? For instance, J. A. Spender, the eminent editor of the *Westminster Gazette*, an important person in political circles, a confidant and adviser of Lord Rosebery, Campbell Bannerman, and Asquith, told me the following story. During the months before the Boer War the Prime Minister, the Cabinet, and Governmental circles were perturbed by the strong line taken by the *Daily Mail*, amounting to an incitement of popular opinion in favour of war. Spender, who was known to be much liked and respected by Alfred Harmsworth, not yet Lord Northcliffe, was asked to go and see the great proprietor with a view to inducing a more peaceful attitude. When Spender arrived, Harmsworth greeted him cordially, and Spender diplomatically explained his mission.

"No, no, Spender," said Harmsworth. "We are right." He then pressed one of a semicircle of buttons on his huge oak desk, and sent for the circulation-book. He turned over the pages to the date when the campaign in favour of war had begun. "Look, Spender, up—up—up—up and up! No, no, Spender, we are right!"

Arthur Pearson occupied a small room in the Tudor Street building when he was not somewhere else; and he generally was somewhere else. Even in those days the man who afterwards went blind with such wonderful courage, who founded St. Dunstan's, and who never gave in to his disability, was rather short-sighted. He made a point of being an immediate yes-or-no man, and of living in a whirl of hustle which to him appeared to be the essence of efficiency. There is a story that one morning the messenger-boy who sat just outside the door of his private office was missing, because ten minutes before Pearson had sent him on an errand. Pearson exclaimed, "Where's that boy? He's never here when wanted! Find him!" About six smart young men scattered after the boy, who in due course returned.

"Where've you been?" said Pearson. "I don't care where you've been. Go downstairs and get your money. You're sacked!"

After the remainder of the morning whirl, much inconvenienced by the absence of a messenger, Pearson hurried out to lunch. Turning the corner of Tudor Street, he ran into a boy and nearly knocked him down.

"What is your name, boy?" he exclaimed. "I don't care what your name is. Do you want a job? Go to 8, Tudor Street, and say you're engaged as a messenger for Mr. Pearson." And away went Pearson before the boy had time to say anything. After lunch Pearson returned and found his familiar messenger sitting on his high stool.

I hope this story is true. It is accepted in Fleet Street.

There have been very few striking successes in sporting journalism, and fewer still that have sent up the circulation of a newspaper. Journalistic successes are often flukes and do not necessarily prove merit. E. V. Lucas in a friendly moment laid down that the success of my columnist stuff in the *Evening Standard* was due to the combination of authority, zest, and wit. I am still hoping that he meant what he said and that what he said was true.

How it came about was thus. The *Evening Standard* had heard that several newspapers contemplated a new line with regard to dealing with Test Matches between England and Australia in 1934. The idea was to engage distinguished novelists and playwrights to write fiction and drama about the Australians. The *Evening Standard*, not to be left behind, invited E. V. Lucas to write. E. V. could not manage this in addition to *Punch*, and suggested my name. I had not been near first-class cricket for thirteen years. But E. V. was keen that I should reappear in print. So I agreed. Just when the season was starting the *Evening Standard* also engaged Douglas Jardine. This was a good stunt, owing to the recent excitement about body-line bowling. So the *Evening Standard* had two experts. I did not quite see this, and was on the edge of resigning. Then Percy Cudlipp, the editor, asked me whether I would do my part on the lines of an American columnist. I said I had never seen American columnism, but if he would send me a specimen I would let him know whether I could surprise the secret of its success and translate it into cricket English. After severe use of an American dictionary I decided that I could. So in due course I sped away in a fast car to Worcester to see the opening match of the Australian tour. The day before I happened to meet E. V. who told me not to forget the sauce; and I told him all right, so long as he supplied the Lamb.

I arrived at Worcester about an hour before the match, and having found a bedroom in a small hotel, thought well to write out about a column in advance, sitting on the bed. This took me half an hour. I stuffed the sheets into my pocket and crossed the Severn and the Rubicon. Just before noon a young man from the *Evening Standard*, sent down to help me, boarded me with, " Will you be able, sir, to let us have half a column in an hour's time?"

" Oh yes," I replied, "and here is something meanwhile."

Before the hour was out, and before I had sent in anything about the actual play, I got a telegram from headquarters as follows: " Splendid stop great success stop this is the stuff to give the troops stop Editor."

One of the marvels about our great newspapers is the amount of space they feel able to devote to sports and field games, coupled with the amount of ignorance displayed by many of them about the psychology of the public they suppose they are pleasing. In the matter of sport you cannot fool all the people some of the time, nor some of the people all of the time. You cannot fool them at all.

Can it be that the higher editorial staffs and even the great Press Lords behind them are under the skin of politics and world affairs, but not of sport?

Perhaps sport has too thin a skin for them.

CHAPTER IX

A LIFE'S WORK

IN one of the numerous biographies of F. E., first Earl of Birkenhead, I found a remark attached to our contemporary careers at Oxford to the effect that he tried to persuade me to go in for the Oxford Union and undergraduate politics, but failed to do so, with the result that whereas he made history, I made only runs. That remark shows what a perfect ass a biographer can be. The fact that a coeval and not always defeated rival of Lord Birkenhead, Sir John Simon, and Lord Justice Roche did not later on emerge into eminence in politics or the law does not prove that he has done nothing with his life.

Once, standing in the *Mercury* rose gardens at Hamble, Lord Birkenhead said to me, "This is a lovely place and a fine show, C. B. But for you it has been a backwater."

"The question remains," I replied, "whether it is better to be successful or . . . happy."

You will not find the *Illova* among the China tea-clippers of heroic performances such as the *Cutty Sark*, but she was a beautiful ship, barque-rigged, teak-built and shapely, and famous in the trade to the East. After the trade lapsed for the sailing ships, and steamers began to multiply on the old sea routes, the *Illova* went home to rest after her last voyage to London Docks. There she remained in excellent condition till she was discovered as likely to suit the purposes of a remarkable man who had decided to devote himself to the training of boys for the sea. So after a few years as a sea-going training-ship in home waters, or at furthest to Villefranche on the Mediterranean coast of France, she was finally moored as a stationary schoolship in the Hamble river, opposite Calshot, on Southampton water. She had changed her name when she became the training-ship *Mercury*. She bore her new name with no small honour from 1885 till the War. Having been replaced in the establishment of the training-ship *Mercury* by H.M.S. *President* (old), formerly the composite sloop H.M.S. *Gannet*, she was sold to the Admiralty, went to sea again with cargoes of coal, and was sunk off Beachy Head.

She may have been still at sea in her barque-rigged splendour of bellying canvas when I was a boy at school, and who could have guessed that this swift ship, searching for wind in the China Seas, or scudding up the Channel towards London river, was to be the centre of my life?

The man who bought her in order to convert her into a training-ship was Charles Hoare, a partner in the Fleet Street bank which to this day is one of the few remaining important private banks. He was in his time one of the best-known Masters of Foxhounds, principally of the V.W.H., a leading figure in the coaching world, a connoisseur of furniture and antiques, a capable water-colour painter, no mean amateur architect; and he was once described by a Bishop under the uncommon classification of "a religious genius." There are very few interests, pursued by intelligence and ambition, on which he could not converse with the knowledge of an expert. I never met his equal in all-round capability. But his most outstanding characteristic was a quite wonderful genius for kindness; and this perhaps was the quality which, as specialised by a peculiarly searching and penetrating mind, persuaded the Bishop to clarify him as a religious genius; that, and an all-round originality.

This quality of originality certainly was translated into the kind of training-ship which he established in the *Mercury*. Although the founder has been dead these thirty years, his manner of mind and the tenor of his aims for the benefit of other people still exist in the training establishment on the Hamble river. The original ship is replaced by a bigger one, and the adjoining shore buildings and grounds have been enlarged and added to in the course of the years; but his spirit is there still. This I can vouch for, because for the last thirty years I have been and still am responsible for helping to carry on this man's work. And I regard it as one of the most remarkable experiences of my life that the ideas of a man should be able of their own initial force to endure in all their original liveliness when carried on many years afterwards by other and very different people.

After maintaining his ship at sea for several years, the founder of the *Mercury* decided that the life on board was too constricted for the kind of training he wanted to give the boys, so he secured some forty acres on the right bank of the Hamble river half-way between Hamble Village and Bursledon. There across the lane, on the other side of which is the present great Air Service Training depôt, he built a house and made playing-fields, gradually added the nucleus of a shore establishment, and moored the ship head and stern off the sea-marsh which forms the shore of the estuary.

For twenty-three years at his own cost he maintained the establishment, which gradually grew by various additions, including a small church and a theatre—building designed by Romanes Walker in miniature imitation of the Wagner Theatre at Bayreuth. The maintenance must have run into about six thousand a year—that, of course, on the pre-war value of money—and the establishment and plant must have involved a capital cost of £50,000. As the sea-training in the *Mercury* proved uniquely successful, and the boy recruits sent to the Royal Navy were soon recognised as about the best that the naval authorities obtained throughout the country, the founder of the *Mercury* in those twenty-three years was responsible for a work which nowadays would be described as of national importance. But I never heard that he received any thanks for what he did; at any rate, not from the nation. As, however, what he had in view was nothing whatever beyond giving his boys the best possible chance of realising in the sea-services what they had it in themselves to become, it is improbable that he himself ever expected any recognition of his work. The after record in the Royal Navy and Merchant Service of the boys he trained was so exceptional that this in itself must have seemed a fair reward.

When I first saw the *Mercury* in the 'nineties it appeared to me in a class by itself as a training establishment, in respect of the results it obtained relatively to the raw material dealt with. It was then and is now the only training establishment which did and does for boys mainly from the wage-earning

world what the great Public Schools say they do for boys from
the salaried and leisured world. That was why, in 1908, when
the founder died and the *Mercury* was about to be closed
down, I thought it worth while to put other things in life
aside and offer to try to carry it on. The real reason why I did
it was simply annoyance at the sheer stupidity of allowing
such a work to die.

What actually happened was this. Charles Hoare was supposed, as a partner in Hoare's Bank, to be a rich man, but
though his will was proved for over £200,000, the whole
of this was hypothecated, and no money was left for carrying on the *Mercury*. The establishment was left in trust
for two years with a request that the trustees, who were the
Bishop of London, the Bishop of Southampton, and Mr. J. C.
Moberley, a leading solicitor in Southampton, would try to
find some "public person or persons" to take it over, and the
executors of the estate were requested to find sufficient funds
meanwhile. The executors, after a few months, informed the
trustees that they could not find the necessary funds, so the
trustees applied to the High Court to be relieved of their trust.
This is where I came on the scene. But had not Mr. Moberley,
who, with Sir Russell Bencroft, was the chief supporter of the
fortunes of the Hampshire County Cricket Club, been one of
the trustees, and had he not harboured (no doubt at the back
of his mind), shall we say, a vague idea that if I took on the
Mercury successfully I should have to give up playing for
Sussex (and perhaps therefore play for Hampshire), I very
much doubt if I should have been able to intervene.

Anyhow, what I did under Moberley's advice was to enter
a cross-petition in the High Court, asking to be allowed to
try to re-establish the *Mercury*. I cannot say that I got much
advice, but I observed that under the deed of trust I might
have to figure as a "public person or persons." So, being put
to it for time, I telegraphed to half a dozen people whom I
knew to be likely coadjutors, asking them to form a committee
and governing body. This with the scheme I presented was
the nearest I could get to being a public person—other, indeed, than a rather well-known cricketer. The outcome was
that the High Court Judge accepted my scheme, but he

decided quite apart from it that I came within the category of a public person, so the Court handed over the *Mercury* to me personally for two years, with the proviso that if the establishment could be put on a reasonable financial basis it should then be turned into an educational charity under a scheme to be settled by the Court. The end of it was that within six months we succeeded in getting together about £2,000 in subscriptions and donations. We applied to the Court, and the *Mercury* was formally established as an educational charity, in which category, by the way, are some of the most famous schools in England; and the *Mercury* has gone on with continually increasing success and no crippling deficit ever since.

Under this settlement I was appointed Honorary Director for life. The term "honorary," by the way, while it implied no pay, by no means implied no work; under the scheme, the list of my duties is such as would make the Headmaster of Eton retire immediately. I have carried out some of them.

Looking back, I am appalled to realise, as I refused to do at the time, that had we not succeeded within the two years allowed by the Court in putting the *Mercury* on her sea-legs, I should in the meantime (owing to the heavy liabilities I had immediately to assume in the matter of a very onerous lease) myself, my heirs and my assignees, have been saddled for nine hundred and ninety-nine years with a liability of about a thousand a year. Such is the sanguine nature of youth, by which I mean the middle thirties. The successful event of what was rated by my family solicitor as a prodigious gamble does not corroborate the value of the maxim "Look before you leap," nor old Mr. Smiles's good words on the paramount virtue of prudence.

Now after thirty years we have a foundation fund, the income from which is enough to keep the establishment open even if empty, and the *Mercury* ought to be able to continue for as long as anybody has any right to look forward. That is to say, provided there is someone with the energy and interest to take care of it. That foundation fund we secured only a few years ago—about twenty-five years after we took over the ship; but we really won it in an interesting little struggle at the start.

The terms of the trust were that the ship and its appurtenances be vested in the three trustees. These terms were necessarily transferred to the new trustees who came into being in the scheme of management settled by the Court. The founder during his lifetime had made a collection of ship models, about two hundred in number, including some fifteen gems, notably half a dozen Stuart Admiralty scale models. The collection was valued for probate at under £3,000. The curious question arose as to whether the collection was an appurtenance of the ship; otherwise it did not go with the establishment, but to the estate. Naturally, the executors did not regard it as an appurtenance of the ship. Our lawyers, one of the leading firms in London, advised me that in their opinion we had no chance whatever of getting the collection. But a "public person" with no idea where he was to get an income of £5,000 to run the ship, and who had hypothecated the whole of his future on the prospect of carrying on a training-ship, a work of a kind entirely outside his previous experience, was not to be diverted on a point of inappropriate terminology.

So what I did was to draw myself six affidavits, the substance of which I obtained from six people who understood the value of the models and their historic interest; affidavits in proper form—"I, So-and-so, of So-and-so, make oath and say as follows. . . ." I included one on my own, in which I made oath and said, among other things, that the term "ship" in this case meant training-ship, which included not only the floating vessel, but the shore establishment. For example, a shore establishment was included under the name of a ship— H.M.S. *Ganges*; the island of Ascension was cited as a ship in the Navy List; the gunnery school on Whale Island was called H.M.S. *Excellent*. I further made oath and said that in my opinion the collection, as being of atmospheric interest to boys under training for the sea, should properly be regarded as an appurtenance of the said training-ship. I have these affidavits written in my neat handwriting (and in green ink) in my desk at Hamble to this day.

The opposition produced only one affidavit by a valuer, who was also an estate agent. The High Court Judge said that he would as soon have his own opinion as that of an estate agent in the matter, but that our affidavits were made by sailors whose opinions he regarded as very relevant. He decided that the collection was manifestly an appurtenance of the training-ship.

So this beautiful forest of little masts stayed where it was in a large room adjoining the house at the *Mercury* for the next quarter of a century. During that period we had various offers to buy the collection, starting at £6,000 and going up to £14,000. With increasing difficulty I dissuaded the governing body from selling.

Finally, Sir James Caird—who provided the funds for H.M.S. *Victory* at Portsmouth to be reconditioned into her pristine glory and preserved as a national monument—decided to offer another gift to the nation in the shape of the National Nautical Museum at Greenwich. After many passages of arms with Sir Geoffrey Callender, the naval historian, the expert promoter of the scheme and quite unscrupulous in pursuit of that good end, we finally sold the collection to Sir James for £30,000.

Up to the final settlement by the Court I can fairly say that I did this, that, and the other, because nobody else did much except offer advice, particularly as to the madness of taking on the impossible task of running a training-ship without any assured income whatever. The small fund we collected to justify our appearance in Court consisted chiefly of single donations. Only about £200 of the £2,000 came under the head of annual subscriptions, and we certainly could not run the place under £4,000 a year. We had no Lord Nuffield to appeal to in those days, although he was up at Oxford "in another college" at the same time as I was. The majority of our donations came from the racing world, curiously enough; because of some lively assistance in collecting given us by Mr. C. I. Robson, brother of the well-known trainer. I take peculiar pleasure in recording that the only donation of any size given us—that is, £100—came from Sir Samuel Montagu, grandfather of the present Lord Swaythling. He was the kindest of men, and with his splendid white beard accorded with one's idea of Moses. All the kinder of him in that we were nominally a Church of England training-ship and he was a strict Jew.

It is not generally realised that the running of this sort of establishment, though the object is moral and not material profit, is just as much a business as running Harrods Stores in its early days. Success depends on a continual effort of financial ingenuity, and otherwise upon the quality of the domestic economy. Anyone with reasonable qualifications who is really on the job can secure a pretty high standard on the instructional side; this, though the instructional staff has also to be used for executive work and the supervision of routine duties, and must be capable of co-operation in the whole main idea of the work. This means that you have not merely to obtain competent instructors; you have to train them into the attitude of mind required by the whole character and intention of the institution. The kind of man, very common in schools and training establishments, who wants to turn up and teach mathematics or seamanship during instruction hours and otherwise lapse into independent leisure, is quite useless. While it is necessary to secure as high a standard of instruction as possible in school and technical subjects, the gist of success resides in the quality of the whole life of the place, and this itself depends upon the way in which routine duties are carried out and on the quality of the domestic economy. Such results are difficult enough to achieve and are often missed in schools well furnished on the financial side; they are a work of art in an establishment which is never sure of sufficient funds year in and year out and has to live by its wits.

I found out at the start of this adventure that there was a great confusion in the public mind about training-ships. Sea training had been discovered to be appropriate to reforming troublesome and even so-called bad boys, so there was a general notion that all training-ships were in the nature of reformatories. On the other hand, the Royal Navy and the Merchant Service required as recruits the very best sort of boy they could obtain. The Royal Navy in particular, at any rate in those days, was not manned but " boyed "; all the recruits for its important branches were entered before the age of 16. Only picked boys were required.

Having spent thirty years of my life in trying to produce

the best result obtainable from boys of any and every sort, I hope no one will accuse me of being a crusted Tory. So in a world which is trying to call itself democratic, and in days when a main idea is that all our Services should be careers open to talent, my own conclusions in this respect may be of interest. It is not true that breeding, environment, and the atmosphere of home count for nothing. It is true that in the Royal Navy the broad gold stripe and curl of an Admiral are in the ditty-box of every seaman boy who joins the Service. But it is also true that whereas out of the boys at a good Public School—say, Repton or Uppingham—up to the age of 16 you can find at least 40 per cent. capable of making first-rate officers, on the other hand, out of a similar number of boys who come from the council schools and the environment of wage-earning homes you will not find more than 10 or 12 per cent. This may be an unpopular opinion, and it would not do for the platform of a prospective Member of Parliament, but it is nevertheless factual. The ultra-democratic proposition which inclines to suggest the general equality of youth as material for the responsibility of an officer is all very well on paper, but in real life it does not work. The whole question is obscured by the equally certain fact that, especially in stirring times, transcendent ability and force of character will emerge into striking prominence, whether they are exhibited by the son of a tinker or by the son of an earl.

What the founder of the *Mercury* had seen was that pre-service training was of crucial value to a boy who wished to go to sea, and that, whereas there were a number of training establishments for troublesome boys, there were only two or three which offered the advantage of pre-service training to the very type of boy that the Services required as recruits. There were plenty of training-ships for the persistent truant and the young semi-delinquent, but if the well-behaved fifth son of the farm labourer wanted to get sea training, his only chance was to raid his father's employer's orchard. Moreover, while a boy who somehow or other had come on the rates was provided with a fine chance of sea training, the son of hard-working parents with not a penny to spare or to owe had practically no chance at all offered to him.

That was why the founder of the *Mercury* started his training-ship for boys of good character. When I inherited the adventure, I persuaded *Punch* to publish a cartoon with a sturdy lad looking at Mr. Winston Churchill and asking him whether he could not be trained for the sea without robbing a till. Mr. Churchill was then Home Secretary, and it is curious to relate that years afterwards, when he was First Lord of the Admiralty, he proved to be the best friend in high office the *Mercury* ever had. We owe it to his attentive interest that H.M.S. *President* (old), our present commodious ship, was added to the establishment on perpetual loan from the Admiralty. When we took over the *Mercury*, I discovered that the founder had some years before applied to the Admiralty for the loan of a ship to enlarge the establishment in addition to the *Mercury*. There had been extended correspondence, and the Admiralty had several years before definitely offered the loan of a gunboat called the *Magpie*.

Where was the *Magpie*? I wrote to enquire whether the offer still stood. Yes, the offer had been made several years ago. Where was the *Magpie*? At this juncture I discovered, but not from the Admiralty, that the *Magpie* was one of three hulks lying about half a mile above us in the Hamble river, forming an establishment for experimental work of some kind, but popularly believed to be a mysterious rendezvous of the Admiralty Intelligence Service. This idea was reinforced when a yachting party, including Gregory Robinson, the well-known marine artist from Hamble, went ashore to buy bread near Cuxhaven and were impounded for searching enquiries by the German naval authorities.

At any rate, there was the *Magpie* a few cable-lengths away from us, and I never discovered why she was not on our moorings. However, the Admiralty wrote suggesting that instead of the *Magpie* would we not prefer to have an old frigate, the ship that saw the sea-serpent, which was just going out of commission as the R.N.R. drill-ship at Bristol.

I posted down to Bristol to see the ship and at once accepted her. When could we have her? After an interval the Admiralty wrote proposing that possibly the H.M.S. *Presi-*

dent, the R.N.R. drill-ship in the West India Docks in London, would suit us better.

I posted to London and inspected the *President.* As this former composite sloop had her upper deck housed in for training purposes as well as any amount of accommodation, I accepted her with alacrity. But we did not succeed in extracting her from the West India Docks. There she stayed, even more distant than her predecessor, the *Magpie.* We knew where she was, and that was all.

After several years it happened that one Sunday afternoon a messenger came up to my room in the house at the *Mercury* to say that a marine was at the office window, and could he speak to me. I stepped down, and the marine, saluting as the Royal Marines salute, informed me that the First Lord of the Admiralty would like to come and inspect the establishment.

I asked, "When?"

"It would be, sir, in about ten minutes."

So I said, "Certainly," and fired off a message to our officer in charge that the ship's company were to be on parade in Number One kit within five minutes. I proceeded to the end of the pier to receive the First Lord, who was coming up in a steam launch from the Admiralty yacht off Hamble Spit.

The party arrived in well under ten minutes, and I observed Mr. Winston Churchill, his brother Mr. Jack Churchill, Admiral Hood, and none other than my familiar friend Lord Birkenhead. The First Lord inspected the boys and the establishment and was much interested. What is more, he asked by far the most intelligent questions ever put to me about the place and the boys by any civilian. Admiral Hood, who inspected the ship's company with Mr. Churchill, delighted us by saying when the party said good-bye that he had never seen better discipline on parade. He was at the time one of the finest senior officers in the Royal Navy, and later went down with his ship in the Battle of Jutland.

Just on leaving, Winston asked me if there was anything the Admiralty could do for us.

I said yes, would he please send round the ship which was loaned to us some six years ago.

This reply excited his swift attention, and he went away leaving me certain that he would find out all about it. The result was that in the course of the next few weeks the *President* was removed from the docks and got as far as Chatham. But she got no further.

It happened that in the same month next year the First Lord made a similar visit to the *Mercury*, and immediately on arrival wanted to know where the *President* was. I reported that she was now at Chatham. Winston pursed his lips with an expression minatory for somebody. Within a fortnight the *President* was towed round to Portsmouth by H.M.S. *Queen*; I believe as a special exercise in towing.

A good deal of correspondence intervened before we finally had her moored opposite our foreshore astern of the *Mercury*. We got the *President*. She has been a fine success as a harbour training-ship. When any political opponent says anything derogatory to the statesmanship of Winston, I remark that at any rate he got a ship round from London to the Hamble river in a year and a fortnight, after everybody else had taken over ten years in failing to do so.

The position of training-ships and training establishments, outside the Royal Navy, which train boys for entrance to the Royal Navy is peculiar. The Admiralty has no direct responsibility for them. They are called mercantile training-ships; even those that do nothing but send boys into the Royal Navy. The Merchant Service consists of a number of independent shipping lines, and they have no responsibility as regards mercantile training-ships.

Where are the training-ships in this new world of National Service? Perhaps in the air. Yet the boy of 15 is to the sea Services what a youth of 20 is to the Army.

When we first took on the *Mercury* there was no Board of Education Grant for nautical schools as there is now. There was a very small grant obtainable from the Home Office under the head of Industrial Training. It was payable on boys who went through three months' training, so if you trained four boys successively for three months you could get about £12 a year for the four. But this, of course, did not provide effective sea training, and was quite useless for an establishment like the *Mercury*, which trained a boy for at least a year and sometimes two; if you trained a boy for two years you still got only £3 for him. There was no grant from the Admiralty, but if immediately on entry a boy passed advance class, the Admiralty made a capitation payment of £25 for him; this was in the nature of a payment for services received on the ground that the Admiralty was saved three months' training of the boy. It was really a compromise from the days before the Navy inaugurated the advance-class boy system, when the £25 was paid for the boy who passed merely as first-class on entering. To qualify as a first-class boy, the boy had to pass the required test in seamanship, rifle drill, swimming, and a very moderate standard in school. The subsequent advance-class boy was required to pass a high standard in school, as well as to qualify in seamanship, rifle drill, signals, and swimming.

When we took over the *Mercury* the average number of boys passing advance class was four or five a year. Before the end of our second year we were entering sixty boys a year to the Navy, and passing fifty-five of them advance class. This success in the advance class soon gave us an income of between £1,000 and £1,500 a year. But some ten years afterwards the examination was conducted on lines that prevented our getting so high a percentage. What happened was that if a boy failed to pass advance class during his first fortnight, he might pass at the end of the next fortnight, and the Royal Navy got an advance-class boy for nothing. At any rate, we made this higher percentage of advance-class boys in our early years one of the mainstays of our finance. Nowadays the grant has been reduced to £15, and is not at all easy to obtain. On the other hand, the Board of Education now and for some years past gives an educational grant nominally of £20 a year per boy for two years, which actually is worth from £8 to £10 per boy. The real basis of our finance in early years was that I persuaded the local education authorities to give sea-training scholarships, so that about half the boys under training were subsidised up to at least half their cost from these scholarships. Neither grants nor scholarships ever work out at their face value, because the cost of training an individual boy depends not on what amount is available for him, but on the total amount available for the expenses of the establishment. You cannot train one boy. You have to train a reasonably full complement, say a hundred, so that the overhead charges can be distributed.

One thing I found out very quickly was that if you were trying to provide proper training for the picked boys—that is to say, the boys the Services wanted—you could not do it on the basis of a charitable appeal. If you appealed for funds on an eleemosynary basis you would no doubt collect a nice round sum; but then your appeal would have to take the colour of pretending to rescue poor little starving boys and make them into great brown-necked able seamen, and you would not get the kind of boy required for the Services. Moreover, you would stamp your establishment as a charity, and the parents of the sort of boys you wanted would not care to send their sons to you. So my policy was to get each boy financed individually, either by scholarships or private assistance for him in addition to such grants as were available. This sounds rather complicated, and in fact the financing of the *Mercury* has always been a complicated task.

If you take on an adventure like running a training-ship you must expect to stand some of the racket. The *Mercury* finance would certainly have failed had the full complement of staff been paid. The fact that my wife and I between us have, ever since 1908, performed the functions of Captain Superintendent, Second-in-Command, Organising Secretary, and for a good part of the time Head Schoolmaster, has in that period saved about £40,000 of cost. As we have also found about £24,000 towards the cost of running the establishment, it will be seen that a ship like the *Mercury* cannot be run, or anything like it, from the State grants or the usual available sources. As there are, I believe, a number of people who fancy that my wife and I have been advantaged by taking up this work and carrying it on for the past thirty years, I take this occasion to exhibit that this is not so. In fact, we have paid heavily for such satisfaction as we may derive from having helped to carry on one of the best training establishments of its kind in the world.

The remarkable atmosphere and spirit of the *Mercury*, even more than such efficiency as it has on the instructional side, are the real secret of the success of its boys in the Royal Navy and Merchant Service. This atmosphere and spirit are due to the fact that my wife happens to be a genius in all that concerns routine work and domestic economy; and that she has for the past thirty years started her day's work at six o'clock in the morning. It is quite likely that the incessant work of a genius for three decades would produce an exceptional result; and it has.

For my part, I have been mainly employed in the organisation of the instructional side and in foreign relations. The *Mercury* is the only example I know of two captains of a ship with a successful result. Although nominally I am the head of the establishment, my wife and I have always acted as two persons in one—like the consuls at Rome; which shows that the Romans knew something even before the days of Mussolini.

The outstanding feature in the success of the *Mercury* is that it has successfully established a training régime which produces from the boy of the wage-earning classes a type that is fit to be made an officer in the sea Services. The number of *Mercury* boys who have risen to commissioned rank in the Royal Navy, entering by the lower deck, is remarkable; so also is the number who have risen to be masters and first and second officers in the Merchant Service. This is due to the boys under training in the *Mercury* being given responsible work every day of their lives, and being effectively introduced to the idea that it matters very much indeed how they do it.

Lord Birkenhead asked me once how we got such results. I told him that a boy in the *Mercury* discovered in his first fortnight that it is worth while to make a fine art of cleaning a bucket. He said it was a pity he and I had not been brought up like that.

The *Mercury* is very different from the general idea of a training-ship. Most people figure to themselves a dull hulk with chequered sides, moored in a muddy estuary. The shore establishment of the *Mercury*, with the church, the house, the theatre, the seamanship hall, and central block containing the dining-hall, bathrooms, school-rooms, and day-rooms, is better found than the majority of private schools where boys cost their parents perhaps £250 a year. Then there is the ship and the boats and all the strictly nautical appurtenances. The big cutters plying between ship and shore run alongside a long wooden pier spanning the sea-marsh through an expanse of tall Japanese bamboo. The Hamble river is a smaller edition of Southampton Water, running north and south instead of west and east. The village of Bursledon is a mile upstream, the village of Hamble a mile downstream, both nowadays much frequented by yachts. From the red brick *Mercury* house, itself a landmark from sea, as well as a pylon for denizens of the air, one can see the liners entering and leaving Southampton Water as they pass Calshot. I myself happened to see the *Titanic* moving outbound like a floating castle on her fatal voyage. There in the south distance are the round hills of the Isle of Wight, and to the left the flatter expanse of the New Forest. It is an historic neighbourhood. The reedy marshland at Warsash opposite Hamble used to be a waterway where warships were moored in the time of Henry VIII. At Bursledon in the old days the king's ships were built. Nelson's ship, the *Agamemnon*, was launched there with all her guns on board. Just above Bursledon bridge a Danish dragon-ship lies embedded in the mud, visible on a bright day at low water. The Forest of Bere, which extended for miles inland north, east, and west of Bursledon, supplied the shipbuilders with inexhaustible timber. The huge woods, called the Liberties, near Wickham on the way to Portsmouth, are a relic of this great forest.

The Hamble river is a typical English estuary such as supplied the Romans, Saxons, and Danes with convenient entry inland. There is a big rise and fall of tide, and the ebb and flood often run fast enough to hold up a strong swimmer. In summer the very salt water looks properly suited to pleasure, but in winter-time, especially when the south-westers are blowing, it can be rough and uncomfortable. There is plenty of scope for watermanship and boatwork on the tideway of the Hamble. The boys under training at the *Mercury* have the freedom of the shore establishment and playing-fields, combined with enough contact with the sea to make the whole place a ship. When a match is in progress on the terraced cricket ground, a fieldsman who does not happen to be attending to the game is looking across the pergolas of the rose garden and away over the waving jungle of the sea-marsh to the big ship at her moorings. The guns are showing from the square port-holes. The blue ensign is fluttering from the signal mast. Perhaps a white steam yacht is passing upstream to Bursledon.

A better place than an ordinary school, and a better life.

One feature in the régime of the *Mercury* is unique and has had much influence on the kind of boy produced—music as a regular item on the instructional side. Every boy goes to his hour of practice and theory of music just as he goes to his hours of mathematics, seamanship, signals, physical training, and gunnery. He does not regard music as an accomplishment. He accepts it as part of his training. The effect is that the training has had a standard fine art incorporated in its routine.

During my thirty years at the *Mercury* I have seen it proved that music has a remarkable educational value: in this sense, that you can see dull boys growing intelligent under its influence. This is not a matter of supposition. I have noted any number of cases where, the moment a boy began to improve in music, he also began to improve in all other subjects, especially in mathematics. I have also noticed that in the examinations at the end of the year more prizes in all subjects go to the best musicians in the picked band than in any other direction. In most establishments the band boys are trained separately to be entered in army bands. In the *Mercury* the picked band are simply the twenty-five or thirty best instrumentalists of the time being, and most of the best musicians are boys destined for the Royal Navy or Merchant Service.

The question of the value of music may be of interest to education authorities. When I first had to do with the Board of Education I was disturbed to find that the Board did not permit hours of instruction in music to count as hours of instruction at all. The *Mercury* system was evidently in advance of its time, but the authorities of to-day have discovered that the Greeks were not altogether off the spot in this matter. All is well.

On results, there is no sea-training establishment superior to the *Mercury* in school and technical instruction, but if I were asked what, in my experience, is the most valuable educational instrument of the *Mercury*, I should say music and what we call gunnery, which amounts to rifle and field exercises. Of music I have spoken, but I have also to say that ordinary military drill, provided—and this is of the essence of the matter—that a rigorously high standard is insisted on, has an altogether remarkable effect on the character and mental outfit, especially in the matter of alertness. This point may be useful in commendation of national military service. After all, the quality of being wide awake is decidedly one of the success qualities. You can soon test this by considering the people around you who are doing well and those who are doing otherwise. Half-and-half military drill is just about useless, but first-rate military drill is a powerful instrument for training the kind of man who is worth while anywhere and everywhere. There is no more fat-headed notion than that of the drill-sergeant being just a necessary nuisance and useless outside the Regular Army. You give me a hundred boys for a month, and give me also a seaman gunner to drill them on parade, and I guarantee that the whole lot will be far better citizens in every capacity than they were at the start.

That is one reason why I have never been able to understand the objection of our free democracy to compulsory military service. Such compulsory service for, say, a year ought to be the university of the ordinary young man.

The Royal Navy has always been a self-sufficing world within the circle of a suppressed major premise that no one exists for the Service until he is inside it. There has never been a shortage of boys applying to join. But the quality of the boys has varied from time to time, and the recruiting authorities have accordingly varied the physical standard required; but the standard has always been pretty high. More or less recently the Admiralty has instituted a highly efficient and well-informed Department of Personal Service, which

among other things has established relations with the schools
of the country. But there was in the past, and still is, a very
valuable function open to training establishments (outside the
Royal Navy, but supplying it with recruits), in that such
establishments are continuously in direct relations with the
local educational authorities and the schools.

My experience during my first fifteen or twenty years at
the *Mercury* was that, as to the general entry of boys at the
recruiting office, not more than 50 per cent. joined the Service
because they wanted to go to sea. The truth was that the
whole system of naval recruiting was founded on the unemployed boy labour market. Every year a large number of boys
between the ages of 15 and 16 became unemployed simply
because they were finished with boys' jobs and were not old
enough to be taken on at men's jobs. The number of boys
from this source was so large that the Royal Navy could
obtain a sufficient number of good specimens. Since, moreover,
the training in the Royal Navy was admirable, and the whole
atmosphere not only stimulating but also backed by traditions
as lively as they were ancient, the personnel of the seaman
branch has never been other than first-rate.

The consequence was that it never appeared that the recruiting system could be improved. It would seem, however, that
since the Royal Navy declared to require the picked boys of
the country, its recruiting might well have been founded on
the educational system of the country and not on the unemployed boy labour market. Boys from the latter source, except
as to physical qualifications, could not be otherwise than
unknown quantities, whereas in the schools every boy was
known for what he was worth.

When Mr. Winston Churchill was First Lord of the
Admiralty, I put this idea forward to him, and he arranged
for conferences, to which I was invited, with Sir Dudley de
Chair, who was then Admiral of the Training Service. My
idea was that relations should be established with all the local
education authorities, and that every schoolmaster should be
supplied with register books in triplicate, and that any boy
who had formed the wish to go to sea should be able while
still at school to report to his headmaster in the council

school, and general particulars about him be entered. Then one copy of the entry could be kept by the school, two sent to the Director of Education of the town or district, and one of these forwarded to the central recruiting authorities. The result would be that the Admiralty would have a register of all the boys in the country of suitable age genuinely desiring to go to sea, and each local authority would have parallel information. Among other useful results of such a system would be the possibility first of raising all the mercantile training-ships to a high standard of efficiency, and then of organising the allocation of the registered candidates for a pre-Service period of at least a year. In sum, the Admiralty would have a well-trained body of boys available annually up to the number of between two and three thousand. These recruits would be not only well trained up to the point possible outside the actual Service, but also every one of them would be a known quantity who had been through the mill and tested for character and ability.

From the point of view of the boys themselves and their prospects, both in the Royal Navy and the Merchant Service, pre-Service training gives a very distinct advantage. Other things being equal, a boy going into the Navy from ordinary life has no chance of competing with a boy from the *Mercury*, especially as the latter has a chance of coming to the front and being noted for advancement within his first few months in the Service. As for the Merchant Service, the moment a boy joins a ship from shore, whether as a cadet apprentice or as a seaman boy, he is pretty sure to be a complete nuisance to everybody for some months; whereas a trained boy is found useful from the moment he puts his foot on board. During the War a *Mercury* boy who had joined a merchant-ship about ten days before she was torpedoed by a U-boat off the south coast of Ireland, although only about 15½ years old, got away with a boatload of survivors and as nobody else appeared to be in command, he took charge himself, and after a day and a night of navigation successfully brought his boat into Cork harbour.

As the training-ship *Mercury*, what it has done and what it stands for (although a small item in the composition of a

great Empire and the sea services which are the mainstay
thereof), has eaten up the lives of at least three people and
has bitten large pieces out of the lives of a score of others, and
as the work is certainly unique and certainly of outstanding value, and as, moreover, by a curious anomaly, in all the
circumstances, the subject of sea training is not generally
understood, it seems worth while to add an exposition of its
meaning and intention brought up to this very day. And this
may even be of interest to quite a number of British parents
who do not know what to do with their boys.

Ashore, wherever we move, hedges and ditches, brick walls
and barriers keep us to the beaten track; we are fenced all
about. At sea there are no such restrictions, and a ship may
wander whither she will or wheresoever a man may guide her;
seamen are free, while landsmen are bound.

Every ship upon the sea is a little kingdom—self-contained,
isolated; in it men are close neighbours, whether they will or
no, and each must give the other room, for all must heave or
haul together; seamen in their ships are shackled, while
landsmen can roam. So it has come about that a discipline,
dating back beyond all kings and parliaments—the Law and
Custom of the Sea—has made of seamen a race apart.

In the old days boys embarked straightway to meet experience butt-end first; in modern times training-ships have
been designed to soften the impact, to give to the youngster a
hint as to what is before him, to impress early the necessity
of exercising those virtues of obedience, self-reliance, watch-
fulness, and comradeship which are the essentials in the
character of a good seaman.

The prime importance of a careful compounding of these
elements has been ever in the mind of the training-ship
Mercury. Necessity for strict obedience, yet readiness to think
and act independently in any unforeseen change of circumstance; readiness to command others, yet consciousness of
being oneself commanded; constancy towards the whole ship's
company, yet ability to fend for oneself—all these mysteries
come into the day's work as well as the technicalities of the
seaman's vocation.

To-day, more than at any time for years, it can safely be

said that a boy who adopts a maritime career is entering a
profession which is of vital necessity to our prosperity and
existence as an island Power. Apart from the fact that, after
a long period of depression, there is to-day work for all in the
Merchant Service, the Royal Navy has just embarked upon a
vast rearmament scheme, and scarcely a day passes without
the newspapers referring to the urgent need for recruits in
His Majesty's Navy.

In recent years changed conditions have made it difficult
for many parents to meet the heavy expense entailed in
education, and consequently more and more boys of sterling
character and good bearing are seeking advancement in the
Navy by way of the lower deck. The Service will gain if such
boys are given an opportunity to rise as high as their ability
will carry them, and a scheme is in force whereby the right
sort of boy can attain commissioned rank after a very short
sojourn on the lower deck. What in old time was called
" entry through the hawse-pipes " was indeed a rough road to
the quarter-deck. Conditions have changed, and to-day a lad
will experience no more hardship than is good for him, nor
need there be any fear that an officer will suffer because
achievement has been by this route, for the day is past when
folk suspected poverty to be near relation to vice and believed
that riches could incontestably claim cousinship with virtue.

The *Mercury* maintains that no training, however good, is
too good for a future member of the sea services. It holds that
pecuniary disability in the parents should be no bar to ability
when accompanied by right conduct in the sons.

At sea, now as ever, the call is for leadership. The *Mercury*
aims at producing this power by daily practice in all boys
who have the germ of it within them. It is an art.

And what is life without adventure?

As for the adventure called T.S. *Mercury*, the late Bishop
of Winchester said that it is the best thing that ever came out
of cricket.

CHAPTER X

ROUND ABOUT W. G.

THE upper regions of cricket, and especially the well-fenced area known as Test Match cricket, are inhabited by familiar names that appear to be its natural denizens. All the same, in many instances the entry into this select world is in the nature of an adventure. If Dr. W. G. Grace had decided to retire from Test cricket before the first match of 1899 instead of after it, the chances are that I should not have slipped in by the wicket gate for several years. W. G. would probably not have been on the Selection Committee, and Lord Hawke would have been in undisturbed control.

My entry in 1899 came about as follows. Except that I had done well in South Africa with Lord Hawke's team of 1895-6, and had scored a reasonable number of runs for Oxford University in four short seasons up to June and for Sussex in the August fag-ends of subsequent seasons, the big boys of the cricket world did not know anything about me. All they knew was that I had been selected to play for the Gentlemen at Lord's as a fast bowler. In 1898, for the first time, I was able to play a full season for Sussex—a different opportunity from a mere month of wet wickets in August. Consequently I made 1,788 runs with an average of 54, and was second in the batting averages. But that was not enough in that season to give me a place in the Gentlemen's eleven at Lord's; they had another fast bowler. I recall that J. A. Dixon, the Nottingham captain, condoled with me about this, and said, "It takes a long time to become recognised in big cricket, and just as long to be dropped from it."

When the Australians came over in 1899 and I started the season with a century against Hampshire and, what was far more important, an 80 against the Australians for W. G.'s team London County, the same W. G., being at the age of 49 still captain of England, plumped for me as his first choice as a batsman and co-opted me on to the Selection Committee. The only two other certainties W. G. would look at were F. S. Jackson and Ranjitsinhji. This for me was sudden promotion. Lord Hawke, Chairman of the Selection Committee, did not favour me as a batsman, nor Ranjitsinhji—was it as a bowler? He gave way to W. G., saying that, if the Old Man wished it, let him have Fry and Ranji for the first match, but it would be the only one they would play in. On figures, however, the Old Man was immediately justified, because I made top score in the first innings, and Ranji not only made top score in the second, but saved the match. So, as they say, we justified our inclusion. We afterwards together made a surprising number of runs against Yorkshire.

This was the first year of a Selection Committee proper as now known. Hitherto there had been only three Test Matches, not five. The M.C.C. Committee had selected its team for the Lord's match, and similarly the Surrey and Lancashire Committes their England teams for the Oval and Old Trafford. The reason for the change was that it was obviously an inadequate system, especially as with five Test Matches two more county committees would appear, with possible further difference of opinion. Moreover, a salient absurdity had occurred in 1896, when Ranjitsinhji, the phenomenally successful batsman of the year, was included in the teams selected by Lancashire and Surrey, but omitted from the team chosen by the M.C.C. As there was no doubt of Ranjitsinhji's merit, clearly the M.C.C. had decided that an Indian ought not to play for England, while Lancashire and Surrey had decided that he ought. I am quite sure that it was good luck for me that in 1899 there was a single Selection Committee and that W. G. was on it.

All the same, this original type of single Selection Committee had one bad fault: with its co-opted and unofficial members it was too large. We used to meet on Sunday at the Sports Club, either for lunch, in which case we separated barely in time for dinner, or for dinner, in which case we separated barely in time for bed. Any one of us could easily have selected the right England team; or right enough. What happened with such a band of experts was that each came along expecting someone else to have the necessary clear-cut ideas. The discussions were interminable. And what were they about? The difficulty was to know which of the available top-notch fast bowlers to include and which of the available top-notch batsmen to leave out. Strictly speaking, the whole problem was whom to leave out. But for the first Test Match in which I played the curious situation was that, whereas England was extremely strong in fast bowling with Lockwood, Tom Richardson, C. J. Kortright, and Mold all eligible, we found that, either from injuries or indisposition, not one of them was available. The end of it was we chose George Hirst, who was a left-hander and not a fast bowler in the same sense as the others.

Now the result of the five Tests that year was that Australia won one and four were drawn; and the distinctive factor in the Australian single victory, as well as in the drawn matches, was the fast bowling of their Ernest Jones. It was an era of fast bowling, when the critical phase for the professed bats-man was to escape an accident early in his innings from the fast bowler. This although all the medium-pace bowling was of a very high standard. Before the first Test Match I said to Ranji that we should have trouble with the Australian bowl-ing; look at the magnificent medium-pace bowlers (lively medium, that is)—Hugh Trumble, Monty Noble, and W. Howell. All of them quite in the first rank by the highest standard. I added that I regarded Noble as about the best of his kind I had played against. "Yes," said Ranji, "but the man we have to fear is that chucker." This reference to Ernest Jones did not mean that Ranji thought that Jones's action was unfair, but that his pace was dangerous. As Ranji was one of the master craftsmen of all time in dealing with very fast bowling even on fiery wickets, his judgment of the situation is interesting. If he did not fear fast bowling for himself, he feared it for others.

On the history of that series of Test Matches he was abundantly right. Jones did the damage; yet all the batsmen who played for England that year were strong players of fast bowling. Here in parenthesis I may remark that with the exception of Larwood the modern generation of batsmen have never seen anything like fast bowling as this term was exemplified in E. Jones, Lockwood, Richardson, C. J. Kortright, Mold, S. M. J. Woods, J. Sharp, and one or two others of that era. Just as the batsmen of those days had no conception of leg-break bowling as it is known now.

Day in, day out, Jones was the fastest of the fast; but not faster than Kortright on his day. In the first Test Match played at Nottingham that year the wicket was of perfect Nottingham marl, just as good as nowadays. I made 50 in the first innings and was batting for about an hour in the second, and I saw plenty of Jones's bowling. I never received a ball from him which appeared to be short, and never one much more than waist high. Yet when I went to look at the wicket at lunch-time on the first day the marks he made with the ball were perfectly distinct, and his usual length was just about half-way down the pitch. I was fond of hooking the short ball, but I did not get a single ball from him which I could hook. The simple fact was that Jones, with his pace, could pitch the ball half-way, and yet that ball was of good length.

It is notable that on this perfect wicket with powerful batting on both sides the scoring was not high. Australia made 252 and 230 for 8 declared, England 193 and 155 for 7. But in our second innings the only score of over 30 was made by Ranji, whose 93 not out was not only a brilliant effort, but also saved our bacon. But for him we should have been beaten. All the main Australian batsmen, especially Joe Darling, Monty Noble, S. E. Gregory, and Clem Hill, batted well; but no one except Hill scored over 50 in either innings. This shows that against batsmen of such high calibre our bowling was good. Our successful bowlers were Wilfred Rhodes and J. T. Hearne in the first innings, and Rhodes and F. S. Jackson in the second.

It happened that my Madame, who came with me to every cricket match I played in, and would never sit in the ladies' pavilion, or indeed anywhere but somewhere where she could see, was over by George Parr's tree at Trent Bridge. Next to her sat Arthur Shrewsbury, and next to him sat Sir Julien

Cahn, then a youth. I asked Arthur what he thought of these
Australians. Now I must tell you that Arthur was an exceptionally sound, sober, and accurate judge of cricket. He had
a surgeon's eye for the anatomy of the game. His answer was,
"Their batting is stronger than in Murdoch's time, but their
bowling is not as good." Arthur's comparative assessment of
the merits of Spofforth, Boyle, Garrett, Palmer, and Giffen, as
against those of Ernest Jones, Trumble, Noble, and Howell, is,
I think, of interest. No cricketer I have ever known was more
likely to be correct in his judgment than Arthur Shrewsbury.
Arthur at that time was still a great batsman, and he would
most certainly have been selected to play in that match but
for the fact that the team could not carry both W. G. and
him, since both of them could field at point and nowhere else.
For that reason alone William Gunn was preferred to Arthur
Shrewsbury. Arthur was, I know, rather hurt. He said to me,
"I think you might have played me on my own ground." So
high had been his position as a batsman in the eyes of me
and the likes of me that I felt half ashamed that Arthur was
there by George Parr's tree instead of in the middle of the
Trent Bridge ground.

Now there is a little story connected with his omission. We
nearly left out William Gunn as well, and, mind you, in those
days it was a big thing to leave out Arthur Shrewsbury and
William Gunn. They figured in the general mind as do
Walter Hammond and Maurice Leyland nowadays—fairly
senior but still dominant. But we all remembered a certain
match at Sheffield Park in 1896. This was the first match
played that year by the Australian team captained by G. H. S.
Trott, and it included the redoubtable Ernest Jones, whose
first appearance it was. In that match W. G. went in first with
Arthur Shrewsbury. I was playing too, and I vouch to you
that it is true that in the first over a ball from Ernest Jones
did go through W. G.'s beard, and that W. G. did rumble out
a falsetto, "What—what—what!" and that Harry Trott did
say, "Steady, Jonah," and that Ernest Jones did say, "Sorry,
doctor, she slipped." Body-line bowling! W. G. topped the
twenties, and his huge chest was black and blue. F. S. Jackson
made a score and had one of his ribs broken. Ranjitsinhji

made 80, and flicked Jonah's fastest rising ball off his nose.
The wicket must have had a sandstone subsoil so viciously
did the ball fly. But about the first over. W. G. played it,
partly, as I say, with his beard. When Arthur Shrewsbury got
to that end, having watched the first two balls, he deliberately
tipped the next into the hands of second slip, and before the
catch was held had folded his bat under his right arm-pit and
marched off. Then the 6 feet 3 inches of William Gunn walked
delicately to the wicket. His first ball from Jones whizzed
past where his head had just been. William withdrew from
the line of the next ball and deliberately tipped it into the
slips, and he too had pouched his bat and was stepping off
to the pavilion before the catch was surely caught.

Later in 1896 I was a master at Charterhouse, so I saw only
one Test Match. I missed Ranji's brilliant start in Test
Matches when he scored 62 and 154 not out. But I supported
him as a spectator in the Oval match. The later stages of this
match were a cataract of wickets. When Ranji and I left the
Oval overnight a few wickets, including Ranji's, had fallen.
The next morning Ranji, who had had a bad night with
asthma, indulged in a leisurely uprising, and we were driving
past the oak palings of the Oval about an hour after the start
of play. Standing up in the hansom cab I saw on the score-
board: Total 14 for 7 wickets down. Heavens! This could not
be England, because England had scored more than that overnight. Again Heavens! When we drew up at the main
entrance gates I helped Ranji out of the cab and lent him my
arm as support. It appeared that he had trodden on an upturned carpet-nail at the hotel on his way to the bath. His
foot was quite bad, and he limped in county cricket for the
next fortnight. This was the match in which Jack Hearne
and Bobby Peel bowled Australia out for 44. Only their last
man, T. R. McKibbin, scored double figures. He was a bad
bat and made 16, otherwise Australia would have been out
for 28.

The upshot of the first Test Match of '99 at Nottingham
was another Sunday with the Selection Committee at the
Sports Club. The hour was the hour of luncheon. I was a
few minutes late. The moment I entered the door W. G. said,

" Here's Charles. Now, Charles, before you sit down, we want you to answer this question, yes or no. Do you think that Archie MacLaren ought to play in the next Test Match?"

Now, Archie MacLaren had in the winter of 1897-8 been the most successful batsman in the team taken to Australia by A. E. Stoddart. He had scored two centuries in Test Matches and had divided a thousand runs with Ranjitsinhji with an average of 54. He had played Jones with great success. He was on top of the Australian bowling as a whole. Our batting had not shown up well at Nottingham. In our summer of 1898, however, he had not played nor in the early matches of 1899. It happened that I had been thinking about Archie MacLaren, so I answered without hesitation, "Yes, I do."

"That settles it," said W. G.; and I sat down at the table. Then, and not till then, did I discover that the question W. G. had asked me meant, "Shall I, W. G. Grace, resign from the England eleven?" This had never occurred to me. I had thought it was merely a question of Archie coming in instead of one of the other batsmen, perhaps myself. I explained this and tried to hedge, but the others had made up their minds that I was to be confronted with a sudden casting-vote. So there it was. I who owed my place in the England team to W. G.'s belief in me as a batsman gave the casting-vote that ended W. G.'s career of cricket for England. Consider that W. G. was a greater name in cricket in those days than Don Bradman is now. Consider, too, that he was still one of the best change-bowlers in England—about as good then as C. V. Grimmett is now—and consider, too, his tremendous personality.

Fortunately for my peace of mind I found out afterwards that W. G. himself felt that he ought to retire, not because he could not bat or bowl to the value of his place, but because he could not move about in the field or run his runs. At Nottingham he had missed a catch at point which he could have taken with ease if he could have bent. This gave Clem Hill a crucial second chance. I was in with W. G. while we put on 75 runs for the first wicket. Had I been in with Joe Vine of Sussex the score would have been over 100. We lost innumerable singles on the off-side, and I never dared to call W. G. for a second run to the long-field. When we were walking out from the pavilion as first pair for England in my first Test the Old Man said to me, "Now Charlie, remember that I'm not a sprinter like you." There is no doubt that it was best for W. G. to retire. But I still think that some other instrument of his fate might have been chosen.

Another point missed at this fateful meeting of the Selection Committee was that, in discussing before I arrived whether Archie MacLaren, in spite of his recent absence from first-class cricket, should come in instead of W. G., it was quite forgotten that by order of seniority and on the score of at least equal merit, F. S. Jackson ought to have had the reversion of the captaincy, even if Archie MacLaren was brought in to raise the batting strength. It was true that Archie possessed a full knowledge of the Australian personnel owing to his recent experience in Australia, but I do not believe that any of those present at the Selection Committee realised that in bringing him in in place of W. G. they were going over the head of F. S. Jackson. I did not. In a case like this where one distinguished cricketer is passed over for the captaincy of England in favour of another, any feeling of dissatisfaction there may be is not a personal matter between the two men. The whole point is that when the senior is passed over in favour of the junior, the process may seem externally like a vote of want of confidence in the former.

Archie MacLaren, it must be remembered, although he ranked at the top of the tree as a batsman, did not play as much county cricket as other leading batsmen of his time. The body of his success was achieved in Australia; the Australians regarded him as the finest English batsman who had ever till then visited Australia. Stanley Jackson, too, though recognised as a batsman of outstanding class, as well as the best all-rounder in English cricket since the prime of W. G., did not play very regularly for Yorkshire and never went to Australia. His success was registered in Test Matches in England. It was accidental that up till 1899 Archie MacLaren had figured in the public mind as an established captain, whereas Stanley Jackson, playing under Lord Hawke in the Yorkshire eleven, had not.

C. B. Fry says . . .

A Mother's Son

Repton, arranged for Mr. Chips

"F.E." and "John"

A Record Long Jump

A Good 'Un on Exmoor

"Madame"

The Future Royal Navy

"Jacker"

The Conquering Don

A Committee of the Nations

"Ranji", H.H. the Jam Sahib

*Some Male Stars – C. B. Fry and Gubby Allen with
Herbert Marshall, Nigel Bruce and Melvyn Douglas*

The second match, played at Lord's, was a triumph for Australia, due to great batting by Clem Hill and Victor Trumper and great bowling by Ernest Jones. This was the match in which Victor Trumper made his name. On our side Jackson, MacLaren, Tom Hayward, and Jessop made runs, but the rest of us did poorly. Just before the match Ernest Jones came to our changing room and borrowed a flannel shirt from me. I had invented a shirt which gave freedom to the arms and did not pull out at the waist. Also, by the way, I invented and wore for one season amid derision, the universal modern trouser made with pleats and a self-contained belt. Jones said he always tore his canvas shirt under the arm-pit. So I lent him a shirt, and I never saw it again. And no wonder; it served him well. In the first innings he had me caught in the slips in the crook of Hugh Trumble's elbow off a fast high-riser which I tried to avoid but which chased my glove. In the second innings a very fast ball hit the flap of my pad, tore it, made a nest for itself, fell out on my foot and cannoned into the wicket. That was not enough. Afterwards at Manchester in the fourth match Jones, as the papers say, "caused me to play on," but it was a very curious play-on. In the second innings of that match I was caught in the country off Hugh Trumble by Frank Iredale from the best straight drive I ever made in my life. Iredale, going full speed, collected the ball on two fingers of one hand, falling over. Jones said, "That's the shirt, Charlie."

This match at Manchester was a draw in favour of England. So also had been the previous match at Leeds. At Leeds none of the leading Australian bats did much except Jack Worrall, who played a fine hitting innings of 76 on a slow wicket. In their second innings they were saved by the batting of Hugh Trumble and Frank Laver. Hugh Trumble was such a name as a bowler that people never properly realised that he was a valuable batsman who often made runs in Test Matches, especially when they were badly wanted. On our side Tom Hayward, Lilley, and myself made most of the runs. But the feature of the match was the gorgeous hat-trick achieved by J. T. Hearne, who beat Monty Noble, S. E. Gregory and Clem Hill with successive balls. The best hat-trick in history. Noble was finely caught by Ranji in the slips off Jack Hearne's faster ball. Gregory was out in exactly the same way, caught by MacLaren. Clem Hill was bowled by what to him was a vicious leg-break. The wicket was not difficult. It was dead and rather slow, but Jack Hearne screwed life out of it with his elastic action and strongly cut spin. Two victims of the hat-trick, Noble and Gregory, being two of the best batsmen who have ever played for Australia, were further distinguished as each of them was out for nought in the first innings, and therefore they collected a pair apiece.

An interesting newcomer to the English side in this match was H. Young, the Essex left-hand fast medium bowler. Young was one of Archie MacLaren's " spots." He had been an Able Seaman in the Navy and had only played one season in first-class cricket. MacLaren picked him out on inspection as likely to get out the two dangerous left-hand batsmen, Clem Hill and Joe Darling. This Young did, one in each innings, and in the match he took 6 wickets for under 100 runs. He was selected again in the fourth match at Manchester and again got 6 wickets in a fairly high-scoring match for 160 runs; but he never played for England again.

For this match at Leeds we, the numerous band of selectors, picked Johnny Briggs instead of Wilfred Rhodes as our slow left-hand bowler. This choice won no approval in Yorkshire. As it turned out, Yorkshire was right. The excitement of the match was too much for Johnny Briggs, who fell out of the ranks after the first innings and never played again—a sad ending to a brilliant career in cricket. Had we played Rhodes I think we should have won that match.

In retrospect I cannot quite follow the mind of the numerous Selection Committee, including myself, in the matter of our bowling. It is true we were bothered by not being able to avail ourselves of the very strong fast bowling we should have been able to call on. In the first match we played George Hirst as our fast bowler; in the second we dropped him and played Gilbert Jessop; in the third we played no genuine fast bowler, though both Jack Hearne and Young were of fairly lively pace; in the fourth we played W. M. Bradley, of Kent, who was distinctly fast but not nearly as fast as Lockwood,

Richardson, C. J. Kortright, or Mold. Then in the fifth match
at last Lockwood was available, but we played W. M. Bradley
as well, and left out both Young and Jack Hearne. In this final
match it was shown what a difference Lockwood would have
made, as on a perfect Oval wicket in the first innings he took
7 wickets for 71 runs. Even in those days, with abundant
talent available, there was the ever-recurrent difficulty of
organising a team with a fixed set of bowlers. If we could
have played Lockwood, Jack Hearne, Rhodes, and Young or
George Hirst throughout, with F. S. Jackson, an excellent
bowler, as an all-rounder, our bowling would have looked as
good as that of the Australians.

Nevertheless, England showed up well in the fourth Test
Match at Manchester and in the fifth at Kennington Oval.
At Manchester we got a big lead on the first innings, chiefly
due to a great innings by Tom Hayward of 130. Hayward
played beautifully against some superfine bowling by Jones,
Noble, and Trumble. Ever afterwards on the morning of a
Test Match I was glad to see Tom Hayward's ruddy-brown
countenance and sergeant-major's moustache. The Australians
made a good recovery in their second innings, thanks to fine
performances by Noble and Trumper. But on the whole
England looked the better side. Ranji bowled for England in
this match and got a wicket; this is interesting because a
bowler who is put on for England and gets a wicket cannot be
bad. Actually Ranji was quite a good bowler, medium-pace,
right hand, with lots of tricks.

At the Oval we won the toss and saw one of the finest first-
wicket partnerships in the history of Test Matches, by F. S.
Jackson and Tom Hayward, both of whom made centuries.
After that we all made runs except Bradley, and some more
hundreds would have been made had we not tried to force
the pace. As it was, the total was 576. Nothing nowadays, but
quite a good total then. In spite of Lockwood's magnificent
bowling, we could not get the Australians out twice. For
them S. E. Gregory made a century in perfect style, and I
account him quite one of the greatest batsmen produced by
Australia. Joe Darling, Monty Noble, and Jack Worrall also
made runs; but the man who spiked our guns just at the

finish was C. E. McLeod, an accomplished strokeless player who, according to Ranji, had the widest edge to his bat of any class batsman. Ranji used to advise me if ever I went to Australia to play like Charlie McLeod.

This season of 1899, so interesting to me as my first in Test Matches, happened to be a landmark in both England and Australian cricket. The men who played on both sides formed the body of a great era of cricket. Almost every man on both sides contributed something to the history of the game. As the matches went no one could show that one side was appreciably stronger than the other; but English cricket in those days was very powerful, and I think that had circumstances permitted effective organisation we should have beaten the Australians.

It was, as I have said, the last year of W. G. in Test Matches.

W. G. always reminds me of Henry VIII. Henry VIII solidified into a legend when he had already involved himself in several matrimonial tangles and had become overweighted with flesh and religious controversies. Yet Henry in his physical prime had been, even allowing for the adulation of courtiers, the premier athlete of England, a notable wrestler, an accomplished horseman, and a frequent champion in the military tournaments of his time. So it is with W. G. He figures in the general mind in the heavy habit of his latter years on the cricket fields, a bearded giant heavy of gait and limb, and wonderful by reason of having outlived his contemporaries as a giant of cricket. Even when disputes in clubs and pavilions canvass the relative merits of W. G., Ranji, and Don Bradman, the picture in the minds of the disputants is of a big, heavy Englishman, a slim, lithe Oriental, and a nimble lightweight Australian. Even those of us who wag our heads and utter the conventional and oracular statement, "Ah, W. G.! There will never be his like again," do not properly realise who it is who will never be like whom. Incredible as it may appear, I myself never saw W. G. till I played against him for Sussex at Bristol at the age of 22 and the great man himself was 46. So my own memory of him begins only five years before he retired from Test Match cricket, and he was already corpulent and comparatively in-

active, though he was yet to enjoy one of his most successful
seasons as a batsman and score 1,000 runs in May. But I came
into first-class cricket soon enough to meet many of the leading cricketers who had played with W. G. in his early prime,
and who talked first-hand of the W. G. we ought to have in
mind when we institute comparisons between him and Don
Bradman.

The only photograph I have ever seen of W. G. as a young
man is an illustration in a book by Alfred Lubbock of a
cricket team which made a tour in Canada. This was the tour
when W. G. made his famous speech—seventeen times—in
the form : " Mr. Chairman and gentlemen, we have much
enjoyed your . . . and I hope we shall enjoy similar . . .
treatment wherever we go. Thank you." He filled up the
blank with an appropriate term, such as " hospitality," " bowling," or "pretty girls." W. G. also made a lot of runs. He
appears in that group a slim and graceful young man, wearing
indeed a beard, but the not unbecoming beard of the better-
known Greek statues of Hercules. It is curious that most of
us think of Hercules as a colossal figure with huge bulging
muscles, but if you look at a statue of the Greek god of
strength, and subtract his beard with a barber's eye, you will
find that the residue might be mistaken for an Achilles or
even an Apollo.

I am quite sure that W. G.'s beard has done definite injustice to his memory. It is difficult to imagine a first-rate
large-scale natural athlete with a big beard. But W. G. for
more years than fall to the lot of most of us was just as much
a magnificent large-scale natural athlete as Don Bradman
is in a far lighter vein. W. G. was a fine runner and hurdler;
he made good times and won numerous races at the
quarter-mile and also over the sticks. He was a quick mover
and had quite exceptional stamina. In Alfred Lubbock's
book—you will remember that Alfred Lubbock was an
Etonian batsman good enough to play for England—it is
casually mentioned that in Canada W. G. was particularly
singled out by the admiring colonials, French and English,
for his excellence as a dancer. None of the English cricketers
could waltz like W. G. If you do not happen to have come

across Alfred Lubbock's book, I wager that this little piece of information surprises you.

There is another illusion quite common about W. G. People have talked so much about him that they have manufactured a species of second-hand familiarity with him. I would even say that, whereas such familiarity has unproverbially produced admiration, it has nevertheless induced the error that W. G. was—how shall I put it?—a great big sort of bar-parlour hearty whom anyone could smack on the back and address as Gilbert. I would have you know that W. G. was hearty, but he was not that sort of hearty, and I do not know that I have ever met a man, except perhaps Lord Nelson in his pictures, with whom it would have been more dangerous to take a liberty. The idea that W. G. was a prodigiously grown-up schoolboy at heart who might be inclined to elephantine foolery is about as true as that Lord Nelson's column in Trafalgar Square is made of putty. Except for his real friends W. G. had a formidable eye and a beetling brow; he had the merry heart of the full-blooded English yeoman type, but he knew who he was and who you were, and he possessed, when it came to it, an Olympian dignity.

One saw him at his best against fast bowling. In the days of Richardson, Mold, Lockwood, and Kortright, I once asked him who was the fastest bowler he had played. He answered without hesitation, "George Freeman." If W. G. in his youth treated George Freeman as I saw him in middle age treat Tom Richardson, all I can say is that George Freeman went home a wiser if not a better bowler. There were no fireworks or extravagances. W. G. just stood at his crease to his full height (and everyone who wishes to play fast bowling well should so stand) and proceeded to lean against the ball in various directions and send it scudding along the turf between the fielders. No visible effort, no hurry; just a rough-hewn precision. He was not a graceful bat and he was not ungraceful; just powerfully efficient.

For a very big man specially addicted to driving he was curiously adept at cutting fast bowlers very late. He did not cut with a flick like Ranji or a swish like Trumper. Before the stroke he seemed to be about to play the ball with his ordinary back stroke, but at the last moment he pressed down quickly with his wrists, with an almost vertical swing, and away sped the ball past all catching just clear of second or third slip. I remember seeing him make about 80 at the Oval against Richardson and Lockwood at their best; he scored at least half his runs with this late cut peculiar to himself, and eventually he was caught in the slips off it. When he came up to the dressing-room, hugely hot and happy, he sat down and addressed us: "Oughtn't to have done it. . . . Dangerous stroke. . . . But shan't give it up. . . . Get too many runs with it." He then changed his shirt and his thick undervest and went away to have a chat with Charlie Alcock, the Surrey secretary, who was a crony of his.

In his later years, when he was handicapped by his weight, he went in for one unorthodox stroke. W. G. never played the glance to leg or the modern diversional strokes in that direction. The ball just outside the leg stump, if he could reach it, he hit with a plain variant of his great on-drive, and the ball went square with the wicket a little in front of the umpire. If the ball pitched on his legs, he played the old-fashioned leg hit with an almost horizontal sweeping swing—but, ye moderns, with his weight fully on his front foot. This was the stroke with which in his later years he hit the ball from outside his off stump round to square leg. The young Gloucestershire bloods used to call this the "Old Man's cow shot." What actually W. G. did was to throw his left leg across the wicket to the off ball and treat it as if it were a ball to leg bowled to him from the direction of mid-off or extra cover. I fancy he introduced this stroke to himself in his great year of revival in the latter part of some of his big innings. The original exponent was the noted Surrey batsman, W. W. Read, who used it with much effect on fast wickets against accurate slow bowlers such as Peate, Peel, and Briggs. In fact, the stroke is the genuine leg-hit. Ranji told me that Walter Read had shown him how to do it at the nets and that it was an easy stroke, but I never saw Ranji try it in a match; he had plenty of strokes without it.

Thinking back on what I have written, I am wondering whether I have succeeded in conveying the individuality of

W. G.'s batsmanship, his tremendous physique, his indomitable precision, and the masterful power of his strokes. At any rate, there they were, these characters, and no one who ever saw W. G. play will admit the near equality of any other batsman, even though he thought, as I do, that in pure technique Ranji was a better.

It was a great disappointment to W. G. that his eldest son, W. G. junior, as he was called, did not inherit any eminent skill in the game. W. G. junior wore glasses and was a very fair batsman and bowler who got his blue at Cambridge. His other son was in the Royal Navy and retired as an Admiral. He had a beautiful and delightful daughter, who, he declared, ought to have been born a boy, because she would have been the best athlete in his family. This daughter died about the time when W. G. left Gloucestershire and went to the Crystal Palace as manager of the London County C.C. The loss was a great blow to him. Lord Riddell, who was very fond of W. G., told me that never afterwards would W. G. stay even a night away from home, because the loss of this daughter had so affected his wife, to whom he was completely devoted.

Above all else, W. G. was a very kind man.

CHAPTER XI

THE GOLDEN ERA

1899 marked an era for the Australians, too. In Joe Darling they had a resolute and sagacious captain, one of the best. Were I to be asked for the Australian equivalent of W. G. Grace for combined personality and power as a batsman I should nominate Joe. Like W. G., he was a countryman. He came from the wide farm-lands of Australia and was the sort of batsman who could turn up in a State match and make a century after one knock at the nets. He was of medium size and sparely built, but very strong. He had a heavy brown moustache which made him look thirty when he was twenty-one, and a pair of the far-seeing blue eyes found in sailors and men of the plains. I rank him as one of the three or four great left-hand batsmen. There was a touch of ruggedness about his style, but a notable competency; he could sit down and defend like a rock, or he could lash out with terrific power. There has never been a better man at a pinch. Against our teams in Australia he was a great match winner.

Possibly on technical grounds Clem Hill, his left-hand colleague, was a more accomplished batsman, but there was not much in it. Actually most critics would select Clem Hill as the best left-hand batsman there has ever been. He had a slightly crouching stance, but he could hit hard. He scored most of his runs by late and square-cutting and by forcing the ball away on the leg side, but he also played the left-hander's peculiar off-drive past cover point. In every way a batsman and a character. He was nicknamed Kruger from a fancied likeness to Oom Paul—Oom Paul, of course, when a boy. Clem had a long, solemn, irregular face, but a busy, merry, alert mind.

Besides these two there were six high-class right-hand batsmen in the Australian side of 1899. The best of these was the triumphant Victor Trumper, then quite young. But both S. E. Gregory and M. A. Noble were little behind him.

Victor Trumper used to walk to the wicket and start making beautiful strokes from his first ball onwards. No matter how good the bowling, he made it look easy, and he never permitted any wicket to appear difficult. Trumper was tall and shapely with slightly sloping shoulders and a rather long body. He had a natural grace of movement and played his strokes with a swing from the wrists which was not a flick but rather, as it were, a stroking effect. Of all the batsmen I have seen except Ranjitsinhji, he most made the bowling look easy. He was not as sound a bat as Ranjitsinhji nor as quick with his blade, but whereas Ranji at his best was sleekly venomous, Trumper gave one the impression of generous abandon. The relative merits of the greater batsmen can never be settled. Many of the cognoscenti on the double basis of style and efficiency put Trumper first. I suppose the argument would be between W. G., Trumper, Ranjitsinhji, and Don Bradman. My summary would be that W. G. had more power than the other three put together, and one stroke for every ball the bowler could bowl. Victor Trumper had the greatest charm and two strokes for every ball. Ranjitsinhji had the greatest finesse and three strokes for every ball; Don Bradman has made the highest number of runs and has strokes of his own which the other three had not; he may be briefly scheduled as a phenomenon. He alone rivals Ranjitsinhji in originality. All the other three were better bats than Trumper when all were out of form. This omits the very near excellence of batsmen such as Walter Hammond, Charlie Macartney, F. S. Jackson, A. C. MacLaren, and a few others.

If Trumper was a stylist for charm, S. E. Gregory was a stylist for correct technique. This very great Australian batsman, a little man with beady black eyes and as neat as a domino, had no superior in technique as a cutter and off-driver. No man who has ever played cricket could have more usefully been offered to a young cricketer as an example for the standard strokes. He was rather fond of running himself out.

Then comes Montagu Alfred Noble, whose category really

is an all-rounder, and as such at least the equal of George Giffen. He was quite one of the soundest batsmen Australia has yet produced. He did not like leg-break bowling, but otherwise his wicket was very hard to get. He had all the strokes, but was specially good at the cut and the off-drive.

Another batsman of a different sort was Jack Worrall, who was one of the best pure hitters I have ever seen on a dead wicket.

In F. A. Iredale this Australian team had another stylish batsman of the Lionel Palairet type. He did not do himself justice in England, but when he made a century he made it in the grand public school manner.

There were two more good bats on the side, both bowlers. Hugh Trumble was good enough to go in first if necessary. F. Laver, another six-footer, was a peculiar bat, who made cricket look a difficult game and was recognised in Australia as a dangerous customer.

So, all in, this Australian team must be regarded as one of the strongest of their batting sides. Its bowling might appear to be short of variety. They had no left-hand bowler and no slow bowler. What they had was the best genuinely fast bowler Australia has ever had backed up by three medium-paced bowlers, each of them different from the others, and all of them of the best brand.

W. P. Howell was the fastest of the medium-pace men. He was a bee-farmer and made the ball buzz. He was loose-limbed and genial and had a rotary action and unique finger-power with which he gave the ball a kind of half-cut, half-twist, the effect of which was a smart break from the off on a perfect fast wicket. He got more work on the ball on a plumb fast wicket than any bowler I met until R. O. Schwarz turned up for South Africa with his standard googly.

Monty Noble ranks as a great bowler. He varied his pace from almost fast to slow-medium, with artful disguise of the change. He could make the ball swerve and he could make his slower ball duck, an artifice he learned from pitching at baseball. I played against George Lohmann, W. Attewell, and Sidney Barnes along with other medium-pace bowlers of the lively type, but personally I consider that in his day Noble was the most troublesome on a good, fast wicket.

Hugh Trumble also ranks as one of the great bowlers of all time. His height and high action made the flight of the ball towards you steep downwards, so that you could not easily judge its length. He had complete control, was very accurate, and he was an artist at slight changes of pace and direction. He was not apparently difficult to play, but he had a subtle knack of getting one out off one's best stroke; indeed, he purposely bowled for this effect.

One feature of this team of bowlers was that Jones was uncomfortably fast, so that when one got to the other end one felt inclined to let loose the painter against the driveable medium-pace bowler. Hence Jones often deserved wickets which were credited to someone else.

The point often mentioned about the solidarity of the Australian team and the fluidity of our own team was a characteristic of this period of English cricket. We had more batsmen and bowlers than we knew what to do with. If a Test Match went wrong there was a constant tendency to try someone new; but this, on logic, was unlikely to improve the team; there was appearance of fairness in giving the other fellow a chance, but it unsettled the combination. For instance, in 1899, whereas the Australians could rely on four bowlers, no fewer than nineteen bowlers went on for England, of whom fifteen would be accounted regular bowlers in their county sides. Looking backwards one can see that we ought to have stuck to J. T. Hearne, Wilfred Rhodes, either Young or Hirst, Lockwood or Kortright, if fit, otherwise W. M. Bradley, with Jackson as the fifth bowler.

Then as to the batting. We had a powerful nucleus in Maclaren, Jackson, Hayward, Ranjitsinhji, and J. T. Tyldesley; and, if you like, myself. Both Lilley and Storer, the wicketkeepers, were strong batsmen. Yet we actually played fifteen professed batsmen in the series. One of the poignant subjects of discussion at our ponderous Selection Committees (Lord Hawke in the chair, divided in his mind between Yorkshire and England and with numerous newspaper cuttings in his pocket) was whether or not to play Gilbert Jessop. Here was perhaps the greatest outright hitter of all time, who was also the finest cover-point or extra cover of his day and a good enough fast bowler to be chosen once that year purely in that capacity. MacLaren always wanted Jessop on the score that his hitting might turn a game topsy-turvy in under an hour, and that even if he made no runs he was worth his place on the chance that he might throw out a couple of the Australian batsmen in each innings. This was a definite tactical point in Archie MacLaren's mind; a psychological point; he maintained that Clem Hill, Trumper and S. E. Gregory had declared to run singles to Jessop at extra-cover. Stanley Jackson had an equally high opinion of Jessop as a hitter, but always thought that his inclusion was intrinsically a gamble. In retrospect it looks absurd ever to have left Gilbert Jessop out of an England eleven, but not so absurd when one reviews the names of the other batsmen. The Australians used to say why play Jessop when you have got Palairet? They always declared that they were not afraid of Jessop and knew how to get him out, but they used to dot the country with a considerable number of fieldsmen when he went to the wicket, and did not quite know where to place them.

When it came to choosing the batsmen, Archie MacLaren used to shake his head and maintain that the number likely to show up well against the Australian bowling was limited. On paper, he said, we could find two teams of batsmen, but when it came to the pinch he believed in only four or five. Actually, there were seven batsmen available who over the years proved capable of making history in Test Matches against Australia, and that does not include Jessop, William Gunn, myself, or even W. G. Moreover, A. A. Lilley, the wicket-keeper, you will find on his record to have been a distinctly successful bat in Test Matches. There is no doubt whatever that with the exception of Walter Hammond, no present-day England batsman can be ranked on a level with Ranjitsinhji, F. S. Jackson, A. C. MacLaren, Tom Hayward, or J. T. Tyldesley.

Ranjitsinhji once said to me that nobody is so soon forgotten as a successful cricketer. No one who saw him performing at the wicket in those days is likely to forget him. He had the same kind of reputation for being a marvel as Don Bradman has now. Nothing is less possible than to appraise outstanding batsmen of different periods; they play under different conditions and up to different standards. Both these super-eminent players in making a hundred runs seemed to me to devastate the bowling more thoroughly than any other batsman I have seen. But whereas Ranjitsinhji sliced it to pieces with a razor-edged scimitar, Don Bradman whips it to shreds with a cane. Don Bradman's enormous scores far surpass Ranjitsinhji's figures, but Ranjitsinhji played under the necessities of three-day cricket and against bowling which, whether or not it was more likely to get you out, was beyond all question much more difficult to treat contemptuously by way of strokes. I have seen Don Bradman tear the bowling to pieces in astonishing fashion, but I have never seen him make a century on a fiery wicket against good-length bowling that kicked as well as broke. And I have never seen him make 260 not out on a difficult mud wicket when no other batsman on the side that day scored double figures.

At his best Ranjitsinhji was a miraculous batsman. He had no technical faults whatever; the substratum of his play was absolutely sound. What gave him his distinctiveness was a combination of the perfect poise and the suppleness and the quickness peculiar to the athletic Hindu. It is characteristic of all great batsmen that they play their strokes at the last instant; but I have never seen a batsman able to reserve his stroke so late as Ranji nor apply his bat to the ball with such electric quickness. He scored his runs on dry wickets very fast. I have often been in with him while he scored eighty to my twenty. It was impossible to bowl him a ball outside the off stump which he could not cut, and he could vary the direction of the stroke from square to fine. It was almost impossible for the best of bowlers on a fast pitch to bowl him a ball on the wicket which he could not force for runs somewhere between square leg and fine leg. These strokes were outside the repertoire of any other batsman I have ever seen. It was not only that he made strokes which looked like conjuring tricks; he made them with an appearance of complete facility. So distinctive was Ranjitsinhji's cutting and wrist play on the leg side that one almost forgot to notice his strokes in front of the wicket; but not only was he a beautiful driver on both sides of the wicket in the classical sense, he could drive if he liked hard and high just like a professed hitter. Old Bob Thomas, the first-class umpire who probably saw most cricket from 1870 to 1900, and who was reckoned a fine judge of the game, told me that " the Prince was a greater batsman than the Doctor because he had more strokes."

When it comes to the two amateurs, A. C. MacLaren and the Hon. F. S. Jackson, one meets excellencies. MacLaren's cricket in England was much broken up by other calls and pursuits, and Jackson was concerned with the large business founded by his father, Lord Allerton, in Leeds, and with other interests, including politics. That was why neither of them figured in ordinary English cricket as compilers of huge aggregates and averages. Both of them came most to the front in big cricket. Both of them as batsmen alone would be candidates for places in the best eleven of all time. Besides that, MacLaren was one of the finest of slip fielders, and Jackson was a premier fastish right-hand bowler. There have been few bowlers as likely as was Stanley Jackson to come on as a change and get out a high-class batsman well set on a plumb wicket. This he did repeatedly in Test Matches.

Archie MacLaren, in spite of Jack Hobbs and Walter Hammond, is still regarded by many of the cognoscenti in Australia as the finest batsman England ever sent there. That is a big saying. He played in the Grand Manner. He lifted his bat for his stroke right round his neck like a golfer at the top of his full swing. He stood bolt upright and swept into every stroke, even a defensive back-stroke, with deliberate and dominating completeness. He never hedged on his stroke; he never pulled his punches. Like all the great batsmen, he always attacked the bowling. He had all the strokes on the card, but perhaps his distinguishing feature was a sublimated use of the orthodox thrusting forward stroke; this stroke he made as a well-coached Harrovian should, but he converted the usual tentativeness of the public-school stroke into a full-fledged swinging lunge. If he was bowled, he was very clean bowled. If he was caught, it was not off a foozle. He was an aquiline type of player who seemed to swoop down on the ball from a mountain height. We one and all immensely admired his play.

Stanley Jackson was another Harrovian who captained Harrow when Archie MacLaren was a squeaky-voiced kid just on the edge of the school eleven. He began his unrivalled success in English Test cricket while still at Cambridge. He made 91 in his first Test March innings as an undergraduate in 1893, and followed it up in his second match with a century. He had an average in Test Matches that year of 66, being second to Arthur Shrewsbury, who averaged 71 in that series. Pretty good for a University batsman! Ever afterwards till he retired he was a certainty for the England side. In his last year against Australia in England in 1905 when he was captain he won the toss in every Test Match, his England team won the rubber by two wins to·three draws, he headed the Test Match batting averages with an average of 70 and a total of 492, and he headed the Test Match bowling averages with 13 wickets for 15 runs apiece. This 1905 season, by the way, gave me my happiest Test Match year. I delighted in Stanley Jackson as a captain; I was second to him with an average of 58. Jackson was exceptionally good-looking in the Anglo-Saxon Guards-officer way; blue eyes and a neat golden-brown moustache. He was always turned out, flannels, pads, and boots, to perfection. He used a lighter bat than most of us, and he used it also to perfection. His style was compact of neatness and strength and his technique in cutting, driving, and back play was a model of easy correctitude. In addition to the ordinary repertoire of orthodox strokes which he relieved of their orthodoxy by forcible facility, he was one of the few even of top-notch batsmen who could play the high drive equally well to the off and to the on. In this respect I think he was the next batsman to W. G. in his prime. Another interesting character of his batting was that it was as good on wet wickets as on hard. He played exactly the same game on mud as he played on marble. Indeed, he is the only great batsman I have known who did not alter his method in accordance with the state of the pitch.

These three protagonists are worth my while to talk about because they were the three great amateurs of my period of big cricket.

The two great professional batsmen of my period, which may be roughly described professionally as after Arthur Shrewsbury and before Jack Hobbs, were Tom Hayward of Surrey and John Tyldesley of Lancashire. Both of them proved their outstanding merit in Test Match cricket and no other professional batsmen of the time was a rival of either. In so far as John Tyldesley coincided with the early Jack Hobbs, I do not hesitate to rank him as a rival, in style and execution, of the Surrey champion. But the best part of Jack Hobbs was rather after my time, and although he was in the England team I captained in 1912 I did not see the period of his big success in Australia or in record-breaking. Again, it is difficult to compare two such batsmen, the more so as Tyldesley spent half his time in the rainy area of Old Trafford, whereas Jack Hobbs enjoyed the smiling southern Oval. Archie MacLaren used to maintain that Tyldesley was as good a bat as Trumper, or at any rate that he had seen Tyldesley play innings which Trumper could not have bettered. I would say at least, and for certain, that Tyldesley was nearer to Jack Hobbs in merit than is usually supposed. I doubt whether there has ever been in the whole history of cricket a better batsman on a sticky, rain-spoiled wicket. On fast wickets he was a thoroughly vivacious and amusing player and enterprising to a degree. He was of medium height and stood up to play on the tips of his toes. He was a beautiful cutter and off-driver, but his speciality was driving in front of the wicket by hitting not at the pitch of the ball but at the ball on the rise. This stroke enabled him to deal unmercifully with the best kind of bowling of perfect length. His back play was as sure as that of Arthur Shrewsbury. On the worst of wickets he never looked to be in difficulties.

Tom Hayward was a different type of batsman but a grand one. He was more phlegmatic, but peculiarly certain and sound in all his strokes. He did not astonish one by brilliance, but once he got going on a fast wicket one was astonished if he got out. On a wet wicket he changed his game and went in for hitting, which he did well. But his speciality was to walk in first against the best bowling on a fast wicket and make that bowling look plainly playable. His best strokes were in front of the wicket; he could drive in all directions along the ground with a nice but slightly studied certainty of timing. Tom Hayward was a tallish fellow with a drooping light brown moustache and a long healthy face. He had a habit of keeping his mouth open when he was particularly on the job, which gave him an inconsequent sort of air; but he was not at all inconsequent. A thoroughly reliable and imperturbable hero.

These five batsmen stand out in my experience because, although they were superficially quite different in style, every one of them in addition to any particular brilliance was fundamentally sound in method. Not one of them had the trace of a basic fault. That is where the great batsmen of that period differed from all but the rarest of the leading batsmen of to-day. Those batsmen were strong against every type of bowling. How they would have shaped at first had they been confronted with the modern leg-break and googly bowling I do not know —except that Ranji would have clouted it to smithereens: for one thing because he would not have allowed some of it to pitch at all. But be sure they would soon have learned to deal with it as well as the best of the moderns.

Another batsman who played for England in 1899, this first year of the post-W. G. period, was the left-hand amateur C. L. Townsend of Gloucestershire, who made stacks of runs in county cricket, but did not do justice to himself in Test Matches. He was very tall and thin, and when afterwards he went to the North of England and appeared for a League team a spectator remarked, "Yon lad hasn't enough fat on him to grease a gimlet."

Then there was the ever-disputable Gilbert Jessop, also of Gloucestershire. He comes in the category of phenomena. No one has ever batted in the least like Jessop. He held his bat with one hand at the top and one at the bottom of the handle. He crouched over his stance like a cat about to pounce; then he launched himself yards down the pitch with quick short steps and literally flung his bat at the ball, with the result that it went vastly hard and high somewhere between extra cover and long leg. Or else after a preliminary

chassée he chivied back to his crease and threw his bat at
the ball in a rasping square cut. His hitting was prodigious,
but he was not a slogger. He watched the ball as carefully as
did Arthur Shrewsbury. His tactics were first of all to run the
bowler down to induce him to bowl short, and then to apply
his square-cut. He was double-jointed all over, and though
his drives looked like long far-flung sweeps at the ball, he
really got his power from a highly developed wring of the wrists
at the moment of impact. He won at least one Test Match in
England off his own bat and did well in others, but he was
always being left out of the team in favour of orthodoxy.

This year of 1899 being the key-year of a period, one ought
to consider the bowlers. First of all there was Lockwood of
Surrey, who played in only one match, but who was without
qualification the best fast bowler I ever played with or against.
His performances on paper do not look as good as those of his
club-mate Tom Richardson, or even of Arthur Mold of
Lancashire, but in reality he was superior. In sheer pace
Richardson and also C. J. Kortright of Essex were faster.
What distinguished Lockwood was the peculiarity of his flight.
He varied his pace deceptively without effort and got many of
his wickets with what we called Lockwood's slow ball—a ball
which W. G. characterised as "not so very slow either." He
also had a natural inward swerve from the off; many batsmen
who thought they had been bowled out by his off-break, which
even on a good wicket was considerable, were really beaten by
the in-swing of the ball in the air. Nor did he require a new
ball for this. But in those days we did not talk about in-swing.
Another peculiarity of his bowling was that he had not the
usual fast bowler's line of flight: straight line from hand to
pitch and straight line from the pitch upwards. He had a
curved flight in the vertical plane of the kind common to
medium and slow bowlers. All the leading batsmen who
played against Lockwood and Richardson and the other great
fast bowlers of the time were agreed that Lockwood was the
most difficult. Ranji once said, and I concur, that one could
be 120 not out on a plumb wicket and then be clean bowled
by Lockwood and walk away to the pavilion not knowing
what one would have done if one had another chance at the

ball. Like Larwood, Lockwood got his pace not from mere physique and strength, but from perfection of poise and swing both of arm and body in delivering the ball. Lockwood took a rather long springy run; he seemed to bounce off the fore-part of his feet. His run flowed rhythmically into a high-over swing of the arm from an easy shoulder. As he delivered the ball with the facile grace of the expert discus-thrower, the right side of his body swung round in one piece. Except Larwood and Macdonald of Australia, no other fast bowler has made so graceful a performance of fast bowling. He was of medium height and compactly built but not big. He had a natural knack of balance and of easy controlled movement. Do not forget that Lockwood was also a first-class bat who made his forties and fifties in Test Matches, and his centuries for Surrey.

Tom Richardson had by 1899 begun to go off. In 1896 Tom had bowled magnificently in the Test Matches. He was a much bigger man than Lockwood. He was dark and black-haired—a cheerful brown-faced Italian-looking brigand with an ivory smile. Most genial, and an inexhaustible worker. He depended for his success upon sheer pace, perpetual ac-curacy, and an abrupt natural off-break.

Besides F. S. Jackson, there were two standard medium-pace bowlers of exceptional quality, J. T. Hearne of Middlesex and Walter Mead of Essex. Personally, I found Mead more troublesome than Jack Hearne, as he had a genuine occasional leg-break of a pace just as fast as his off-break. But Jack Hearne was the outstanding length bowler of the time, and I do not think that an England team ought ever to have taken the field without him. He had a beautiful easy action, elastic and lively. He was impeccably accurate but never mechanical. Valuable on all wickets, however good, he was deadly either on a dusty or on a sticky wicket. George Lohmann was a great artist, and W. Attewell of Nottingham consummately accurate, but I think perhaps that Jack Hearne, of all our English medium-pace bowlers, most closely rivalled and maybe equalled for accuracy, variety, and quick off-break the great Australian, Charlie Turner. Jack Hearne, like all the Hearnes, was of the Anglo-Saxon type, pale and blond. He never appeared physically strong, but he was. An equable and kindly soul, but a hostile bowler.

We need not have looked further than Wilfred Rhodes for a slow left-hander. I doubt whether at that time he was quite as difficult and tricky as John Briggs on a difficult wicket, but he was a better bowler on hard wickets. He was accurate with a deceptive flight and plenty of spin, and he did not care how much he was hit on plumb wickets such as gave his spin no chance. His subsequent career is enough testimony to his value. In those days he was a chubby, ruddy Yorkshire lad willing to bowl all day, but he was not allowed to show how good a batsman he was. When he replaced the famous Bobby Peel in the Yorkshire side, a northern sportsman told me that previously in club cricket they had regarded Wilfred as a very good bat, but not much of a bowler. For Yorkshire he was just required to bowl and to go in last.

In the Test Matches of 1899 George Hirst got 1 wicket for 62 runs. He had not then developed the swerve which afterwards made him terrible to all but high-class batsmen. He was regarded as a fast left-hand bowler of the normal kind. He was often deadly on a bad wicket, but I do not think he was then as formidable on good wickets as Sailor Young of Essex.

At this time England had two fine wicket-keepers in W. Storer of Derbyshire and A. A. Lilley of Warwickshire. Storer, on his day, was just as good as Lilley, but he had rather tender hands and was not as reliable. Lilley afterwards became the standard Test Match wicket-keeper and achieved a great reputation. He was a good bat and did very well in Test Matches as such. But I do not rank him quite with the best wicket-keepers; I do not, for instance, find him as good as Leslie Ames or Oldfield. He was supposed to be a wonderful judge of cricket; such he may have been, but in that respect his main asset was a good crease-side manner and a wise look.

In the winter of 1901-2 Archie MacLaren—this was before the days of M.C.C. management—took a team to Australia which was not fully representative, lost by one match to four, and discovered Sidney Barnes.

The Australian invasion of 1902 was again led by Joe

Darling. The England captain was again A. C. MacLaren. The series of Test Matches was won by Australia by two to one, with two matches drawn, both washed out by rain, one of which England had in her pocket. Compared with modern figures, the totals for completed innings seem small. Out of thirteen completed innings three were under 100, seven under 200, and only two over 300.

It is strange that England should have lost the rubber, because the eleven who took the field in the first match at Edgbaston is generally agreed to have been the strongest that ever at any time represented us. The batting order was: A. C. MacLaren, C. B. Fry, K. S. Ranjitsinhji, F. S. Jackson, J. T. Tyldesley, A. A. Lilley, G. H. Hirst, G. L. Jessop, L. C. Braund, W. H. Lockwood, W. Rhodes. Lilley, who went in fourth wicket down, had been a successful batsman in Test Matches. Wilfred Rhodes, who went in last man, was even then as good a batsman as he was when later on he went in first with Jack Hobbs for England and created history. Lockwood, last but one, was a fine bat who went in high up for Surrey. Braund, last but two, was a century maker in Test Matches. But it was not merely the strength of the batting which distinguished this eleven. We had four bowlers, each of them with fair claims in his own style to have been the best ever. Lockwood among cricketers would be at the top of the poll for the best genuine fast bowler in the history of the game. George Hirst would at any rate be near the top as a fast left-hand bowler. Similarly Wilfred Rhodes as a slow left-hand bowler. And certainly Braund has claims as one of the three or four best leg-break bowlers. I myself consider Braund as good a leg-break bowler as I ever played; none has ever been more accurate in length: not even Grimmett. It was not merely the class of these bowlers; it was the combination of ideal variety which they presented. In addition we had F. S. Jackson, and he proved to be one of our very best bowlers in Test Matches. Then there was Gilbert Jessop, a good enough fast bowler to have been chosen on that account alone for England. Jessop could also bowl good medium-pace stuff. Thus the side contained no less than six top-notch all-rounders. Nor was this all. We had a competent fielder for every place in the field and at least seven exceptionals. We had five men who could field in any position whatever with credit. We had three superb slips in MacLaren, Ranji, and Braund. In a Test Match Braund at first slip made a catch at fine leg off Hirst. Not a cocked-up catch, but one slick off the edge of the bat. He anticipated it, of course. There has never been a better first slip than Leonard Braund.

We started off at Birmingham by scoring 376 for 9 wickets declared. The chief scorer was Tyldesley with 138. Jackson and Lockwood made 50 each; and Hirst and Rhodes scored well. I made 0; MacLaren, Ranji, Lilley, Jessop, and Braund were got rid of much under their value in runs. It rained during the night. We then proceeded on an unpleasant but not too terrible wicket to evict Australia for the exiguous total of 36. Of this Trumper made 18, and no other batsman more than 5. Hirst got 3 wickets for 15 runs, Rhodes 7 for 17. Curiously enough, it was Hirst who was most troublesome to the Australians; their batsmen hurried to the other end and tried to hit Rhodes, without success. Well as Rhodes bowled, it was Hirst who was responsible for the debacle. This is the best instance I know of the bowler at the other end getting wickets for his colleague. But this often happens. In the second innings we had 2 of their wickets down for 46, and the whole side would have been out for about 130 at most. But rain interfered and finally washed the match out.

The next match at Lord's was a complete wash-out. The only feature was that both Ranji and I were out for 0 in a couple of overs. The ground had been too wet for play, and most of us had gone to our hotels. At about five o'clock we were telephoned for. We won the toss, and what upset the apple-cart was that Joe Darling, for some reason which he could never explain, started with a bowler named A. J. Hopkins, when, in addition to Ernest Jones, he had declared good bowlers on his side in Noble, Armstrong, and J. Saunders, the latter a left-hander specially suited to a wet pitch. I had never seen Hopkins, who was a fair bowler of the practice description, but in his first over I was caught at fine leg by Clem Hill, who was on his way from second slip to square leg by the umpire. The ball and he happened to coincide in transgression. In came Ranji, and he was promptly bowled by an innocent straight ball from Hopkins, which the bowler had endeavoured to break back with a prodigious amount of finger-work. After that MacLaren and Jackson played out time with the greatest of ease, although against them Joe Darling tried all his six bowlers. It was a dead easy slow wicket. They scored 100 runs in 100 minutes. The rest of the match was a flood.

In July the Australians beat us fair and square at Sheffield by 143 runs. We were short of Ranjitsinhji and Lockwood, both damaged, though this time Ranji had not trodden on a nail. But we had Sidney Barnes, and he took 7 wickets in the match for 99 runs. The Australian advantage in runs was due to Monty Noble and Hugh Trumble in their first innings, and to Trumper, Clem Hill, and Hopkins in their second. Clem Hill played a grand innings of 119, and Trumper made a brilliant 62. Only two batsmen on our side did any good— MacLaren and Jessop. The former played finely for 31 and 63; and in our second innings Jessop punched a redoubtable 55. With the exception of Bobby Abel and Tyldesley in our first innings, no one on our side scored 20 runs. During both our innings it happened that the light was atrocious. When I was stumped in the first innings I literally saw no ball at all to play at. The Sheffield smoke-stacks were in fine form, and the light was otherwise grim. Gilbert Jessop was l.b.w. to Hugh Trumble to a ball which hit him in the middle of his chest on the lower shirt button; he was trying to hit a straight ball to square leg from the position of a doormat. For us, besides Sidney Barnes, Wilfred Rhodes bowled well. For the Australians, Noble and Saunders were well on the spot in the first innings, and Hugh Trumble and Noble in the second. Noble took 11 wickets for 103 runs; he bowled beautifully.

The result at Sheffield disturbed the Selection Committee, and they began changing the team. This resulted in the historic victory for Australia by 3 runs at Manchester in the match known as Fred Tate's. Had it not rained overnight for our second innings we should have won the match with ease. The Australians scored 299, due to a lovely century by

Trumper, and good scores by Duff, Clem Hill, and Joe Darling.
We replied with 262, of which F. S. Jackson scored a splendid
128 and Braund a fine 65. Then we got them out for a paltry
86 on an easy wicket. Lockwood had taken 6 wickets for 48
runs in the first innings. In the second he did one of the
finest bowling performances in the history of Test Matches by
taking 5 for 28. His bowling was truly magnificent; the more
so as the ground was so wet that no other fast bowler I have
ever known could have found a foothold. His beautiful bowling in the circumstances proved how perfect were his swing
and control; a mere strong-man bowler would have been
sliding all over the place. So we had 124 runs to make in our
second innings. Of these 89 were made by our first four
batsmen, but after MacLaren got out for 35 no one made
another double figure. Hugh Trumble did the damage.

Why Fred Tate's match? Because the unlucky Fred Tate
had to walk in last with 8 runs wanted to win. He snicked an
uncomfortable fourer between legs and wicket. Then the rain
came, and he had to sit in the pavilion for three-quarters
of an hour before again facing fate. This time Saunders, the
Australian left-hander, sent his off-stump flying, and Australia
won by 3 runs. But Fred Tate was otherwise unlucky. In the
Sussex eleven he never fielded anywhere but in the slips. The
difficulty of providing for the deep-field with a right-hander
and a left-hander when Joe Darling was in with Gregory
caused MacLaren to put the unfortunate out in the country
at deep square leg. Joe Darling immediately hit a colossal
skier. Fred Tate, on the boundary near Old Trafford Station,
carded wool beneath it. The ball hit his chest. This miss
really lost the match. But another chance which was held
really won it when Clem Hill brought off a miraculous running catch along the pavilion rails at deep square leg, to the
detriment of Lilley off Trumble.

Now I must tell you that the only reason that Fred Tate
was playing at all was that at the Selection Committee before
the match Lord Hawke objected to our taking Schofield
Haigh, of Yorkshire, as one of our thirteen and as the proposed wet-wicket bowler. It was gorgeous sunshine at the time
the selectors met, and we had chosen Rhodes and George

Hirst as well as Stanley Jackson from the Yorkshire side. It seemed as if Schofield Haigh would be a mere twelfth man, *honoris causa*. When someone proposed Fred Tate instead of Schofield Haigh, I distinctly told my colleagues that Fred Tate could not field anywhere except at slip, and that, though he was a careful slip in a county side, he was not up to the standard required in a Test Match. Lord Hawke was huffy, and we gave way to him, me protesting. So the truth is that this remarkable match ought to be called Lord Hawke's match. But there is more to say. When we got to Manchester and rain was in question, Archie MacLaren decided to leave out George Hirst of all people, a strong bat and prospectively the most dangerous wet-wicket bowler we had. So Fred Tate, whose forte was medium-pace bowling on fast, dry wickets, though no doubt he was useful in county cricket on wet ones, was included instead of George Hirst; because Archie Mac-Laren was pardonably annoyed with Lord Hawke for, as he said, foisting Fred Tate on him as a wet-wicket bowler. Archie said, "Martin chose Fred Tate for a wet wicket, and it will rain." In addition, the selectors left me out in favour of Bobby Abel. This was all right because I had not been making runs. But as it happens I was for value at least 25 per cent. a better batsman on a wet wicket than on a dry, whereas Abel was preferably a dry-wicket batsman.

The events of this match in combination with others are the origin of the caustic saying that Lord Hawke lost more Test Matches than anyone who never played for England. This is rather severe. Lord Hawke was chairman of the selectors from 1899 to 1909, and again in 1933. He was not a good chairman. He was too much concerned with the fortunes of Yorkshire; he regarded the Test Matches as spoiling the county championship, and he was much too observant of what he thought was public opinion. He has been much misrepresented as a strong man of cricket.

Whoever's name ought to be allotted to the fatal Manchester match, there is no doubt about whose name should distinguish the fifth Test Match at the Oval that year. This, the most dramatic game ever played between England and Australia, was won by Jessop's hurricane century. I have seen

the spectators at Test Matches strained and excited, but this
is the only Test Match in which I have seen a spectator burst
into tears when the winning run was scored. The Australians
won the toss and played a fine first innings against fine bowling
by Lockwood, Hirst, Braund, and F. S. Jackson. They scored
324, and against such bowling this was a performance. Hugh
Trumble with Trumper and Noble were the chief scorers.
George Hirst took 5 wickets for 77, and I never saw him bowl
better. England followed with the poor total of 183, but the
wicket had been damaged by rain. Trumble took 8 of our
wickets for 65 runs—a masterly piece of bowling. He was also
top scorer with 43. We then shot out the Australians for the
small total of 121. Lockwood bowled at his best, taking 5
wickets for 45. Only Clem Hill and Warwick Armstrong
scored over 20 runs. So we were left with 263 runs to get on
a wet wicket. A. C. MacLaren, L. C. H. Palairet, Tyldesley,
Hayward, and Braund were all out for less than double figures
each. Stanley Jackson, however, played a fine innings of 49.
His certainty on an unpleasant wicket was superlative. Then
Jessop let himself loose like a catapult at the bowling and
scattered it to smithereens. He offered one scanty chance in
the deep off a giant drive. If ever an innings ought to have
been filmed, that was the one. I should say that Jessop's
104 must rank as the greatest innings by a pure hitter ever
played. The other batsman who made a difference was George
Hirst with a brave and skilful 58 not out. The match was
pulled out of a very wet fire. I am bound to say that when
our last two men were in Hugh Trumble planted a likely-
looking l.b.w. on George Hirst. He was bowling round the
wicket, and there was a scintilla of doubt, but I have never
been able to feel comfortable about that decision. Hugh
Trumble picked up the ball without a sign of discontent.

When the England team went to Australia in 1903-4, the
ideal thing would have been for F. S. Jackson to captain the
side. Jackson, however, could not go, and I was asked to be
captain, but I was much too busy with extraneous affairs at
home. So Pelham Warner took the team and was able to write
his book *How We Recovered the Ashes*.

England won the series by three to two. The Australians

were a fine team. They had lost their dangerous left-hand bat, Joe Darling. Ernest Jones had lapsed from his full pace as a fast bowler. But Trumper had become a magnificent batsman, and Reggie Duff had blossomed into improvement. Monty Noble as a batsman was better than ever; the great Clem Hill just as good. They still had Syd Gregory, and Warwick Armstrong was beginning to be a giant batsman. In bowling, A. Cotter, perhaps on his day as fast as Jones, but with a plainer flight, was a good substitute. Hugh Trumble, M. A. Noble, and W. P. Howell remained. The English batting was sound. R. E. Foster scored his pre-Bradman record of 287 in the first Test Match. Hayward, Tyldesley, Pelham Warner himself, George Hirst, and Braund batted well throughout. Our bowling was strong. Wilfred Rhodes was at his best; Arnold, of Worcestershire, a high-class bowler, fast or medium-fast as required, and an artist, did well; Braund with his leg-breaks and Hirst with his quick left-handers were useful; but the unique performer was B. J. T. Bosanquet, the father of googlies.

Then came the Australian visit of 1905, when Joe Darling reappeared in command of Australia, and England under the captaincy of Stanley Jackson enjoyed a triumphant season. This was the season when Jackson pre-emulated Walter Hammond by winning the toss in all the Test Matches. We won two matches and drew the other three. Jackson was head of our bowling averages and of our batting figures, the finest all-round record in the history of England *versus* Australia. Our batting all through showed fine figures; I was second with an average of 58, Tyldesley third with an average of 53, and Rhodes, R. H. Spooner, and A. C. MacLaren all averaged over 40. On the Australian side only Duff averaged over 40 for batting, and the most successful Australian bowler, Frank Laver, could not do better than an average of 31 runs per wicket. These figures indicate the superiority of the England eleven. Australia felt the loss of Hugh Trumble as a bowler. Cotter, for all his slinging pace, could not emulate Jones; Noble was out of form with the ball, and though Warwick Armstrong and C. E. McLeod were good bowlers, they could not make up the leeway. The Australian batting, however, was formidable; the names of Duff, Armstrong, Darling, Gregory, Hill, and Trumper all in a row prove that much. Of our bowlers besides F. S. Jackson, both Walter Brearley and Rhodes did well, and B. J. T. Bosanquet won one match to his own fingers. Walter Brearley was a fine, steady, fastish bowler, but he was not fast in the same sense as Lockwood, Richardson, and Mold; his merit was that he could bowl well for a fast bowler on slow wickets. And he could talk the hind leg off a giraffe. We again had Arnold, but the best bowler in England, Sidney Barnes, did not appear.

Our first Test Match at Nottingham was a great game. You must know that the marl wicket at Nottingham was as good then as it is nowadays. But in our first innings we made only 196, and John Tyldesley was our only individual success. The damage was done by the baseball bowling of Frank Laver, who got 7 wickets for 64. Australia replied with 221, and the reason it was not nearer 421 was a dramatic spell of bowling by Stanley Jackson. He did not put himself on till fifth change; then, with Clem Hill and Monty Noble well set, he dismissed both of them and then Joe Darling in a couple of overs, and ended off with 5 wickets for 52 runs.

I was not playing in this match. My thumb had been squashed to a jelly while practising on my home ground at Hamble to the bowling of a small boy. So I was sitting on the grass by George Parr's tree at Trent Bridge in company with Sir James Barrie, A. E. W. Mason, and E. V. Lucas. This was the occasion when I asked Lucas what sort of a bowler Barrie was, and he said, "Slow—very. High—very. Left hand—very." Then I asked Barrie what sort of batsman Lucas was, and he said, "Lucas lays on the wood—two duck's eggs." Sometimes it is fun looking on at a Test Match when you ought to be playing. Not often.

The unexpected success of Laver's bowling had upset the reckoning; it was much spoken about in the England dressing-room between the innings. So next innings Archie MacLaren agreed to go in first and take the bull by the horns. This he did. He smashed the good Australian bowling to the tune of 140 runs, and I have never seen more dominating batsmanship in a Test Match. As Tom Hayward and John Tyldesley

played finely for 47 and 61 apiece, and Stanley Jackson himself
with pleasant Nordic ease collected an impeccable 82 not out,
he was able to declare at 426 for 5 wickets. We scarcely
expected to get the Australians out in the time available, but
Bosanquet was even more surprising with his googlies than
Frank Laver had been with his baseball swerves. None of the
Australians except Joe Darling and Syd Gregory could tackle
him. It looked like a game of diddling. Australia made only
188, and we won with time to spare. I do not ever remember
having enjoyed a match more. We all admired and liked the
Australians of those days, but, by Jove! we did like beating
them.

There was one incident of this match which ought to be
recorded. Towards the end of the Australian second innings,
when they were well in the soup, the light became very poor.
Charles McLeod, when his partner got out, ran to the
pavilion and signalled. The big brown moustache of Joe
Darling emerged. There was a consultation at the gate. Joe
Darling surveyed the quarters of the sky as a farmer would,
then shook his head, slowly indeed, but not without emphasis,
turned his broad back, and went in. McLeod had wanted to
know whether he should appeal against the light. The light
was bad. If Joe Darling had allowed the appeal I think it
certain that the umpires would have stopped play, and Australia would have drawn the match. Joe Darling was a sportsman of the best. We had by that time morally won the game,
and Joe Darling was not the man to slide out on a side-issue.
And, mark you, McLeod need not have discussed the question; he could have appealed himself, but he, too, felt disin-
clined to escape on an appeal when his side was beaten on
the play.

Would that happen nowadays?

This was the match in which Warwick Armstrong introduced his method of bowling wide outside the leg-stump to a
numerous leg-side field. He was rather angry with me for de-
scribing this as "defensive bowling." But such it was.

The second match, at Lord's, was drawn. The wicket was
dead, but not wet, when we won the toss. We scored 282 in
our first innings. A. C. MacLaren, Tyldesley and I made

the runs. I was very much annoyed (of course in private) because when I had made 73 and was well set for a century, that obstinate umpire Jim Phillips gave me out caught at the wicket when I hit the toe of my front boot at least a foot away from the ball. His heavy, autocratic explanation was that he heard a click. I asked him—of course, after the match— whether he was sure it was not the slamming of a door in the pavilion. Jim and I were slight enemies, because years before he had no-balled me for throwing. That was all right if he disliked my slightly bent arm action, but it was no reason why he should have no-balled me for my other nine balls of the over when I delivered slow round-arms and slow over-arms with an absolutely rigid elbow. This elaborate incident occurred in a match at Brighton between Sussex and Oxford. Before the second innings I had my right elbow encased in splints and bandages and took the field with my sleeve buttoned at the wrist. But old Billy Murdoch, our captain, who had ostentatiously put me on to bowl in the first innings at Jim Phillips' end, because he knew that Jim had come down to Brighton to no-ball me, twisted his black moustache, showed his white teeth, and refused to put me on. I was both astonished and annoyed, but he refused further particulars. Jim Phillips was a famous umpire. He was an Australian who came over, qualified for Middlesex and was a second-rate elephantine slow-medium bowler. He was quite honest, but was ambitious to achieve the reputation of a "strong umpire." His other ambition was to qualify as a mining engineer, and he used to go about with a Hall and Knight's Algebra in his pocket.

To return. The Australians had to bat on a wet, easy wicket, and we dismissed them for 181. They would have got more had not Stanley Jackson forgotten, when he went on to bowl, to put a third man for Trumper. It was just an oversight. Trumper had made 31 and was hitting superlatively. Jacker bowled a rather short good length straight ball. Trumper, seeing the opening, tried to cut it and saw his off-stump disturbed. Jacker would not have got that wicket but for his oversight. In our second innings Archie MacLaren and I, chiefly he, pushed the score up to 151 for 5 wickets, and I was still in. So had the rain not come we should have put the Australians in to get over 300. The draw was distinctly in our favour.

So, too, was the third match at Leeds. Jacker as usual won the toss, and our totals were 301 and 295 for 5 declared. Jacker and Tyldesley both made centuries. Hayward, Hirst, and I put up some runs; and we had the match in hand. Good work by our fast bowler, Warren of Derbyshire, had accounted for the Australians for 195. Only Armstrong and Duff put up much of a show. These two batted well, especially Armstrong. We could not get through the Australian batsmen a second time. They scored 224 for 7; so morally we were on top. Noble played a fine innings in his second attempt, and saved the match for Australia. Armstrong, too, had a good match. He scored 66 and 32 and took 7 of our wickets, including all the five we lost in our second innings. Warwick was becoming a matchmaker. Well as Warren bowled in the first innings, I think we should have won this match if we had had Walter Brearley as our fast bowler. I could never understand why he was left out.

At Manchester, England won by an innings and 80 runs, a big feat against any Australian team. Stanley Jackson scored his usual century and a beauty it was. Everybody else except Walter Brearley made runs, especially the ever-reliable Tom Hayward with 82 and Reggie Spooner with 52. This was the first time that Reggie's charming style and thorough craftsmanship were seen in a Test Match. Brearley, Arnold, Rhodes, and Jackson all bowled in a winning vein. Walter Brearley was the spearhead of our bowling with 4 wickets for 72 and 4 for 54. Walter had the confidence of the archangel Gabriel and the stamina of all the saints. He was not as fine an artist in bowling as Ted Arnold, who backed him up at the other end, but he had more inherent vice. Walter Brearley genuinely expected to get a wicket with every ball he bowled, and if he was allowed he would bowl all day.

The Oval match was drawn, but it was another triumph for the England batting. We made 430 and 261 for 6. In the first innings I much enjoyed making 144, and I much enjoyed my partnerships with Tom Hayward and Stanley Jackson.

In our second innings John Tyldesley scored a not-out century, and Reggie Spooner settled himself as a Test Match batsman with a perfect 79. Cotter bowled very fast for Australia in this match, and although the wicket was a dry Oval wicket, some of us got some rib-ticklers. He got 7 wickets in our first innings, which was good on such a pitch. Australia scored 363 and 124 for 4. So the draw was fairly even. For them R. A. Duff played a splendid innings of 146. The only other distinguished batting for them was by Joe Darling. Reggie Duff, who had a face like a good-looking brown trout, and was full of Australian sunshine, was an entertaining batsman of excellent class. He had all the strokes and a native knack of timing. Like John Tyldesley, he was specially good at the high drive on both sides of the wicket played at the good length ball on the rise. He did not hit at the pitch of the ball. He hit on the rise with his eye genuinely watching the ball. This is an uncommon stroke. John Tyldesley was the best at it I ever saw, and Duff the next. The bowling in this final match on our side was good, but just not good enough to press home our advantage. We were short of a leg-break bowler. Brearley's performance, however, of 5 wickets for 110 runs in the first innings was one of his best.

So ended a fine series of Test Matches with honours to both sides and a personal triumph, never better deserved by any cricketer or captain, for Stanley Jackson.

This was the then Honourable F. S. Jackson, son of the first Lord Allerton, the great Secretary of State for Ireland. Afterwards Jacker was Chairman of the Unionist Party and then Governor of Bengal; he is now the Right Hon. Sir Stanley Jackson, P.C., G.C.S.I. An excellent Englishman.

The England team which was taken to Australia in 1907-8, with A. O. Jones of Nottingham as captain, had points of distinction, but it was no match for Australia. They beat us by four to one. A. O. Jones unfortunately fell ill, and after the first Test Match our team was captained by F. L. Fane of Essex. Our most successful batsman was George Gunn, nephew of the great William; a wayward genius, but a genius. George Gunn was an original, and he ended up the tour with an average of 51 for Test Matches; he went to Australia for his own health, and was incorporated because of A. O. Jones's ill-health. In point of fact, he kept none other than Jack Hobbs out of the first Test Match, on results not unjustifiably, because he made 119 and 74 in a match of moderate scores. All the same this tour was the full dawn of the great career of Jack Hobbs.

Other successful batsmen on our side were Joe Hardstaff, father of our young Joe, and known in Australia as Hotstuff, and that very brilliant amateur, Kenneth Hutchings of Kent. F. L. Fane and Wilfred Rhodes also did well. Our bowlers who got the wickets in Test Matches, but not cheaply enough to win, were J. N. Crawford, Fielder of Kent, and Sidney Barnes. Crawford was then only 19, and he topped the bowling averages with 30 wickets for 24 apiece. He came from my own school, Repton, and on his record there was the best schoolboy cricketer there has ever been. He was a right-hand bowler of lively medium pace and of exceptional natural talent, and a strong bat.

On the Australian side there were still the great names of Noble, Armstrong, Hill, Gregory, and Trumper; and two brilliant new batsmen in left-handed Vernon Ransford and Charlie Macartney. These two did well, but Macartney had yet to develop the eminence as a batsman which later promoted him to rivalry with Victor Trumper. It is of interest that Hanson Carter, remembered now as one of the expert Australian wicket-keepers and as a perpetual judge of the game along with his friend J. A. O'Connor, was second to Armstrong in the Australian batting averages with 42. To this day the passenger list between England and Australia when cricket is afield is incomplete without Carter and O'Connor.

Montagu Alfred Noble captained the Australian eleven in England of 1909. Archie MacLaren captained England; Stanley Jackson was absent. Jackson was available, but diplomatic difficulties caused him to stand out. England won one match, Australia two; the two draws were rather in favour of Australia.

We had a good wedge of the old brigade, but our team did not do itself justice. I was kept out of two Test Matches through a law case. In this Lord Reading, then Sir Rufus Isaacs, was our leading counsel. When I was introduced to

him on the first day in court he suavely said, "I wish I were
as distinguished in my profession as you are in yours." Sir
Rufus prided himself on his diplomatic gifts; but that is the
one and only time I have been called a professional cricketer.
No; now I remember there was one other time. In a county
match, Sussex against Lancashire at Old Trafford, when I
was fielding on the boundary, a local commentator spent the
whole of the first Lancashire innings telling me, "Fra, Fra,
you bluidy amatoors is no good." Then I made a lot of runs,
and he spent the whole of the second Lancashire innings
in saying, "Fra, Fra, th'art nowt but a bluidy professional
thysel'."

Lord Hawke was still Chairman of the Selection Committee
and I was on it, but I have not much good to say of our meetings. To begin with, Archie MacLaren was not playing cricket
regularly, and he was not his true self. In the five Test Matches
his total was only 88, with a top score of 24 and an average of
12. A Selection Committee needs more than anything a successful captain with personal prestige. But of course MacLaren
was still a formidable potential.

We started at Birmingham with a fine win by 10 wickets.
It was a wet wicket match. Hirst and Blythe dismissed Australia in their first innings for 74. Only Armstrong scored 20
runs. We did not do much better. We were all out for 121
against the bowling of Macartney and Warwick Armstrong.
John Tyldesley, A. O. Jones, and Gilbert Jessop scored twenties. Jack Hobbs and I both made ducks, both defeated by
Macartney. Then Hirst and Blythe again routed the Australian
batsmen for a total of 151, of which Syd Gregory and Vernon
Ransford scored 86; 43 apiece. The wicket was reckoned to
be difficult. Archie MacLaren was pessimistic about our
chances of getting the 115 runs required to win. I asked him
to let Jack Hobbs and me go in first to bustle for our pairs
of spectacles. After sucking his pencil Archie agreed. The
result was that we knocked off the runs without loss of a
wicket. Jack Hobbs scored 62 not out, and as a spectator at
the other crease I have to say that this was as great an innings
as I ever saw played by any batsman in any Test Match, or
any other match. It is the only innings I have ever seen when

batting the other end that I rank with some of the innings I saw Ranjitsinhji play when I was in with him. Jack Hobbs, on the difficult wicket, took complete charge of the good Australian bowling, carted it to every point of the compass, and never made the shred of a mistake. His quickness with his bat and his skill in forcing the direction of his strokes made me feel like a fledgling; and when it comes to it, I was not so dusty a driver in those days.

The Australians had their revenge at Lord's. They won easily by 9 wickets. I did not see much of the match as I was hobnobbing at the other end of London with Sir Rufus. On our side only John Tyldesley, J. H. King of Leicestershire, and Lilley, the wicket-keeper, did any good with the bat. For Australia, Ransford, the slim left-hander, played a magnificent not-out innings of 143, and it was his batting that put Australia on top. The only other good batting on the Australian side was by Warren Bardsley, who thus introduced himself to big doings in Test Matches. England was short of bowling. I did not like our team when we chose it, and I was glad that Albert Relf of Sussex, whose inclusion I rather forced on my colleagues, took 5 wickets for 85 in the first innings and got the only wicket in the second.

We had a wet wicket match at Leeds and lost to Australia by 126 runs. There was no high scoring. For Australia, Syd Gregory, Ransford, Bardsley, Armstrong, and Trumper made twenties, thirties, and forties. For us nobody but John Tyldesley and Jack Sharp of Lancashire and Jack Hobbs in the second innings did any good. Jack Sharp came in by substitution, and collected 61 in our first innings, the highest individual score of the match. The winning factor was the medium-pace left-hand bowling of Macartney. This redoubtable little cricketer was afterwards so prodigiously successful a batsman that we are liable to forget his bowling, which made him one of the finest all-rounders ever. Our second innings was not worthy of us; we made only 87, of which Jack Hobbs made 30. Leeds has always been unlucky for us. In 1921 Jack Hobbs developed appendicitis there, and had to be operated on by Lord Moynihan. And there it was that Johnny Briggs went off his head and never played again; Colin Blythe had an epileptic fit; Gilbert Jessop shockingly ricked his back and was out of cricket for some time; and, in harmony, Mrs. J. W. H. T. Douglas had appendicitis which prevented Johnny from playing. Headingley is a fine ground, but I have played there in a snowstorm in May and in several floods in other months. It was at Leeds, too, that at a critical moment in a game all the Yorkshire Committeemen and their wives tramped out to be in time for lunch, and one of them, when I protested, said, with a heavy foot still on my toe, that after all I was only a guest. It was at Leeds that having made six successive hundreds at the end of the previous season I forgot about this, and also about the future of Don Bradman, and ran myself out when well set at 68. So you see what Leeds is like. I now invariably stay at Harrogate.

The fourth match, at Old Trafford, was drawn, decidedly in Australia's favour. I was not there, and nothing much happened. Ransford, Trumper, Armstrong, and Macartney batted well for Australia, but the top score was 51. Barnes and Blythe bowled well for us in their first innings, and Rhodes in their second. Nobody at all batted well for us, except Reggie Spooner, who scored 25 and 58; the only two others to score 20 runs were Lilley and Pelham Warner. Of the Australian bowlers none did anything to speak of except Frank Laver, whose lanky limbs and angular action emerged into 8 wickets for 31 runs in our first innings.

The Oval match, as so often, ran into runs. Australia scored 325 and 339 for 5 wickets declared. We scored 352 and 104 for 3. Warren Bardsley, with his studious left-handed proficiency, scored 136 in the first innings and 130 in the second. Trumper played a characteristic 73. Syd Gregory ought to have made a century, but this blackberry-eyed slip of accomplishment cheerfully ran himself out at 74. Macartney and Noble both scored first-rate fifties. For us Wilfred Rhodes made 66 (and ran me out) and 54. I hit 62 with every intention of proceeding at least to a century when Wilfred played a ball quietly to mid-off, invited me to change places with him, and then went back on it. Jack Sharp, whom Archie insisted on having in the team as our fast bowler because he had batted so well at Leeds, justified his captain with a fine century. K. L.

Hutchings hit beautifully for 59. I scored 35 not out in the second innings, and no one listened to me when I suggested that we might go on with the match for a fourth day. I saw runs in the offing. The Australian fast bowler, Cotter, did a good performance in our first innings by taking 6 for 95. Our only successful bowler was D. W. Carr, who, with his medium-pace leg-breaks and googlies, more than any other England bowler resembled the great South Africans of this type. There had been much eleventh-hour discussion about the final composition of our team. Buckenham of Essex had been selected as our fast bowler. It was a dry wicket and this was what he was for. But Archie MacLaren made up his mind that if Carr was played it must be as an opening bowler; he also objected to Jack Sharp, after his success at Leeds, being only twelfth man. A standing idea with him, and a right one, was that a captain could not use more than at most five bowlers; and we already had an approximation to a fast bowler on the side in Sidney Barnes.

This was the last year in which the masterful figure of Archie MacLaren appeared on the England side.

Our team in Australia of 1911-12 ought to have been captained in the field by Pelham Warner, but he was prevented from adding another brick to his edifice of service to cricket by an unfortunate illness. His successful mantle fell on the shoulders of a very different man, J. W. H. T. Douglas. Douglas was a strong cricketer, but everybody found fault with his captaincy, the result of which was a triumph for England over Australia by 4 to 1.

Monty Noble's solid name was absent from the Australian elevens. His eminence, Charlie Macartney, appeared in only one match, but with Clem Hill as captain, backed up by Trumper, Armstrong, Bardsley, Ransford, and Kelleway, Australia was strong. Their bowling was good but did not pull its weight, except that a great slow bowler appeared in Dr. H. V. Hordern, to back up Cotter's speed. I never saw Hordern, but Wilfred Rhodes ranks him as the best leg-break and googly bowler he ever played; and Wilfred should know, as he averaged 57 runs per innings against him in Test Matches.

The English victories were a succession of triumphs for Jack Hobbs and Rhodes as first-wicket batsmen, and for Sidney Barnes and F. R. Foster as opening bowlers. Frank Woolley, George Gunn, and young J. W. Hearne, not to mention Foster, were other fruitful run-makers on our side.

In parallel, Barnes and Foster did wonderful work as bowlers. Between them in Test Matches they bowled 572 overs and took 66 wickets. They were two superb bowlers. Frank Foster was a left-hand bowler with a short run and an accelerated delivery which made him nearly a fast bowler; he had an abrupt swing of the body following his arm which caused the ball to swing across the line from wicket to wicket. The peculiar quickness of his arm-swing made the ball come from the pitch like lightning.

There is no doubt that the combined success of Frank Foster and Sidney Barnes in Australia was due to the pace of the Australian wickets exactly suiting their style. Both of them could pitch the ball a foot or two shorter there for a good length than in England. This especially applied to Sidney Barnes. The one way of getting on top of Barnes—it was not often done—was to drive him over his head. But in Australia this was more difficult to do, as he could keep the good length ball out of reach of the good batsman's natural swing. I found myself that unless one drove Barnes over his head he would be knocking at the door all the time. The opinion in the cricket world of Australia is that Barnes is the greatest bowler England ever sent to Australia, and they rank him with their own F. R. Spofforth. Both of these princes of their craft are often spoken of as fast bowlers. Both of them could bowl a fast ball, but their standard pace varied from medium to fast medium. Spofforth earned his soubriquet of " The Demon," not because he was fast, but because he was difficult. His average ball was about the pace of our J. T. Hearne, or, say, Maurice Tate. Sidney Barnes's average ball was rather faster, but he too varied his pace within a wide margin. Barnes is 66 in this year of 1939; but he still takes his 100 wickets for about 5 runs apiece in good club cricket. He is tall, loose-limbed, and a deliberate sort of mover, with easy hips after the manner of the African races. He takes a long loping run and swings his arm over with disengaged carelessness and consummate control. He could swerve the ball in and out, but did not much use this device. He relied on disguised changes of pace and of break, which he never overdid. His best ball was one, very nearly fast, which pitched on the leg-stump to hit the top of the off, sometimes even on a good wicket. He had the knack of making the ball rise high from the pitch. I never batted against a bowler more interesting to play.

In the series England lost the first match against a century by Trumper and fine hitting by Clem Hill. Frank Foster promptly cabled home that this was the only match that Australia would win, and he was right. He was one of those bowlers who expected to flatten the middle stump of a Trumper or a Clem Hill every ball.

There were good years to follow; but I do not think England cricket has ever again been quite as strong as in this period.

CHAPTER XII

AND AFTER

IN 1912 we had the one and only Triangular Tournament with Australian and South African teams in England together. The experiment has been voted a failure; in fact, what made it so was not any inherent disadvantage of a Triangular season, but the execrable weather of that summer. The three England *versus* Australia matches were played on wet wickets, and two of them were washed out. The other one we won in style. We beat South Africa in all three Test Matches, but because of their difficult bowling I myself feared their eleven more than I feared the Australians. The South Africans did not realise how strong a batting side they were, and they did not do themselves justice either against England or against Australia.

I happened to be captain of England that year; happened is the right word. By seniority I ought to have been captain in 1907 when the South Africans were over, but I had snapped my Achilles tendon in May, 1906, and was supposed to have finished my career; indeed, that knowledgeable critic, Sir Home Gordon, had written of me some ten years previously "his book of first-class cricket is now closed." I was not popular at Lord's, being regarded in the light of a rebel. The only possible alternatives as a captain in 1912 were Pelham Warner and R. H. Spooner; both of them junior to me in captaincy and on bare figures not superior as performers. Pelham Warner was ailing and a doubtful starter. Reggie Spooner disliked the responsibility of captaincy.

So after much debate the Board of Control accepted the situation. Lord Harris was Chairman of the Board of Control. He wrote me a tentative letter asking me in hypothetical terms whether I would accept the captaincy of England in the first match. Previously no England captain from the time an independent Selection Committee had been established had

249

been invited otherwise than for the whole series, but there had been rather a muddle in 1909 due to Archie MacLaren's indifferent health and form and inability to play first-class cricket regularly when he was captain.

I wrote back to Lord Harris and said no: I would accept the captaincy only for the whole of the matches and on condition that I myself was one of a Selection Committee of three, the other two to be suitable men neither of them a candidate for a place in the eleven. No others to be co-opted. I pointed out that both the Board of Control and any Selection Committee were bound to release the strings the moment they appointed a captain; he became the executive and they had to rely on him; that in my view the idea of appointing an England captain on appro., especially in the case of a senior man like myself, was ridiculous. But I added that I had complete confidence in him, Lord Harris, and I proposed that if they appointed me captain for the series he should be at liberty to hold a meeting with my two colleagues if they had any doubts about my competence or form, and if the verdict went against me I would accept the opportunity to resign.

Lord Harris read my letter out to the Board of Control with the preface, "I think this fellow Fry is right."

In the result nothing went wrong. We won the tournament hands down and never at any point in any of the matches did we look like losing. A slightly amusing sidelight was that never in any species of representative match from Oxford and Cambridge onwards have I ever been on the losing side as captain.

I would like to add that throughout the season Lord Harris stood by me loyally. The Board of Control offered me the choice for my two colleagues of J. R. Mason, H. K. Foster, and J. Shuter. I chose Jack Mason and Harry Foster; but Jack Mason did not fancy the job, as he was not seeing enough first-class cricket. So Foster, Shuter, and I met once in May, chose a definite team with definite substitutes if required for the whole series of six matches, and we never met again. This did not provide much fodder for the scribes, pharisees, and dramatists; but it worked.

Our first match at Lord's against the Australians was extinguished by rain. After we had scored 310 for 7 wickets and declared, rain intervened and there was little prospect of getting the Australians out even once. The wicket was dead and easy. In our innings Jack Hobbs scored one of his proper centuries, and Wilfred Rhodes and I made another hundred between us. I ran myself out trying to hurry up the pace. In point of fact, I tried to run two to the bowler. When it came to the Australians' innings I gave my critical friends in Lord's pavilion a fine run for their subscriptions. I knew very well that we could not get the Australians out even once and that it was quite likely we should have wet-wicket matches throughout the series. I therefore thought well not to unmask the strength of the England wet-wicket bowling. I used Wilfred Rhodes little, and Frank Woolley, our best left-hander for a wet wicket, not at all. This to the unintelligent no doubt appeared preposterous mismanagement. I never came across a word detecting my tactics until Douglas Jardine mentioned them in his book twenty years afterwards. But it happened that I guessed right, because in the final Test Match against Australia at the Oval, which was decisive of the rubber, we had a bad wet wicket, and Frank Woolley settled the issue by taking 5 wickets for 29 in the first innings and 5 for 20 in the second. The Australians had three dangerous batsmen on a wet wicket: Charlie Macartney, Syd Gregory, and a powerful hitter, D. Smith. A good wet-wicket bat who is allowed a fancy-free go at a slow left-hander on an easy wet wicket has a much stronger hand when he meets him on a difficult one. As it was, at Lord's Macartney was at the top of his form for 99 runs, and we had a lot of bother with the unmitigated defensive powers of C. Kelleway. Macartney had bad luck. He was caught on the leg side by the wicket-keeper standing back at 99; if the ball touched his bat it was the most delicate touch a batsman ever perpetrated. I would not have given him out from short slip. But of course the facts of cricket are the honest subjective interpretations of the umpires' perceptions. In this match Jack Hobbs was bowled out at 107 going strong by the Australian fastish leg-break bowler Emery with one of the few unplayable balls I have seen; it was a perfect length on the leg stump, came fast off the pitch, and hit the off stump low down. Jack Hobbs, being a batsman, played back at it, but was late; a lesser player would have scraped forward and might have snicked it.

Our second match against Australia at Old Trafford gave us one innings and the Australians none. We played on pure mud and with muddy clouds in the offing. For us Wilfred Rhodes, to the manner born, dug a skilful 92 out of the slush. The rest of us chanced our arms with balloon strokes and were caught in the country when we did not miss the ball. Wilfred did not lift a single ball off the ground. This was the second wettest match I ever saw in the rainy region of Old Trafford.

Our final match with Australia at the Oval was a proper final. It was a straight knock-out fight, the other two matches having been drawn. The preliminary atmosphere was tense. The Press was on one of its pessimistic and critical wavelengths. A rival evening paper explained my incompetence in two columns. The weather enhanced the situation. So much rain fell that, although the first day was fine, the field was quite unfit for play. A crowd of 30,000 was sitting expectantly in the sun looking at a wicket which they did not know was a quagmire. The junior groundlings had been slowly proceeding to and fro with the pent-houses.

Early in the afternoon Syd Gregory, the Australian captain, came to me and proposed that for the sake of the crowd we should make a start. The officials at the Oval were becoming anxious at the crowd's disappointment. Now this was a good gamble on the part of little Syd. The wicket was bound to be wet even if we played, not on the prepared pitch, but on another. Syd knew that his side was done against our bowling unless he had the luck to win the toss with a chance for his batsmen on the wicket while it was in its easier state, and a chance for his bowlers if they got us on a drying sticky wicket. I knew that with equal conditions of a mud wicket my team was bound to win. So with the rubber depending on the one match I refused to start until the turf was genuinely fit.

We did not start until late in the afternoon, and then I won the toss. Thanks to Jack Hobbs, Rhodes, and Frank Woolley, who made 177 runs between them, we registered the fine total in the conditions of 245. When I walked out to the wicket I was unanimously booed by our 30,000 supporters. The news had got around that I was the captain who would not start earlier. Sidney Barnes and Frank Woolley easily accounted for our opponents for a total of 111. No Australian batsman except Kelleway made double figures. Our two heroes took 5 wickets each for 6 runs apiece. Frank Woolley made the ball break away with his left-hand finger-flip, and Barnes was quite unplayable. Had the Australians been able to play him they would have made fewer runs. In our second innings we lost Rhodes and Spooner quickly. Then Jack Hobbs and I attacked the bowling as in 1909 at Edgbaston. After making 32 by sheer hitting Jack Hobbs punched a long-hop into the stomach of point. Having again been booed properly on my way to the wicket, I was very much on the job, and with the help of Johnny Douglas the other end I may say that I performed in quite the right sort of way on the bowling. I think I should have got a century instead of 70 odd if I had not divoted the turf in attempting a full drive. No one else made runs and our total was 175.

I started the Australian second innings with Sidney Barnes, but I saw in a couple of overs that he was not the Barnes of the first innings. Great bowler as he was, he was liable at that stage of his career to be stiff and angular at the start of his second attempt. He had a slight rheumatic tendency, especially in damp weather. So I said to him, " Barnes, what about trying the other end?" This brought on Frank Woolley, and he and Dean of Lancashire bowled the side out for 65 runs. Glorious victory. Immense applause. And in ten minutes down came the rain.

Just when we were finishing them off, Jennings, I think it was, one of the good Australian batsmen, in trying desperate measures, hit too soon and projected the ball vertically above himself to the height of a steeple. I shouted " Wicket-keeper!" and Tiger Smith stood arms akimbo. Rhodes was at silly mid-on. I shouted " Wilfred!" and the immobile Wilfred looked benignly at the sky. I shouted " George!" to Hirst, who stood star-gazing at silly short-leg, like the Royal Observatory. The ball was well on its way down, so from silly point square I projected myself and arrived just in time to pouch it about a foot from the ground with a dive. I regard the catch as almost a fluke, but it looked all right as I casually tossed the ball into Wilfred's disobedient tummy.

This added the last straw to the growing burden of my popularity. But when the crowd gathered round the pavilion and shouted for me I would not go on to the balcony, because I felt that the time for them to cheer was when I was walking out to bat as captain of my side to try to win the match on a foul wicket. Ranji was in our dressing-room and he said to me, " Now, Charles, be your noble self." But I said, " This is not one of my noble days." All the same it was a great match, and I never saw the Australians again till 1921.

The South African team of 1912 did not do themselves justice.

Their first invasion in force had been in 1907. In that season their bowling had been exceptionally strong; indeed, all the England batsmen who met it agreed that it was the most difficult bowling they had ever met. We had to face three of the best leg-break and googly bowlers ever known— in my opinion the best ever—in Aubrey Faulkner, A. E. Vogler, and G. C. White; a phenomenal purely googly bowler with no leg-break in R. O. Schwarz; a fine medium-pace right-hander of the Hugh Trumble type in J. H. Sinclair; and quite one of the fastest bowlers who have ever appeared in J. J. Kotze. Their batting was really strong down to number ten, but for some reason they never made good in runs to their proper value. Against the counties in the early part of the season their bowling demolished the batting opposed to them. There was much pessimism as to what would happen to the representative England team.

These South African bowlers of 1907 were a landmark in cricket. On the matting wickets of the Cape, Bosanquet's invention of the googly had been developed into a standard type of bowling. They were not the ordinary type of high-tossed slow leg-break bowlers. Their pace was slow-medium to medium. To my mind A. E. Vogler was the best of them. He could bowl in two styles. With the new ball he bowled medium-pace right-hand stuff with a peculiar dipping and swerving flight and a good deal of hand-cut spin. He also bowled leg breaks and googlies at a slower pace, but not so very slow, with uncommon accuracy. Aubrey Faulkner bowled medium pace with precision of length and an abrupt break both from leg and from the off. He delivered the ball so that no one could tell whether it was a leg break or an off break. Jack Hobbs said he could see which way the ball was spinning in the air after it left Faulkner's hand, but Jack Hobbs on his day is a humorist. White was a slower edition of Vogler in his second style; he did not use much break, but his length was peculiarly steady. Some of our batsmen considered him to be the most difficult of the three. R. O. Schwarz, who had once upon a time played for Middlesex and was an international footballer, was a curiosity, and private secretary to Sir Abe Bailey. He could not for the life of him bowl a leg break, but with the leg-break action and the dropped wrist changing the axis of spin he bowled the most prodigious off break on a hard wicket ever achieved by a mortal. He would pitch the ball on the off stump and break across outside the legs of a right-hand batsman. Some of our county batsmen feared him like Old Nick. It was the success of these bowlers and the sensation they caused that inaugurated the modern era of so-called spin bowling.

R. E. Foster had been elected captain of England very soon after Christmas, 1906. It was not expected that I should be available, owing to my accident the previous May. Playing at Lord's against Middlesex on a hard wicket I made a stroke to long leg, and when I started to run there was a crack like a pistol, and I could only stagger half-way towards the other wicket. After carefully running me out, the Middlesex team collected me and carried me to the pavilion, Pelham Warner walking in the rear like a mourner, bearing my boot rather as if it were infectious. A consultation of distinguished surgeons in the Long Room, including Sir Alfred Fripp, decided that I had ruptured my Achilles tendon. So I motored home, looked up Achilles tendon in the Encyclopædia Britannica, and decided to have my leg put into plaster of Paris. The tendon joined and healed up in a period quite contrary to the rules. A doctor friend of mine said that he would never have thought that anyone but a convict would have mended so quickly. I was walking about by the end of July. Then I had a boot made with an iron upright and a strap round my knee, and I went hunting in November. The next spring I went to consult a specialist in London as to my prospects. He told me that I had had a great career, but must never again go in for anything athletic. I paid him three guineas. I consulted another specialist. He said the same thing. I paid him three guineas. I consulted a third. He said that if he were I he would forget about the accident and go on as if nothing had ever happened. I paid him three guineas. So I started cricket in May with a score of 80 against Yorkshire on a wet wicket, and developed an off drive of a kind I had never before professed, due to the iron stanchion supporting my left leg. As I went on making runs, I was asked to play for England. After a month I took off the iron stanchion, and I have never felt the injury again.

Contrary to expectations, the batting of England in the first Test Match at Lord's was a success. We scored 428, of which Braund made 104 and Gilbert Jessop 93. We had a good batting side, with Tom Hayward, John Tyldesley, R. E. Foster, George Hirst, and Jessop, not to mention J. N. Crawford, Arnold, and Lilley. In this match we all made runs except Foster, Hirst, and Arnold. Vogler bowled finely, taking 7 wickets for 128. Then Arnold ran through the South Africans for a total of 140, of which David Nourse and Aubrey Faulkner made 106 between them and no one else double figures. Arnold's 5 wickets for 37 on a good wicket against such strong batting was worthy of his class. But the South Africans drew the match in brave style, chiefly owing to a memorable century by their wicket-keeper, P. W. Sherwell.

The second Test Match at Leeds is historic as a nightmare needle match. The wicket at Headingley was the most difficult sticky wicket ever played on in a Test in England. Genuine glue. We won the toss and were promptly bowled out for a total of 76 by Faulkner, Sinclair and Vogler. Faulkner took 6 wickets for 17 runs. Tom Hayward made 24, George Hirst 17, John Tyldesley 12; nobody else double figures. We then accounted for the South African batsmen for a total of 110.

Colin Blythe with his slow medium left-hand artistry got 8 wickets for 59 runs. At this stage there remained three-quarters of an hour's play that day in a poor light. R. E. Foster wanted to put in some of the lesser batsmen, but I persuaded him to let me go in with Tom Hayward. I always believed in doing the bold thing and standing by the regular batting order. As usual, this came off; Tom and I played out time. When we returned undefeated to the pavilion, R. E. Foster was one of the happiest captains I have met in a Test Match. Next day I knocked up 54 runs, and I choose to flatter myself that this was a good innings. Tyldesley made 30 and Foster 22, so we finished off with a score of 162. In the fourth innings Colin Blythe figured as unplayable. He took 7 wickets for 40 runs. So we won by 53 runs. The strain of the match was severe, especially on Colin Blythe, who was completely knocked up. From start to finish he never bowled a single ball except of impeccable length. The situation was that three bad overs could have lost the match. This was the tautest cricket match in which I ever played.

The third match at the Oval was played on a most uncomfortable wicket; nearly as bad in the earlier stages as that at Leeds. I look back on the match with fine self-appreciation, because I scored 129 without a chance against very difficult bowling on a foul wicket. Tell it not in Gath, but this was the best innings I ever played in my life. R. E. Foster scored 52 runs with more discomfort than this fine batsman usually displayed. Our total ran to 295. It might easily have been a bare 100. The wicket rolled out better, and South Africa scored 178. This time Colin Blythe took 5 wickets for 61 runs. S. J. Snooke, who in 1934 was manager of the South African team in England, played very well indeed for 63. David Nourse and Sinclair also played well for thirty-odd apiece. Our second innings realised only 138. Vogler did the damage, getting wickets not only for himself, but for Schwarz and Nourse. In the fourth innings South Africa saved the game by good all-round batting. They finished off only 138 behind, with 5 wickets in hand on an improving wicket. We all of us on the England side thought very well of the cricket displayed by South Africa in this match. It was good enough to stamp them as a powerful team. In a way it was a pity they did not bring off a win, as it would have put South Africa on the map of cricket where South Africa belonged.

Again in 1912 the South African team did not succeed in Test Matches against England in showing their true value. The England team was specially strong in possessing sound batsmen right down to number ten, and a set of dangerous wet-wicket bowlers. The appalling weather of this season played entirely into our hands against cricketers who came from a sunshine country and their own quick matting wickets. We won all three Test Matches against them.

At Lord's on a mud wicket Frank Foster and Barnes were too much for their batsmen. We won by an innings and 62. In the first innings Foster got 5 wickets for 16 runs and Barnes 5 for 25 in a total score of 58. Only David Nourse made double figures. He was a solid yet powerful left-hand bat after the type of Philip Mead, of Hampshire. Our first innings score was 337. Reggie Spooner played one of his classic innings of 119, and Frank Woolley was in his best vein for 73. The South Africans did better in their next innings, because C. B. Llewellyn, who had come from Natal into the Hampshire county team, whipped Foster and Barnes at their best all over the field for a remarkable effort of 75. Llewellyn was a left-handed wristy hitter who scored very quickly. He was qualified by Hampshire as a medium-pace left-hand bowler, and, strangely enough, had been selected as a reserve bowler for England against Australia. A very talented cricketer. This time Barnes took 6 wickets for 85 and Foster 3 for 54. Llewellyn certainly gave us all a lesson in how to play Sidney Barnes on a wet wicket.

The South African team was, on paper, as good as in 1907. Their one loss was Vogler, but in his place they had a new bowler of exceptional quality in S. J. Pegler. He was a peculiar leg-break bowler. He did not toss the ball in the air, but as to pace looked like a regulation medium-pace off-break bowler. In this match he took 7 wickets for 65 runs. When we had the situation in hand in this match I tried to produce Jack Hobbs as a fast bowler. My experiment did not win the approval of the critics. Jack Hobbs was a batsman, therefore he could not possibly be a bowler. All the same, but for his innate modesty, I would have made one of him.

We won the second match at Leeds by 174 runs. For us Jack Hobbs, Reggie Spooner, young J. W. Hearne, and Frank Woolley all did well in batting; especially Reggie Spooner, who was in his best form and made a first-rate job of dealing with the troublesome South African leg-break bowling. He is one of the very few first-rate batsmen whom I have seen able to play the classical forward stroke successfully at leg breaks. But his forward stroke was not a thrust; it was a circular swing with his wrists as a centre; moreover, he kept his eye on the ball right up to the instant of impact. My belief is that if he had been able to go to Australia he would have proved one of the biggest scorers in the annals of Test Match cricket. In this second match Sidney Barnes again dominated the opposing batsmen. His craftsmanship and control were a delight.

In the third Test Match at the Oval we enjoyed a foul wicket. Sidney Barnes enjoyed what he described as " a veritable beano." Barnes rarely said anything, and he was not by nature an enthusiast, so the phrase has weight. We got the South Africans out for totals of 95 and 93. None of their batsmen except H. W. Taylor, S. J. Snooke, and the impermeable David Nourse could do much. The wicket did not suit Frank Foster. Barnes and Frank Woolley took 5 wickets each in the first innings, and Barnes 8 for 29 in the second. We won easily by 10 wickets, but we owed our runs chiefly to Jack Hobbs, whose skill in dealing with difficult bowling by Pegler and Faulkner was a lesson in technique. No one else except Spooner and young Hearne made runs.

So England won the Triangular Tournament. We were a very fine side and the bad wet wickets played into our hands.

This was the only season in which I saw much of the batsmanship of Jack Hobbs. His grand career was spread over the years rather after my time. When one remembers the War cut out four of the seasons of his prime, his record in big cricket is the more admirable. But there have been other great run-getters who did not rival Jack Hobbs in polish and finish and mastery. He sailed along through sunshine and

storm on a perfectly even keel with an alert pair of aristocratic hands on the helm of the game. His quiet gentility
disguises a thoroughly resolute and pugnacious subsoil of
temperament. Jack Hobbs is an able fellow who can make a
first-rate speech, and he has drooping eyelashes which would
be invaluable in Hollywood. He deserves his iron gates.

There was no more big cricket till the winter of 1920-1, when
Johnny Douglas captained an England tour in Australia and
lost all five Test Matches. This was the era of the two great
Australian fast bowlers J. M. Gregory and E. A. Macdonald.
Their batting was powerful, with Macartney, Armstrong,
Collins, Bardsley, J. M. Taylor, Kelleway, and Pellew.

In 1921 Warwick Armstrong brought his strong side to
England and won three matches for Australia, with two
drawn. Our cricket was in an inchoate state. Johnny Douglas
was a fine all-round cricketer, but in his captaincy no idea ever
emerged. Being then in my fiftieth year, I was astonished on
April 25th, which happened to be my birthday, to get a letter
from H. K. Foster, asking me what sort of form I was in and
whether I was inclined to take on the captaincy of England.
I wrote back telling him I could play bad bowling very well,
but could not see much fun in taking on Gregory and Macdonald so early in the season. However, the Selection Committee—Foster, Spooner, and John Daniell—wanted me to
play in the first Test Match at Nottingham under the captaincy of Johnny Douglas, with a view to taking over the
captaincy for the remainder of the matches if, as they anticipated, things went wrong. I replied that there was sense in
resuscitating me if they were bunkered for a captain, but no
sense in producing a man of fifty to lion-tame two of the finest
fast bowlers ever known in Test Match cricket. So it was
agreed that if things went wrong at Nottingham we should
reconsider the situation for Lord's.

At Nottingham things went wrong, about as wrong as they
could go, so I agreed to play at Lord's under Douglas's captaincy provided I made runs against fast bowling in the
interval. I was duly selected for the England eleven at Lord's,
but I did not meanwhile get runs against fast bowling and
did not fancy taking on the Australian fast bowlers on a fast

wicket. Had there been likelihood of a wet wicket, I would have played.

I was playing for Hampshire just before the Lord's Test Match, and I had a brain-wave. I went up to London by an evening train and saw the selectors. I said to them that their difficulty was to find a batsman likely to knock off Gregory and Macdonald, who appeared to be on top of our batsmen. "Take my advice," I said, "and play Lionel Tennyson. He is much more than a mere hitter. If he likes he can play proper cricket. He has a fine knack of hitting fast bowling. If you play him he may bat like a cow till he has made 15, fire a couple over slips' head, edge a couple between his legs and the wicket; but if he survives he will proceed to make 75 and you will have another Jessop." They took my advice. Lionel Tennyson was played at Lord's. He did precisely what I had prophesied. He scored 74 not out. But we lost again.

The next move was that I should take on the captaincy at Leeds. To this I consented, having seen the English batsmen at Lord's and perceiving that I could not be less valuable than some of them against fast bowling. I consented because Hampshire were playing the Australians in the next few days and I could try myself out. I made 59 and 37, and none of their bowlers bothered me except Arthur Mailey, who, being one of the greatest of all leg-break bowlers, bothered other people as well. It happened that in this match Bardsley scored one of his left-handed double centuries. Just as he was on the edge of his second century it occurred to me that when he had registered it he would have a go. I guessed, too, that as he was not a straight driver he would have a go with his favourite square cut. So I crept in from deep square cover to backward point rather near in as that was where a mis-hit would go. Sure enough he did exactly what I had anticipated, and offered me a dolly sliced catch which I caught; but I caught it on the tip of my crooked little finger. With a damaged hand I did not care to take the field in a Test Match, so I had to cry off the Leeds match.

Thus it was that the selectors made Lionel Tennyson captain, and he split his hand in the Australian first innings at Leeds and was more severely incapacitated than I should have been. All the same he scored 63 and 36. Lionel Tennyson did not succeed in beating the Australians, who won all three Test Matches which were finished, but he proved an excellent captain. Had he chosen to devote himself to mastering the formal technique of batting instead of amusing himself with hitting a long ball at least once an over he would have been a great batsman. He had a fine eye and a fine natural talent. Whenever he went in early on the list with me for Hampshire his back play was excellent. When he went in later he abandoned science and carted straight good-length balls over the square leg boundary.

So my connection with big cricket ended on a merry if vicarious note.

Much has happened in the world of cricket since then. Don Bradman has arrived, of whom everything that it is possible to say has been said, and much of it is self-contradictory. They tell me that it is because Don Bradman has revolutionised batting that nobody now drives to the boundary in any direction between cover point and forward short leg, and not often in the latter direction, else forward short leg would not be there. With this I cannot agree, because I have often seen Don Bradman drive a very long ball over the bowler's head when the bowler brought himself to pitch the ball far enough up for this stroke.

The truth is that the prevalence of swerve, leg-break and googly bowling has substituted the numerical success of Herbert Sutcliffe and Ponsford for the poetry of Palairet and the magnificence of MacLaren. Herbert Sutcliffe is undoubtedly one of the most accomplished batsmen of all time, but modern bowling has not allowed him to make his runs in the way that runs were made by the Lytteltons, A. G. Steel, and William Gunn. Had he not accommodated his methods to the modern form of attack so artfully he would not have defeated it so signally.

There is much discussion as to whether the protagonists of modern cricket are or are not as good as their forefathers. Such disputes are fruitless because one cannot equate the conditions. When I see Walter Hammond playing an innings I am afraid I doubt whether any of the batsmen of my day could play better, and I am not at all sure that even Trumper had a greater charm; and when it comes to pure mastery of technique I incline to give the palm to Hammond.

As for the comparative merits of English and Australian cricket to-day, I do not think any of the young Australian batsmen are as good as Hutton and Compton. But we shall know more about our batsmen when O'Reilly retires to a headmastership, and much more about our bowlers when Don Bradman devotes himself exclusively to the Stock Exchange.

There is a quantity of remarkably good young batsmen in first-class cricket. I dare say, too, that young bowlers will appear if and when the wickets give them a chance. But why it is that fast bowling has died out and slow left-hand bowling has become so scarce, is a mystery.

One thing that strikes me is that all but a handful of the best batsmen of the 'nineties would have had to go through an apprenticeship before they could tackle successfully the best of the swerve and leg-break bowlers we see to-day, and all but a handful of the modern batsmen would have to alter their game materially to cope with the genuinely fast bowlers and the impeccably accurate slow and medium-pace bowlers of the 'nineties.

I have a notion that the cricket of the 'nineties and early nineteen hundreds was more amusing to watch, but I am not at all sure that the game of to-day is not more difficult to play. The fast bowling, however, were it here, would make a difference. If you look at the score sheets of big matches of the older period you will see that quite often your Tom Richardson or your Lockwood accounted for two or three of the half-dozen picked batsmen very early in their innings. The modern batsman has only himself to blame if he does not play himself in; the modern bowler gives him time to do so. The old-fashioned fast bowler often had you out before you had time to orient yourself.

Cricket remains a great game; and, in the absence of crises, perhaps the greatest common interest of the Empire.

CHAPTER XIII

CORINTHIAN AND SAINT

WHEN I made contact with first-class football the Association world was in a turmoil. Payment of players was at the time entirely illegal, but everybody knew that in the Midlands and North there was any amount of professionalism and surreptitious persuasion.

The situation was paradoxical. In London and the South the game was genuinely amateur, and, as may be seen from the composition of the International teams, the playing strength of the clubs was decidedly greater; but here the authorities were in favour of pulling the ostrich's head out of the sand and legalising professionalism. The Midlands and the North, where the sand was provided, were altogether against it. The issue was finally decided by campaigns in the Press and a growth of what is called public opinion, which really means public sentiment. The root of the difference was that football in the Midlands and North was played by wage-earners, whereas in the South most of the strong clubs were composed of relatively leisured men.

The special case that pushed the ".antis" over the edge was when the famous Preston North End Club was summoned to the cross-bar of justice. Their patron and manager, Mr. Sudell, presented himself to the court and opened his defence by genially stating that his club certainly did pay their players, and what about it? Nowadays, when there are so many professional clubs which so entirely monopolise public attention, and when football stars are bought and sold at sidereal figures, all this sounds very long ago.

Having afterwards in my time played for what was then one of the strongest professional clubs, Southampton, for several seasons, including two when the club headed the list of the Southern League and one when we got through to the final of the Cup-ties, and having immensely enjoyed all the strenuous League and Cup-tie football along with a band of fine players and fine fellows, I am about the last highbrow amateur to be prejudiced against professional football. What is more, for the Corinthians and Casuals I played against most of the best professional clubs of the day from 1888 to 1902, and enjoyed magnificent games. All the same, I must say that in the early days of professionalism one knocked up against a lot of foul play in the Midlands and North, especially minor foul play on the part of the minor football teams. This big difference of attitude was not due to professionalism: it was due to the way everybody all round up there looked at things. The proof is that the modern professional teams, most of them, so far as I have seen, have an altogether different mind. But then they come from a far more cultivated class. When the Arsenal players stay at the Grand Hotel at Brighton you would not distinguish between them and the generality of other leisured young men. It must be remembered, too, that the early professionals were very near the days when the Old Etonians and Old Carthusians were Cup winners, and played a game which we should now call very foul. All sorts of roughnesses were allowed, such as hacking and tripping. The Old Etonian Lord Kinnaird reckoned the finest player of his day was famed for his ruthlessness. One day Sir Francis Marindin, at one time President of the F.A., called upon his mother, who expressed her fear that Arthur would some day come home with a broken leg. "Never mind," he consoled her, "it will not be his own."

C. W. Alcock, for many years Secretary of the Surrey Cricket Club, captain of the Old Harrovians, in a pause in a game, while rubbing his shins, pointedly asked Lord Kinnaird, "Are we going to play the game, or are we going to have hacking?"

"Oh, let us have hacking," was the bland reply. And they did.

The cheerful ruthlessness of football as played by Lord Kinnaird and Charlie Alcock and their contemporaries was soon legislated out of the game when professionalism swept over the world of Association Football. Accidents and injuries became too expensive.

A feature which escapes appreciation is that the earlier heyday of professional football, between, say, the middle 'eighties and the middle 'nineties, produced a standard of play in the leading teams of the Midlands and North at least equal to that of the best modern professional clubs. I am quite sure that the old triumphant Preston North End team, together with Aston Villa, Everton, Sunderland, and suchlike, would at the very least have played the best modern professional teams level, and my own feeling is that the best team of that day would beat the best team of this. It is true that modern tactics produce an apparently faster game, but there is not the same precision and control of the ball. In particular, modern half-back play is not as good as in the great professional teams of the early days.

Even more interesting is it that though the first powerful era of the professional class produced a standard of play certainly equal to that of to-day, nevertheless the best amateur team then could show a standard of football equal, if not superior, to that of the professionals, whereas nowadays the professionals have quite obliterated the amateurs. I very much doubt—though, of course, one can never substantiate these comparisons—I very much doubt whether in the history of Association football from the beginning right up to the present any stronger teams have taken the field than those of the great Corinthian club round about the middle 'eighties.

The Corinthian F.C. was brought into being by the cleverest man who ever appeared in connexion with the promotion of football. This was the famous N. L. Jackson, universally known as " Pa." He had been a protagonist of the historic struggles between professionalism and amateurism. When professionalism won the day and began its swamping growth, he saw that, if the amateurs were to hold their own, at least one club of selected players must be formed. Why not build up a club of picked players from all the Old Boys' teams? This could be done if the select club did not go in for the Cup, and so left the Old Boys' teams undiminished for the competition which was the main interest in the football world of the day.

" Pa " Jackson was admirable. When in my fourth year at Oxford I was sustaining the rôle of the Prince of Morocco for the O.U.D.S. in the "Merchant of Venice," "Pa" wired to me to play for the Corinthians on Saturday in the position of outside right. I like to think I would have been a good outside right had I ever played there; but as it happened I had never played anywhere in first-class football but full-back. Anyway, we had a matinée on Saturday, and I wired inability. "Pa" wired back: "Please manage to play stop sake of amateur football stop you will probably get your international cap against Scotland at outside right if you play stop Jackson." "Pa," I may say, was on the Selection Committee, so he was not telegraphing through his hat. It was a temptation and, come to that, "Pa" Jackson was not unlike a mild Mephistopheles in appearance. But I could not disentangle myself from the matinée.

The Corinthians went through several successive phases of power. Its first prime was from 1884 to 1887. The forward line I have never seen equalled, and the brothers A. M. and P. M. Walters at full-back, with W. R. Moon in goal, formed the best defence England has ever had against Scotland.

The main forwards were W. M. Cobbold, E. C. Bambridge, Tinsley Lindley, and George Brann. Cobbold, an Old Carthusian, was a positive genius. A spare body on tremendously powerful hips and legs, he was a magician as a dribbler. He had a shuffling run and seemed to wriggle through his opponents, and he had a knack of shooting unexpectedly from impossible angles. His partner on the left wing, E. C. Bambridge, had a fairy left foot for centring the ball, was always spotless, and was known in the North as "The Dude." Once, after he had broken his leg and was not expected to play in a big match, he turned up, and he turned out wearing a big shin-guard. The Corinthians never wore shin-guards, and this, apart from other characters, always made their white-shirted, blue-knickered teams appear to advantage against the armoured bare-legged professionals. Everybody expected Bam to get crocked. But he survived the game and scored the winning goal. He had worn his shin-guard on the sound leg.

This left wing played repeatedly for England against Scotland, together with their centre-forward and colleague, Tinsley

Lindley, now His Honour Judge Lindley, of Nottingham, reckoned to be as fine a centre-forward as ever played. Lindley was slightly built and skilfully elusive. Half-backs seemed to be chasing a shadow. He had a pair of conjuring feet and a trick of timing a shot at goal from a crossing ball, after the manner of Ranji's glance to leg. George Brann, the inside right, was afterwards one of the best batsmen in the Sussex cricket eleven in the time of Ranji and myself. He also played creditably in the Golf Amateur Championship and took a successful team to South Africa when he was over seventy. He was one of the finest forwards who ever played for England against Scotland. In the famous England v. Scotland match of 1886, with Cobbold, Bambridge and Lindley on the same side, the Scottish critics picked him out as the best forward on the field. This England team is said to have been the best that has ever played against Scotland.

The brothers Walters as a pair of backs I never saw equalled. There have been as good players individually, but together they have never been surpassed. Each weighed about 13 stone, all muscle and bone. They were fast and were very accurate in kicking, and very good with their heads. Their defence was daring. They played close up to their half-backs, trusting to their own pace to overhaul any fast forward who might break through. They tackled their man like charging bulls. When they got the ball, unless their goal was in danger, they did not boot it down the field, but pushed it through along the ground or quite low to one of their forwards.

Round about the time of these players the Blackburn Rovers were at the zenith of their Cup-winning career, but the Corinthians beat them 8—1 at Blackburn in the season of 1884-5, and again 6—o in the season 1885-6. The England eleven of 1886 v. Scotland, already mentioned as probably the best England has ever produced, contained nine Corinthians.

In the second prime of the Corinthians their great defence of Moon and the two Walters at first remained; so, too, for the most part, did Brann and Lindley. But a new great line of forwards came into being, among them J. V. Veitch, of the Old Westminsters, G. H. Cotterill, of Brighton College, both of Cambridge, both six-footers of splendid physique. The physique of the line as they came on the field was heroic. Norman Bailey, the great half-back of the previous period, was gone; he was replaced by C. Wreford Brown, the Old Carthusian. The Corinthians of this phase beat the all-conquering Preston North End team by 5—o in a match at Richmond. North End was at its zenith, and its team is still regarded by many as since unequalled by any professional club.

C. Wreford Brown, apart from being, perhaps, the best centre-half of his day, presents a difficulty as to what day was his day. He was playing for England against Scotland at centre-half before I began first-class football, and he was still going strong in good-class football years after I stopped. I saw him playing an excellent game against a strong school team when he was well over fifty. I believe he was playing at the age of 59.

Another half-back of this period was A. G. Henfrey, who started as a forward. His nickname was "Cocky," and he was a wit. On tour with the Corinthians in 1891, I saw Henfrey win a bet off a Scotsman. He had sat down to take off his boots on a locker in the changing-room. The locker-lid was off its hinges. He wagered the Scot that he would sit down dressed as he was on the small red-hot stove in the corner. The Scot took him. Cocky Henfrey rose, with the lid of the locker hidden behind him under his coat-tails. He sidled up to the red-hot stove and sat down on it just long enough for a cloud of blue smoke to rise. The Scot remarked, "Verra guid," and paid up.

Along with the giants Veitch and Cotterill entered another magnificent forward, R. C. Gosling, of the Old Etonians, very fast, skilful, and unselfish. Otherwise he was an M.F.H. with a princely income, and played in perfectly valeted brown boots which must have cost him a fiver. He aided the Corinthians in their reputation up North as a team of toffs. We were suspected of being Guards officers and young squires. Certainly we were a presentable lot, and I am not sure I would not rate R. C. Gosling as the best-looking man of my acquaintance. In the blond Viking style, George Cotterill might be a rival. John Veitch was an ivory-faced hero with a black moustache. The brothers Walters were both exceptionally fine-looking fellows of the Nordic type.

The great event, or series of events, of a Corinthian season was the Christmas tour in the north of England and the south of Scotland. Sometimes two teams took the field on the same day, and there were matches every other day for a fortnight. The game of games was on New Year's Day at Hampden Park, Glasgow, against the crack Scottish amateur club, Queen's Park. There has never been finer football played for the sport of the game than between the Corinthians and Queen's Park in the New Year matches. The Scottish supporters took a keen interest, not only in the game, but also in the personalities of the Corinthian side.

The first time I played at Hampden Park was just after I had done my then world's record of 23 feet $6\frac{1}{2}$ inches in the long jump. That day my partner at back was F. R. Pelly, a great player and a great man weighing in the neighbourhood of 18 stone, and very active at that. As we walked on to the field a solemn-looking Scot with a bristly moustache said, "Yon's the laddie who jumped twenty-three feet."

"Hech! A bonny height!" was the reply. "And he must ha' made a hole when he came doon." He had supposed that if anybody was to jump 23 feet high it must be the giant.

We had tremendous fun on these Corinthian tours, but it was often stiff going. On one journey our train broke down on the field of Bannockburn; that is to say, one engine could not pull it through the snow. So our engine went off to get another. When we got to Stirling the locals had thawed the iron ground with salt. This created a lake of mud, to the depth of six inches, with an iron bottom. When the two teams lined up they looked like twenty-two men on wooden legs; not a boot was visible.

The giant forwards, Veitch, Cotterill, and Gosling, overlapped into the third great Corinthian phase, but this became the era of that marvellous centre-forward, G. O. Smith, the most famous perhaps of all Corinthian forwards.

There is dispute whether he was a better centre-forward than Tinsley Lindley, but he was certainly the best of his day, and a long day at that. The secret of his consummate skill, his adroitness in trapping and controlling the ball, his mastery in dribbling, his precision in passing, and his deftness in shooting was an altogether uncommon faculty of balance and poise, coupled with an altogether uncommon neatness of foot. It was by his poise that, without being a sprinter, he moved so quickly.

A little later on appeared another typically Corinthian forward in R. E. Foster, who captained the England cricket eleven in 1907. He would have been an ornament alongside Bambridge and Cobbold. " Tip " Foster was tall and long-limbed and quick without being fast. He had fine dexterity of foot, and controlled the ball, caressed and persuaded it with an almost manual cunning. His feet had, as it were, the Oxford accent.

Of the wing forwards during my Corinthian days, perhaps R. R. Sandilands on the left, and R. Topham, who also played for Wolverhampton Wanderers, were the most prominent.

My usual partner at full-back was W. J. Oakley, who repeatedly played for England against Scotland. Oakley was an eminent all-round performer. He won the inter-Varsity hurdles on wet grass over real obstacles in 16⅓ seconds, and as my second string in the long jump he did well over 22 feet. He was a good oar in the Christ Church boat at Oxford, and was not far off his Blue for rowing.

All this time C. Wreford Brown was pursuing his ubiquitous career as a centre half-back.

Just at the end of my Corinthian days two exceptionally fine forwards came into the line. One was Stanley Harris, much admired by the selectors of England teams; the other the Cambridge and Kent cricketer, S. H. Day, who, though he did not play cricket for England, was up to England form as a batsman.

The equivalent, when I was actually playing, of the great games in earlier times between the Corinthians and Preston North End, one team the flower of the professionals, the other of the amateurs, were the matches played for the Sheriff of London's Shield. This was first of all called the Dewar Shield. In 1898 " Pa " Jackson persuaded Sir Thomas Dewar that Sir

Thomas's idea of a trophy to be played for by the best professional and the best amateur side of the year for charity
was first-rate, and how very clever of Sir Thomas to think
of it.

Sir Thomas (afterwards Lord) Dewar once said to me,
" C. B., you get more advertisement gratis per annum than
I could buy for £10,000."

I wanted to know why.

"This way," he replied. "You are in the newspapers all the
year round, and on the posters all the summer. If you make
a century, it's 'Another Century by Fry' all over London; if
you don't, it's just as good—'Fry Fails.'"

This perhaps has nothing to do with the Sheriff's Shield.
Advertisement or no, the result was a series of fine football
matches. I do not think that the best professional teams of
the time were as good as the old Preston North End, nor that
the Corinthians were equal to the Corinthians of the early
prime of the club. The increase in the number of professional
clubs had tended to distribute talent, and the Corinthians,
good as they were, did not exhibit the same exceptional
standard of physique. Nevertheless, the Shield matches
probably staged the finest football of the season outside the
internationals.

In the first match we played Sheffield United, then as ever
at the top of the tree in cup-tie football. Despite the rain, the
match drew a huge gate to the expansive Crystal Palace
ground, which was to other football grounds as garden cities
are to other cities. The end of a great game was a pointless
draw.

Sheffield agreed to a replay, and we met again a fortnight
later. We were stronger, because the international R. Topham
came in at outside right. The result was another draw, this
time one goal each, but the Corinthians had the better of the
game. We wanted to play extra time. The Sheffield players
were willing, but their directors were not. So the honour of
the Shield was bisected.

The next year our great rivals, Queen's Park, Glasgow, were
preferred to the Corinthians to represent the amateur clubs.
Aston Villa represented the professionals. Again the match

was a draw, with no goals, in spite of an extra half-hour's play.

The third year the Corinthians played Aston Villa at the Crystal Palace. We had more than half of the same team playing, but at last Wreford Brown was absent. We had R. E. Foster along with G. O. Smith in the forward line. The Villa team was full of Internationals, and we had half a dozen, but the Villa was short of the player whom I couple with W. J. A. Davies, the Rugby International of the nineteen twenties, as the greatest natural genius at football I ever saw—namely, Crabtree. He could play in any position at half-back, and generally played centre- or left-half for the Villa, but he was chosen for England against Scotland at full-back. The ground was a quagmire, but the game was played at a racing pace. We won a brilliant match by 2 goals to 1. Since the time of the brothers Walters, I doubt whether the Corinthian defence has ever put up a stronger game. If Oakley and I had not been able to sprint as fast as the Villa wingers, we should have been done in. Athersmith, the Villa outside right, is considered by many to have been the fastest wing forward the game has ever known.

The next year we again opposed our old friends Aston Villa at the Crystal Palace. Again the ground was sodden; and there were pools of water in places. Once more it was a heroic game, but this time the Villa beat us by 1—0. Right at the end of the game Athersmith for once outpaced Oakley and went through with his long raking stride to score the only goal of the match. The match would have been drawn but for Oakley being tricked by John Devey, who drew him while Athersmith, the outside right, switched across to the centre. Please note that the dodge of "switching," which the modern professional teams have discovered, was not unknown to the Villa team of 1901.

In the fifth year of the Shield the winners of the previous year, Aston Villa, rather surprisingly were not chosen. Lord Dewar's Charity Committee gave the preference to Tottenham Hotspur, who had won the English Cup. Another innovation was that the match was played not at the Crystal Palace but on the Tottenham ground. The result was a huge gate and

defeat for the Corinthians. We were short of Oakley as well
as G. O. Smith. Their absence made a hole as big as Old Bill's
in our defence as well as in our attack. We were short, too,
of M. Morgan-Owen, our Welsh international half-back, who
was an assistant master at my old school, Repton. The 'Spurs
had their complete Cup-tie eleven of the previous season.
Throughout the first half it was an even game, but we scored
twice from good shots by H. Morgan-Owen. In the second
half, however, we were outplayed, chiefly because our half-
backs cracked, and were beaten by 5—2.

The fine games played by the Corinthians against the best
professionals of the year were remarkable because the Corinthians had practically no training except in Saturday matches,
while the professionals were in training all the week and all
the season. It is quite worth noting that in these great and
gruelling matches the stamina of the untrained amateurs held
out everywhere except in the half-back line. When the Corinthians lost, it was generally because the half-backs could not
quite go the distance.

Before bidding farewell to the glories of Corinthian football
—a long farewell, because the club has now lapsed into an
amalgamation—it is well to recall an unparalleled achievement of the club: their feat against the Barbarians, their
counterpart in the Rugby world. In 1892 we challenged the
select champions of the other code to a tournament—Association, track athletes, cricket, and Rugby. I was a Barbarian as
well as a Corinthian, but I played for the latter. We won
the Association game easily by 6 goals to 1. The Barbarian
methods were robust, collectively aggressive, and not half bad,
but were rather misapplied in sending the ball into touch.
We won the athletics by one event. The cricket match was
played some time afterwards, and was won by the Barbarians,
but I could not play in the game and do not remember the
scores. It was the only one of the contests the Barbarians
won.

Marvellous to relate, the Corinthians beat the Barbarians
at their own game.

We, the Corinthians, won this historic match by 2 goals
and 2 tries to 2 goals and 1 try, a result which a newspaper

described in original terms as "certainly a surprise to everyone." That is to say, at the time, the match created much more than a mild sensation. The Rugby world was inclined to regard the whole thing as a freak and a lark. I can assure you it was a very proper and first-rate rugger match. The explanation of the result is this. The game was played at Queen's Club on turf which, without being hard enough to be unfit for rugger, may be described as in summer condition.

Rugby players have no conception what can be done with the feet by a dribbler of the class of Tinsley Lindley. He manipulated the oval with the same control and certainty as he did the globe. This match was won because the defence and running of our back division was nearly as good as that of the Barbarians, and because our forwards outclassed their opponents with the ball on the turf in the open. On the usual heavy turf familiar to the Rugby game, no doubt we should have been beaten. But I am not too sure. Nor must you rate me as prejudiced. I had played for the Barbarians as well as for Oxford and for Blackheath; and, what is more, I offer my judgment that of the two, Rugby is the better game.

The first Lord Birkenhead, when he wrote anything autobiographical (a great strain on one so loath to unbushel his light), always honoured me by introducing me as entirely his pupil at the Rugby game. This is partly true, because he had more to say than anybody else in the Wadham College Rugby fifteen, where I learned the game. He had much more to say in encouragement and disparagement of the rest of us than anyone else in the team, both when he was our captain and when he was not. But so far as first-class Rugby was concerned, my education was a full season in the Oxford University fifteen—bar the last match, which unfortunately for me was against Cambridge, so though I earned my Blue for Rugby, I did not get it. In the last match but one, against, I think, the Harlequins, I strained the big muscle of my thigh. The Oxford fifteen was very strong, captained by the international forward W. J. Carey, afterwards immortalised under the soubriquet of "The Bull" in Alec Waugh's "Loom of Youth." Our full-back played for Scotland, and also one of our half-backs. The other played for England. Our left-wing three-quarter played for Wales, our two centre three-quarters, Leslie Jones and E. M. Baker, for England, and I was unofficially told, though never able to verify this, that I was chosen first reserve for the South against the North at right-wing three-quarter.

The Rugby fifteen at Oxford the year I played and the year before was among the first in England to adopt the new Welsh four three-quarter formation properly in the Welsh style.

The year before I played in the Oxford fifteen the captain was a Welsh international, Conway-Rees, and an accomplished centre three-quarter. He induced his pack of forwards to play the Welsh game, and his colleagues behind the scrum to adopt the Welsh method. So the fifteen in which I played inherited the complete Welsh dogma. Being a wing three-quarter and a hundred yards sprinter, with a knack, derived from much practice in the cricket field, of accepting easy catches, I had the time of my life.

After I came down from the University I played for Blackheath. The club was the strongest in London, with an outstanding pack of forwards. The captain was a forward, and Blackheath played the old forward game very successfully. The forwards used to score most of the tries.

On tour with the Barbarians, a grand collection of internationals, we had some splendid games, especially down in Wales against Newport and Cardiff. That I ever quite learnt the knack of falling on the ball in a maze of speedy Welsh boots I would not say. But one did learn a thing or two about how to do it facing the spritely Cardiff and Newport packs in a quagmire.

As the number of extravagants who have played in first-class company in both the Rugby and Association game is minute, and as I was one who wandered over the border-line, it may be of interest to offer one or two relative remarks. I am quite sure that anyone capable of reaching a good standard in the one game could do so in the other. It is simply a matter of opportunity and industry. The qualities required in either game are the same. It does not follow that a man is not likely to be better in the one game or in the other; but if he is any good in the one he certainly could be some good in the other.

Having been bred and educated in the Association game, I would like to be allowed to pay a very generous tribute to the grandeur of the Rugby game. In my heart I wish I had learnt to play Rugby at school. I should have been a better man at that game than at Association. Lord Birkenhead once said to me, " A fellow as contentious as you are, who runs as fast, with his knees as high, could not have failed to get his cap." He also told me, when I first played for Wadham College, that I tackled like a schoolgirl fainting.

Another tribute I would like to pay is to the virtues of professional football from the point of view of sport. When I played for Southampton it was commonly thought that a blue-blooded Corinthian must feel *déclassé* on a professional side. Nothing of the kind. True, my home was within four miles of Southampton, so I was a genuine local and not a mere importation; but at the time I was one of the very few amateurs who had played for a first-class professional side.

For several seasons I played with Southampton right through the Southern League fixture list, and I have nothing but happy memories of that exacting football. We had a fine side captained by the old Wolves international, Harry Wood. One year our goalkeeper, Jack Robinson, my colleague at left back, Mollineux, and myself were chosen *en bloc* to represent England.

A commonplace of Association football in newspapers is that there is some sort of basic difference between League matches and Cup-ties. After a fair dose of both I cannot recall any difference between a major League match and a Cup-tie. That is to say, if you are playing. But no doubt if you are spectating you excite yourself much more for a Cup-tie.

The best dose of Cup-tie football I enjoyed was in 1902, playing for Southampton, when we played eight matches in five rounds, to lose the final, after a replay, by a single goal.

In the first round we were drawn against Tottenham Hotspur, the Cup-holders of the year before. The Spurs were a fine team, with three exceptionally accomplished half-backs.

We met them on a bright afternoon on their own ground, and we finished off a hard, even game all square one-all. The end of a ding-dong return match was another draw, this time two goals all. An extra half-hour was played, but neither side could score.

By this time both the Spurs and the Saints, as we were called, had become two hard-bitten, thoroughly well-knit teams who knew every move in each other's repertoire, man for man. The third game of the series was played at Reading. The countryside was deep in snow. The nearer to Reading in the train, the deeper it seemed to be. But the neat little ground had been swept and garnished. It was hard as iron, and when we lined up powdery snow was still falling. The touchlines were marked with blue paint.

The referee told us before he started the game that we had got to play to a finish, extra time *ad lib.*, half-hour by half-hour. This was a fine prospect on a ground like a skating-rink. You could run straight ahead, but if you tried to turn in your tracks, either you had to stop dead or sit down.

Both sides went at it again full bat, and after Sandy Brown had scored a clever goal for the Spurs the pace almost caused a thaw. In a cool moment in the midst of the fever our veteran forward, Harry Wood, made a clever opening for his outside right and we equalised. After that the play was vigorous to the point of desperation. A couple of minutes before time the ball hit their goalkeeper on the knee-cap and bounced out, and our Brown, known to us as " Jigger," delivered a cannon-ball into the net. So the Saints tribulated into the second round. And, mind you, by this time we were polished into a proper team.

In the second round we beat the League champions, Liverpool, at the Dell. Interesting, because we ourselves were the champions of the Southern League. Liverpool owned a grand centre-half-back in the Scottish International Raisbeck. But we scored four goals to their one and won on our merits. All the same, Raisbeck did the work of three men and played in superb style.

Our next round match was at Bury, when we played on a ground thawed with salt into a sea of slush. Often when the ball fell from a long kick it made a splash of mud and sat there. We were completely outplayed, but won the match by the odd goal in three, scored in the last minute. Believe it or not, midway through the second half Bury had seven corner-kicks continuously one after the other, but the Lord was with us. About the only two times we got within range of the Bury goal we scored.

We recovered, however, our best form in time for the semi-final against Notts Forest at Tottenham. The Forest, led by the celebrated Frank Forman at centre-half, were well worth their progress to the semi-final. It was a lovely spring day. The turf was sound and elastic. No goals were scored up to half-time. Then after a quarter of an hour the Forest scored. After that our forwards took charge and scored three goals— " Jigger " Brown very prominent.

We had to wait a month before we met Sheffield United at the Crystal Palace in the final. Had we played a fortnight earlier, when the grounds were still heavy, we might have won. As it was, the turf at the Crystal Palace was like a cricket field; our veteran forwards were not as good on a hard ground as they were in the mud. All the same, we had the better of a very fast game which ended in a draw of one goal each. Sheffield had a powerful defence, organised by their captain, Ernest Needham, at left half-back.

The outstanding feature of the match was the miraculous goalkeeping of Foulkes, the gigantic Sheffielder. He was the burliest, the heaviest, and the most rubber-like goalkeeper known to history. Some of his saves were incredible. His attractiveness was enhanced by his fondness for a gamble : rather like the Bank of England backing horses.

Between that game and the replay I became a year older. It was a summer day at Sydenham, and the ground was still more like a cricket field. Unfortunately, there was also a high wind, and the ball bounced about prodigiously. Nevertheless, the football played on both sides was far superior to that of our first attempt. Sheffield United scored at the very start, within two minutes of the kick-off. It was the result of in-genious manœuvring by Needham. So we were a goal down in the first two minutes, with a gale to fight against up to half-time. All the same, our forwards did just as much attacking as the Sheffielders. Giant Foulkes from their goal punted a huge distance down-wind; some of his kicks fetched first bounce within shooting range of our goal. The two Sheffield backs, Thickett and Boyle (an Irish International) played a most determined game. Half an hour after half-time our "Jigger" Brown equalised from a jumble in the goalmouth. Then, with the wind in our favour, I thought we should win. Indeed, we had the better of the play, which was at a great pace. But luck was against us. The referee gave a free kick for hands against our captain, Harry Wood, about forty yards out from our goal. Actually the ball bounced against Wood's elbow by accident. Needham placed the ball into the goalmouth. I headed it a good way towards the left. Needham got hold of it again and took a long shot, which swerved across our goal almost parallel with the cross-bar. Our goalkeeper, Jack Robinson, perhaps the best in England, took a swing at it, but the ball seemed to "slip" his punch, like Len Harvey's head. So, with six minutes to go, Sheffield gained the lead that won the match.

For me, an uncommon sequel. Having played in the said final on a Saturday, I played in a first-class cricket match on the following Monday—for W. G.'s London County eleven against Surrey at the Oval—and made 78 runs and got some wickets.

Where is Don Bradman?

Whatever else he has done he has never played Cup-tie or League football.

Nor has he played a part in another and a larger League. But he yet may as Prime Minister of Australia.

CHAPTER XIV

GENEVA

THE first four or five years of the League of Nations were the period of its accepted importance. It represented an integral part of the Treaty of Versailles, and indeed really owed its existence not to international idealism, but to the necessity of providing an international instrument by which alone many of the main terms of the Treaty could be rendered operative. The afterthought, widely entertained, that the seeds of its failure were sown in the fact of the Covenant of the League being part of the Treaty leaves out of view that the Treaty would never have been signed at all without some means of satisfying all sorts of national aspirations which could only be settled in the future. Either the Peace Conference in Paris would have had to go on for years and years, or else some such instrument as the League had to be instituted.

In those early years, too, the League had scarcely had time to become translated in the minds of many well-meaning people into a species of secular religion. When its critics blamed the League for being idealistic, in the uneminent sense of having its head in the clouds, they forgot that it was instituted by a collection of statesmen, all of whom had been thrown up into positions of authority by the bitterly practical exigencies of the war. True enough, even in the early years, quite a number of people in England persisted in regarding the League as a super-national entity which inhabited a caveful of Idola at Geneva, missing the point that the League as such simply consisted of the governments of the nations which composed it. A tennis club consists of its members, and is not something that lives at Wimbledon independently of them; and, of course, if enough of the members refuse to play, then there is little tennis, and not much of a club. This simplicity pretty well explains the so-called failure of the League.

To those who attended Geneva in its first year of 1920 the League certainly appeared a vastly important political structure in the making. The Delegations of the 41 nations represented at the First Assembly consisted of a body of exceptionally able statesmen who had been tested in the strain of the war, even if they came from neutral countries; for in those days no nation could afford to leave its affairs in the hands of any but competent men. It may be added that, as nations cannot get together except by the contact of their leading men, the early Assemblies in particular (and otherwise all of them) had much importance quite apart from anything done by the League, merely in virtue of the personal relations established between the leading and most representative men of nearly all the nations of the world.

Attending the First, Third, and Fourth Assemblies as an acting Substitute Delegate on the Indian representation, I came in for a good chance of knowing what it was all about, and what sort of men were about it. There is not the slightest doubt that there was the fullest intention on all hands to build up the League into a successful solution of the difficulties of the world with fair dues to friend and foe alike. The mistakes and miscalculations which in after years have been cast in the teeth of the League did not arise from any foolish and unpractical conceptions at the start. The truth is that presently some of the members began to refuse to play tennis, and others never did like tennis at all as a game.

Nowadays, in spite of the general agreement as to the failure of the League of Nations, quite a number of the members chiefly concerned are hurriedly reverting to the principle of collective security which was one of the main objects of the League. The fact that nowadays collective security is to be backed with armies and armaments only rehabilitates the League principle in the form in which France tried hard to establish it at the outset. What would have happened if the League had possessed an army as the French advocated? Would Germany have been allowed to re-arm and engineer a situation for Europe at least as bad as she imposed in 1914? French logic about the law court without any police certainly had, as nearly every speaker in the League Assembly said of the arguments of another speaker which he was about to demolish, "a very great deal of force."

Be all that as it may, Ranjitsinhji took me with him in September, 1920, into a vividly interesting new world. He took me because he said I could speak French and was sure at any rate that I was the kind of Englishman who would not be afraid to try. He also knew that if he gave me his points on a subject and we discussed them for a quarter of an hour, I could produce a speech which left none of them out and would if necessary last for an hour.

Ranjitsinhji himself was a very able speaker: indeed, one of the best extempore speakers I have heard, but he always liked someone else to compose for him probably a less effective speech than he would have composed himself. He had cultivated the art of reading out a prepared speech so skilfully that if you did not see he was reading you would have suspected him of speaking without his manuscript or even notes. One of his dodges was to pencil in a very large comma wherever he was going to take a breath or make a pause.

We both of us took a lot of breaths on the way from London to Geneva. The arrangement of our journey was supposed to have been made by the Government Hospitality Bureau in London. We did receive ten tickets instead of five at the eleventh hour. All went well as far as Calais. That is to say, we got there. This was because there was an empty compartment reserved for two of the British delegates who travelled by another train. From Calais to Paris again was all right because of the absence of Mr. H. A. L. Fisher and Mr. George Barnes. But there were no *wagons-lits* at Calais as advertised. Again, at the Gare de Lyon on the Geneva night train there were no *wagons-lits*. I boarded the train through a window, and occupied three sleeping compartments with sixteen suitcases. But when Ranjitsinhji arrived with his customary leisured dignity the Japanese Delegation arrived too with their tickets, and as Ranjitsinhji wrote in his report, "I caused my assistant to evacuate his entrenchment." He added, "My assistant made a valiant and fluent attempt to put on more wagons, and nearly succeeded." The English Bishop who was travelling to Geneva to preach an inaugural sermon told me that when he was my age he had commanded a fair flow of vituperation, but he gave me best. Anyhow, thanks to the Government Hospitality Bureau, we should have travelled all night in the corridor sitting on our sixteen suitcases but for the kindness of some of the Dominions representatives.

When we arrived at the Hôtel de la Paix at Geneva, we found again that either the Government Hospitality Bureau had failed or else that the Japanese Delegation were there first, because the Japs had snaffled nearly all the bedrooms and quite all the sitting-rooms in this abode of peace. Perhaps they thought it was Manchukuo. They had some excuse to be expansive, because they took to Geneva a total staff of 170 little bodies, and the Rising Sun fluttered from dawn to eve in every street in Geneva.

As the Japanese later on so dramatically repudiated their connection with the League, it is interesting to recall that in the earlier days their representatives and staff were prominently industrious in the work of the Assembly. Nothing happened without one of them being present, and there was always one Japanese secretary or more taking down very full notes of everything everywhere. Their accumulation of detail must have been immense. One of their Substitute Delegates, afterwards a Delegate, Mr. Adatci, afterwards a Baron, their Diplomatic Representative in Belgium, can scarcely ever have gone to bed; he was ubiquitously employed in producing reports for committees and with making speeches whenever Japan had anything to say. He was a very small man, and smoked the largest cherry-wood pipe known to history; and was extremely clever. As against this, the three main Jap Delegates, all Ambassadors, listened with industry but said nothing. Viscount Ishii, their Ambassador in Paris, made one or two pronouncements in the Assembly. Baron Megata made one speech to the Finance Committee, and this was a notable speech because it was in a language that nobody understood. He ought to have spoken either in French or in English, but he did not. When he sat down the interpreter came round and asked Ranjitsinhji whether the Baron had made his speech in French or English. Ranji whispered, "French." He then asked me, and I whispered, "English." That was because we were both sitting very close to the Baron. I then whispered to the interpreter that perhaps a little Japanese secretary sitting on the other side of the room might know. This turned out true. On being whispered to, the little secretary blandly produced from his regulation portfolio a typewritten copy of the speech in French and then one in English. The interpreter then read out both for the information of the Committee. Baron Megata never spoke again.

Baron Hayashi, the Ambassador in London, was easily the most silent Delegate at Geneva. He never spoke at all. When the Japanese Delegation came to dine with Ranjitsinhji, I asked Ranji whom I should put next to Baron Hayashi. Ranji said, "Put yourself, and if you can get him to talk I will give you a diamond ring." It was a large and conversational dinner. I tried to tempt the Baron, but he only nodded with great courtesy. Half-way through, however, I got into a lively argument about Arab horses with Sir Arthur Priestley. Suddenly the Baron chipped in by way of correction. He then gave us the history of the horse from Ghenghis Khan down to the last winner of the Derby. He went on for half an hour in a quiet voice amid universal silence. Then he stopped. This is the only occasion on which he is known to have said anything during the three Assemblies I attended. Even Sir Arthur Priestley was impressed. Ranji did not give me a diamond ring. He gave me a large black pearl, which he bought from a Russian refugee, and which claimed to have belonged to Lucrezia Borgia.

Ranjitsinhji's hospitality at Geneva was celebrated. When he first arrived in this world of universal politics he was regarded by all the other Delegates with awe as the only autocratic sovereign present. But he was also regarded with interest owing to his reputation as a cricketer; and this was enhanced (if I may say so) by his having me as his Assistant. Nothing surprised me more at Geneva than that all the Delegates from all over the world knew both of us as cricketers. Indeed, in our first week or two, this allocation of our value was rather embarrassing, but it did not take long for a hundred and twenty or so of the ablest men in the world to discover Ranjitsinhji's ability. In so democratic a collection of humanity it was natural that a ruling prince should be very much admired, but he established his reputation purely on merit, and in the third Assembly was elected one of the Chairmen of Committees, not at all *honoris causa*. The Spanish-speaking bloc offered to get India elected to the Council if we could assure them that Ranjitsinhji would be the Indian representative. Lord Balfour, consulted by Ranji, said it would not do to have another member of the British Empire on the Council.

At the reception given by the city of Geneva in the Opera House during the first days of the first Assembly it was taken for granted that everybody knew everybody else. So when Ranjitsinhji arrived nobody presented him to anybody. This would not do, so I stepped forward and presented His Highness to H.E. Monsieur Paderewski of Poland, whom I knew at least by sight. Then Ranji presented me to H.E. Monsieur Paderewski, whom he knew at least by sight. This worked well. So I found out from an official in uniform the names of a dozen or so eminences, and we repeated the reciprocal presentation with each of them. It was then that we discovered that the most unexpected eminences were acquainted with the names of English cricketers.

It was curious that Ranjitsinhji's first new acquaintance at Geneva should be Paderewski, because these two took to one another at once and became close friends. Paderewski had been a great figure at the Paris Peace Conference. He told Ranjitsinhji that it was as big a nuisance to him to be known as a pianist as it was to Ranjitsinhji to be known as a cricketer. It was due to his personal force and diplomatic ability that Poland achieved so large a measure of attention in Paris. He had the advantage of a distinguished presence and a powerful eloquence to render effective his statesmanship and intense patriotism. He was certainly one of the half-dozen finest speakers I heard in the Assembly. He spoke English well, but made his speeches in French with a finished command of dramatic eloquence. A notable figure.

If anybody at Geneva at all rivalled Ranjitsinhji in hospitality it was Paderewski. He had a tall red rectangular villa, like a giant doll's house, on the shore of the lake a few miles away at Morges, near Noyon. There was a long garden lead-

ing down to the lake where Madame Paderewski maintained
the largest collection in Europe of every variety of bantam.
There was one pen of birds about the size of larks, called
Mille-fleurs, of which she was specially proud. We often
dined at Morges, and sometimes Paderewski played to us;
always before dinner.

One Sunday there was a special entertainment. We began
dinner at half-past five in the afternoon, and left the table at
about nine. I have never seen so many different kinds of food,
nor so many different kinds of wine. What about the enormous lake-trout and the Château Yquem? Paderewski was a
magnifico. Evidently the chauffeurs were equally entertained
below decks, because the journey back to Geneva was a series
of hairbreadth escapes. We damaged two lamp-posts, and ran
over a large heap of stones at the side of the road at an angle
of 45 degrees. The road was flat and straight, parallel with
the edge of the lake, but the third Indian Delegate, Sir Ali
Iman, Prime Minister of the Nizam of Hyderabad and a
distinguished barrister, was lost on the way home somewhere
up in the mountains and search-parties had to be sent out to
recover him. One of our party, Colonel Berthon, a former
high official in the Political Service in India, who always wore
a bowler hat, had that hat concertinaed against the roof of
the car three times during the drive, each time worse than
the last.

Sir William Meyer, Chief Delegate of India in 1920, Finance
Minister of the Government of India during the War, and
then High Commissioner in London, when he heard that Sir
Ali Iman had been lost on the way home, remarked that
this was the first time he himself had told a valuable lie.
He had excused himself on the ground of a severe attack of
indigestion. Sir William Meyer was an Indian Civil Servant,
affectionately known in India as "Bloody Bill." He was small
and unobtrusive, with a little white moustache, beady eyes, a
parrakeet's beak of a nose, and large owlish tortoise-shell
spectacles. He could desiccate half a dozen pages of budget
at a glance. He was probably the greatest authority on finance
at Geneva, but much to his disgust he could not allot himself
to the Finance Committee because he had to be elsewhere

for questions closely concerning India. A sly humorist, he nominated His Highness the Jamsahib to the Finance Committee on the ground that an Indian Prince should know all about that.

This indirectly led to my having to do more work at Geneva than I have ever done before or since. I had to call upon Sir William at eight o'clock in the morning every day to be briefed for the information of Ranji in complicated interrogation and criticism of the accounts and budgets of the League. Ranji attended the Committee twice, and then decided that it was no good for the complications to be dealt with three times over—first by Sir William, then by me, and then by him, so he left me in charge of Indian interests on the Committee as his Substitute Delegate. The Finance Committee seemed to sit every day and all day. It was always a problem how to escape from it in time for the important dinner I was responsible for to His Highness almost every evening. Ranjitsinhji considered that he could do good work, since he had the means to do so, by bringing all the Delegations into social contact; and he was desirous of proving to the representatives of the nations that Indians in general, and particularly the Indian Princes, were very different from the mistaken notions commonly entertained of them. He certainly succeeded. He did big work for India at Genéva; no Delegate was better known or better liked.

For my engagements with the Finance Committee I was thoroughly and patiently educated by Sir William Meyer. I naturally became, armed as I was with all his acute and varied weapons, quite a troublesome critic in the Committee. Even though Sir William was not there in the after years, India continued to frighten the League financiers. Sir William left his sting behind him.

He had a caustic manner. One of his proposals was that, since several member nations of the League were behindhand with their subscriptions, would it not be well to institute a Calvin Casino at Geneva in rivalry with Monte Carlo? The profit from gambling Delegates would soon ease the situation.

Early on, the Swiss at Geneva started the idea that the city should erect a monument in memory of the victory in the Great War and the inauguration of eternal peace. This was considered a fine neutral gesture. The monument was to be of granite covered with oblong copper plaques with the signatures of all the Delegates of all the nations, each of whom was to subscribe some such motto as, "*Dulce et decorum est pro patria mori.*" Representatives called on all the Delegates to obtain their autographs and mottoes. One called upon Sir William during my matutinal briefing. Sir William, in crisp French, asked a score of searching questions as to detail, but finally observed with a beady glance that he could scarcely see to write his own name and was absolutely stumped for a motto. After protestation the emissary offered to retreat, accepting defeat. Just as I was bowing him out of the door, Sir William called him back with, "*Un moment, monsieur.*" He selected a pen with meticulous care, lowered his spectacles to within an inch of a piece of notepaper, and then handed the minute writing to the visitor. He had subscribed his autograph and the motto, "*Point d'argent, point de Suisse.*" Sir William Meyer was never at a loss. When a long and animated discussion was just closing, as to whether Spanish, as well as English and French, owing to the number of Spanish-speaking Delegates, ought to be included among the official languages of the League, he proposed an amendment that as the standard of education at Geneva was so high, would it not be best to have only one language—Latin? Once, in the Assembly, in following Lord Robert Cecil on the Mandates question, he began, "There is much force in what Lord Robert has said. '*Ex Africa semper aliquid novi.*'" The point was that Lord Robert, an original British protagonist of the League, was introduced to Geneva as a Delegate not of Great Britain but of South Africa. This sally raised by far the biggest laugh I ever heard in the tawdry Salle de la Reformation. So, after all, Latin might have been a good *lingua franca* for the League.

In those early days the Assemblies of the nations of the world met in this large hall. The walls were as thin as many of those in the Swiss hotels where winter sports enliven the Alps. The entrance, in fact, was mixed up with the front door of a hotel. If any lobbying occurred it was within a very confined space.

The great Secretariat itself was a converted hotel, but anyone who has a grievance against the League ought at any rate to concede that the personnel of the Secretariat has never been rivalled. One soon saw at Geneva that the success of any International Conference depends decisively upon the skill with which questions and facts are prepared and documented. In such matters, and also in the circulation of records of proceedings, the Secretariat of the League did wonderful work. They were a picked lot, embracing an elegant percentage of women.

Dame Rachel Crowdy, ex-Commandant of the V.A.D.'s in France, was the head of one department. She was slim, fashionable, and not at all like one's idea of a lady politician. She was a very good dancer. She certainly held her own in a select company of departmentalists.

But beyond doubt the remarkable reputation of the League Secretariat distributed all over the world by the Delegates was due to the presiding genius of the Secretary-General. Never was there such talent in smoothing over difficulties and persuading co-operation. I once heard Lord Balfour say, "Eric Drummond never puts a foot wrong." Afterwards as the Earl of Perth and our Ambassador in Rome, he must have had another fine *campus* for his directive tact and suave candour.

Among the individual personalities of Geneva, the English Delegates always seemed to me to stand out in a class by themselves for force of character and power of presentation. Among them Lord Balfour was pre-eminent. But he had a near rival of a different type in Lord Robert Cecil. There was no one like Lord Balfour for the easy treatment and yet dominant conduct of large questions. Never was there so iron a hand in so velvet a glove. But when it was a matter of principle, Lord Robert Cecil brooded over the Assembly like a great eagle of peace. Sir William Meyer described him as " a benevolent vulture," but Sir William had spent many years in India, and had forgotten about eagles.

One feature of early Geneva was the possibility of an individual Delegate of a comparatively unimportant country exercising personally large influence. One of the speakers who was always listened to with great attention when he mounted the rostrum was the accomplished negro Delegate for Haiti, M. Louis Dantes Bellegarde, witty and polished to a degree in exquisite French.

But the prime instance of purely personal influence, apart from national importance, was M. Edouard Benes of Czecho-Slovakia. Lord Balfour went considerably on his advice, and so did the French leaders. He was always noticeably alert and equipped with exact knowledge, and his handshake was positively crippling in its attachment. It was like a quintupled thumbscrew. He rarely made a speech, and then it would be a short one.

In the matter of forthright oratory as distinguished from businesslike statement of a case the French had no rivals. Their two great guns were the incomparable René Viviani and his under-study, Henri de Jouvenel.

Viviani was a barrister, and had been Prime Minister of France in 1914. His magnificent voice had a range of inflection like the stops of an organ, and I doubt whether any man in modern times has been a finer orator in the excellent sense of the term. Henri de Jouvenel was similar in style, and at his best exhibited nearly an equal power.

The French always studied the precise requirements of an occasion. They had the venerable Léon Bourgeois, President of the Senate, for quiet persuasion; Gabriel Hanotaux, of the French Academy, for definite exposition; and the other two for dramatic thunder.

The French appropriateness extended outside the meetings of the Assembly to those of the six full Committees. They provided a separate specialist Substitute Delegate for all the many main questions in which they were interested, but if by chance some side-issue arose at all affecting the terms or the interpretation of the Covenant, or the Treaty of Versailles, by some adroit Gallic mechanism the specialist disappeared and you found his place taken by one of the premier Delegates: usually Gabriel Hanotaux, a former Minister of Foreign Affairs.

Certain countries may have regarded the League as an airy

experiment, but the French and all the small countries of Europe took it seriously enough. In the small countries it figured as their main hope of salvation. It was indeed their certificate of existence. To the French the League stood for the integrity of the Treaty of Versailles and its implementation. Great Britain and the Dominions were equally sincere, but in a more general tone. They appeared to regard the League mainly as the best available political prop of peace, and as a valuable buttress of British policy. Incidentally, the British subscribed much more than anyone else towards the cost of the League.

In spite of the large proportion of the expenses of the League subscribed by Great Britain, it was not the Delegation of Great Britain who led the campaign on behalf of businesslike and economical management of the finances of the League. The discussions in the Finance Committee were lively and lengthy on all hands for the first few meetings, but after that the energy of the Continental and South American Delegations evaporated and they subsided into relative impassivity. Subsequently the work was done by the representatives of New Zealand, Australia, South Africa, and—India.

Much trouble arose from the curious claim of the International Labour Bureau to be financially autonomous. This was a naïf claim, inasmuch as its revenues came from the contributions of all the members just as did the money for all the other organisations of the League. The Labour Bureau, however, had a Secretariat and establishment of its own, and what is more a Director of its own, and was autonomous in that it differed from other and smaller organisations of the League in not being under the authority of the Secretary-General. Its own Director, who might better be described as a Democratic Dictator, was the famous Monsieur Albert Thomas.

This admirable young Frenchman, with bushy head and whiskers, had been the Lloyd George of France in the War at their Ministry of Munitions. For him the enormous political problems facing the League scarcely existed. Among other features of his peculiar position, his Labour Bureau absorbed one-third of the total budget of the League. He introduced his budget to the Finance Committee of the League, which had to find the money, with a descriptive eloquence such as surely never before had adorned the presentation of mere figures. He submitted inadequate details, but explained everything with the force of a fairy-tale. Everybody knew that the Labour Bureau was a sort of international spoiled child, but everybody knew that it was highly efficient and that its Director was as honest as he was enthusiastic. So the Labour Bureau always won the appropriation it claimed.

Albert Thomas proposed his first budget in a speech lasting an hour in the nature of a dithyrambic ode. He spoke in his native flowery French. Then his very clever second-in-command, Herbert Butler, now the head of the new Nuffield College at Oxford, stood up and calmly gave a verbatim translation without a single note. He just began, " The Director has said . . ." and he repeated in English, word for word, precisely what the Director had said.

Apart from his figures, what Albert Thomas claimed for his Labour Bureau was that though it was inside the League it was also outside it. That though it derived its revenue from the League it was entirely independent. That this position had been approved by the Council, confirmed by the legal adviser of the Secretariat, and conclusively assumed in a pamphlet which he himself had written. He clothed these paradoxical claims in a sparkling mantle of lucid logic. This is the way that some of the best French minds sometimes work. What is more, he made a success of everything he touched.

This now seems long ago, but at the time it was all very exciting and interesting. When the representatives of some two-score different nations pool their objections to nearly everything, even a statement of accounts becomes dramatic. On one occasion I was required, as advised by my chief, to deliver a speech in French on the question of the size of the salaries of the Secretariat. The subject was technical, and many of the recipients of salaries were friends of mine. So I began, " *Messieurs les Délégés, je parle français non pas sans reproche, mais sans peur.*" I was then free to slip in English words and phrases whenever I was out of French.

One of the difficulties about the salaries of the Secretariat was that of the cost to them of living in Geneva, which was much higher than it was to the natives. The Swiss could not disembarrass themselves of their habit of regarding foreigners as a commercial proposition. A Spanish Delegate remarked that the ladies and gentlemen of the Secretariat did not come to Geneva to look at Mont Blanc but were expected to pay up as if they did.

Apart from the hurly-burly of financial discussions, the most exciting episode in which I was involved at Geneva was when Signor Mussolini sent his ships to bombard a corner of Corfu, including a monastery, and to occupy the island. During the Paris Peace Conference one of the principal Italian claims was for ports on the eastern shore of the Adriatic. This was their equivalent of the French Rhine frontier. The French did not get the Rhine, nor the Italians their ports; and it was on this account that Signor Orlando was recalled in a huff from the Paris Conference. The Italian claim was that the Italian shore of the Adriatic was shallow and sandy; they could not even maintain submarines there; the eastern shore was full of fiords from which another power could control the passage of the Adriatic. When the French went into the Rhine, Signor Mussolini went into Corfu. To him it was a stepping-stone to Valona.

This happened while the Assembly was in session. Greece was perturbed, because Valona was like a bridge-head leading straight into Greece. Similarly, Jugo-Slavia and the Danube countries were afraid of an open backdoor. Greece, having a defensive agreement with Jugo-Slavia, was fairly well ready to fight, but as the Assembly of the League was in session Greece appealed for the protection of the League, and requested to be relieved of Signor Mussolini's presence.

Signor Mussolini instructed the Italian Delegates to state that this particular military operation was entirely outside the competence of the League. As Italy was a member of the League and had signed the Covenant this was rather thick.

You can easily realise the hubbub at Geneva with a new war so early in prospect. But the situation was seriously inflamed because the many smaller countries in the League

all saw that if the League was not competent to relieve Greece
of the Italian threat it would not in the future be competent
to relieve them of similar unpleasant contingencies. All
ordinary business at Geneva went to blazes. The Italian question brooded over the citadel of peace.

One afternoon I was in the lobby of the Salle de la Reformation talking to Wilson Harris, the journalist, when a messenger
came to tell me that His Highness wanted me.

His Highness said briefly, "Charlo, we have got to make a
speech."

"What about?"

"Lord Balfour wants me to make a declaration on behalf
of the British Empire that, in the opinion of all its Delegations,
the Corfu question is within the competence of the League."

I said, "When?"

He said, "Now."

"But we can't get it typed."

"Never mind. Write it out large and legible."

So down I sat and wrote out the speech which I shall always
claim turned Mussolini out of Corfu. I used a green pencil
as thick as a walking-stick, which some wag had given me,
and the writing was large and legible. Ranjitsinhji delivered
the speech within half an hour.

The speech meant that the British Navy would not permit
Mussolini to stay in Corfu; and he came out. But his face
was very cleverly saved, because although the decision of the
League Assembly was the operative factor, the final negotia-
tion of the fiat was transferred to the Council of Ambassadors
in Paris, on which Italy was represented. Our small but
momentous speech sounded quite well in English, but when
we heard it translated by the interpreter into French it
sounded superb. Lord Balfour, having conveyed his request
to Ranjitsinhji, choosing him for the job as the least likely
of any British Empire Delegate to give offence, had gone off to
his hotel, and I could not find him to submit for his approval
what we had written out.

The more immediate result of the speech was that three
Italian Delegates, who were coming to lunch with Ranji next
day, wrote to regret that they had headaches. I watched the

members of the Italian Delegation as they listened to the speech. They were visibly perturbed, and one of them appeared to be trembling with suppressed emotion. The truth was that the Italian Delegates, under Signor Salandra, were in an absurd position. They knew well enough that they ought not to be sitting there while Italy openly contravened the Covenant. What is more, they did not at all agree with the wisdom of the Duce's excursion. No wonder they had headaches. One of them went down daily by the night train from Geneva to Rome to convey to the Duce the impossibility of the situation.

The little speech in which I was concerned in opposition to Signor Mussolini and his threat on Valona via Corfu was not my only connection with Albania. I do not say that I received a specific and definite invitation to become King of Albania, but in the indirect manner which so often characterises any affair in which an eminent Indian is concerned it amounts to this—that I was well in the running for the billet.

You must know that Albania was not an original member of the League, but had applied to join. In pursuance of this policy, Albania had sent a deputation of three to attend to her interests at Geneva. One of the representatives was a Mahommedan, one was nothing in particular, but the head man was very much of a man. He was a Christian Bishop, and he was the nearest replica of W. G. Grace I have ever seen. His beard was jet black instead of W. G.'s dark brown, and his eyes were black. He was not quite as big a man as W. G., but had he dressed up in cricket flannels with a red and yellow M.C.C. cap and walked out on to the pitch at Lord's, he would have been accepted by the crowd as W. G.

So it was that one day when I went to see him at breakfast in bed, Ranjitsinhji enquired casually, " Carlos, would you like to be King of Albania?"

I accepted on the nail. I was willing to be king of any willing nation.

" Well," he said, " the Bishop is coming to see me about it to-morrow."

It is a strange coincidence that between the writing of the last paragraph and this one, on April 6th, 1939—that is to say, nearly twenty years afterwards—I picked up my morning paper and noted a headline indicating that Signor Mussolini had the day before walked into Albania.

To return. The story Ranji told me was this. At the beginning of the war of 1914 the acting King of Albania was a German Prince, yclept Wilhelm of Wied, but this King, scenting some discomfort in remaining, decided to go for a holiday to his ancestral castle in Germany. At the end of the War, Albania, in consequence, did not possess a King. British prestige at the moment was high. With a degree of intelligence I should not have attributed to the Albanians until I saw their Bishop (though they are a very warlike people), they had decided that the best thing they could do for a king was to obtain the services of " an English country gentleman with ten thousand a year."

Among its other duties at Geneva the Albanian deputation was charged with the task of finding this eligible contradiction in terms. Why the Albanians thought that Geneva was a good place to find an English country gentleman with ten thousand a year was never discovered. It is quite easy to understand that as the personal friend and assistant of the only Sovereign Prince at Geneva, illumined by the reflected light of his magnificent hospitality, and being pretty busy all over the place without any careful solicitude to hide my own light under a bushel, I was spotted by the lambent eyes of the Bishop as an eligible Englishman. Nor would it be wholly improbable that somewhere or other an income of ten thousand a year was knocking about. The upshot was that the Bishop had proposed to call the next day at 11 a.m. for an interview with His Highness. So, said Ranji, would I please to see to a proper *bunderbuss*.

My preparations consisted in obtaining the use of the largest salon in the Hôtel de la Paix, persuading the proprietor, M. Albert, to adorn it with all the best furniture selectable from other salons, and I told Ranji's four personal servants to be ready, in full Nawanagar State livery, with a good supply of every kind of refreshment in the background. I was not supposed to know anything about the diplomatic visit, so Ranji instructed me to get ready my very best behaviour and to receive the deputation with excuses on his behalf for some few minutes on account of Delegational business. He impressed upon me the necessity of trying to look English and, if possible, a country gentleman, and further, if I could manage it, one likely to possess £10,000 a year. The fact is, he was balancing in his astute mind the relative advantages of finding £10,000 a year and planting me as King of Albania, or of retaining me on his political staff with a considerably less salary, with a view to future political activities in India. I was by this time so used to all sorts of social adventures with the eminent inhabitants of all sorts of nations that I had no qualms whatever about receiving the Albanian Bishop, myself in the guise of an unwitting but appropriate candidate for the crown.

Punctually at 11 a.m. next day the Bishop arrived. He was met at the front door (which looks across the stone esplanade away over the lake to the fountain of Eaux Vives and the Alps) by two resplendent Rajputs. I received him with my best bow, quick down and slow up, with a resounding click of the heels, and conducted him to a circle of stately chairs. After compliments and general conversation, I invited the Bishop as to whether he would take some refreshment.

The Bishop would be delighted, and he combed his fine black beard with his fingers exactly as W. G. used to.

Bhimji, the Rajput servant who was afterwards my gun-bearer in India, and who at the moment looked enough of a prince himself, advanced carrying an enormous silver tray on which there was a powerful battery of decanters. Another servant, Mohan, followed with another silver tray, charged with about two dozen wine-glasses and tumblers. The Bishop did not hesitate. He would have Irish whiskey. I selected a decanter on faith, hoping it was not sherry, and began pouring the liquid into a tumbler.

It was whisky all right.

I suggested to the Bishop to say when.

The Bishop did not say when until I had half filled a tumbler.

Would he have soda-water or plain water?

" No," said the Bishop.

So Bhimji handed him the neat whisky on a silver salver. The Bishop with his left hand pushed his great black moustache conveniently upwards and tossed off the liquor in two gulps. I had never seen W. G. do this, but I could not help thinking that he could have done it equally well. The magnificent physique shared by the Bishop with our own national hero made it appear a trifle to swallow half a tumbler of whisky in two gulps.

After that the Bishop and I conversed for ten minutes with mutual esteem. The Bishop subjected me to what I interpreted as appreciative scrutiny. In short, nothing could have gone better. The more so as the Bishop refreshed himself again with another half-tumbler without turning a single shining jet-black hair.

Then Ranji appeared in a leisurely hurry of courteous excuses, and, much delighted to have had the honour of meeting His Lordship, I bowed myself out backwards, and went to wonder which of the many lines of procedure he was quite sure to have been turning over in his mind Ranji would adopt. Beyond telling me that the Bishop was quite favourably impressed with me, and that the matter was now under full consideration, Ranji never revealed to me what had occurred—except that the Bishop had enjoyed another half-tumbler.

How long I remained as the first candidate in the field for the crown of Albania beyond the first fortnight I do not know. If I had really pressed Ranji to promote me, it is quite on the cards that I should have been King of Albania yesterday, if not to-day. Nor would Mussolini have disposed of me as easily as he did of King Zog. Remember Corfu!

After about a fortnight I could see that the prospect either of losing my services or of having to find the £10,000 a year was beginning to weigh down the balance in Ranji's mind against my elevation. When he casually laid stress upon the inconvenience of having to live in a lonely castle on an island, and perhaps of a bullet in the ribs, I could see at once that his lively affection for me had decided him against the adventure. At any rate, for some reason or other the proposal gradually faded out, in the way that so many projects

fade out in Geneva—and in India. What remains true is that
I was a great deal nearer a crown than happens to the majority
of people not born in the purple.

The Albanian episode was altogether exceptional. For the
most part, the actual work on a delegation staff at Geneva
kept one much less romantically employed from early morning till late at night; how late one could never anticipate. One
of Ranjitsinhji's main ideas was to ensure that India and the
Indians should have every possible chance of being understood
and appreciated in the convenient circumstance of so many
nations of the world being collected together in one place.
Among other means to this end he gave a series of luncheons
to all the representatives of the Press. I fathered this job off
on the Yuvraj of Limbdi, the clever and accomplished son of
H.H. the Takhor Sahib. This young man was attached to our
staff as Ranji's military secretary, but he was also a very good
tennis player and not always to be found. He came to me
with a reply from an American lady journalist named Miss
Drexel, who, in answering the invitation to lunch, had written
that she would much rather come to dinner. I suggested to
the Jam Sahib that she should be invited to dinner, and put
next to the Baron Hayashi, the Japanese Ambassador, who so
rarely spoke. Ranji agreed, and the alternative invitation was
sent. But the lady came to the luncheon as well, and Ranji
would not let me put her next to the Baron at dinner. He put
her next to me.

The dinner was protracted, and at about 10.30 p.m. Miss
Drexel asked me whether I thought His Highness would
excuse her, as she had a date with an Egyptian prince at the
Kursaal. I wrote a note to Ranji on the back of a menu.

He wrote back, "Certainly. And kindly escort the lady
there yourself." The result was that I got back to the hotel at
5 a.m. next morning.

On the other hand, the lady, who had succeeded in ex-
changing about a dozen words with Ranji, wrote two columns
and a half of highly decorative literature about him in an
American newspaper. Where she got the information from—
and most of it was pretty authentic (with embellishments)—I
cannot conceive; although she had asked me a lot of questions

during the dinner, she never gave me time to answer one of them, and talked all the time herself about every conceivable aspect of her impressions of Geneva. When we got to the Kursaal, though I found the Egyptian prince and his party, she immediately disappeared, and I never saw her again. None the less, the Egyptian prince entertained me all right and all night. Moreover, I won 50 francs off him in a bet that I would persuade the girl who went round dressed in a white Oriental costume distributing programmes to dance with me, which was rigidly against the rules.

Another excursion of Ranjitsinhji's in the direction of propaganda was the entertainment of members of the Secretariat. He succeeded in this way in making contact with the leading figures of all the departments—a considerable feat; and, what is more, the personnel of the Secretariat was well worth knowing. Two of the most interesting were M. Avenol, who was then the Assistant and is now the Secretary-General of the League, a quiet, adroit, and extraordinarily well-informed Frenchman; and the other Assistant Secretary-General, Dr. Nitobe, who was more nearly like a European than any other of my Japanese acquaintances, and a first-rate brain.

At that time Philip Noel Baker, now an eminent M.P. on the Labour side, was an important official in the Secretariat, but he was afterwards seconded to act as private secretary to Lord Robert Cecil. He is probably the best intellectual who was also a champion athlete in the Olympic Games. One of the best milers ever turned out by Cambridge, he was also highly distinguished in the Schools and a Fellow of his College.

With Dame Rachel Crowdy we had a great deal to do outside social amenities. She was head of the department of the Secretariat which dealt with the opium question, and our Delegation was up to its neck in this. Although the Government of India, years before, had made the export of opium illegal, the main result had been that other countries, especially Persia, acquired the reversion of the commerce while India lost the revenue. Nevertheless, India was supposed to be the prime source of dope. The United States, although not a member of the League, sent a special deputation to take part in the opium discussions. We had a great job to persuade the Americans, especially the lady deputy, that India was not engaged in a colossal drug traffic.

Ranjitsinhji, however, produced figures to prove that much more opium was consumed per head in the United States than in India, and that none of it came from India. He also discovered that Switzerland contained several very large distributors of deleterious drugs, and this much shocked the Swiss Delegates.

There were interminable disputes and recriminations on the opium question. The main fact that emerged was that the greatest distributor of deleterious drugs was Japan. Much of the difficulty of international control was caused by the system of transhipment in Japanese ports. It appeared that in one year alone enough cocaine was shipped from Japanese ports to China to provide four injections for each of its 400,000,000 inhabitants.

Dame Rachel Crowdy assisted at the Opium Committee with elegant ability. She and her several women assistants had to deal with a tangled question. The Indian opium expert remarked that after much experience of intrigue in India he found at Geneva that he had yet a thing or two to learn.

It may be of interest to remark that the main deleterious use of opium consists in smoking it, and that there is a negligible amount of opium smoking in India. Opium is largely used in India as a veterinary medicine; and with regard to this use, it may be mentioned that the number of cattle in India alone is about 180 millions. The practice of eating opium in small quantities may fairly be said to correspond with the Western habit of drinking tea or beer. At one time a small ration of opium, with medical approval, was served out to the sepoys in the Indian Army, because it was found that it increased their stamina on the march, or at any rate for a special effort. The country postmen in India, who often walk great distances, eat opium to enhance their endurance.

It was in connection with the opium question that Lord Chelmsford, the chief Delegate of India in 1922, was described in one of the Genevese newspapers as a Hindu. He happened to make a speech in the Assembly, which he opened by saying

that he had come to Geneva sceptical of the value of the
League, but a fortnight's acquaintance of its working "had
made him hope that his scepticism was unwarranted."

Ranjitsinhji made a much better speech on the subject,
which he opened by saying that evidently Lord Chelmsford
had suffered a double conversion. Ranjitsinhji much objected
to popular misconceptions about India and opium. It seemed
to him, he said, that people entertained a sweeping and easy
belief that every Indian grows opium and every Chinaman
smokes it. He pointed out that a large proportion of opium
grown, though used in modern medical practice, was credited
to the abuse of opium, and besides, opium has always been
used in India as a home-made medicine, just as various herbs
and simples are even now used by the Western nations.
Another point of his was that, though the loss of revenue to
the Government of India of £40,000,000 in the previous ten
years might be cited as a considerable sacrifice, even intelligent
opinion overlooked the fact that the loss to the producers was
not £40,000,000 but £120,000,000 in that time.

Ranjitsinhji reckoned that the consumption of opium by
human beings in India amounted to about one-third of a lump
of sugar per head per annum; and it is worth noting that an
Indian postman on the march would need a weekly dose of
opium the size of a coffee-bean to keep him up to his arduous
work. Another argument of his was that, whereas in Europe,
a cold region, something in the nature of a stimulant is necessary, in India, where it is very hot, a sedative is required. He
spent hours trying to convince the American lady representative that eating opium was different from smoking it. The
lady, an ardent disciple of uplift, retorted that it was just as
bad to chew tobacco as to smoke it. She also annoyed Ranjitsinhji by including him under the term "you natives."

There were several women acting as Delegates to the Assembly, but they did not figure so effectively in the work of the
League as the women in the Secretariat. Much the best
speaker among the lady Delegates was Helène Vacaresco of
Rumania, who, indeed, had she wished, might in years gone
by have been Queen of Rumania. She had a reputation as a
poetess, and there was no doubt about her gift of choice

phrases. She had been very beautiful as a young girl, but her charms had matured and, if one may say so, had broadened. She was still, as to stature, quite petite. Whenever there was a mixed dinner at the Delegations there seemed to be a conspiracy that Ranjitsinhji should take her in. He maintained that she was the most interesting woman in Geneva. She arranged on behalf of the Rumanian Delegation by far the most brilliant banquet and ball given at Geneva in the three years I was there. She imported musicians from the remote corners of Europe, including Paris. Probably she was easily the most experienced political lady at Geneva, but she succeeded in never figuring as a politician. She was without any taint of the woman Member of Parliament.

Another lady of note, who, however, had nothing to do with League work, was Mrs. Wellington Koo, the wife of the Ambassador and Foreign Secretary of China. Wellington Koo had been educated at an American University, and spoke perfect English with an American accent; but in spite of those two disabilities his speeches in the Assembly were as successful as they were clever. Mrs. Wellington Koo was the daughter of a wealthy Chinese merchant and proprietor in Java, and was the best-dressed woman in Geneva. It was said, with what truth I do not know, that she always made her own hats. These were as successful as her husband's speeches, and as clever. She was very attractive, and never interfered in politics.

What with the multitudinous staff of Japan, the princely hospitality of India, and the social ability of China, the Eastern Delegations figured well at Geneva. The Siamese Delegation, though it did not project itself at all prominently into the hurly-burly of the Assembly and Committees, achieved wide popularity. Their chief Delegate, Prince Charoon, was the Siamese Ambassador in Paris. But perhaps the best known of the Siamese was a secretary on the Staff whose name was Stephanie, and who was the daughter of H.E. Pluja Bibadh Kosha, their representative in Rome. She was about the size of a large doll, spoke goodness knows how many languages, more or less ran the Secretariat of Siam, wore the neatest black silk stockings imaginable on the neatest of legs, drove an enormous racing car, and used to dance the tango with an A.D.C.

on the staff of an Italian Military Adviser, only an inch or two taller than herself, to unstinted applause. When these two were dancing, everyone else stopped and looked on. I should myself rank her as the wittiest tongue of those days in Geneva.

Such are some of the highlights of this international interlude of my life.

If a grandchild ever asks me what I did after the Great War (I mean the 1914 Great War), I shall tell him that I composed a speech which turned Mussolini out of Corfu and ran prominently in the race for the Kingship of Albania.

CHAPTER XV

INDIA OF THE PRINCES

EXTREMES meet; in the sense that one leads to another. For me, the path from Geneva, with its European and democratic preoccupations, led to India, Rajputana, and the world of the Indian Princes. And this is what I have to say about India.

After I had worked with him as his assistant and as a substitute Delegate on the Delegation of India at the Assembly of the League of Nations in 1920, Ranjitsinhji wanted me to continue as one of his Secretarial and Political Assistants, both in the government of his own State and also and particularly in his work connected with the Chamber of Princes. He was on the Standing Committee, and was one of the most able and energetic members.

He believed that a right settlement of the constitutional questions in India, including the relations between the Indian States and the British Government, was of supreme importance to the British Empire. He himself was immediately concerned with the second of these matters. He knew, too, that in parliamentary circles in England, and even in governmental circles in India, the influence of the Indian Princes in important parts of British India was not appreciated. For instance, many thousands of the leading Indian merchants and financiers in Bombay were actually subjects of his own State, and similarly a large number of the rich and influential Marwari merchants and bankers in Calcutta were subjects of His Highness the Maharajah of Bikaner. When the Prince of Wales visited India in the cold weather of 1922 I myself saw Ranjitsinhji exercise his influence effectively in dissuading the leaders of the Congress Party from the projected demonstration in the shape of a hartal, or public strike, in Bombay.

The position of the Indian States was never well understood. The majority of people here at home used to look upon the whole of India as "belonging to England." The distinction between British India and Indian India was and still is quite vague. More than one-third of India territorially, including about a quarter of the population, has never "belonged to England" at all, nor been governed by the British Government. Its people are not subjects of the King-Emperor, but of the rulers of the Indian States. There is a type of old Indian Civil Servant who writes to the papers from Cheltenham and would have you believe that the rulers of the Indian States rule "under the advice of a British Resident." The suggestion is that the ruler does not really rule. This is quite misleading, except in the occasional instance of a weak or quite youthful Prince.

The relations between the British Government and the principal Indian States are based upon Treaties. The gist of the Treaties between the principal States and the Crown is that the States are internally independent and sovereign, but their external relations are vested by agreement in the British Government. Nearly all the principal States made their Treaties with the old East India Company; so the agreements were originally drawn up between one independent territorial power and another, however much greater the one power was than the other. Then came the Mutiny. In the Mutiny our power in India was saved by the loyalty of the Indian States. Then the British rule in India was transferred from the Company to the Crown. Queen Victoria assumed the title of Empress of India, and her Government was declared to be paramount. The character of the Treaties, in spite of the fact that there was an Imperial declaration that they remained sacrosanct, became coloured by the new status assumed by the British Government and implicitly accepted by all the Princes. Nevertheless, formally, the Treaty position remained the same. All the major Indian States retained their internal sovereignty, and their peoples were the subjects not of the British sovereign but of their own ruler.

By 1920, when I first visited India, a new situation had followed the Reformed Constitution introduced when Mr. Edwin Montagu was Secretary of State. This set up partial representative government in the Provinces of British India, with the promise of further concessions in the direction of responsible government at the end of ten years. This brought the Indian States face to face with the possibility that at no distant date the Government of India would be some species of representative Home Rule, with the further possibility that their relations would be not with the Crown but with some sort of Indian Elected Government in India. It was agreed among constitutional lawyers that the Crown could not without consent of the other party divest itself of its Treaty obligations to the Indian States, and that these could not be transferred to an Indian Home Rule Government; but the Indian Princes were much exercised in their minds, because their status and internal sovereignty depended entirely upon their Treaty position.

This was a clear issue, and the Princes had every right to believe that their claims would be respected; but they also knew very well that in the complicated turmoil of establishing any sort of reform in British India, their own position might be left doubtful and susceptible of severe encroachment in the future by a Government in the hands of the Indians of British India.

But there was another and more immediate matter for anxiety. During the period of over half a century since the Crown had assumed paramountcy in India, there had gradually grown up in the relations between the British Government and the States a vast body of precedent—various interpretations of rights which were summarised under the title of Political Practice. The task of administering the Government of India partly by the central Government and partly by the provincial Governments often resulted in a clash of interests between the paramount power and the individual Indian States. It must be remembered, too, that there are over a hundred first-class Indian States, as well as several hundreds of secondary importance, and that such great States as Hyderabad, Jodhpur, and Kashmir are comparable in size with European countries.

Gradually, in all sorts of ways, the Indian States had seen their Treaty rights eroded. On the one hand, every new Viceroy and every Royal visitor to India made a point of publicly declaring that the Treaties with the Indian States were inviolate and inviolable; but the great machine of the Government departments pushed forward plans and policies with the most benevolent intention, on the general principle that an Indian State, however inviolable its Treaty might be, must not obstruct the work of the Government of India. It is easy to see that over some question of a railway, or customs, or coinage, or port rights, the interest of the smaller power might be divergent from that of the Imperial Government.

So an Indian Prince often found that in some to him important respect his inviolable Treaty was in practice required to remove itself conveniently in order not to be violated. In short, what the Indian Princes said was that Political Practice superimposed upon their Treaties had severely encroached upon their full Treaty rights.

This general aspect of the matter had developed in the case of a number of important States into particular grievances. Many of the States held that the Government of India had subjected them to injustice, and had forced them to forgo important rights. Thus, in addition to the common anxieties entertained by the Princes, almost every one of them felt he was suffering from some wrong that ought to be put right. Many of the grievances of individual States dated back for years. From necessity in earlier times, before the territorial power of the British in India had been thoroughly established, the policy of the British Government was based on the principle of " divide and rule." Further, as by the Treaties all external relations were vested in the Government, the Indian States were precluded from making common cause with one another or even from negotiating with one another on any common interest. Each State was required to make individual representation to the Government of India, and when the matter was one of dispute between the Government and the State, the peculiar position was that the comparatively powerless State was addressing itself as plaintiff to an all-powerful Government, which was also the judge, and in extreme cases not only the judge, but the executioner.

There was one point in particular which often led to difficulty. One of the great departments of the Government of India, say the Public Works or Railway and Telegraph Department, being required to push through an important work, was concerned only with doing its job. It was not concerned with Treaty rights and political relations, which belonged to the Political Department. So the one Department might do something to which a State objected, and meet the representations of the State by saying that the Department knew nothing about that, and must refer the State to the Political Department.

However benevolent and fair the intentions of the Government of India, there was always the difficulty that the paramount power envisaged a particular case as involving the establishment of a precedent. On the other hand, in the eyes of the Prince, this question of precedent was always a considerable grievance, because often a governmental decision in the case of a small, backward, and out-of-the-way State was afterwards produced to colour a decision in the case of a major State of entirely different character. For instance, something that had been done in the case of a minor hill State in Assam, the size of Rutlandshire, might be cited as a precedent in the case of Hyderabad, a State the size of Italy.

In theory the paramount power fully accepted the treaty position and the internal sovereignty of the major States, but with the proviso that the whole situation was subject to the obligation of the paramount power to preserve order and good government throughout the whole of India. This led to considerable interference in the internal affairs of States, as the Government would say, with the most benevolent intentions and in the interest of the States themselves. Granted that the Government was much more often right than wrong in what it did, this was no consolation to a State which in a matter of dispute happened to think that it had not received just treatment in accordance with its treaty.

A curious difficulty in which a discontented Prince was placed was that the Viceroy and Governor-General himself held the political portfolio in the Government of India. The case of the State would be presented to the Political Department and dealt with by the Political Secretary, but if the

Prince himself went to see the Department he often found himself dealing with the Viceroy, and the Viceroy would then figure, not as the representative of the Political Department, but as the representative of the King-Emperor. So the Prince found himself dealing, as it were, with the King-Emperor himself, to whom he owed personal fealty and allegiance.

On the other side, the Government of India was presented with the difficulty that the State Governments were conducted by individual rulers of varying capacity and character. It can easily be seen that over a period of years in a subcontinent the size of Europe, with hundreds of Indian States of varying importance, not to mention variations in the character of their treaties and rulers, there was an accumulation of grievances.

Leading cases between the Government of India and the Indian States are not easy to expound briefly. One may, however, put one or two typical cases as they present themselves to the latter. Perhaps the most notable, owing to its magnitude, is the case of the Nizam of Hyderabad in the matter of the Berars.

The Berars are two large tracts of country more or less in the central hinterland of the Mahratta country to the northwest of Hyderabad. The Nizam of the time was our principal ally in our wars in Southern India, first of all against the formidable Hyder Ali of Mysore, and afterwards against the Mahratta power of the Peshwas. It was the defeat of the Mahrattas, whose confederacy covered the country of the Western Ghats inland of Bombay and parts of Central India, that finally gave us our undisputed territorial dominance in India.

As a reward for his adherence the Nizam was given the Berars in the carve-up of the Mysore and Mahratta territories. Now it happened that in earlier days, when French influence had been strong in Hyderabad, the Nizam was fortified by a French contingent under the command of the famous soldier Bussy. When the French opposition in Southern India was dissipated and we became dominant, it was thought well between us and the Nizam—though whether the Nizam had the thought or whether we had it is not quite clear—that the

Hyderabad contingent should be under the control of British officers. In any case, the Nizam, as a weaker ally, could not well refuse internal "assistance" from us. The Nizam, of course, had to pay for the contingent, and the scale of pay for our officers was princely. The cost of the contingent was heavy, and the Nizam got behind-hand with his payments. So we took over the Berars, administered them, and collected the revenue, which, owing partly to our excellent administration, but largely to the more peaceful and settled times, increased beyond expectations. The agreement was that we should hand over to the Nizam any surplus of revenue above the debt.

The Nizam, as soon as possible, began to represent to us that his liabilities had been liquidated many times over, and could the pledged area be returned to him? He did not receive a very immediate answer, but when it did come it amounted to a representation that there would be considerable difficulty in handing back to native rule a large district now accustomed to the beneficent administration of the Raj. Thus after pigeon-holing we demurred, and the Nizam said, well, at any rate, could he have the surplus?

The divergence in the course of lengthy correspondence over the years became greater and greater. Nizam succeeded Nizam, but without success. Finally, when Lord Curzon was Viceroy, the matter presented itself to his Government as requiring effective treatment. Lord Curzon invited the Nizam to meet him for a private discussion. The Nizam of the time had to come alone, without the assistance of his Prime Minister.

The result of the discussion was that he was persuaded voluntarily to sign in our favour a perpetual lease of the Berars—about the worst voluntary bargain in the history of India. The subsequent development was that the next Nizam, when an opportunity occurred (and it occurred in particular when the whole question of the Indian States came up in modern form in 1920), very respectfully represented that this lease had not been voluntarily signed, but had been unwarrantably and forcibly imposed on his predecessor. The final decision up to date, given by the late Lord Birkenhead, amounted to telling the Nizam that the lease had been signed, and that the matter could not be reopened.

The Nizam who voluntarily signed the perpetual lease did not feel as voluntary when he returned home to Hyderabad as he did when he went to call on Lord Curzon. It was reported to him by a Minister that another Minister had said something sarcastic about the part the Nizam had played in this voluntary transaction. The Nizam sent for the dissatisfied Minister, who admitted his criticism and tried in vain to explain it away. The Nizam called for his guards and had him lashed to a charpoy, a sort of low stretcher-bed. He then sent for a riding-whip and thrashed the air around his victim, enquiring the while, " Now, Minister, can you prevent me from beating you?"

The Minister kept on saying, " Please, your Exalted Highness, no."

" Ha!" said the Nizam. " Now you know what is meant by voluntarily signing a perpetual lease at the request of Lord Curzon. Go home and be a wiser man. You are not deposed."

Another case, not quite so dramatic, was one which concerned Ranjitsinhji. His State of Nawanagar lies on the north coast of the bowl-shaped peninsula of Kathiawar, about two hundred miles north of Bombay. Within easy reach of his capital are the ports of Rozi and Bedi, easily connected with the railway running eastward through Kathiawar and with the railways leading into Rajputana, thus also with one of the main broad-gauge systems of India. There was no treaty limiting Ranjitsinhji's internal sovereignty. There was no formal restriction on the use of his ports, but indirectly he was balked of their value.

Ranjitsinhji, when he became ruler of his State, set about developing its resources. He succeeded within a very few years in improving and extending the standard of agriculture by a hundred per cent. Among other things, he was much impeded by not being allowed by the British Government to build a railway connecting his capital with other parts of Kathiawar; the years of delay between the time of projection and the completion of the railway about trebled its cost to the State.

Ranjitsinhji was naturally very much annoyed. He said the

British Government professed to encourage Indian States to develop their agriculture and commerce; but what was the good if a State was not allowed to develop transport for its products? However, as soon as the railway was finished, after some ten years' delay, the question of export and import by sea became even more important. It was impossible to develop the port without freedom to impose reasonable port dues and Customs duties. He was allowed to exercise such rights provided that he did not charge less than the British schedule at Bombay, and for some time all went well. But when the trade through Bedi increased, the Government, after offering him a somewhat inadequate compensation, imposed a second Customs line where the railway from his port entered British India. This annoyed Ranji, who had from the first foreseen that something of the kind might happen, and had endeavoured to provide against it by getting an assurance from the Government. But the terms of the assurance were not clear, and the Government denied that the assurance meant what Ranji said it did. He could always be pinched if the Bombay Government withdrew his liberty of transhipment from ocean-going ships to coasting-ships in Bombay. His claim amounted to this: that the ports belonged to his State, which was internally a sovereign State, and he and his State ought to have untrammelled use of them. Government, on the other hand, said that his trade was no good without the hinterland of their territory, and that he ought not to expect too much profit.

Naturally, the Bombay authorities preferred that all goods for Kathiawar should be landed there and pay Customs duty there, and that the railway connecting Bombay with that part of India which could be served by Ranjitsinhji's ports should enjoy the freightage, not only to other parts of India, but to Kathiawar itself. The difference of revenue to the Nawanagar State amounted to a very large sum per annum. Ranjitsinhji's argument was that his State ought not to be deprived of an inherent geographical advantage.

All sorts of reasons were produced by Bombay against this; among others, the necessity of controlling the importation of seditious literature.

Ranjitsinhji said he did not want to import pamphlets; he wanted to import perambulators and umbrellas.

For over twenty years the dispute continued, and Ranjit-sinhji was not allowed his full port rights until about 1930, when, through the situation created by the new constitutional importance of the States, he was able to get the dispute trans-ferred to an arbitral tribunal in England, which decided—to the unconcealed dismay of Government—that his claims were completely legal and just. Unfortunately, this long-postponed success was not achieved until a few months after his death. His successor was induced not to take full advantage of the victory, and compensation was never fully made. Ranjitsinhji had proved himself a highly competent ruler and was deeply admired and beloved by his subjects. His life was sadly em-bittered by what he regarded as the injustice inflicted on his State by the Government.

Another sort of story concerns the deposition of the late Maharajah Holkar of Indore. Indore is a rich Mahratta State in Central India. The ruler is a descendant of one of the great generals of the Mahratta confederacy.

It happened that the late Maharajah, in addition to his Ranis, had, as is permissible by Hindu custom, several mor-ganatic wives. Among these was a Mohammedan lady named Mumtaz Begum, who had once been a dancing girl in Lahore, but had transferred her art to Indore. It should be under-stood that a Mohammedan wife cannot be the Rani of a Hindu Maharajah, but she has a properly regulated position.

After Mumtaz Begum had been in Indore for several years her relatives in the Punjab sent her surreptitious advice to the effect that she was now rich and enjoyed a lot of jewels because the Maharajah was still fond of her; but the time might soon come when the Maharajah would not be equally fond of her. Now was her chance.

Mumtaz thought so too. She succeeded just in escaping across the border into British India. Directly her absence was discovered the Maharajah sent some trusted men to catch her along the railway, and he said something to the effect of " Who will catch me this turbulent woman?" A female Thomas à Becket.

The emissaries, having missed the lady at the frontier, took it upon themselves to follow Mumtaz down to Bombay. Very soon after her arrival there Mumtaz took up with a rich merchant. The emissaries from Indore had been keeping their eye upon her. The lady's behaviour, apart from other aspects, was a gross and flagrant insult to their master. As one might say, she had spat upon his beard in public, except that Holkar did not wear a beard.

The Maharajah wrote to the Governor of Bombay, requesting him to return Mumtaz to Indore. The Governor was unable to do this, for she was on British territory.

The Maharajah then wrote to the Governor, asking whether, if he could not return the lady, he would return the large quantity of valuable jewels the lady had taken away. For as the lady, by His Excellency's decision, did not belong to the Maharajah, undoubtedly the jewels did.

The Governor replied with great courtesy that there was no evidence that the jewels were not a free gift to the lady.

The sequel was that the Indore men took upon themselves to waylay Mumtaz when she was out driving with the merchant, and tried to kidnap her. Two young British officers who happened to come on the scene rushed in with golf clubs, and in the fracas the merchant was fatally stabbed and the face of Mumtaz severely slashed. The assailants escaped, but were afterwards arrested and hanged.

There was no evidence that the Maharajah had given any instructions beyond that the lady should be captured inside his own State. There was a strong presumption that anything his men did in Bombay they did on their own judgment and in an excess of loyalty to their master.

But feeling in Bombay ran high, especially among the rich and influential merchants. Obviously it was extremely improbable that a clever man like Holkar would be so foolish as to instruct his servants to do anything flagrantly illegal in British India. But there was a sense in which the Maharajah could be held responsible for anything done by his servants.

Whatever the actual truth, the Maharajah preferred to abdicate rather than to undergo the indignity of a public enquiry. The story is that when he left India from Karachi he went on board ship in a bath-chair which contained, in addition to His Highness, many bags of diamonds. Except for the last item, the above account of the affair is the one current in Indian India.

This Maharajah Holkar of Indore was not the first ruler of that State to lose his throne. The Indore ruling family has a sardonic wit. A former Maharajah, being much annoyed with the merchants of his capital, who refused to pay their proper taxes and were otherwise troublesome, made a public exhibition of some of the more recalcitrant leaders by harnessing them to a State carriage and making them draw him round the streets of his capital. In a similar vein, this Maharajah himself was recalcitrant to the advice of the British Government, so he was deposed in Lord Curzon's time. He was living in Bombay on a liberal allowance when Lord Curzon himself was obliged to resign his Viceroyship after his differences with Lord Kitchener. When Lord Curzon was on the eve of leaving India via Bombay, the Maharajah sent him a telegram saying, "Your late Excellency, now we are both deposed may we not meet as friends and fellow-sufferers?"

Piquant stories always obtain a wider currency than serious history, but they are rarely representative. This should be recognised here in England, where there is a pretty general ignorance about the character of the Indian States, and a complete misconception about what kind of men the Indian Princes are. A Maharajah or Rajah is often referred to as "an Eastern potentate," the term implying a vague background of the Arabian Nights. Moreover, if any Indian—say a Risaldar of an Indian Regiment—appears in Indian dress in London, near Buckingham Palace, one might easily hear the remark, "There goes a Rajah." Among the hundreds of rulers of Indian States of all sorts and sizes, there are no doubt some who from a European point of view are "Eastern potentates" in the ancient sense. But the rulers of the important States can be of first-rate ability, capable of holding their own with European statesmen, both in personal attainment and in mental calibre. It would have been easy at any time to pick out half a dozen or more who, had they not been rulers of Indian States, could have sustained with credit the position of Cabinet Minister in England or of Governor of a Dominion.

The common practice here in London of dismissing the ruler of an Indian State with some such phrase as "Oh, he's a Rajah," is as mistaken as it is misleading. Even more mistaken and misleading is the idea that because the rule of an Indian State is in form autocratic, the ruler, as the individual embodiment of the Government, is irresponsible.

Individual rulership is the form of government that conforms to the indigenous social and religious fabric of India. Hindu kingship is surrounded with all sorts of restraints and obligations of tradition and religion as binding as the restraints and obligations of a constitutional monarchy. A ruler may be incompetent and rule badly, but the consequences will certainly be visited internally in the State, if not upon him, upon his successors.

We must remember, too, that even in British India our own Government was in form autocratic, after the type of the Roman Empire and in continuation of the imperial system of the Moguls. Yet throughout our rule we succeeded in establishing the enormous blessing of the Pax Britannica in a vast country which for a thousand years had been afflicted with the successive calamities of invasion and internal war. We increased the prosperity and well-being of the population beyond all recognition, by public works such as roads, railways, and irrigation, as well as by excellent administration. The paradox is that although there was always a considerable body of feeling in India against the alien rule of the British, it was not the Indians themselves who asked for representative government and the forms of democracy. We ourselves put the idea into their heads: and this in a peculiar way. The supreme authority over the autocratic government in India was the British Parliament, and our statesmen and publicists at home were always laying stress upon the principle that our rule in India was intended to be for the good of the Indians, and that we were educating the Indians for the day when they would be able to rule themselves.

What the Indians were really asking for was that they

should be given back their "face," and not be treated as an inferior people. This was the only widespread " political " feeling in India, and at bottom it was social and not "political." Although much has been made of India not being a nation but a congeries of races, creeds and castes, there was in a certain sense a united national feeling in India against alien rule. But the truth is, democratic institutions would have made no appeal to Indian sentiment had not we ourselves presented them in the light of a future ideal, so that they became to India a symbol of a return of social and political self-respect. It may be said that the gradual education of the Indian mind towards political institutions on the Western pattern was the only way to prepare India to rule herself, but the idea that the Indians have all along been crying out for political emancipation on Western lines is quite mistaken.

It is also worth bearing in mind that out of the three hundred and fifty million people of India, nearly three hundred millions live in the villages, each of which is from ten to fifty miles from anywhere else; and that in a sub-continent the size of Europe, the cities can be numbered almost on the fingers of two hands. The result is that whereas the cities form a minor part of India, they are the only part that makes any noise. No doubt by now a good deal of political-mindedness has spread about among the villages of the more populous regions, for instance in Bengal and the valley of the Ganges and in the Punjab. But even in 1920, anyone who took the trouble to busy himself about an Indian village found the villagers entirely concerned, as from time immemorial, with their small local affairs, with their crops, and with the water-supply; their only interest and anxiety as to the form of government being limited to its appearance in the person of the tax-collector. There is no better instance of complete local self-government than an Indian village under its elected council of five and headman, the patel. Provided that the local moneylender is not on its back, an Indian village is remarkably free from interference.

Generalities about the huge and diverse world of India are bound to be incomplete. One might as well talk wholesale about Europe. Nevertheless, India is not just a bigger and more easterly England, inhabited by innumerable trade-unionists and working men who are brown instead of white.

There were two main sources of agitation for Reform. On the one hand, the politically minded intelligentsia of the towns, backed up by a quantity of Westernised applicants for careers which did not exist, avidly seized our flag of democracy and waved it in our faces. On the other hand, the Indian merchants and financiers, together with a few industrialists, backed up the cry for some sort of Home Rule, chiefly because they regarded our authoritarian Government as a ring-fence protecting English trade, finance, and industry. When an Indian commercialist complained hotly that British trade and finance were exploiting India under the protection of the British Government, what he meant was that he would very much like the liberty to do the same without interference.

In sum, political agitation in India for " swaraj," or Home Rule, did not in the least mean that the Indians wanted responsible government of our home breed. What they really wanted was no Government at all that interfered with their own interests and activities, and yet at the same time some Government that ensured justice and good administration.

In the long run, however, political agitation took the form of a demand that we should give India what we had promised; and we had promised India not the form of government native to India, but the form which we had adopted as best for ourselves. The result in the end was the immensely complicated political situation which even now is not finally solved by Federation.

The Indian Princes and their States were nominally outside the political operations of British India. But they could not be left out of the picture, since geographically and racially the States could not be separated from the rest of India. For one thing, most of the fighting races of India either inhabit the Indian States or are very closely connected with them and, so to speak, look towards them. A considerable part of the strength of the Indian Army is drawn from this source—for instance, the Rajput, Sikh, and Jat regiments. Moreover, as previously mentioned, many of the subjects of Indian States go to the large towns in British India to pursue their avocations in trade and finance, while continuing to regard the States they come from as their home.

About the time that I joined up with Ranjitsinhji in his political affairs, the Chamber of Princes had recently been instituted in consequence of the recommendations of the Montagu-Chelmsford Report, the result of Mr. Edwin Montagu's visit to India as Secretary of State in 1919, while Lord Chelmsford was Viceroy. When Mr. Montagu went to India for the purpose of collaborating with the Indian Government in discovering the best means of implementing the promises for constitutional reform made during the War, the Indian Princes suddenly discovered that, although their States made up a third of India, they were in danger of being left entirely out of consideration. It was due to the energy of a small number of the Rajput Princes, especially the Maharajah of Bikaner, the Maharajah of Alwar, and the Jam Sahib (Ranjitsinhji), and the Sikh Maharajah of Patiala, that hasty conferences were more or less exacted from the Secretary of State and his collaborators. But these Princes and some of their very able Ministers succeeded in presenting the importance of the general case of the Indian States so well that one chapter on the subject, with recommendations, was embodied in the Montagu-Chelmsford Report.

One of these recommendations was that the informal Conference of Princes, which some years before had been instituted by a previous Viceroy, should be converted into a formally established Chamber of Princes. The Chamber, although neither in constitution nor in procedure conforming with the hopes and wishes of the Princes, did present a platform where the affairs of the Princes could be discussed. The chief objection of the Princes to its constitution was that the agenda of its meetings were entirely controlled by the Political Secretary of the Government of India, so that, as the Princes anticipated, very few of the really important matters that concerned them were ever allowed to be discussed. But here it must be added that some of the most important Princes in India did not approve of the Chamber of Princes at all, because in their opinion it was likely to derogate from their status and independence. Notable among the dissentients were the two great

Mahratta Princes of Gwalior and Baroda, and the Nizam of Hyderabad, the premier State of India. The main supporters were the Rajput Princes of Rajputana and of Kathiawar.

The Chamber of Princes, owing to its constitution, could not do very much in the way of improving the position of the States in the directions they desired. On the other hand, to its Standing Committee was allotted the task of thrashing out the vexed questions of Political Practice with the Political Department. As might be supposed, the codification of Political Practice did not advance with any celerity.

When I went to India in 1922, the Reformed Constitution of British India under the India Act of 1920 had been established with its ingenious compromise called diarchy, and the Chamber of Princes with its Standing Committee was in being. As every Indian of British India had interpreted the promises made during the War in the light of the removal of his own personal grievance, and as a period of economic depression followed, not surprisingly many of the Indians felt that they had been cheated. There was a fertile human garden for the seeds of agitation and discontent wide-strewn by the Congress Party. As for the Indian States, they were principally occupied in marking time and hoping for the best.

It was mainly due to Ranjitsinhji that some of the leading Princes decided not to mark time. They knew that there would be a parliamentary review of the constitutional questions of India in 1929. That had been promised. Ranjitsinhji determined that, so far as he could promote it, the whole of the case of the Indian States, as distinguished from British India, should be well prepared in advance. So it was that in 1922 he asked me to come to India as his assistant in his work of mustering collective attention to the matter by the leading Princes of Kathiawar and Rajputana. This led to many visits and conferences based on the case of the Indian States as presented to the Secretary of State in 1919.

What struck me most about the matter was that the Indian Princes would never obtain the full and unbiassed hearing they merited unless their case was presented to the highest authority in England and well understood in parliamentary circles at home. But most of the Princes were so used to the idea that nothing about India affecting themselves could ever be done except in India that Ranjitsinhji could not move them much in this direction.

Within the next two years Lord Birkenhead became Secretary of State for India, and I was able to present to him personally, though of course informally, how important was the case of the Indian States, and how considerably it was misunderstood at home. In consequence, Lord Birkenhead interested himself to find out what it was all about, and invited Ranjitsinhji to a series of private conversations. So it came about that Sir Warden Chilcott, who was Lord Birkenhead's Parliamentary Secretary and a friend on whose judgment he relied, went to India in 1924 to investigate on the spot.

Sir Warden and I visited a number of the chief Indian States, and there were many conferences with the Princes and their Ministers. Needless to say, all this was interesting and informative. The principal result was that when we returned home much more became known about the Indian States in the right quarters than ever before. Sir Warden Chilcott is a very able man with an uncommon talent for obtaining attention and getting things done. The other result was that Lord Birkenhead approved of a suggestion which originally emanated from the Maharajah of Bikaner that a Commission be sent to India in 1928 to enquire into the question of the Indian States in parallel with the Parliamentary Commission which was to go and report on the whole constitutional question of India. This Indian States Commission eventually went to India and was known as the Butler Commission, its Chairman being the eminent ex-Lieutenant-Governor of the Central Provinces and ex-Governor of Burma, Sir Spencer Harcourt-Butler, who previously had been an Indian Civil Servant and Political Secretary of the Government of India.

Among interesting visitors to India I met at this time were Paul Cravath, the great American corporation lawyer, Chairman of the Metropolitan Opera, and Harrison Williams, then and perhaps even now a good-looking pale-faced American millionaire. They were looking round to see what could be done with railways, and, having the luck to fall in with me, they saw much of the inside of several Indian States. What they did in British India I do not know, but I happened to meet them in Bombay just before they left, when Paul Cravath said, "Well, sir, thank you very much. And after having seen India, I will never again run down the British."

When the Butler Commission was due to start its work the Princes invited Sir Leslie Scott, K.C., now Lord Justice Scott, to go out to advise them in presenting their case, and Sir Leslie asked me to go with him as his assistant. So in 1928 I saw the final development of this effort on behalf of the Indian States to obtain a full and proper regulation of their status. Meanwhile an energetic and comprehensive preparation of the case had been made in India by the Standing Committee of the Chamber of Princes. In this one of the ablest Englishmen in India took a leading part—namely, Professor Rushbrook Williams, who had been in charge of the Government annual publication called *Moral and Material Progress of India*, and was at the time Foreign Minister of the Patiala State. He had had a brilliant career at Oxford, and was a Fellow of All Souls. When Sir Leslie Scott arrived in India the Maharajah of Patiala lent him his Foreign Minister as an assistant. The result was that the case for the Indian States was admirably prepared. Apart from his other qualities, Sir Leslie Scott was a tremendous worker, and he could not have had a more admirable coadjutor than Rushbrook Williams, than whom I have never come across an abler exponent of documentary organisation. But when it came to fundamentals Ranjitsinhji was a main source of efficiency.

It is interesting to record that it was from Sir Leslie Scott, in his endeavour effectively to formulate the case of the Indian States, that the idea of Federation first came to the front. All the time we were there the Indian Princes were mainly occupied in their minds with their treaty status and their individual dissatisfactions, and regarded Sir Leslie Scott as their champion in these respects. But Sir Leslie Scott could not see a solution except in a comprehensive settlement of the whole Indian constitutional question, and he was aiming all the time at the formulation of a scheme of Federation which would include the Princes in accordance with their rights and privileges. When in the end the recommendations of the Simon Report were abandoned by Parliament in favour of Federation, the curious result was that the great difficulty of establishing Federation was, and is, to persuade the Indian States to come in. Whereas until the Federation scheme was adopted the whole question of the rights and status of the Indian States had been relegated to the background as a matter of comparative unimportance, it was discovered after Federation was adopted that the Indian States were important enough to be both the crux and the key of the whole problem.

Sir John Simon's famous Commission was in India at the same time as the Butler Commission, and I saw a good deal of Sir John. I do not think that Sir John Simon, outside inner circles, has ever received proper recognition for the monumental work that he did in India. The first volume of his report is by far the greatest exposition of India that has ever been produced. This has been disguised because his recommendations in the second volume were not accepted. His exposition and explanation of facts was by general agreement perfect. The inevitable conclusions from the facts and their necessary implications were neglected. Nevertheless, volume one of his report was a best seller.

In any case, I was privileged to see the inner working of a large making of history, and my own small activities in the matter enabled me to see Ranjitsinhji's too little recognised force of character and talent for statesmanship, and also contributed, I should say materially, to my own enlightenment.

CHAPTER XVI

THE PRINCE IN INDIA

IN India it is the man that counts.

India presents many paradoxes. The unit of Indian life is the village, and nowhere better than in the Indian village is local government by committee exhibited. The village *panchayat*, or committee of five, rules the Indian village in all its internal affairs, and its only external affair is the payment of taxes. Ninety per cent. of the life of India is in the villages, but when we come to government in the larger and wider sense India does not believe in assemblies and committees; it believes in the man. Even an Indian Prince is never happy till he has obtained access to the Viceroy. The humble cultivator in a village in British India wants to get to the presence of the Collector of the district himself. I have always thought that India could easily be ruled through the microphone if the King-Emperor would occasionally talk to every town and every village over the air.

It was during the early stages of all the goings and comings that eventually emerged in Federation that H.R.H. Edward, Prince of Wales, visited India when I was there with Ranjit-sinhji in 1922. It was not a very opportune time for the visit of the Heir-Apparent of the King-Emperor to India. Nor, perhaps, was it good policy for the Prince of Wales to visit India at all, since it happens that heirs-apparent are not regarded in India with the reverence one would expect among a people devoted to the idea of kingship. In a great Indian State the heir-apparent is so entirely overshadowed by the ruler that he does not figure in the Indian mind as does an heir-apparent in a Western country. It was inherently impossible for the Prince of Wales, even with all his personal advantages, to achieve in India anything like his success as an Ambassador of Empire in the Dominions and Colonies. The plain truth is that India wants the Man himself or nobody.

Moreover, the unsettled state of India at the time threw a heavy responsibility upon the Governments of India and of the great Provinces in conducting a tour for the Prince of Wales. Not that there was any feeling at all in India, even among the bitterest agitators, against the King-Emperor and the Royal Family; in fact, a peculiar feature of the Indian world was an intensely loyal and affectionate feeling towards the King-Emperor, combined with a poignant dissatisfaction with the Government of India. Edward, Prince of Wales, was sure to be personally welcomed everywhere, but it was impossible to expect that the occasion of his visit would not afford a ready opportunity to the militant agitators for what they were bound to regard as effective demonstrations. A few sporadic demonstrations there were in the big towns, but the reports circulated in England representing these as directed against the Heir-Apparent were entirely misleading.

I arrived in Bombay about ten days before H.M.S. *Renown* steamed into harbour with the Prince of Wales on board. There was one considerable riot in the bazaar quarters, started by a band of hooligans imported for that purpose. This ended in a lively clash between Mohammedans and Hindus. It had nothing whatever to do with the arrival of His Royal Highness except as an occasion. Nevertheless, I saw reports in English papers representing it as an outrageous exhibition of disloyalty. The riots occurred in the neighbourhood of the Byculla Club in the morning and afternoon, but when I went to a function at the Club in the evening I did not see anything in the streets to suggest that anything at all had happened. When the Prince of Wales landed on the Apollo Bunder and was received by the Viceroy and the Governor of Bombay, enormous crowds lining his route welcomed him with every sign of respect, which in India does not consist of making a noise. Indeed, when there is a public procession in a city of India, great or small, on a public occasion in honour of a personage, the most respectful and reverential treatment that the Indian crowd can accord is silence. So that if you read that His Royal Highness was received by the huge concourse in complete silence, by European standards this would appear to present an exhibition of unpopularity or disapproval, whereas in India it would be evidence of exactly the contrary.

I have only mentioned the small irrelevant disturbance in Bombay because so much was made of it in newspapers at home that there was quite a widespread belief in London that the political discontent in India had expressed itself loudly against the Royal Family.

The story that the Prince of Wales sent a cable to King George, "Magnificent reception; one killed, fifty-five wounded," is on a par with the equally witless story that when Ranjitsinhji cabled the news to his uncle, the then Jam Sahib of Nawanagar, that he had made his first century, he received the reply, "Good. I have sacrificed a hundred slaves." It is notable, though, with regard to the latter story that in England at the time, while nobody quite believed it, it was accepted as not outraging the verities in the case of a rajah.

Staying as I was in Bombay with Ranjitsinhji when the Prince of Wales was there, I was present at the public functions, and I was also well informed of everything that happened so far as known to the leading Indians in Bombay; but I never heard of a single instance of discourtesy or discontent directed against the success of the royal visit. The only serious demonstration I heard of afterwards occurred at Allahabad; but this, too, had nothing to do with the royal visit except in so far as the agitators took advantage of the occasion for publicity.

In my first few weeks in Bombay as the guest of Ranjitsinhji I was much struck by the peculiar position in which a guest of an Indian Prince found himself. If he behaved at all naturally as a loyal friend of his host, he ran an uncomfortable risk of being regarded as pro-Indian. I earned some small disgrace at the Royal Bombay Yacht Club by adverting to the difficulty at that stage of history of being genuinely pro-British without being sensibly pro-Indian. One could see with a quarter of an eye the basis of the political troubles. The Indians understood the British extremely well, whereas too many of the British did not even want to understand the Indians. Not that there was any intention of being other than perfectly just and friendly.

I remember the second day I was in Bombay I met an English lady whom I had known at home; extremely clever, charming to a degree, and the female equivalent of a man of the world. She astonished me as follows. She asked me what I was doing there, and I said I was staying as the guest of Ranjitsinhji.

What other Indian Princes did I know?

I mentioned one, a close friend of my host.

She said, " Oh, that horrible man!"

To which I replied that he had always been very nice to me, and I liked him.

" He is a horror," she went on; " he pours petrol on dogs, sets fire to them, and shoots them in the dark with a pistol."

What struck me was that so delightful a lady should think fit to tell me this, even if it were true, about a man I had just mentioned as a great friend of a great friend of mine, and in some degree a friend of my own. If he had been an Englishman she would not have told me the story, but because she was English and I was English and the other man was Indian, she told me the story without compunction.

I told her I simply did not believe it. Afterwards I found out from Ranjitsinhji that the story was a curious perversion. What had really happened was this. The young Maharajah in question wanted to clear his capital of stray pi-dogs. He did not want to displease his Jain citizens, who do not like any-thing to be killed, so he ordered the dogs to be collected within a large walled compound on the outskirts of the city, and sardonically allotted to the Jains the task of feeding them. The panthers in the neighbouring jungle decided that they, for their part, would feed on the dogs. They jumped over the wall at night and helped themselves. The Jains found this out and complained. So the Maharajah built a small tower at each corner of the compound, had arc lights sus-pended, and sat up at night with his rifle. He gave orders that no one from the town was to go near the compound after dark. The combination of the shooting and the lights in the distance was the basis of the story told to me and commonly told in the clubs all over India. Whatever sort of fellow this Maharajah may have been, that particular story is a good example of any number of similar *genre* one came across in clubs and coteries in British India. Such stories are not a good foundation for the understanding of India and the Indians.

In Bombay, and, I expect, in the other capitals of Provinces he visited, the Prince of Wales was chiefly engaged in functions organised by the governmental and official world, but he certainly tried his best to make contact with the available sections of Indian life. In this he must have been an anxiety to the officials responsible for his tour. I remember one occasion in Poona when he eluded the official grasp. After an anxious hour he was discovered walking about unattended in the Indian crowd on the racecourse. He had a strong wish to become acquainted at first hand with the people, and he must have been much struck by the difference between the world of India and the worlds of Canada and Australia, where there are no divisions between the governors and the governed, and even the Heir-Apparent could go about everywhere like an ordinary individual and make his own friends wherever his own pleasure prompted him.

It seemed to me in India that the Prince of Wales, although accommodating and genial in carrying out the public functions of the official world arranged for him, somewhat chafed against not having complete liberty to do what interested him personally out of school. The word " official," you note, keeps on turning up. One of the distinguishing characteristics of British India is that everything that matters is official, and even for an ordinary visitor it is not easy to go anywhere or do anything without official assistance. A friend of mine, who happens to be High Sheriff of a county, told me that, in his experience of India, it was no good going there except under the shadow either of a great official or of an Indian Prince.

I was fortunate enough always when I went to India to be under the shadow of a great Prince, for Ranjitsinhji, whom we ought really to call H.H. Sir Ranjitsinhji Vibhaji, Maharajah Jam Sahib of Nawanagar, although his State was not territorially large as the big States go, was regarded personally in India both by the British and by his brother Princes as one of the most important rulers, and he certainly was one of the most influential. It was under his shadow that I saw the celebrations of welcome to the Prince of Wales, not only in Bombay, but also in Delhi and in several of the Indian States.

It was in the Indian States that one saw the real India of the Indians, where it was not overlaid by the concomitants of the British Raj, which, though vastly important in themselves both to the Empire and to the well-being of India, always embody a self-contained European atmosphere not intended to be chock full of prestige, but in effect unable to be otherwise. So far as an onlooker could judge, the Prince of Wales found himself much more at home, at any rate for the purpose for which he had come to India, and also enjoyed himself much more in the large Indian States such as Jodhpur and Bikanir than in British India.

Outside his formal engagements, he was interested in riding and in polo rather than in any other form of entertainment in India. He rode and played polo a great deal, and always looked very fit and hard. I doubt if he had a more interesting time than in Jodhpur, the large State of Rajputana, where the everyday pursuits of the relatives of the Maharajah and of the young Sirdars were polo and pig-sticking. There was, I was told, no small anxiety among his staff and the officials about this pig-sticking. But H.R.H. certainly went pig-sticking.

The life in and around the young Maharajah's palace in Jodhpur would astonish, by its Spartan activity and simplicity, our common notions at home about Indian potentates of the Purple East. Old Sir Pertab Singh, uncle of the Maharajah, the famous soldier so much liked by Lord Roberts, was about the hardest nut I have ever come across. Even at the age of nearly eighty he lived in riding boots and breeches in the day-time, and at night he slept on a pallet in a small bare apartment like a saddle-room. Being charged with the welfare of the young Kumars and Sirdars, he turned them out on the polo-ground or in the pig-sticking field at dawn, and took very good care to eliminate anything in the nature of softness or luxury. He also took very good care that they lived the kind of life befitting older days, when they might at a moment's notice be required to ride with the Jodhpur cavalry against a neighbouring State.

The Jodhpur Lancers are still famous for their dash; nor was there any chance of their being otherwise under the eye of Sir Pertab. At one time he went away from Jodhpur, of which he was Regent during the Maharajah's minority, to be himself the ruler of the State of Idah, but he tired of that and went back to Jodhpur. He was a shortish man, sparely built but very powerful, and he walked about looking as if he ought to be on a horse. He was very simple, direct, and pungent—when he chose to say anything, which was not often. He had no particular interests except in soldiering, pig-sticking, and polo; but he was a strong character. He was extremely fond of his nephew Ranjitsinhji, whose sister had married the late Maharajah; he figured to exercise as an elder relative no small authority over him, which the Jam Sahib accepted with affectionate and obedient courtesy, whether he was going to follow his uncle's advice or not.

When I was at Jodhpur I had a feeling that Sir Pertab did not altogether approve of life in the unpretentious bungalow where the present Maharajah lived, and would have liked to transfer the whole outfit to the tremendous ancient castle on the one hill in the plain of Jodhpur city. There are many great castles in Europe still standing which must have been impregnable in the days before heavy cannon, but I have never seen any stronghold as solid and menacing as this elephantine military building, standing yellow on its yellow hill, dominating the expanse of yellow plain under the brazen Indian sun. The walls are monumentally thick, rising sheer in continuation of their rocky foundation. How in the old days an attacking army ever succeeded in forcing an entry one cannot imagine. There is no way of getting in except by forcing the huge main gates at the bottom of a winding narrow declivity between the high walls. Just beside the inner gates on the face of the terrific yellow stone are the red shapes of the small delicate hands of the Ranis of Jodhpur, imprinted as they went from the castle to mount the funeral pyres of their lords, who are unlikely to have died other than in battle. A most pathetic and inspiring relic of dead nobility.

Anyone who harbours illusions about the mild Hindu would be enlightened had he ever seen the castles of Jodhpur and Bikaner, or old Sir Pertab Singh, or that fine soldier and magnificent specimen of humanity the present Maharajah of Bikaner. These castles and men are only two out of many such exemplars of the fighting races of India.

One saw plenty of the potential military might of India when the Prince of Wales visited the capital of the Government. There all the functions and celebrations passed off successfully and in complete tranquillity. Nowhere in India did the reception given to the Prince of Wales reach the same standard of elaborate magnificence.

The most striking function was the Durbar held in the Old Fort at Delhi, in the great hall where the Mogul Emperors, Akbar, Shah Jehan, Aurungzebe, and the rest, seated on the jewelled Peacock Throne, had received the homage of their dependent Princes and high officers of State. There was a great gathering of the Indian Princes, and the appearance of these powerful men in their full regalia and in the historic setting opened one's eyes to the full importance of Indian India. The addresses on behalf of the India rulers were delivered by the Maharajah of Gwalior, the Maharajah of Patiala, and by the Jam Sahib. I thought Ranjitsinhji's speech was best, but then he had asked me to write it for him. The function was followed by a military tournament, viewed from the windows of the State apartments of the Mogul Emperors overlooking the flat dry sands of the Jumna. A fine display of the horsemanship of India.

New Delhi, with the new Viceregal Lodge and the Parliamentary buildings, was not yet complete, but the best part of it, including the main buildings, was there to see. Sir Edward Lutyens travelled up with Ranjitsinhji in order to explain his new capital of India to the royal party. In one of the halls of the Secretariat he had constructed a large model with a periscope fitted from underneath, so that one could look up through it and visualise the wonders of his work as they would finally appear. Lutyens took Ranjitsinhji and myself to see this one afternoon, and we found the Maharajah of Alwar there, and also Admiral Sir Clinton Baker, Commander-in-

Chief of the East Indies. Ranjitsinhji went below to look through the periscope, and the Maharajah of Alwar, who always called him "uncle," pencilled on a visiting-card, "You are an ass," and held it in front of the periscope.

A subterranean voice of commanding timbre shouted up, "Quite true. But who the devil are you?"

It was the Admiral. The Maharajah of Alwar, affecting consternation, hurriedly disappeared and was away in his Hispano-Suiza down the wide main avenue.

Had New Delhi been complete at the time, such functions as the Viceregal Ball would have been trebly magnificent. As it was, the ball was held at the old Viceregal Lodge, and was still a superb sight, with many of the Indian rulers on the dais, including the Begum of Bhopal, her face shrouded in a lace veil with only her eyes visible, and all the officers of State, and the ballroom thronged with resplendent British uniforms.

The unique feature of the ball was the entry of the Viceregal party. A fanfare sounded, the floor of the ballroom was cleared. The Viceroy's bodyguard formed up as a barrier all round the room. Then, to the tune of "God Save the King," played as a slow march, the Viceroy, the Prince of Wales, Lady Reading, and several Governors of Provinces slowly made their entry. The idea was a good one, but the slow march, even with disciplined troops, requires a certain amount of practice. It was then, I suspect, that H.R.H. began to be amused. Later on a Royal Quadrille was staged. Again the Viceroy's bodyguard cleared the floor and formed a picturesque hedge. The ballroom was surrounded by a tightly packed mass of resplendent uniforms and gorgeous confections. It happened that I had been dancing with the lady who is now Mrs. Tom Sopwith, one of the most superior blondes of my acquaintance, in whom I was taking a special interest because, for a lark, I had been called in to help design the dress she was wearing. It was a most successful peach-coloured creation, with white slashings. This lady, as clever as she was beautiful, being connected with the Viceregal Staff, knew that the Royal Quadrille would be worth watching. She had arranged with the bandmaster to view it from the band gallery, which gave onto the ballroom rather high in a side wall through a narrow aperture. So I, too, had the luck to be there.

The Royal Quadrille was performed and received with ceremonial reverence. The participants had evidently thoroughly schooled themselves in the elusive and stately manœuvres of this dance—all except His Royal Highness. His Royal Highness, in the uniform of a Scottish Regiment, with a scarlet tunic and tartan trousers, had relied on his partner, Lady Reading, "she in mauve." By this time his internal amusement had gathered too much volume for suppression, and although Lady Reading playfully tapped him on the shoulder as though to say, "Naughty boy," he went through the various visitations and swappings of partners ruddier than David with laughter, and preserved his equanimity only by stuffing his pocket handkerchief into his mouth. Nobody else turned a hair, and there was no let-up of ceremonial dignity. The Viceroy himself, in knee-breeches and white silk stockings, was the beau ideal of punctilious accuracy and Oriental grace.

I completely forswear any irreverence. The Royal Quadrille was one of the finest ceremonial exhibitions of dancing in circumstances and surroundings of impressive dignity, and at the same time one of the funniest things I ever saw in my life. I have blessed Mrs. Tom Sopwith ever since.

Another adventure that befell the Prince of Wales, this time out of doors, I happened to see. One afternoon Ranjitsinhji drove me off in his car to what he believed were camel races. We threaded the maze of the ancient city and arrived eventually at some sort of maidan where there was a huge crowd and a quadrangle of temporary stands. What was really going on we never discovered. The crowd was so thick that we could not reach our seats, so we got out of the car and penetrated the crowd on foot. Ranjitsinhji was in full Indian dress, patient and unperturbed as ever. We were jammed in the crowd long enough for the function, whatever it was, to conclude, and for the assembly to try to disengage itself. When we began slowly to accompany the dispersion in the direction of where we thought our car was, some sort of a stir occurred behind us. We did see some camels' heads whose legs we supposed had been engaged in races. Along with the camels there came a respectful eddy in the dense throng. So it was that near by us emerged H.R.H. on foot, accompanied by his Military Secretary riding a bay charger which mercifully behaved as well as a police horse in London.

How this happened I never heard. H.R.H. was proceeding among the rag, tag, and bobtail of Indian Delhi. Cultivators in homespun cotton and a variety of multi-coloured Indian whatnots were respectfully allowing as much passage for H.R.H. as the rest of the crowd would allow them, and gradually H.R.H. disappeared from view.

Ranjitsinhji, in his Rajput safa and pale blue silk aitchkan and pearls, and I, in a black tail coat and white topi, were liberated to find our car about half a mile away. That was the end of it. We never heard any more of it. But that this should have happened to the Heir-Apparent of the King-Emperor within rifle-shot of the Throne Room of the Mogul Emperors was the kind of surprise introduced into the ponderously dignified imperial life of the British Raj in its capital by this unconventional and democratic young man. I can still smell the smell of the camels.

The next time I saw the Prince of Wales under brilliant circumstances was when he was the guest of His Highness the Maharajah of Bikaner, away in his pink city in the wide rosy expanse of the Bikaner desert. The Maharajah's modern palace, marvellously built of red stone, with its central courtyard surrounded by lapidary lace-work supported on light marble pillars, housed a number of distinguished guests. There was a State banquet in the stupendous hall of the ancient palace, within the strong crenellated walls of the old fortress. At this banquet the Maharajah was at his best. He was the first Chancellor of the Chamber of Princes, and was then still a young man. But he had served with distinction with the British Army in China as well as in France in the Great War on the staff of the Commander-in-Chief. I have never seen a man who better looked the part of a distinguished soldier. He has a fair complexion for an Indian, brilliant large eyes, a moustache only just less military than Lord

Kitchener's, a voice of melodious thunder, and withal a fine athletic figure. He walks like a king and rides like a Rajput. He has decision and authority in everything he does, and his ability in any kind of staff work is reflected in the results he exacts from his own staff. The functions in his capital were magnificently done. He made a speech at the banquet, which, had you heard it broadcast without knowing the speaker, you would have allotted in your mind to an English statesman educated at Eton and Oxford.

A typical Indian entertainment was given in the inner courtyard of the Fort, which was cunningly illuminated, the outline of the battlements being picked out with innumerable yellow flames floating in small terra-cotta saucers. In the course of this entertainment appeared a strange giant, seven feet tall and powerfully built, who exhibited his skill in entirely eliminating his weight. He walked about on a heap of the Indian sweets which are so fragile that they break into dust with slight pressure between one's fingers like meringues. The sweets were placed in a cloth and wrapped up, and the levitationist, after lifting first one foot and then the other in a slow dance, while emitting a sound like "zip-zip-zip," stepped on the heap and went through the motions of treading grapes in a wine-press. Not a single fragile sweet was broken. He then proceeded to walk about on the upturned edges of a rack of sharp Rajput scimitars. The blades were fitted on a slant, and he walked up and down the curved edges. When he stepped off there was not a mark on the soles of his feet. I inspected them myself, as one does a horse's hoof. He also danced about with equal success on a square two yards of the points of a rack of lance-heads. There was no nonsense about the show, which I afterwards saw at close quarters three times when I was staying at Bikaner.

Another interesting performance was that of the fire dancers, who walked, leaped, and ran upon a broad heap of live embers. But this was not so magical; the skin of their feet was hardened by perpetual disuse of shoes; and the sand round the heap was damp. The skill of the dancers consisted in the rapidity with which they moved from one foot to the other in the proper style of an educated cat on hot bricks.

After these indoor shows the Maharajah transferred the whole company of guests to his ancient palace of Gujner. This lies twenty miles away across a desert of red earth covered with thorn and scrub. Gujner is a kind of oasis on the banks of a large lake. Except for internal modernisation, the palace of Gujner must be as it was hundreds of years ago in the days of Rajput chivalry. It is a castellated Indian château, with an immense baileyward, a finely timbered garden surrounded by high thick walls with a parapet all round from which the place could be defended. The wild pigs come up to the walls to be fed; and that is the one time when they are tame. Ordinarily they are scattered over miles of country round the palace, and do not obtrude themselves except that when there is a sand-grouse shoot they approach the butts through the scrub and pick up and eat the fallen birds.

The Maharajah takes his guests to Gujner for the shooting. There are thousands of duck on the great lake, and though the duck shooting cannot last long because the birds soon scatter to the smaller tanks across the desert it is excellent for one or two days. The guns are placed in butts round the edge of the water, and there are half a dozen floating butts on small rafts. The guns can get to the butts without disturbing the innumerable duck, which feel safe swimming in the lake. When the signal gun is fired the duck rise and swirl round in all directions, and gradually swing away higher and higher in separate flights. They are shot only while they are clearing away, and after an interval they begin alighting on the lake again, but no one shoots the birds as they return. The process can be repeated two or three times.

The pride of Bikaner in the line of sport, however, is the Imperial Sandgrouse, which come in from the desert any distance up to a hundred miles for three dips of their beaks in the lake at Gujner. The shooting of the Imperial Sandgrouse is without doubt the most wonderful bird-shooting in the world. The grouse arrive in incredible quantities and are marvellously quick on the wing.

It was a pity that the Sandgrouse were not in Bikaner when the Prince of Wales was there. I saw this shoot several times, and once the bag amounted to over five thousand birds. But

it is not the size of the bag that makes this shoot so distinctive; there are about forty guns in the tactically disposed butts.
It is the swift swooping flight of the birds and the difficulty of
hitting them. The birds are not driven over the guns; they are
kept away from the water by outlying stops all round. The
packs presently make up their minds to do a dash for their
drink and seem to arrive like volleys of grey cannon-balls out
of the blue. The Maharajah is a fine shot and always puts
himself in a difficult butt. His eldest son the Maharaj Kumar,
at the shoot when Lord Reading visited Bikaner, accounted for
nearly six hundred birds between about eight o'clock and half-
past ten in the morning. He is a notably quick shot and has
three loaders. I also saw the Maharajah of Kashmir shooting
very well. Ranjitsinhji, too, was a brilliant shot even after he
had lost the sight of his right eye and used twenty-bore guns
with pronouncedly bent stocks. One is liable to regard the
huge bags at Bikaner as somewhat of a slaughter; but this mis-
represents them, because shooting is so difficult. I have never
seen such difficult birds as the Imperial Sandgrouse, when
they whirl away after the packs become broken up.

I should say that the Maharajah has no superior in the
world as the organiser of a shoot. He has many trained lieu-
tenants among his sirdars, but the master-mind is his. Magnificent as he looked at the head of his cavalry when these
fine troops, together with the world-famous Bikaner Camel
Corps, were reviewed by the Prince of Wales, I think that one
obtained a more vivid insight into the tremendous asset that
an Indian Prince of his calibre should be to the Empire when
one saw him managing the success of any kind of shikar.
Dressed in his simple suit of green shikar-cloth, away on a
small expedition in the early morning over the plains to some
little tank where the bag might be small, but could be obtained only by the exercise of practical intelligence and hard
work in the craft of the hunter—there one saw the man.

Sometimes in the evenings at Gujner, the Prince of Wales,
Lord Cromer, Admiral Sir Lionel Halsey and I played vigorous
games of billiard fives. This is a devastating game. I remember H.R.H. wrestling heavily with the Admiral underneath
the billiard table for possession of the ball. Once the Prince

drove a ball so hard that it leaped off the cushion onto the wall and made a round hole. The next evening the Maharajah discovered that some careful house-wallah had filled up the hole with plaster. The Maharajah's eye never misses a detail. He had the hole regouged.

Why obliterate the traces of a royal guest?

*   *   *   *   *

Bear in mind that in India the Viceroy takes precedence over all the relatives of the King-Emperor. In harmony with the sun of India a fierce light does rather more than shine upon Viceroys. Personally I saw something of four Viceroys. Each of them in his own way was a success. Both Lord Hardinge and Lord Chelmsford were from the Indian point of view the right kind of men for the exalted position of Viceregent of the King-Emperor. Both looked the part, which matters in India. Lord Hardinge had the advantage of a diplomatic training and no quality is more needed in a Viceroy than the right kind of autocratic diplomacy. When it comes to it India has not much use for anything but autocracy, but it prefers its autocracy gilded by manners. Lord Chelmsford I knew at Oxford as Freddie Thesiger; he had been captain of cricket and took a first in the Law School. He was somewhat cold and statuesque in public appearance, but, like Lord Hardinge, he was regarded as a sahib of sahibs; he relied on his officials, and his favourite phrase was " the matter had better be kept fluid." The fluidity often congealed into the rigidity of the Indian system. An honest sportsman who regretted that Indian political leaders had not been to Eton.

Lord Reading was a far cleverer man than either Hardinge or Chelmsford. He steered his ship adroitly through many rocks and shoals and weathered many a storm by detecting its centre and manœuvring to its outer fringes. His ambition was to travel through his term without a row. He held the scales of justice so even that he himself sat on the tongue of the balance.

Lord Willingdon as Viceroy I did not know. He was Governor of Madras when I was in India, after having been

Governor of Bombay. He was by the Indians the best-liked Governor and Viceroy of modern times. Slim and aristocratic, with the background (some would say the foreground) of a brilliant, clever and kindly wife, he succeeded in winning the friendship of all classes in India.

An Indian will do anything for you if he believes that you like him; he will never show you that he knows whether you do or not, but he knows.

CHAPTER XVII

SHIKAR

BESIDES princes and politicians, India contains tigers and snakes. This is well known. The snakes are not as easy to find there as politicians, nor the tigers as princes. Some people talk as though there were no tigers left in India; but there are. In the jungles of the Central Provinces and the sunderbunds of Bengal and all along the foothills of the eastern Himalayas, as well as in Southern India, there are still plenty of tigers; but India being a vast country the individual animals are often some distance apart. Anyone who has had the fortune to be a guest of the late Maharajah of Alwar would be unlucky were he not to see a tiger. Alwar is within easy reach of the populous districts of Delhi and Agra. There are tigers in the forests and hills of Alwar quite close to the capital. As for snakes, I saw only two: one not anywhere in this world, and the other puffily swaying in a charmer's basket. Thousands of barefooted villagers die every year from snake-bite, so it is remarkable that I should have spent hundreds of hours in the jungle without ever seeing a snake there.

In Indian India, shikar holds a prominent place when important events bring important visitors, and in quiet times no guest of an Indian Prince would be considered even fairly entertained without being taken out to shoot.

Ranjitsinhji's State of Nawanagar in Kathiawar, being for the most part flat and open, was not all its ruler would have liked it to be in the matter of shikar. There have been very few keener hunters and fishermen than Ranjitsinhji, and I cannot think of one more skilful in the pursuit of any form of game, great or small, furred, feathered, or scaled.

It must have been a regret to Ranjitsinhji, who in latter days was far keener on fishing than on shooting, that the few rivers of his State were not of the sort to provide sport. Nor did he himself pursue the gentle craft in India; he did not

even seek out the rivers of India where the fiercely running
mahseer can be caught. He would have liked, I expect, to
frequent the trout-streams of Kashmir, and his friend the
Maharajah would have been very glad to see him. Ranji, however, found that the high country of Kashmir was bad for his
asthma, and I believe he only went there once or twice.

Then he went in the old Maharajah's time, and to play
cricket. What is more, with the honours of Test Matches in
Australia thick upon him, he travelled all the way up to
Srinagar at the old Maharajah's request, and was caught at
the wicket first ball. When he returned to the pavilion the
Maharajah said to him, "But, Ranjitsinhji, you have not
made duck surely. I never make duck." Presently the
Maharajah went in sixth wicket down and was bowled in his
first over in spite of the tender efforts of the bowler. The
Maharajah just picked up the bails and went on with his
innings.

The old Maharajah, uncle of the present ruler Sir Hari
Singh, was a humorist. Once when a visiting Viceroy was
being conveyed up the Jhelum valley to his capital in the
gilded State barge, His Excellency adverted to the banners
displayed in every village.

"Yes, Your Excellency," said the Maharajah; " welcome to
the Viceroy in very big letters."

Presently after passing half a dozen villages the Maharajah
said, "See, Your Excellency, more welcomes . . . All lies,
Your Excellency."

It was a pity about Ranji's asthma because Kashmir is as
beautiful as the books do say. Switzerland, as it were, concentrated into one huge valley with the Alps multiplied by three
on either side. When I was there the almond blossom made
a pink canopy along the banks of the Jhelum. The walled
gardens on the hillsides above the Dahl lake, through one of
which flows the pellucid stream of Shalimar, were full of
flowering shrubs. All the mountain streams and rivers where
I fished were full of trout, the largest I have ever caught except
the rainbows in New Zealand. For Ranji it would have been
a paradise. Otherwise Kashmir is a paradise for everyone; in
spite of its fabled beauties, still a paradise.

But as for shooting, two exceptional examples he had in his own State. One was an island near his port of Rozi, where, contrary to all advice and all expectations, he had succeeded in raising an abundant stock of partridges. There are various kinds of partridges all over India, but Ranji's was the only partridge shoot in the English sense of the term. No walking up; proper drives with hundreds of birds whizzing over the guns, and a bag at the end of the day worthy of Six Mile Bottom.

Then the panther shooting. There were panthers in nearly all the outlying districts of his State, but his show spot was around his shooting bungalow about seventy miles from the capital in the southern corner along the borders of the State of Porbandar; his famous panther jungles in the Burdar Hills. These hills form a wide circle, heavily jungled with bamboo and all the common smaller trees of Western India; a huge saucer, in the centre of which was his bungalow of Kaleshwar. The circle of hills in that outlying part are sparsely inhabited by the wandering herdsmen tribe of the Robaris, magnificent people with Greek features and terra-cotta skin; but there are no villages within the circle of hills; an immense, silent, and lonely amphitheatre.

At Kaleshwar there was an ancient temple a stone's throw outside the garden of the bungalow, surrounded by tall pipal trees, with here and there an aged and expansive banyan tree, under one of which the Jam Sahib used to hold informal audiences of cultivators from the distant villages. Outside the gates of the garden was a row of low buildings, inhabited only when the far countryside made pilgrimage to the temple.

It happened that the first time I was with Ranjitsinhji in Jamnagar, the capital of his State, he had no other guests, and after a busy fortnight, in which I was learning about Indian India from the Jam Sahib and his Ministers, my host suddenly announced after dinner that to-morrow we would go to the Burdar hills. This meant that at six o'clock three Ford cars of the old type and a lorry awaited us under the portico of the white Jam bungalow. We started with the sudden decision characteristic of Ranji, who rarely told anybody what he was going to do till the last moment; he always

knew perfectly well days before. Away we went, past the two
broad lakes with their ancient round fortresses, and past the
high outer walls and the frowning west gate of the city into
the sea of plain beyond. For some miles there was a proper
road. Then we forked off on what was called a fair-weather
road, which meant an earthen track across the plain. Soon
we seemed to be far from human habitation, seeing only
occasional cultivation on one side or the other, and distant
villages, few and far between.

Within twelve miles of the city we began to see herds of
blackbuck dotted here and there, and once, quite close to the
track, a herd of little, brown, gazelle-like chinkara. To one
who had had no experience of bigger game, except fugitive
springbok in the Transvaal, the quantity of deer was exciting.

Within two hours we had traversed the remainder of the
yellow plain to the foothills of the Burdar range, which
seemed to spring from the earth like a sudden island at
sea. We passed close to the site of the ancient and obliterated
city of Ghoomli. Scarcely a fragment remains, but close to
the hillside there are some deep wells, in which, according to
the legend, the inhabitants deposited their treasure. Attempts
to extract the water have failed. One can descend by steep
steps almost to the water's edge, and the water looks dark and
deep enough for anything. We climbed a rough track over a
series of shoulders and wound down towards the green saucer
in the centre.

There was the pink-washed bungalow, square-faced and unobtrusive, rather like the country houses one sees down the
Rhone valley. The rough but well-tended compound was
brilliant with a dozen giant clumps of bougainvillea. There
was shade in the wide verandah and under the big pipal trees.
A grey stone fountain was plashing in front. All round was
the wide circle of the wooded hills, complete silence, and a
brazen blue sky. The quiet experience of arrival was more
than thrilling to one who only knew the woods of Europe and
the treeless stretches of the high veldt. Were there not sambur
and cheetal somewhere in those mysterious jungles, and
panthers sleeping in caves or under shelves where the outcrop
of rock showed on the ridges of the round hills?

That afternoon a score of white-clad cultivators appeared by magic. Under an immense banyan tree, whose wide branches were supported by pendent pillars of itself, they sat and awaited Bapu's pleasure.

The Jam Sahib, impassively patriarchal, sat in a camp-chair and heard their case. It was that they were being oppressed by a moneylender. Shylock was there with all the signed documents and other bundles of legality in the fold of his cotton homespun. Everybody stated his case except Shylock. He merely exhibited his papers with a laconic gesture. There was no doubt that the cultivators had signed themselves into trouble.

The Jam Sahib explained to me that the man had all the law on his side, and the protestants had been very foolish not to take advantage of the Land Bank which he had established. But the *banya* had been outrageously extortionate; and what would I do if I were he? He was always testing me in small matters of practical wisdom in India, and, I think, took sly pleasure in showing me that the ruler of an Indian State had no sinecure in his capacity of Bapu—the daddy of his people.

I knew better than to hesitate. I said that whether the *banya* had the law or not in this case, did not His Highness think that in equity the *banya* could be severely called upon to justify so flagrant a breach of the spirit of His Highness's intention in establishing Land Banks? Why not give the *banya* the verdict and then, on the count of equity, fine him enough to recoup his victims?

To my surprise, the Jam Sahib, in measured vernacular, and in the style of Haroun Al Raschid, delivered his two judgments accordingly. Afterwards he told me that the *banya* had paid up with alacrity and on the nail, and had been glad to escape so lightly. I believe I went up in Ranjitsinhji's opinion quite several pegs over this small incident. And so to tea in the verandah, and then an early dinner, including some excellent fresh fish rather like mullet, which had been brought in by runners from the sea coast in the morning and conveyed in ice on the lorry. Early because we had to be away and hidden in an old tower in the jungle before nightfall.

Directly the sudden night falls with scarcely any interval of twilight a panther which has been lying up in the hills, choosing a coign of wide observation, wakes up and begins to think of coming down to find his dinner. The cunning beast knows very well that the goats will be driven home before nightfall, and that, like himself, the stray dogs, if any, will be prowling round for derelicts of daytime near the habitations of man.

The Ford car drove down a jungle track to within half a mile of the tower and overtook the party of shikaris and half a dozen goatherds. The goatherds had one unfortunate youthful goat on a short tether, and walked ahead calling out their musical summons. "Arree! Arree!" they go, not loud, but audible for miles. This would be a sign to all the denizens of the jungle that the goats were being called home.

When we got to the little clearing with the small two-storied tower of old stone, called a *kotah*, the guns and two servants slipped in by a back door. The theory is that the panther cannot count. Ranji and I mounted to the upper room, where the soda-water and refreshment for the night were laid out, and sat down in two large wicker chairs. Meanwhile the outside party walked on down the jungle path, still calling their goat-call. At last they came back, tied up their goat (which as yet had said nothing) on a large artificial boulder resembling an ancient pagan altar.

Such *kotahs* with the little clearing and its artfully simulated boulder in the middle were disposed at various spots in the jungle. Formerly, when younger and less *rusé*, Ranji used to sit up for panthers in *machans*—that is, shallow Indian wooden beds plaited across and arranged as platforms in the branches of convenient trees. But when he became the ruler and could get things done, he either adopted the existing little old towers or had new ones built at convenient spots where goats could be grazed in the daytime. The panthers, watching from the hills and keenly alive to noting where they would be likely to find a dinner, inferred (with due respect to the psychologists) that a clearing and a *kotah* meant a chance of a random goat after dark.

So the party moved casually around, still calling, and then

disappeared, their voices diminishingly audible afar off. Just before leaving the clearing one of them had lit a big lamp hung up on a high pole. Panthers do not mind a light slung up at a fair height, so there was no need to wait for a full moon. The carbide arc-light made no sound, and sound is what frightens a panther away. Perhaps, too, the panther has learned to interpret the hanging lamp as a nearer and a better moon.

There we sat in silence. The arrangement may seem rather artificial, but when the Indian night falls over the jungle, followed by a spell of silence, and then gradually the distant honk of the sambur is heard from the hillside, and the little various night sounds of the jungle begin, the impression is one of complete loneliness in a mysterious savage world. There we sat for hour after hour until well past midnight. Not easy to keep awake, peering out of the narrow windows. But, of course, the goat, as soon as he found himself deserted, began to bleat; and he bleated on through the night hours with rhythmical monotony.

Suddenly Ranji touched me on the knee and whispered, "He has come." He pointed across to the bushes at the corner of the clearing and handed me his binoculars. Good glasses disentangle and magnify objects even in the darkness.

I could not see anything at first. Then suddenly a pair of phosphorescent lights switched on in the dark. The panther's eyes. There he sat for half an hour in the blackness of the bushes, himself as black. Then the eyes were switched off. Ranji made a pass with his hand to indicate that their owner was circling round us in the bushes. The ground was covered with dry leaves and dry sticks; the bushes themselves, as one knew from moving through them in the daytime, might well have been designed to produce a stage crackling and rustling. But not the least sound.

Presently the brilliant green eyes appeared at another corner; then they disappeared again. Meanwhile the goat had stopped bleating and was standing up. It kept facing round with its nose like a compass-needle in the direction of its circling enemy. Very slowly, but not always correctly. Sud-

denly from the side of the clearing behind it a grey form, as
of a giant tabby on very long legs, moved out into the open.
Just before it stalked from the bushes the form looked dead
black, but the moment it came into the artificial moonlight it
was grey as the ground—so grey and similar as to be invisible
when still. The goat jumped round to face it as it stood for
some minutes as still as stone. Then the panther moved
forward like a grey ghost and leaped with marvellous ease
and grace on to the edge of the boulder. There it sat like a
cat on a doorstep, with its forepaws between its hind legs, and
contemplated the goat. The goat stamped its feet and blew a
succession of snorts through its nostrils.

Ranji had an electric pencil with a light at the end, such
as hospital nurses use. He wrote on a small block: "It is a
lady, but you can shoot her if you like."

Whether from innate gallantry or from sympathy with the
goat—probably the latter—I took the block and wrote: "No.
Let her go." I lowered my rifle on the cushions provided for
the very purpose, and Ranji knocked with his knuckles.
There was a grey streak, and the lady was gone.

Ranji then wrote: "She or the old man will be back in
twenty minutes." So I drank a bottle of soda-water and
relaxed.

Sure enough, the lady came back, but only to sit half-way
between the goat and the edge of the clearing. Again, after
an interval, she did the same from the other side, but this
time she went away for good, and Ranji whispered—he could
whisper without any sound of breath—"The old man is
watching in the bushes. I saw his eyes last time she came."

But the old man did not show that night. Ranji and I took
it in turn to lie down for a snooze on the charpoy, but I was
not good at this, because I kept verging on a snore, and every
time Ranji leaned across and pinched my nose.

Finally the grey morning washed over the hills and the
jungle. Ranji blew a whistle, and presently our overnight
party began threading the jungle path towards us, going
through the same routine as before. You must not let a
panther into the know. Their "Arree! Arree!" echoed
nearer and nearer, we came down, and the whole party, the

reprieved goat now cheerful, returned to breakfast and to bed till noon.

The old man panther had seen us home. The shikari reported that he had followed on the edge of the jungle fifty yards behind us to within a stone's throw of the house.

On our undisturbed way home Ranji told me of a goat which defeated a panther at the very spot where we had spent the night. The panther had jumped on to the boulder. The goat, after pulling back to the full length of its tether, launched itself like a bullet at the panther, which was so surprised that it fell off backwards, made an acrobatic landing, and shot away into the jungle to think it over.

"What is more," Ranji added, "you can see the white goat any time you like in the Zoo at Jamnagar. His compound is labelled *Caper heroicus.*"

For six successive nights I sat up in *kotahs*; different goats but the same performance. Every time either no panther or else a lady.

Ranji was not too pleased; he wanted me to get a panther. He told me next time it did not matter whether it was a lady or not.

But I would not shoot a lady; I had found out that there were not too many panthers in the Burdar jungle. If you shot a gentleman, his successor would soon arrive from the jungles over the Porbandar boundary; if you shot a lady, her gentleman would depart over the Porbandar boundary to find another wife.

Nevertheless, the whole experience was exciting. It is no feat to shoot a panther in the strong artificial moonlight at a distance of twenty yards, but it is intensely interesting to wait while interpreting the mysterious drama of sounds in the jungle at night.

My self-restraint was well rewarded. At the end of the week Ranji announced casually at lunch, "Charlo, you are in luck. There is a panther down on the plain by Moti Gop. We will go and get it." He had known this all morning.

So in the brazen afternoon three Ford cars with canvas hoods—the kind we now call Lizzies—threaded up the hills, out of the Burdar saucer and down over the other side, a few

miles out into the plain, where there was a big, single,
rounded hill like a giant ant-heap and the little village of
Moti Gop.

Directly we got there we saw a ring of villagers in their
white cotton *dotis* on the side of the hill, ringing a mass of
jumbled rock. The panther had come down from the hill in
the night and had been seen in the early morning creeping
up the hill to lie up for the day, no doubt meditating another
try for a stray dog near the village. We began to climb.
Ranji was then quite stout, but he was almost as good a
walker as in the old days over twenty years before, when we
used to tramp the big fields after partridges at Duxford, near
Cambridge.

The panther beat us. He did a bolt when we were about
half-way up. We saw the upper arc of villagers scattering
like white ants over the brow of the hill. They were not going
to lose sight of Bapu's panther.

So we climbed down again, and the head shikari came to
report that the panther had gone over the hill and into a
cave at the head of a dry watercourse in the flats on the other
side. Away we went after him by car. How they got there in
the time was amazing, but the villagers were already standing
at intervals in a big ring round the curious underground
cavity at the head of the deep narrow nullah, which was like
a single-line railway cutting. The villagers were opened out in
a long line on either side, and we found a little thorn zareba
arranged for us on a spur overlooking the nullah. There I
sat with Ranji, while about a hundred yards away the shikaris
insulted the panther with stones and epithets.

Suddenly there was a silence. The panther was under way.
View halloos might have caused him to break back. I saw a
creature like a yellow maggot threading the bed of the nullah
towards us. He crept slowly along, with his white belly
scraping the ground. Very different from the tall, ghostlike
panthers of the night jungle. They were feline greyhounds.
This fellow, until he stood up fifty yards away and began to
lope, was a huge dachshund-mastiff. As he went by, just after
he was past me, I had an easy shot and bowled him over.
One should never shoot while the animal is approaching; if

he is wounded he may up and at you like lightning. A panther can flash from immobility into electric speed of spring.

Shooting panthers on foot is a very different thing from sitting up in a tree or in a kotah. A wounded panther is dangerous. Some say more dangerous than a wounded tiger, because of its savage swiftness. Nor can one readily find an emplacement in the open where a panther cannot climb or spring; both of which evolutions he performs a good deal faster than anything most animals can manage on the flat. But with Bapu's servants one was almost safe. Any one of them would have jumped in front and taken the charge, and even jammed his arm in the panther's mouth, rather than that Bapu's guest should be clawed. That was my first panther.

It happened that two years later, when we were in the Burdar hills again, another panther was reported at Moti Gop. I had been out with a party in the jungle, where a drive was being attempted for General Sir Archibald Montgomery-Massingberd, to give him a shot at a sambur. He was Chief of Staff to the Commander-in-Chief. I got separated from the party in the maze of jungled hillside, and went home.

Ranji, sitting in his shirt-sleeves in the verandah, welcomed me with the words: "Lucky fellow, Charlo. There is another panther at Moti Gop."

This time it happened there was a largish party at the Kaleshwar bungalow, including four ladies, all of whom, as always, wanted to come and see the show. So this time we went away in four Ford cars.

When we arrived at Moti Gop we found that the panther had eluded the villagers from the start and gone away to the nullah cave at the first intention. We all pushed off again and found everything curiously as before. If Sir Archibald had not been high on the Burdar hills hoping for a sambur, he, being a short-time and very important guest, would have been the man to shoot. As it was, Charlo came in for the luck.

But when the ladies arrived with Ranji, and he saw the frail zareba on the top of the spur as before, he decided that this was much too dangerous a spot for them. We were accordingly all moved about a hundred yards down the nullah to a higher, but, for the rifle, by no means as convenient a spot.

The chief shikari shook his head and indicated to His Highness that the panther was likely to break back towards the hill up a grass slope almost opposite our former station.

Ranji brushed this aside in a word, so the noise of dislodgment began at the cave, as before. The panther came out all right, but he did exactly as the shikari had said. He broke back up the grass slope at a gallop. At the top was a long row of villagers who immediately chased him back as if he were a sheep. One youth with nothing on except a loin-cloth ran after him, beating him on the back with a little stick. Meanwhile, four unfortunates had been badly clawed. The villagers were not going to let Bapu's panther escape under the eyes of Bapu. They treated him with positive indignity; and he streaked back to his holt in the cave. He was too far away from me to shoot; and even if I had I might have only wounded him, which would have been bad for the villagers.

Again after a lot of insults he was dislodged. Again he went up the side of the nullah and clawed three more villagers. Then he returned to earth. Ranji sent my gun-bearer, Bhimji, with a bottle of neat brandy to pour into the scratches. Bhimji also took a double-barrelled gun loaded with slug.

This time the panther refused to budge, so in the end the head shikari, a little man with a face exactly like a panther, crept down to the mouth of the cave with a rifle and shot the panther at about five yards. He did this bold feat as though he were merely going into the backyard to unchain a dog. This man had an instinctive knowledge of panthers. If there was one within half a day's march he would find it; he would know everything it had done in the last twelve hours, and everything it would do in the next. He was a quiet little fellow of few words, but he was a panther-man.

The panther-man was not the only interesting character among the cotton-clad shikaris. There was the man with the red beard. These shikaris were scattered all over the State; in general, one to each village, but wherever you happened a party of a dozen or so could always be relied upon to turn up by dawn full of the required information, whether of birds or of beasts.

Ranji had a permanent camp out on the plains among some

shallow rolling hills at a place called Samana. Eminent
visitors, such as Governors or the Viceroy, were taken there
for shooting. The camp contained the biggest marquee on
record, where the large parties used to dine.

Once when there were no big guests Ranji took me there to
see what we could find. News came in that a panther had
been found and ringed. Along with us was an old friend of
Cambridge days, Charlie Rush. We three went out across the
plain for some miles, and stopped at a spot where the plain
dropped in an abrupt clifflet, like one side of a railway
cutting.

At the bottom of the cliff ran the remnant of a river; a clear
stream with a shingly beach, which in the rains would be a
torrent.

The shikaris had ringed a craggy nest of huge sharp rocks
on the side of the declivity. We went round by a narrow path
and were disposed among some bushes on the lower beach
looking across the stream at the face of the steep bank, along
which ran rough narrow terraces like sheep-tracks.

When the ring was open and the *brouhaha* started, out shot
a small panther. It went past me half-way up the bank at
speed. I had a bang and thought I had missed, but it was
afterwards found that I had hit its front paw. A few yards
further on it suddenly stopped, hesitating which side of a
boulder to go, and Charlie Rush brought off a beautiful shot
just behind the ear.

Then our old friend the panther-man came down and maintained that it was the wrong panther; and should he drive
the scrubby bank back the other way towards us?

Bapu nodded assent; so we sat down again. The panther-
man, of course, knew. Almost as soon as the drive began,
about two hundred yards on our right, out loped a big panther,
oiling between the bushes and boulders. Just before it was
within shot it turned back and disappeared again like magic.
It had gone into a slit of a hole scarcely large enough to admit
a big fox-terrier.

The panther-man explained, "Little cave—other hole."

Bapu gave some swift directions, and the shikaris cut down
a sapling with their walking-stick axes. Another fellow clad

in nothing but a wisp of green shikar cloth and a henna beard was looking about for a large stone with which to block the slit. Finding none, he promptly and casually sat down on the hole. Within six feet of his person was crouching an angry panther with a set of claws like meat-hooks. But Red-beard just sat down on the hole.

The panther was poked out. Out it came, as soon as Red-beard had removed his person and the sapling was inserted. Charlie Rush shot it as it was threading the scrub.

Several years afterwards I spotted Red-beard when we were out after sand-grouse. I said to Ranji : " That's the fellow who sat on the hole."

Bapu called his man up and told him that Fry Sahib remembered him.

Red-beard wagged his henna whiskers and chattered something. He was saying that he was much honoured, but the Sahib ought to know that when a panther goes into a hole it sits still.

Even with no such dramatic incident as that of Red-beard and his seat, panther-shooting on foot in the open was always exciting. The cunning of the simple manœuvres never failed to bring the dangerous beasts within shot. One admired the craft and pluck of the shikaris and of the villagers engaged as stops, but the brain behind it all was Ranji's. He had succeeded in educating the natural faculties of the shikaris into disciplined skill. What is more, any of the villagers who turned up to assist always knew exactly what they had to do in the plan of campaign, however varied the circumstances.

As sport, the pursuit of the panther in the open by daylight was far superior to sitting up at night and waiting for the quarry. But the still hunting by night, though the shot itself was simple if the panther condescended to come, had a romantic mystery which was captivating to a degree. There is nothing quite like the silent suspense in the surrounding darkness of the jungle at night. What in the biting sunlight is a desert of thorn-bush, scrub, and bamboo, traversed at rare intervals by dusty tracks, becomes at night a forest peopled by noiselessly moving life, and full of distant sounds which suggest that at any moment some unexpected shadowy form may appear, big or small, harmless or dangerous.

Indeed, even in the daylight there was a peculiar lonely mystery about the house and garden and scanty buildings at Kaleshwar. The more so because of the little temple among the pipal trees at the end of the narrow paved quasi-Italian garden with its purple flame of bougainvillea. It was a small domed kiosk of aged grey stone, in a narrow compound surrounded by a high wall.

One could see the little dome above the wall from the end of the garden beyond a small stream crossed by a wooden footbridge of Japanese dimensions.

Knowing that one ought not to trespass near a temple, I had always refrained from approaching it even in the long mornings and afternoons when Ranji was away and not a soul within sight or hearing; but there was always a temptation to go and find what there was to see. I never saw a priest or any temple attendant near the place. It was always utterly deserted.

But once a strange thing happened.

The day before, out buck-shooting, my bearer had dropped my rifle and the foresight was bent. In the evening I persuaded it straight; and next morning I woke up very early, and just as if I knew what I had planned to do, which I absolutely did not, I made a black blot with ink in the middle of a sheet of foolscap, took a pin, half a dozen cartridges, and the rifle, and walked straight across the verandah and down the garden. The usual sentry who walked to and fro in front of the verandah all night until the household were about was not there. But I took no particular notice of this.

I crossed for the first time the narrow, wooden footbridge, pinned my target against the stem of a pipal tree by the temple wall, walked back about thirty yards and planted three or four bullets more or less in the bull's eye. So the sight was all right.

Then, carefully looking round and seeing not a soul anywhere, I went just inside the entrance of the temple compound and peered about. There I saw through the open front of the shrine the usual stone lingam festooned with small white flowers, evidently regularly tended. I tiptoed back, forgetting even to collect the target. I had the feeling that I had done something wrong.

Not a soul was astir in the house. When I sat down in the verandah a peculiar feeling came over me as if I had been doing something in a dream. I began to wonder why I had ever taken the trouble to go and pin up a target on one of the sacred trees. Why there, of all places? It would have been so much easier to go the other side of the house as I had intended overnight.

Then it occurred to me that the reverberating sound of my shots, exaggerated by the echoes of the surrounding hills, had not been noticed in the house. I had a curious feeling that there was a conspiracy not to take notice of what I had done; and yet that unknown people somewhere around knew all about it. Above all, where was the sentry? I would wait and see. But when Bhimji presently brought me my *chota hazri* he said nothing, and he was a light-sleeping shikar servant who woke at the least sound. He was, I thought, over-innocent when I asked him where the sentry was. Bhimji would almost suggest that the sentry was either there, or was never there.

Later on at breakfast neither Ranji nor anyone else mentioned anything about rifle-shots. This was curious, as the noise at a hundred yards must have amounted nearly to the bang of a bomb in their bedrooms. I felt I had committed a major *faux pas*, perhaps even sacrilege. The incident was never referred to then or afterwards, but I did notice that Ranji looked rather grave at breakfast.

This happened in connection with panther-shooting in the Burdar hills. Several weeks afterwards something else happened. One morning Ranji took me away miles across the plains, saying that there was a report that the quail had come, and he wanted to see. We began by walking up a belt of long narrow fields of sparse corn near a large empty house formerly inhabited by a relative of his who had gone away to another State because he had misbehaved.

After spending a long forenoon walking the fields under the hard sun, we arrived at higher ground where there was a dry torrent-bed. There we found a couple of servants with lunch spread out on the bank of a dry cavity which in the rains was a deep pool in a mountain stream. One lonely tree gave us shade. A dozen yards to the left was a replica of the little temple at Kaleshwar, with its dome showing over the closely girdling walls. Ranji told me that this now deserted and empty pool was a spot of great sanctity where Shri Krishna had bathed; and pilgrimages were made there after the rains by people from all over the State. He then lit a cigarette, and after a few puffs leant back against the tree and apparently dozed off into a siesta. The servants had disappeared down the track towards the cars.

There I sat, feeling rather sleepy and thinking about nothing in particular. No idea had entered my head to go near the little temple. I was looking at the distant, empty, dismantled house, and wondering where its occupant was, and what was the true story of its emptiness. While I was drowsily pondering, quite at a tangent, I was prompted to get up and look inside the temple. Ranji seemed fast asleep.

I went to the flanged entrance and stepped inside. There was the simple but carefully tended furniture of a Hindu shrine. The anointed lingam festooned with wreaths of white jasmine, a spread of flowers on the floor. I had been standing about half a minute not without a feeling of awe, when from nowhere appeared a tall, ascetic priest. He wore the saffron jacket and the close-fitting Phrygian cap of the Brahmins. He took a small bunch of flowers from the lingam, touched me on the forehead, the chin, and both cheeks, and then disappeared without a word. Where did he come from, and where did he go? It all happened with unhurried, silent swiftness.

I went out and sat down again, and in a few minutes Ranji woke up, if he ever was asleep. I told him what had happened; he nodded his head slowly as he did when acknowledging the salaams of his people in the city. So we went after the quail again, and I thought no more of it at the time. Yet in retrospect the incident was peculiarly impressive. I knew no more why I suddenly went into the little temple than I did why Ranji had taken me to those vague, sparse little cornfields to shoot a couple of dozen of rumoured quails.

We shot a few more in the early afternoon, and then went

home. What struck me most about the day was Ranji's remarkable ability to walk miles and miles in the sun over
rough ground; for in those days he was stout and took little
exercise. I was lean and fit, but he walked me off my legs.
The little quails jumped out of the short sparse corn like frogs
and sped over the ears like bullets.

It was about ten days after this, at a big function in Jamnagar city, that I saw for the first time the Hindu High Priest
of the State. It was the priest who had touched my face with
the white flowers in the Hindu temple by the dry pool where
Shri Krishna had bathed.

Meanwhile, a day or two after the incident by the pool, I
noticed one morning when I was brushing my hair that a
round red mark about the size of a shilling had appeared in
the middle of my forehead. At the time, not connecting one
thing with another, I thought it was simply caused by the rubbing of my topi. One evening at dinner in the Jam bungalow,
casually conversing with my next-door neighbour, I was nar-
rating the incident by Krishna's pool, and without any real
connexion of thought, I added, " . . . and do you see this little
red mark on my forehead? That is where the priest touched
me with the white flowers."

There had been a buzz of conversation, but somehow, as
happens, the buzz tailed off as I was telling the story, and the
last sentence or two must have been audible all round the table
to the relatives and Staff of the Jam Sahib. My last words coincided with a frozen silence, which held for several long seconds.
I heard the Jam Sahib murmur, "Just the usual blessing."

This little chain of incidents, I cannot explain why, did not
strike me at the time as other than disconnected. It was only
a long time afterwards and in the light of other knowledge
that I connected them in coherent sequence. To this day I do
not know whether there was a sequence.

Why did I not ask Ranji himself, or some Indian friend?
Well, I felt that it would not be tactful, and that in any case
I should only get an evasive answer. Remember that I was in
India for the first time, and had been there for only a few
weeks.

To me it has always seemed, after a good deal of experience

in Indian India, that most of the stories that suggest the un-
canny verge on the imaginary; but I did meet six first-hand
eye-witnesses in Jamnagar who had seen a fakir walk up and
down a long trench filled with live charcoal, so hot that one
could not approach within yards of it—walk up and down for
several minutes in his loincloth, unscathed. Then he invited
anyone who had faith to do the same. One of the Jam Sahib's
elderly retainers, a sort of senior butler, promptly disrobed
himself and walked up and down the live charcoal with equal
impunity. The evidence of this was as good as one could get,
short of seeing the performance oneself.

Ranjitsinhji had an A.D.C. of the same name as himself, a
Rajput of the Chohan clan from the State of Idah. He took no
part in shikar expeditions or any form of active exercise, but
was much interested in *yoga*, and somewhat of an authority. A
quiet, pleasant fellow of decided but unobtrusive opinions. He
was connected with the first snake—you remember my only
other Indian snake belonged to a charmer.

There was a largish party of guests at the Jam bungalow on
one occasion, and overnight we were all told to be ready to
start early next morning to shoot snipe. At 6 a.m. we buzzed
off on a clear and exhilarating Indian morning in a series
of Ford cars, followed by the little Ford van with the guns and
cartridges. We drew up a quarter of a mile from the marshy
pools on the flat plain of crinkled cotton-land, and were standing around chatting while our guns were brought to us. Everyone was ready, but no one moved off. I was standing about
five or six yards from the little Ford van, now emptied of all
its contents. It was, as I say, a lovely fresh morning, and I was
never fitter, never more wideawake in my life. I remember,
too, that for me I shot particularly well that day, up to my
waist with no waders among the reed beds.

While I was casually standing there by the van I saw a large
cobra slither out of the back, slide to the ground and wriggle
away across the cotton-land. I called out: "Snake! Snake!"
and pointed.

Ranji was standing near, and Charles Rush from Newmarket, and two Army officers from Rajkot. "Where?
Where?" they exclaimed, following my pointed finger.

But in the brief interval, about twenty yards away, the cobra had disappeared. I followed where it had gone and the others followed me. There was no vestige of a hole in the flat black cotton ground where the smallest mouse could have gone to earth.

I noticed that nobody seemed to be at all disturbed about the snake; indeed, they betrayed only a formal interest. I also noticed that the A.D.C. Ranjitsinhji, who never came out shooting, was one of the party that day. He was looking on with quiet inattention; and when one of the cars went back before we started shooting he went with it.

Well, there it was. I distinctly saw the cobra, as real and concrete as the double-barrelled gun in my hands, but nobody else saw it. We went away after the snipe, and had a great day, and I troubled no more about the cobra. At lunch-time I talked a bit about it, and wanted to know what my companions thought had happened. They were singularly lacking in attention or interest.

When we were driving home in the evening I began to think over events. Then I remembered that the previous night, first before and then after dinner, I had been arguing with the A.D.C. Ranjitsinhji and half a dozen other Indians of the Staff about *yoga* and the rights and wrongs of the rope-trick and the mango-plant, and just for the sake of argument had put forward the usual European thesis of hallucination. The A.D.C. Ranjitsinhji and several others were trying to explain to me the metaphysical doctrines about *Maya* and the interconnexion of appearance and reality, and so on. Again, for the sake of argument and to elicit information, I had put myself in opposition on the lines of philosophic doubt. We all went to bed rather late. I remember feeling more sleepy than usual, so that the second I put my head on the pillow I fell asleep. I felt heavy when Bhimji woke me in the early morning with a cup of tea.

There is no explanation of that snake unless I was presided over during the night by one of the expositors of *yoga*, perhaps by the A.D.C. Ranjitsinhji himself; and imbued, according to their practices, with a mental picture of something that I was to see next day. Why was it that for the first time the A.D.C. Ranjitsinhji came out with the shooting-party?

Perhaps I ought to add that I was as good as a teetotaller while I was in India, and was as fit as ever in my life at that time.

Talking of snakes, I was never in India except during the months of the cold dry weather, and snakes are very rarely seen then. It is during the rains that they come out and are seen in the gardens and in spots convenient for them in the jungle. All the same, thousands of cultivators and grass cutters die of snake-bite every year. The local postmen at all times tramp about tapping the ground with a heavy stick to warn any casual snake that someone is coming; and by Ranji's orders, a black bag with all the likely serum was taken whenever we went into the jungle.

Tiger stories, unless first-hand, have little value. Except one. A certain Commander-in-Chief went to Gwalior on his quinquennial visit of inspection. The Maharajah Scindia proposed to offer His Excellency a tiger. The Gwalior tiger-jungles are good.

His Excellency was delighted; and, by the way, would His Highness put his young A.D.C., his nephew Tom, in a machan, where the boy could do no harm, and afterwards be able to say that he had been in a tiger-shoot?

The Maharajah would be delighted.

So next day His Excellency was up a tree in the middle of a jungle valley; His Highness up a tree a hundred yards to the left; and Tom up a tree three hundred yards to the right.

Far away began the tap-tapping of the beaters. It was a long belt of jungle. Presently the peacocks flew out; then a couple of pigs rushed across; then two or three deer walked by. Closer and closer came the beaters; but no tiger.

Just at the end of the beat, far on the right—bang! bang! After a pause the beat was resumed; the men came into sight, but no tiger.

So His Highness blew his whistle; His Excellency climbed down, and they went for refreshment under a big tree. His Highness was intensely sorry, they had made certain there were two tigers in the jungle, but better luck next drive.

Then Tom came strolling up, followed by his bearer with a couple of rifles.

"Hullo, Tom," said His Excellency. "What were you shooting at? What was it—pig?"

"No," said Tom, "I got a brace."

"Brace of what?" asked H. E.

"Tiger," said Tom.

And he had.

One ought to have mentioned lions. Most people think there are no lions in India, but there are, and according to Ranji they used to be common all over India in olden days. In the peninsula of Kathiawar, within easy reach of Ranji's own State, there are lions. They inhabit the Ghir forest, which lies principally in the State of Junagadh. I heard plenty of stories about them from Ranji himself, and also from the Maharajah of Bikaner.

One story of Ranji's is not a shooting story. When Lord Kitchener went to visit the Nawab of Junagadh, the Nawab gave him an entertainment in his arena. There was an elephant fight, but the *pièce de résistance* was the show of a maneless lion of Gujerat. This was because the Nawab had heard Lord Kitchener mention his curiosity as to how a lion kills its prey.

In due course a donkey entered the arena under compulsion. It trotted through the big gates, sniffed the air, flopped its ears, and began cropping the grass. Then from a side entrance emerged the king of beasts. He exhibited no interest in the donkey, and stood by his inlet, slowly lashing his tail. Presently the donkey saw him, pricked up its ears, stretched out its nostrils and drew a long whiff. The smell was novel. The donkey advanced slowly towards his majesty to get a closer whiff. This was a novel experience for the lion, which began to sleer away round the wall, looking back over his shoulder. Gradually the donkey went further, and so did the lion. Faster and faster. The donkey overtook the lion almost at full gallop, wheeled round, and let fly a tremendous rib-roaster, which got home. Then the donkey gave two tremendous bucks, cantered to the middle of the arena, and brayed its triumph fit to make the welkin ring. The lion was not having any, so the donkey went on looking for stray blades of grass.

The Nawab said he was very sorry that the lion had misbehaved.

"No matter, Your Highness," said Lord Kitchener, "no matter. If the asses of Junagadh are such warriors, what must the men be?"

Ranji vouched for this story. He was there at the time as a guest. He added that the fool of a keeper had gone and fed the lion as usual.

It would seem that, in spite of his moustache, Lord Kitchener had a ready wit. He once went down from the War Office for the annual review held by Queen Victoria of troops stationed in Parkhurst Barracks, near Osborne. The battalion advanced in review order to give the royal salute. It then formed up to march past in line.

When the advancing line was about thirty yards distant, Queen Victoria turned to Lord Kitchener and said, "General, we smell a very peculiar smell."

"Yes. Your Majesty," replied the General, "*esprit de corps.*"

It was a hot summer's day. In those days a soldier of the Queen possessed two flannel shirts: one on, and one at the wash.

This story is true, no matter from whom you heard it before. It was told me by the late Surgeon-General Evatt, who was present.

If I had ever met Lord Kitchener, and he had not frightened me at once by saying that it was me that he wanted, I should have asked him why it was that the British Empire did not furnish itself with a superb army in reserve by trusting the Ruling Princes and allowing each of them to provide a highly trained well-armed contingent. It is true that of late years more latitude has been allowed and more encouragement given to the Indian State troops, but they have never been allowed to have artillery or really efficient equipment in arms. There is a tremendous body of soldiers by choice—men, young and old, who feel themselves at a loose end if they are not soldiering, in the Indian States. The idea that any Prince would use his troops nowadays against a neighbouring State or against us is as obsolete as the Dodo.

Not long after Ranjitsinhji was installed on the Gadi of Nawanagar, he was confronted with a rebellion, which had its origin among the piratically inclined people on the West coast. It was a serious business. Ranji took the field himself and conducted a masterly little campaign. He used to tell the story with emphasis on the fact that most of the casualties in his own troops were due to the bursting of the out-of-date rifles, which were the best he was allowed by the Government for their equipment; whereas the rebels were armed with the best modern rifles.

I forgot to ask him whether, after he had rounded up the rebels, he was allowed to transfer the modern rifles to his own arsenal.

I venture to wager that he was not.

CHAPTER XVIII

ADOLF HITLER

O NE day early in 1934, lunching with a friend at the
Junior Army and Navy Club, I found myself (no doubt
by pure chance) seated next to a blonde lady in black,
who spoke good English with a German accent. Half-way
through she discovered my name, and I discovered that she
had been trying to get me on the telephone for weeks past.
Further, her husband was the agent for Armstrong-Siddeley
aero-engines in Berlin.

The story was this. The Fuehrer's head man of his Youth
Movement, Herr Baldur von Schirach, in pursuance of the
desire of the Nazi Government that some sort of *rapprochement* should be essayed between the German Youth Movement
and whatever might be its opposite number in England, had
sent over a representative, Herr Nabbesburg, to manage some
sort of *pour-parler* with the authorities of the Boy Scouts. It
appeared, I gathered, that Herr Nabbesburg had approached
the titular heads of the Boy Scout organisation rather than
the real heads of the working executive.

This led to misunderstanding. Moreover, Herr Nabbesburg
did not speak the English language at all fluently. He
started also with a background of difference of opinion
between the Boy Scouts in England and the Hitler Boy Scouts
in Germany as to what constituted the proper way to be a
Boy Scout.

Shortly, the German Scouts were strong on discipline,
whereas the English Scouts were strong on goodwill. This
difference had in the past obstructed Scout-like co-operation.
Now the main object in view on the German side, and a sound
one from their point of view, was to institute regular exchanges of visits between the two Youth Movements. Herr
Hitler, as he afterwards explained to me himself, believed
that such an exchange would lead to a better understanding

between the younger generations in the two countries. He sincerely believed this at the time, and most sincerely desired to effect such a better understanding.

In the upshot Herr Nabbesburg's visit to London was neither properly understood nor welcomed with suitable courtesy. I have no doubt, too, that he was received with a certain amount of suspicion, which his inability to explain himself did nothing to allay. The newspapers were rather inhospitable—one of them described him as resembling a first-class field-mouse—and the result of his visit was that the German side in the person of the emissary felt itself somewhat rejected, if not also snubbed.

On the other hand, I gathered that when Herr Nabbesburg returned to Berlin his chief, von Schirach, came to the conclusion that this was not intended, and that the mission had resulted in a misunderstanding on the English side. Enter my blonde lady.

She had a son at school in England, and was frequently over here, and someone had told her that I was a useful person to help to recondition the whole affair. Being a political lady, and a very able one, and also interconnected, in the matter of her husband's aeroplanes, with the Governmental authorities in Germany, she had the sagacity to believe that I was worth trying.

That is where we got to at lunch, except that being a political lady she asked me whether I would go over to Germany to see the leaders there and look into the matter. I at once said I would, provided that I saw the leaders, including Herr Hitler, as it would be useless for me to go there to find out about the matter unless when I came back I could speak with first-hand authority derived from the heads of affairs in Germany. There for the moment we left the adventure, and the lunch.

A few weeks afterwards I had an earnest telephone message from the lady in Berlin asking me whether I could come over in two days' time, as everything was arranged for me, including an interview with Herr Hitler. I replied that I could not throw up all my engagements and come over at a moment's notice, but I would come over about the 20th of the month, which was April. In spite of the tears in the lady's voice, I would not budge about the date, and a week later she rang me up again from Berlin telling me that everything was fixed for my date, and I agreed to go.

This arrangement having been made, I took the trouble to go and interview the leading executive authorities of the Boy Scouts in London and find out what it was all about; and I also took the trouble to tell the Foreign Secretary, Sir John Simon, what I was proposing to do. He arranged that I should see the relevant official at the Foreign Office. I also communicated with our Ambassador at Berlin, Sir Eric Phipps, who was a friend of my sister-in-law, Lady Heaton-Ellis. So everything was shipshape and Bristol fashion, and everybody, including the German authorities, was informed of this.

In due course I travelled by Harwich and the Hook of Holland to Berlin, and quartered myself (as, of course, I was running the whole show at my own expense) at the Eden Pavilion Hotel. I was put in the charge of an official of the Propaganda Department, and after various civilities and entertainments I went to see Herr Baldur von Schirach, the Head of the Youth Movement, and he explained the whole situation.

Now it happened that Herr Hitler himself was on his way to Munich to hold the opening ceremony of the great eastern motor-road, and to make an important speech. He had, as usual, gone by air. The blonde lady and the official conductor and I went by train. We had several days in Munich, and were specially conducted over the famous Brown House. We saw the miniature Senate Hall designed by Herr Hitler, which is the Mecca of the Nazi Party. It is an austere room with stone walls and red senatorial chairs. The sort of room in which the old Roman senate of the best time might have sat with dignity. The Fuehrer's private room on the first floor, with little furniture, two pieces of bronze, and two chairs, was also in the style of the old Roman Republic.

In due course we went out by car in the direction of Vienna, and arrived at the scene of the ceremony. Thousands of land-workers in parties were collecting from all directions to join an already immense concourse. They marched with their spades and forks and hoes at the slope after the manner of soldiers.

Herr Hitler made his speech, and it was impressive in a way that is not conveyed when one listens to him at a distance over the air. His voice was troubling him, but he succeeded in making his words forcible and his presence commanding. His voice has a peculiar carrying quality, even with its touch of harshness, and even without loud-speakers and microphones. He had some of his important people with him, notably General von Blomberg. The whole ceremony was simple, and gave one the impression of work, not of display. I saw Herr Hitler for only a few minutes, and then he hurried away in his car.

The huge concourse of landworkers dispersed as they had come, their implements at the slope, and they left behind them the straight wide road leading to unrecovered Austria. If the Propaganda Ministry had thought it well that a humble person like myself should be impressed with what Germany of the early Nazi régime was like, they certainly succeeded. There was no question that the people were devoted to the Fuehrer, and there was no question that the world of the fields and valleys round Munich was a world of work, simple-minded and disciplined. I cannot refrain from saying that the atmosphere of effective discipline strongly appealed to me. No one was running about doing what he was not wanted to do; everybody knew his allotted place and went there when called. Remember that this was the spring of 1934.

After a few days, regretting the Hofbrau House and the Rhine wine, we went back to Berlin. The next day an interview was arranged for me with Herr Rudolph Hess, then Herr Hitler's first lieutenant, but now formal Head of the Political Party.

Herr Hess is a very presentable adjutant. He stands well over six feet, spare and powerful, with close-cropped, wavy black hair, attractive blue eyes, clean-cut features, and charm of manner. He is a Bavarian, and as unlike the common English idea of a German as could well be. No doubt he was sampling me, but he did not show it; rather he succeeded in giving me the feeling that he regarded it as highly worth while that I had come to see him. This he did by manner, not by word; and naturally I thought well of him. I afterwards tried to persuade him that from the point of view of an understanding between Germany and England, far the best thing would be for him to come over to England and stay with me, going about informally, meeting people who mattered, so that they could find out what Herr Hitler's men were like. What is more, I was right. Right, that is, on the hypothesis, which I never saw any reason to doubt in 1934, that Herr Hitler and his men genuinely wished to be friends with us.

Afterwards I met several of the principal ministers, but for specific purposes I was handed over to Herr Rust, Minister for Kultur, corresponding to our President of the Board of Education, except that "Kultur" means not merely the education of youth but every activity in the Reich that has influence in making people what they are, including, I understand, much that we assign to religion. Herr Rust had been in the early days a Professor in a Prussian University, and had given up his position to throw in his lot with Herr Hitler in the days of struggle. Herr Hitler does not forget his friends if they are worth remembering.

In the Kultur Ministry, at what seemed to me incredibly short notice, representatives were collected from all over Germany to hear what I had to say and to ask me questions. Not all of them could speak English, but here as always the blonde lady acted as an adroit interpreter.

When previously I saw Herr von Schirach he had asked me to write a memorandum explaining the situation from the English point of view. This I did, emphasising that there was no unified Youth Movement in England as in Germany, and that they must not expect to find an exact opposite number of theirs. One of the mistakes had been to suppose that the Boy Scouts in England were a nation-wide organisation corresponding to their own Youth Movement. I suggested that if their project of a *rapprochement* by an exchange of youth was to bear fruit, the first thing to do was to establish in England a small liaison committee of a few representative men, provided that this committee was completely seized of the German proposals, so that it could sound all the different organisations in England to see whether any movement could be made to match the already existing German centralised authority.

The memorandum had been typed and distributed to everyone present at the conference at the Kultur Ministry. And everyone present certainly achieved a clearer knowledge of what were the scattered activities of whatever youth movement there was in England. My memorandum was accepted with approval. Then arose the question whether I could suggest some names for the projected liaison committee. I gave them half a dozen, icluding that of Hubert Martin, of the Boy Scouts, and J. A. Spender, the well-known writer, journalist, and publicist, former editor of the *Westminster Gazette*.

There the matter ended, but not quite. Before I had left for Berlin, knowing that Alfred Spender, an old friend of mine, knew all about continental affairs, I had asked him if I could come to see him about the mission in which I was engaged. He had not been at all forthcoming, although I was quite pressing, and I never saw him. When I returned to England I wrote to him and told him all about what had happened, and gave him my impressions. He wrote back saying that I would not be able to persuade him that the régime in Germany was desirable. Then, and not till then, did I discover that a recent book of Spender's had been banned in Germany, and that his freely expressed Liberal opinions at the expense of other political creeds had rendered him *persona ingrata* in Berlin. So far as I know, my unwitting suggestion of Alfred Spender's name for the liaison committee was the only *faux pas* I made in Berlin. But after all it was not really mine.

One grows to hate the word efficiency in connection with everything German, but one could not escape the reality of what the word stands for when one came into contact with the official and executive world in Berlin. The men one met were mostly young and keen. They wasted no time about irrelevancies, were always impersonal and objective, free from

the egoism of self-importance, direct and clear-headed. If
something were mooted to be done there were no delays. When
one turned up to see an official he was always punctual to the
minute and always knew with precision what was the point at
issue. The men at the head of affairs were attractively quiet,
attentive, and courteous. I liked them, and I wish that this
sort of man was not, as things are, in the enemy's camp.

On the social side I obtained a good deal of enlightenment.
Hospitable evenings at the big hotels and restaurants gave a
fair insight into the character of the city. Few people dined
before nearly ten o'clock, because the whole world of Berlin,
however fashionable, started work at nine o'clock in the morning and went on till nine o'clock at night.

Why it surprised me I do not know, but I was surprised to
see how smart and elegant were the ladies of Berlin. What is
more, the German girls have a large streak of that vitality for
which Australia is supposed to be unique; and in spite of re-
putedly hard times, they were as well-dressed as any I had
recently seen in Paris. One of the most attractive German
ladies I met was the young Countess Bernsdorff, daughter-in-
law of the pre-War Ambassador at the Court of St. James's.
Tall and slim, with a real Anglo-Saxon complexion, white with
a glow of red blood underneath. She had quiet blue eyes and
a beautifully poised head. Her yellow hair was long enough to
make a plaited Grecian bandeau like an oblique coronet. She
moved with a swing from the hips which one rarely sees in
Europe. She was a friend of my blonde lady, and both of them
afterwards came to stay with us at our home at Hamble. One
day, motoring to London, we had some time to spare, so I took
the ladies to Windsor Castle, and we happened on the Changing of the Guard. You know how magnificent the Grenadier
Guards show as they march off between the giant walls of the
entrance to the Castle with their band. I had regarded the
Countess as a quiet, self-contained, and much reserved lady.
But soldiers like these were too much for her Prussian ancestral blood. She was out of the car in a trice, and followed
the Guards for half a mile, running whenever she was
obstructed by her fellow-spectators. You should have seen
the flash of flame behind those blue eyes.

The name of Bernsdorff recalls former times, and reminds me of another interesting encounter, this time in England. Although I was cordially invited to go to Berlin again, I never found the opportunity. However, about two years later, being in the Long Room in Lord's pavilion one day, I was approached by Gerry Weigall's brother, the barrister, who is a protagonist of the Anglo-German friendship movement, and he asked me to come up to one of the boxes because he wanted to present me to—I did not catch the name. I went, and in the Distinguished Strangers' Box found a good-looking man of the Guards' officer type, a lady, and a girl of about fifteen. I was presented by name without being told to whom. So I sat down beside the lady, who was attractive in an outdoor, nut-brown way, and I tried to explain the cricket match.

Someone said did I not know that Her Highness was a long-jumper? Then out of her handbag came a certificate that she had passed the Nazi Athletic test in five events, and two picture postcards of herself. On the ground of fellowship in long-jumping, I annexed the photographs, and the lady signed them. She was the Duchess of Brunswick, the Kaiser's youngest daughter. She was extraordinarily nice. I met her afterwards at an afternoon party at Sir Archibald Weigall's house at Ascot. She is a very good dancer.

Much of the social side of Berlin stays up late at night, but it succeeds also in getting up early enough in the morning for everyone to be at his job and her job by 9 a.m. There was a complete absence of the lounge-lizard type of youth, who looks as if he would break in two in the middle, so frequently seen in the entertainment resorts of London. Nor did one see the kind of girl who looks as if she were presenting herself to the late hours of the night as the whole object of her existence. Indeed, Berlin of 1934 gave me the feeling of a world swept clean by a fresh wind which had left it stimulated, energetic, and ready to work without losing its capacity to enjoy itself.

The most interesting formal occasion of my visit was when Herr von Ribbentrop gave a dinner for me at his house, where a number of interesting people appeared, notably von Bieberstein, the Head of the Civil Aviation, and von der Goltz, the son of the famous general. Frau von Ribbentrop was a delightful hostess, although she entirely repudiated my suggestion that it would not be long before she was hostess at the Embassy in London. She said, "No! No—no—no!" But, as you know, it came true.

Herr von Ribbentrop at the time was a special ex-officio adviser of the Fuehrer in foreign affairs; a sort of additional Foreign Minister without portfolio. He struck me as a keen, wide-awake and resolute man. He was remarkably well informed about everything in England, and seemed to have gauged not only the tendencies in our political world, but the characters of our political protagonists. Had I met him without knowing his activities alongside the Fuehrer, I should have summed him up as a first-rate man in big business in the City of London. Not at all the type that suffers fools gladly, distinctly forcible, and quite ready to forgo any effort at unnecessary tact.

Herr Adolf Hitler is a Unitarian prophet of German resurgence with the drive and fire of Mahomet. Herr von Ribbentrop, with his hard, handsome face and cruel mouth, is a dangerous second to the prophet. He goes more by the sword than by the Koran.

A couple of days before I was leaving I was informed that Herr Hitler would be pleased to accord me an interview, as he wished to ask me what had been done in the matter of my visit. A car came to fetch me at eleven a.m. from the Eden Pavilion, and landed me at the Reich Chancellery, where four Black Guards saluted me into the gloomy portal. At the foot of the stairs I was met by a major-domo in evening dress, white tie and white waistcoat. He conducted me up a flight of stone stairs and invited me to take a seat in the long anteroom. At once a messenger in uniform came to report that Herr von Ribbentrop would be with me in a few minutes. So he was, and he conducted me to the other end of the anteroom and then to the right down a spacious and very long passage, such as one threads when one tries to discover an official at our Admiralty. Half-way along we stopped before a pair of large sliding doors; the instant we halted they slid aside and left us framed in the doorway.

In front of me at the end of a long, lofty, narrow room, as it were almost on the horizon, I saw Herr Hitler at a desk in his light brown tunic. He sprang to attention on the instant and gave me the Nazi salute, which I returned still framed in the doorway. He then took two steps forward and halted to let me start; as I stepped off he stepped off, and kept in precise step with me, so that we met precisely in the middle of the room.

He was, as I say, dressed in his khaki-brown tunic, and black trousers, and he moved with quick alert steps and a smart poise. He is not a tall man, but he carries himself with a natural air of command which, even if he were small, would prevent him from appearing so. What struck me about him as he advanced was his alertness. When we met he bowed formally, but with the kind of fine ease with which I have seen Baron von Cramm bow to Queen Mary at Wimbledon. He motioned us to a table at the side of the room, myself to a corner of a settee on the wall side, he himself sitting in a Louis Seize chair at the head of the table, with Herr von Ribbentrop on his left.

He then asked me, through Herr von Ribbentrop in German, to tell him what I had done since I had been in Berlin. I had the feeling that the Fuehrer understood English, but did not care to talk it on a subject, and *vice versa*, I was in exactly the same case. Anyhow, I offered a concise statement of what had occurred.

After this had been restated in German, Herr Hitler said that he would like to explain clearly the object of the Youth Movement, and what he felt about exchanges of parties with England. His first point was that the whole object of the Youth Movement in Germany was to bring up the next generation as first-rate citizens of the National-Socialist State. This was the main object, although training in qualities of mind and body was an important corollary. It was of vital importance to his régime that all class-distinctions should be dissipated, and one main instrument for this purpose was the wearing of uniform by the whole of the Youth Movement. He specially asked me to bear in mind that it would be a mistake to interpret the general wearing of uniform by the Youth Movement as of military significance. As I knew, he went on, it was quite impossible for Germany to exist without a strong army, and naturally he hoped that the Youth Movement would make first-rate material for the armies of Germany when the country was again capable of assembling her forces on a scale proper to her. But he reiterated that the primary intention of the Youth Movement was not military, and he feared that there had been some misunderstanding about this when Herr Nabbesburg went to England to meet the leaders of the Boy Scouts. He seemed to know all about the whole affair.

Herr Hitler then went on to state the case, as he thought it ought to be understood in England, for the military rehabilitation of Germany. He said that people in England did not recognise that Germany had five frontiers, and that in the state of German military strength as prescribed by the Treaty of Versailles, any one of five States could invade Germany, and every German knew it. Unless he was able to furnish Germany with sufficient military strength to convince the people that they were safe from invasion, unless the people believed that he was moving as quickly as he could towards the re-establishment of the military strength of Germany, he would not be able to hold the nation together, and the result would be chaos as little in the interests of neighbouring countries as of Germany herself.

He paused, and said with slow emphasis that we in England did not realise how close to Russia was Germany, both politically and geographically. People in England were inclined to think that he exaggerated the danger of Communism in Germany, but in truth the German State even then was seated on a volcano. That was his phrase. He added that the relative figures of his majority as against the Communists did not truly exhibit the strength of Communism in Germany; it was a perpetual and difficult task to establish and maintain a stable Government.

He then touched upon the Jewish question. He said that we in England did not understand the Jewish question as it existed in Germany. The Jews became good citizens of England, and though many of them achieved powerful positions individually, especially in finance, they were not an organised community within the community: an imperium in imperio. In Germany, he insisted, the Jews had obtained a stranglehold on finance, medicine, law, and all the learned professions. They were organised as a sub-community, and their support permeated all Communistic activities. Einstein, he added—in England no one could understand why a scientist of international celebrity, a harmless scientist, should be treated as dangerous. But Einstein's name, and therefore his authority, would be found in the subversive activities of the Communists. The Communists presented Einstein as one of their leading names. England ought to understand that the National-Socialist State must be all or nothing, and it could not be all unless the antagonism of the Jews—even the passive antagonism—was destroyed. He admitted that there were apparent injustices and hardships in his treatment of the Jews, but that, he added, was their fault because they hung together like a hive of bees.

Herr Hitler, beyond all question, was earnestly desirous that his aims and difficulties should be understood in England, and he said that he sincerely hoped for such an understanding. "If England would give me her little finger," he said, "I would give her my whole hand."

I do not for one moment suggest that Herr Hitler gave any indication that he would depart from the line which he believed would be the salvation of Germany. He said that what he was doing was what he had to do in order to preserve Germany, and that when his actions and policy were not understood in England in their true intention, he was sorry, because he valued the friendship of England.

Herr Hitler listened very carefully to my statement of my idea of *rapprochement* of the youth of the two countries, and I found him approving the line of exploration which I had advocated.

At the end of about an hour and a quarter he stood up, and we moved to the middle of the room. The Fuehrer shook hands and bowed, and indicated a departure of myself and himself in different directions, so I stepped out towards the far-off door. When I got there I turned round and saw that the Fuehrer had timed his arrival at his desk to a split second. As I turned, he was turning, and as I saluted, he saluted. The sliding doors closed in front of me, and as they snapped, the picture of the Fuehrer in his brown khaki coat at his desk registered in my mind as the exact duplicate of what I had seen when I entered.

What did I think of Herr Hitler, for what my ideas are worth? I was attracted by him. He looked fresh and fit, and, as I say, notably alert. He was quiet and courteous and simple. He treated everything that occurred in the conversation with an apt precision that cut out all waste. A characteristic I noted was the economical consecutiveness of his mind. He gave the impression of effective grip. Anything further from the idea, not unprevalent in England, that the Fuehrer is hasty, over-emphatic, and perhaps even noisy, I cannot well imagine on my impressions in 1934. He has an innate dignity, at any rate in such relations as those in which I met him, and he has a knack of making one feel that he gives his fullest attention to anything that one says. I am just writing of this great man as I then found him.

And what did I think of Germany, as I found it in 1934? At that time there was no sign of a renascence of what we used to call militarism. So far as an ordinary visitor could see, what formerly we used to call " Prussianism " (whatever we meant by it) was gone. The claim for freedom in rearmament and military establishment did not appear at that time to imply a State policy of aggression. It was just the outward sign of an inward determination to reinstate Germany as a first-class nation and to rehabilitate national honour. After all, to imagine that the traditions, sentiment and vigour of sixty millions could permanently be held in tutelage was absurd; to expect a great people willingly to remain defenceless within a ring of powerfully armed neighbours was fantastic. I doubt whether at that time, no matter what Herr Hitler had written in *Mein Kampf*, what we call the expansionist policy, and Germans by another name, was more than in the bud. But the new political and social régime was firmly founded and was revered as the heaven-sent alternative to political chaos and social disintegration. Leading Germans at the time would have said that this might be quite difficult for England to appreciate at its

German value; our main troubles and problems, severe enough in all conscience, had differed from theirs; ours had been economic and commercial: theirs, in addition and in poignant insistence, political and social. The English did not realise, they would say, the formidable nearness to them of Russia. To the English, Communism—by which they mean the stark continental species—is a small cloud on the horizon; to Germany it has hardly ceased to be a Damoclean thunderstorm whose premonitory flashes and rumblings had already begun, and whose deluge was barely forestalled by a miracle of effort. This was not rhetoric; it was too close to the stern facts. It was a truth: and one by which any inclination to criticise their means and methods must be tempered.

It seemed to me at the time that, unless one realised this background of the German mind, a correct appreciation of the salient features of Nazi statecraft was impossible. At any rate, it was with this background of declared intention to rebuild and consolidate a unified and coherent State on a racial basis of right-minded citizenship, trained and disciplined, that the Youth Movement figured.

We may dispute about political and social forms and theories, but we cannot dispute the German theory that it is the character of the men who make and administer these forms that really counts. For example, we in Britain have no Youth Movement equivalent to the German. Up to a point the Scouts resemble the Hitler Boys as originally founded, but though the Hitler Boys were originally meant to be the German counterpart of the Scouts, there is this fundamental difference: that the Hitler Boys were trained to become not any kind of good citizen they themselves may elect, but good Nazi citizens of the pattern required by definite Nazi State principles. They were imbued with the doctrines and ideals of a dominant political party which aimed at eventually ceasing to be a party by evolution into the whole State.

There was, too, the difference that the Hitler Boys underwent a formal discipline foreign to our Scout methods, which made the Nazi system much more of a training and less of a game; to my mind a distinct point of superiority on the

German side. I do not believe in training without discipline. There is a discipline of goodwill as well as of insistence, but the best discipline is a compound of both, and cannot be obtained without the second ingredient. Nothing excellent in corporate effort can be achieved without discipline, and no discipline is as good as the best.

What we call the German Youth Movement goes far beyond the original Hitler Boys. It embraces Universities and schools and clubs and societies of all kinds, and purposes to unify and control them all. With us there are the Universities, public schools, council schools, primary and secondary and technical, the training-ships, the cadet schools and Army-type schools, the Scouts (overlapping some of the above), boys' clubs, societies, and brigades, and what not, all of them for the most part self-contained, self-governing, independent, and under no central control. But the German Youth Movement is controlled at the top by the Reich Ministry of Kultur; and the Reich Ministry itself controls a much wider range than our Board of Education, which is not administratively concerned with the Scouts or Boys' Brigades.

There is a further point. The Nazi ideal of education definitely places health and character in front of mere intellectual training, and lays formal stress on physical drill, athletics, and games; and includes all this formally in its Youth Scheme. In fact, the German Youth Scheme is a definitely coherent State method of producing the citizens it wants. We have not any such definite State methods. We may get our own results successfully in our own different way. We say we like liberty. But if we are to achieve a rival efficiency, then we must persuade ourselves to organise a machinery for inter-relating our scattered and excellent activities and societies of youth.

This would be a desirable development. Communism and all its corollaries are a turgid curse of mankind. Whatever storms the Germans have ridden into, they did face and outride that storm: a tremendous feat of national character.

The fact that we have come to look upon the Nazi system as hostile and dangerous to our interests does not prove that the means whereby Germany has reformed herself into such a capacity are not worth our close attention. Whether we like it or not, we do not enhance our own national virtues, however great, by inserting a national ostrich head into a national sand in order to pretend that random voluntariness can obtain the same results as organised discipline.

Such were my impressions and my conclusions when last I saw Herr Adolf Hitler. Whatever may have happened since, I see no reason to withdraw any of them. " *Fas est et ab hoste doceri.*"

CHAPTER XIX

THE OTHER END OF THE EMPIRE

ANY Englishman who thinks that his education is complete without visiting Australia is mistaken. The Australian has rejuvenated the British race in a new world of his own without losing his attachment to the root qualities of the parent stock.

Before I landed in Australia I had only known the Australians in terms of cricket. I had thought of Australia as a vast country, sun-bitten, stark, and flat, except for distant rugged mountains.

What astonished me most about Australia were the flowers and the roads. Who of us at home thinks of Australia as a land of flowers? Disembark at Fremantle in Western Australia—a good thing to do because it is nearly two thousand miles nearer England than that vertical line of four great cities in the East, vertical if one regards the earth as standing on the South Pole, with the North Pole on top. Disembark there and you will discover, after a few days in Perth, that much of the bushland of this huge State is a garden of glorious wild flowers and still more glorious flowering shrubs.

Western Australia is so immense an area that mere detail is swallowed in space. No one, however, could miss the particularity of baby pelicans under instruction in fishing by their mothers in the Swan river, or the arc-lit trotting race-track of powdered oyster-shell.

Perth is, perhaps, the finest city in the Commonwealth; a glorious climate, fresh with a resplendent sun, wide streets, an atmosphere of energy, and a cricket ground. One does not hear so much of the cricket of Western Australia as of the other States, but the cricketers of Western Australia are notable for turning up from all over the place, just dropping their jobs for the day in order to bowl out Walter Hammond or make a century against Verity.

But the flowers! You can see them, too, after three days and nights in a train, in surprising and glowing profusion in the park-like gardens of Adelaide, which is, perhaps, the finest city in the Commonwealth; a glorious climate, fresh with a resplendent sun, wide streets, an atmosphere of energy, and a cricket ground. Adelaide confronts the world from a series of right angles. Stay at any hotel you like, go out of the front door, turn to the left, turn to the left four times more, and you are at the front door again, having walked a mile.

Then, again, the suburbs of Melbourne, which are nearly as large as those of London, differ from the latter in being avenues of scarlet blossom with villas embowered in greenery. Melbourne is, perhaps, the finest city in the Commonwealth; a glorious climate, fresh with a resplendent sun, wide streets, an atmosphere of energy, and a cricket ground. Add, too, that the finer parts of Melbourne are in some respects finer than the finer parts of Kensington. Why, one day a brilliant young Australian dame was whisking me sharp to the left up a boulevard much wider than Portland Place when she suddenly jammed on all brakes, back and front, and exclaimed, "Damn! I'm up the wrong alley!"

Then what shall we say of Sydney? That gargantuan harbour, that colossal bridge—nothing that even an Australian can say about them, could he find the words, verges on exaggeration. The difficulty for a Briton from home is to express his own thoughts and feelings in terms intelligible to the direct realism of the Australian mind. A harbour can be something more than a harbour and a bridge than a bridge in Sydney. With a central core of ancient tradition and narrow streets reminding one of old New York, the vast suburbs rival those of Melbourne under the smiles of Hebe and Flora. Sometimes as one strides along a broad, paved passage between the hibiscus bushes with a mauve-blue jacaranda blocking the horizon like an earthly cloud, one almost feels that a brace of fauns or a leash of nymphs will slip out between the shrubs, following the pipes of Pan summoning them to dance in the twilight—if Australia had a twilight. Surely this is a re-edification in a newer and better world of the outskirts of ancient Athens.

Nevertheless, Sydney is, perhaps, the finest city in the Commonwealth; a glorious climate, fresh with a resplendent sun, wide streets (some of them narrow), an atmosphere of energy, and a cricket ground. But, stay—Sydney has its beaches: sun-drenched sand and Atlantean Pacific rollers, populated by magnificent humanity of all sexes, genuinely putting the fabulous bathing-places of Honolulu and Samoa (and I have seen them both) into the category of the trite and outworn. Indeed, it was the life of the beaches of Bondi, Coogee, and Manly, coupled with the background of urban and suburban vivacity in Sydney, that betrayed me into the remark that the Australians are so full of life that they have forgotten how to live.

We have leapt fifteen hundred miles from Perth to Adelaide, four hundred miles from Adelaide to Melbourne, five hundred miles from Melbourne to Sydney, and now another five hundred to Brisbane, the crown of Queensland. There the beauties of the other cities are reproduced on the fringe of the tropics. It might be a seaside Pietermaritzburg enlarged into some likeness of Colombo. Behind its local patches of flamboyant flowers and brilliant trees there is a background of sun-bitten grey all over Australia, but in Queensland the grey becomes a brazen red. One may say that here, compared with the other cities of Australia, is a *soupçon* of backsliding from stark reality into tentative romance, furtive, perhaps, but unmistakable. There is a feeling of the Puritan conscience, but with loopholes through which an enquiring eye might discover some of the extravagances of the unregenerate East. Were one to follow the clue, one would light upon some touches not only of Colombo and Pietermaritzburg, but of Suez and Alexandria. Nevertheless, Brisbane is, perhaps, the finest city in the Commonwealth; a glorious climate, fresh with a resplendent sun, wide streets, an atmosphere of energy, and a cricket ground.

Let it be understood that Australia, with its five great cities which have engulfed about two-thirds of the inhabitants of the continent, and its boundless open spaces, of which hundreds of thousands of miles have never been open to the eye of white man, strikes the casual visitor as scarcely scratched

by way of development. What of it is developed has achieved
a marvellous, vivid, and energetic value, and is the nurse of a
race of men and women, genuinely a separate race in their
own right and not simply an offshoot of an older civilisation;
though its members refer to England as home. This is a
paradox which enhances the vast value, actual and potential,
of this young and beautiful daughter of an ancient and distant
mother. But how fine it would be if this distance could be
measured in the mind of England as no more than a bare
month in a ship or barely ten days in an aeroplane.

The danger of generalising about countries which are conti-
nents, such as India and Australia, is proverbial. But Australia
is one of the few countries of the world possessing unity in its
type of inhabitant. This general type falls into two sub-
species—the city type and the country type.

From the English point of view the Australians of the
stations, of the back blocks, of the great wheat-fields, and of
the illimitable pastoral lands, are the salt of the earth: hospitable to a degree, kindly past words, and simple in the
eminent sense of the term—the simplicity which always goes
along with great qualities.

The Australian of the cities is also no doubt the salt of the
earth, but this excellence is disguised by his being separated
from the earth by bricks and mortar.

The Australian of the cities has involved himself in an
environment alien to his true nature. The moment he gets
out of the cities for long enough—as, for instance, when he
volunteers for active service in the armies of the Empire—he
does not mind talking about the Empire and reverts to his
proper self. The life of the cities is active and, worse still,
efficient; one feels that the inhabitants have been hurried
into a noisy, strenuous life copied by mistake from the big
cities of America. Having shed their background of the sheep-
runs, the mines, and the mountains, they have not quite had
time to manufacture, in their short life, a proper background
of urban culture.

Perhaps this is the reason why so many of them are liable
to suspect an ordinary Englishman of walking about in their
sunshine with a perpetual desire to outshine them. And so

the Englishman is confronted with the feeling that the ordinary Australian is trying to come it over him. As a side-issue our newspaper readers at home can never quite understand the import of barracking at the big cricket matches. Can an English spectator in Australia fairly interpret the gladiatorial shrieks from twenty thousand fair throats that ought to be emitting golden voices when an English cricketer is caught off a bump ball?

The Englishman and the Australian ought to admire one another because their good qualities are complementary; their defects cancel one another out. Instead of that the Australian has an unwilling way of being betrayed into prickliness, and the Englishman into irony.

We other English find the Australians superabundantly energetic, but their own joke against themselves is that they are bone-lazy. A great fellow named Dicky Keane, who was once a Commissioner for Railways and is probably now a Senator, who weighs twenty stone and has a ready wit as well as a voice that requires no microphone, and is altogether a first-rater, told me this story. Four Australians drove into an up-country town on the usual hot day, and the horse stopped in front of the hotel and leant against a tree. One of the party leant against one wheel, one against the other wheel, and the third against the horse. The fourth could not find anything else to lean against, so he leant against his own shadow. A true story, unless there was a race-meeting on in that town that day.

Most of us from home would suppose that the great cricket fields of Australia are the places to see the heart of the nation, its very essence. Not at all. Where the real Australia flows into evidence is at the races. Race-meetings in Australia are conducted on a scale and in a quantity which put old England to shame.

A modern democracy without racing and cricket in the summer and football in the winter is, of course, unimaginable. In these three requisites Australia can certainly challenge the democracies of the world. And please do not forget that, although we do not hear so much about it, football in the Australian towns is a tremendous institution, and draws bigger crowds than cricket. Withal for the most part they play their own game, and are quite sure it is the best; nor am I quite sure that it is not.

Then again, in Australia, of all democratic countries, one has the best chance of realising what it is to be governed.

I was late for breakfast one Sunday in Adelaide. That is to say, it was ten o'clock. We had been days in the train, and at last I had gained a good night's sleep. No one to provide breakfast. The young man in the bureau added that it could not be done.

Could I not have a boiled egg and some coffee in the lounge?

No. The kitchen was void for any such purpose.

Well, if I could not get even a cup of coffee, I would make Adelaide the laughing-stock of London.

How the young man thought I was going to do this I do not know, but he consulted the proprietor, and from some source in this fine hotel a boiled egg and some coffee were produced by eleven o'clock. No doubt it was my fault. The first law of life in a democracy is obedience to one's own law.

The amazing thing under a régime so democratically restricted is how hospitable and kind to visitors is every public authority in Australia. For instance, the great Cricket Associations of Western Australia, South Australia, Victoria, and New South Wales, not to mention Tasmania, could not do enough for any of us who had come there to describe the virtues of our English cricketers and the defects of their Australian opponents. But may the best team win. As a matter of fact, the English team was the better, but it did not win.

Queensland, from lack of accommodation, cannot be quite so generous to her guests, but she does her best.

Everywhere else we special visitors from England had been given temporary membership. My hosts in Queensland were full members of the cricket club and had the right of introducing a friend, but they were not allowed to introduce me; which was severe, as I was not only an ex-Captain of England, but the senior member of the Marylebone Club out there at the time. Characteristically, the daughter of the house had somehow succeeded in becoming, not a lady member, but a full male member of the club. She had the right of taking in a female friend, and put forward that I did not take up as much room as a fat lady.

In vain. So, in accordance with the rules, I got myself proposed as a paying member, and went round to see the Secretary with a fiver in my pocket. If I had been a chance visitor it would have been all right, but, as it was, the matter had to receive the special consideration of the Committee. The Committee refused my fiver.

Everywhere I went in Australia I was pursued by the feeling that, magnificent as are the five great cities, one was not actually seeing the real Australia. One wanted to be away in the real life of Australia, the stations, the sheep-runs and the cattle country, the illimitable cornfields, and perhaps the mines. One knew all the time that the life of the cities was only there at all because of wool, kine, corn, and gold. Primary products. The kind of men who made Australia are still there somewhere, though they are pretty well taxed out of existence. But nowhere more acutely than in Brisbane did one hanker after the wider world away from the walls; Queensland spreads out into so vast a land of bush and pasture, and even away up to the sugar plantations and tropical products of the north.

It is only in Brisbane that the setting of a Test Match is not on a scale that completely dwarfs our own venerable provision for major games. Compared with the colossal stadiums at Sydney and at Melbourne, Lord's and the Oval and Old Trafford are miniatures. The only comparable arena for games that we can show is the stadium at Wembley; and even Wembley, though it may be a rival in point of the number of seats it provides, is out of the picture for convenience and comfort.

The huge grey amphitheatre at Sydney frowns down on the central grass like a circular range of mountains; from the upper seats the players resemble white ants industriously performing evolutions in a green bowl. The Melbourne Oval, though not so beetling in its buildings, is just as amphitheatrical. At Kennington Oval, and even at Lord's, one might perchance remember that cricket began on village greens as a

game played for pleasure. There it is difficult to believe that
the great game did not spring as it were full-grown from the
thigh of Jove in a Test Match.

Not so, however, at Adelaide, which possesses the loveliest
great cricket ground in the world. Indeed, it is the only cricket
ground in the world which combines adequate accommodation
for a Test Match crowd with a scenic setting ideally attractive
in itself. Seated in a luxurious leather-covered fauteuil in
the middle of the semi-circle of stands, one looks across a
perfect first-class cricket ground, surrounded by perhaps 50,000
comfortable spectators, away over a wide foreground of
wooded parkland to a fine range of mountains distant enough
to give a sense of spaciousness, yet near enough to be impressive. The tall cathedral on the near left has strayed from
an older world and is the only building in sight. Yet we are
within ten minutes' walk of the heart of the third greatest
city in Australia.

In according the finest cricket ground in the world to
Adelaide and to Australia, one must not forget that Tasmania,
too, is an Australian State, even though it is an island. At
Launceston and Hobart are two cricket grounds of uniquely
beautiful aspect, equal to most of our county grounds in
capacity, but not suitably furnished for Test Matches. The
Launceston ground is the nearest to a village green to be
found in Australia, yet it is big enough for a first-class match.
The Hobart ground is on the top of a hill looking down on
one of the finest and bluest harbours in the world, where a
battleship can run alongside the quay, and is overshadowed
by a Highland mountain. In sum, big cricket can be presented in Australia as it can be presented nowhere else in the
world.

The big cricket that I saw in Australia was the tour of the
M.C.C. team, captained by G. O. Allen. The fortunes of that
team, and all the things it did not do, are chronicled in
Wisden. Before it started everybody in England expected this
team to be beaten, and everybody in Australia was sure of it.
To my mind it was a stronger team than the Australians put
forward, because our bowling was the better, our batting just
as good, and our fielding superior. There was only one

objection on the Australian side, and in the end Don Bradman did us in.

But the actual course of the cricket was absurdly out of step with the prophets. The English team played badly against some of the States, chiefly because most of the batsmen behaved frowardly in their treatment of a lot of slow leg-break bowlers who would have been regarded as second-raters in minor county cricket. Then our fellows, having earned the hospitable pity of public opinion in Australia, completely out-played the home champions in the first two Test Matches. They won hands down at Brisbane, where the Australian batsmen surprisingly dropped their bundles, and otherwise played badly against the fine fast bowling of Allen and Voce. Charles Barnett and Maurice Leyland were excellent in our first innings, and Allen's 68 in the second innings when runs were sorely needed was the best batting he has ever displayed.

One is inclined to remember only Australia's powers of recovery in this Test series, which she won after being dormy two. This first Test at Brisbane proved that England was a fighter, too. Voce and Allen bowled us to victory as they did at Sydney, where the rain and Walter Hammond with a double century contributed to Australia's eclipse.

The wet wicket at Brisbane was not a difficult wicket to batsmen educated to appreciate that a little water need not drown one. The wet wicket in the second Test at Sydney offered a difficult, but possible surface. The wet wicket at Melbourne almost justified cricket journalists in their use of the word "impossible." It was bad enough for Allen to declare his innings closed while still 124 runs behind, in the hope of getting another thrust at Australia on it. I am not sure that we saw any better batting on the tour than Hammond and Leyland gave us in a stand of 42 on that treacherous wicket. Hammond was caught by Darling, fending a ball with a dead bat almost off his Adam's apple. After our collapse a week-end of Australian sunshine supplied Bradman with a billiard table for his impeccable break of 270. We were beaten out of sight.

The fourth was the vital Test. It was the only match played on a wholly dry wicket, and in spite of losing the toss we ought to have won. Our batsmen lost us the match and the Ashes by too much respectfulness in the first innings. Barnett hit a Gloucestershire hundred, but Walter Hammond played with unusual solemnity long enough to flatter the good bowling into the appearance of danger. Fleetwood-Smith found the dusty marl on the last day the ideal wicket for his method. It goes without saying that after a poor Australian first innings, Bradman produced one of his most masterly double centuries.

The fifth Test went with the toss. Australia made a wonderful start. They scored 604 in their first innings, but quite as meritorious as Bradman's 169 was Farnes's 6 wickets for 96 in a total of 604. Rain and O'Reilly gave the *coup de grâce* to a tired side which might have taken on one of them but not both.

After the first two Tests we did not enjoy Voce at his best— he could never be sure his back would stand up to a full gallop. Barnett was the only England batsman to come out of the tour with an increased reputation, though Leyland solidly maintained his good name. Hammond batted and bowled as well as we knew he could, but Ames was his true self only as a wicket-keeper, and a superb wicket-keeper.

O'Reilly bowled nearly twice as much and nearly twice as well as anybody else for Australia. But I do not think Australia called upon her other best bowler. Perhaps she was keeping him up her sleeve, not for next time, but for the time after next. He is, of course, that wise little gnome, Clarence Grimmett.

It would be painting the wattle-bloom yellow to accentuate the excellence of Australian cricket relatively to that of England, from a population of six against a population of fifty millions. But the excess of our home population is counterbalanced by the concentration of cricket in four main centres, and by the perpetual sunshine of Australia.

In Sydney, Melbourne, Adelaide, and Brisbane there is not just an Oval, there are any number of ovals. Anybody keen on cricket can from earliest boyhood get as much of the game as he has time for. And there is plenty of time in Australia. Facility for cricket is about the most democratic feature in a country which prides itself upon its democracy. There is not the same heavy line drawn between first-class cricket and club cricket. The backbone of the game is the district club cricket of the cities. A boy on leaving school can join a district club, and if he is of the sort likely to do much can play in, say, the fourth eleven of the club, and next year in the first eleven, alongside a Macartney or a McCabe. Even if he belongs to a country district he will come into the circle of celebrity in what are called Country Weeks, when the leading country sides come to town. He may be invited to stay in town and play in Grade cricket—the open door to Shield and Test Matches. That is how Don Bradman dawned.

The club cricket is very keen, and although few of these clubs are as good as an English county, the sides contain quite a number of players fit for county teams in England. If a young cricketer is of the calibre likely ever to reach the top of the willow-tree, he has this advantage, that the district has a representative on the Cricket Association of the State, who will most certainly push him into consideration for the State eleven; not to mention that the State authorities in each city have all the local Grade cricket under their eye, and are quick to exploit new talent. It took them one year to promote young S. G. Barnes from Grade cricket to the Australian team.

What Grade or Pennant cricket means is this. The city, Sydney, or wherever it is, is divided into so many districts. Each urban territory has a cricket club. These clubs play each other in matches lasting two Saturday afternoons. You begin the game this week; end it next. It is more like League cricket than any other in England; but if there is no Test or Shield game on, all the leading cricketers in the State will be playing for their districts.

We at home are prone to think of the Inter-State games as representing first-class cricket in Australia in normal operation; but this is not so. Rather is it the equivalent of what we should have, were our counties collected together, say, as Northern, Midland, Western, Eastern, Metropolitan, and Southern groups, with a team chosen, say, from Kent, Sussex, and Hampshire, playing against a team from Notts, Derby, Warwickshire, and Leicestershire combined. Our champion county, say Yorkshire, in one of those rare years when York-shire is champion, would play a weaker State eleven on level terms and perhaps beat it, but an average good State team would be much too strong for an average county. The result is that the Sheffield Shield matches between New South Wales, Victoria, South Australia, and Queensland provide something we have not got—a standing system of unartificial and genuine trial matches from which the representative elevens of Australia can be chosen.

There is another aspect of Australian cricket which makes a difference. In our county cricket, any batsman or bowler at all likely to be mentioned for an England eleven, once he gets a place in his county team as a young man, can recline for the rest of his cricket career in a comfortable armchair. But in Australia there is a continual competitive pressure up-wards from dozens of ambitious youngsters, so that a famous player failing to maintain his fame with equal energy may easily find himself displaced from a State side almost as soon as he is dropped from the national team.

Another signal difference is that the whole world of cricket in Australia is amateur; genuinely amateur in terms of Aus-tralian life. All the players earn their livings from some job in a brightly competitive world, and even one who may be more interested in his cricket than in his job cannot forgo the mental activity of having to hold his job down in addition to keeping his form up. It is true that some of the Australian cricketers get their jobs in virtue of their ability to play the game, but none of them can find (as do our professionals) a whole-time living in the game, with no economic interests outside it.

We are familiar in England with the disappearance of the old-fashioned amateur from first-class cricket, due partly to the passing of the old country-house life with its leisured class, but partly also to the increase in the number of first-class matches, and the necessity under which the county clubs labour of maintaining a regular team. But the kind of young man who in Australia corresponds with our amateur of former times is equally absent from first-class cricket there. The young men of the station families and of the equivalent section in the cities rarely appear in State or even in Grade cricket. They do not play cricket after they leave school. Few of them go to the Universities, which in Australia are not places where culture can be leisurely absorbed, but are nearer to technical colleges where degrees are to be obtained to furnish one with a livelihood as a school teacher. This type of station youth prefers to go in for lawn-tennis, golf, polo, or surf-bathing.

The truth is that the bulk of Australia's first-class cricket, although it cannot quite be a profession, comes from the section of Australian life parallel with that part of English life from which most of our professional players are derived. Probably the reason the young men from the station families avoid the higher walks of the great game is that they do not care for the democratic authoritarianism of cricket management in Australia. This management combines a high degree of efficiency with a general tendency to keep the player very much in his place.

Nothing could be more divergent than England's management of county cricket and of Association football. Our management of county cricket is not a business-like coherent system. It is a working arrangement of custom and convention. The Football Association is a co-ordinated organisation. There is no one in England in the cricket world to dictate to an amateur cricketer what he should do or what he should not do.

In Australia, if you allow for necessary modifications, the world of big cricket corresponds with our world of Association football, in that the management is of the same kind. The Cricket Association of each State is governed by a body consisting of representatives of each of the district clubs, and these representatives elect their managing committee. The Board of Control is composed of members elected to represent the Cricket Associations of the States. The playing cricketers as such have no representation either on the governing bodies of the Associations or on the Board of Control. The governing bodies of Australian cricket possess and exercise a pervasive grip. The players are not consulted at all, and do not figure in the management of the game. It is very rare, too, to find a prominent old cricketer as a representative of a club on the Association, and even rarer to find one acting on a Selection Committee.

One upshot is that the Board of Control is exceedingly unpopular with Australian cricketers themselves. There is an excess in the direction of discipline, and a jealousy of authority. The gods of Australian cricket are very jealous gods: even Don Bradman can only be a light-weight demigod. Supposing, say, Stanley McCabe wants to take a team up to play against his home town, he cannot do so without obtaining permission from the Cricket Association, which is quite likely to refuse it. Were he to disobey, he would find himself left out of the State team. Even Don Bradman was fined £50 for a slight technical breach of discipline in writing a book. Arthur Mailey, one of the finest slow bowlers Australia ever produced, was a professional journalist, and was banished from cricket for ever for writing in the course of his duties an impersonal, objective report of a match in which he was playing. He had telegraphed to the Board for permission, and had allowed plenty of time for the reply which he never received. It may all have been the fault of the Australian postal system, another democratic institution. Such straws could be multiplied into the thatch of a haystack; they are enough to indicate the direction of the wind.

No doubt the Australian world of cricket knows its own business and what is best for itself, and the management certainly is efficient, but one cannot help feeling that the easy-going want of system in England is more in character with the game of cricket. In England, we sometimes grumble at the M.C.C. for what it has not done, but we do not find ourselves cursing it for what it has done.

These eager, earnest and accomplished young men who nowadays represent Australia in the cricket-field play the game in a wideawake and devoted spirit, and if there is any slackness anywhere in Australia, outside the operations of the post office, which, without apology, once took three months to deliver a telegram for me, it is not in the cricket-field. One fine characteristic they have is that they always exhibit in their play a hundred per cent. of their actual ability; they tug their best out of themselves in matches played at high pressure. The way in which the Australian team pulled itself together during the Test Matches I saw there was fine.

One found these modern Australian cricketers first-rate fellows, but they are quite different from the distinctive characters of pre-war days. If we leave out the phenomenal Don Bradman on the score of his unprecedented scores, one misses the individuality of the great Australian cricketers of the 'nineties. There is no one to rival the artistic charm of Victor Trumper, the solemn, alert competence of Monty Noble, the busy, enterprising, carefully conducted aggressiveness of left-handed Clem Hill, and still less the rugged, native genius of Joe Darling. Such batsmen as these introduced, each of them, when they walked to the wicket, the prospect of something individual. Victor was Victor, Clem was Clem, Monty was Monty, and Joe was Joe.

What is more, these great cricketers won the personal admiration and affection of our own great men, such as Archie MacLaren and Stanley Jackson, much more intimately than happens now between their moderns and ours. To my mind, bar Bradman, the modern Australian batting, good as it is, is not comparable with that of the older generations.

As for the modern Australian bowlers, O'Reilly and Grimmett alone compare with the old vintage. The race of Australian bowlers up to recent years has been of superb talent. It has never since been as fine as in the days of Spofforth, Garrett, Boyle, Palmer, Turner, and Giffen, followed by Hugh Trumble, Noble, and Jones. Macdonald and Gregory were a powerful interlude, and their earlier leg-break bowlers, such as Hordern and Mailey, introduced a new first-rate type. But in pure class, the older generation of Australian bowlers set a standard which, to be honest, has sadly diminished.

This is not to say that so fruitful a source of fine cricket as Australia is dried up; but it is not flowing with its old-time volume and vigour. When one met in the pavilions such ancient heroes as Tom Garrett, Hugh Trumble, and Charlie Turner, one felt that Australian patriotism alone prevented them from shaking their heads sadly over what they saw going on in the field. I am sure that old Tom Garrett, sitting slimly in his wicker chair, looking like the best type of old-fashioned English gentleman, would have liked his long grey beard to be brown again, and to bowl with renewed youth at some of the batsmen he saw.

There is one of the older brigade who does not merely shake his head. He proclaims his unflattering opinions in forcible language. It is not only in the Legislative Assembly of Tasmania that the Honourable Joe Darling lets drive. That is perhaps why this strong and wise elder statesman of cricket is not included in the management or government of the game. He knows more about cricket than the whole of the Board of Control put together. But perhaps his direct and sanguine energy is better employed in politics and in pastoralism than in combating what he regards as the modern heresies of Australian cricket.

Joe Darling ought to be Prime Minister, and he might even make a good Prime Minister of New Zealand. Not that one notices politicians as much in New Zealand as one does in Australia, though there is little difference in the two countries in the matter of their unpopularity with the grazing and farming interests which have made both countries what they are, and have therefore richly deserved to pay for the privilege.

Go to New Zealand and you feel at home. You are at home. You are not regarded in New Zealand as in need of emendation. There is nowhere in the Commonwealth of Nations where an Englishman feels less out of place. The two beautiful islands are rather like Scotland without the rain and mist. There are the lowlands and the highlands, but there is no difficulty whatever in understanding the language of the people.

New Zealand is not as good as Australia at cricket, but it is equally good at racing and has much better fishing to offer, and very much better facilities for winter sports. That Australia can show snow mountains where one can ski and toboggan quite as well as at St. Moritz is not generally known. Still less generally is it known that the glorious mountains of the South Island of New Zealand can give most of the winter resorts in Switzerland a fair start and a beating.

Perhaps it is not worth while travelling thirteen thousand miles for the winter sports in the South Island, but it is certainly worth while to travel that distance for the fishing in the North Island. There is nothing like the long blue lake at Taupo, with its innumerable lively rivers, anywhere else in the world. And there is no fish as well worth pursuit as the rainbow trout of the region. What is more, I have not yet come across any other spot where one can enjoy a hot bath in a pool below a waterfall on the hillside in the open sunshine. Most stimulating; especially if one can walk away and in ten minutes be fishing in streams as clear and as bountiful as those of Snowdonia, with a good chance of half a dozen trout weighing not five ounces but five pounds apiece. There is no waiting for rain and cloudy days at Taupo. Under the bluest of skies, in the brightest of sunshine, in the clearest of water, one can catch these rainbow trout—but not unless one can fish. The idea that the fishing in New Zealand is so wonderful that a novice can chuck any sort of fly at the end of a muddled line and haul out a monster must be abandoned. In some of the rivers, though the trout are much larger than in the Itchen and Test, the art of the best dry-fly fisherman may be properly exercised.

In the stream of Waitakanui, near Taupo, which received most of my attention, the fruitful method was exactly like fishing for salmon in a quick-running West Highland river. One cast across and downstream, so that the fly would search the water in an arc across the pool, assisted by the pull of the stream. But one had to use finer gut than for ordinary salmon fishing, and exercise a lighter touch and a more careful accuracy. Then again a certain special knowledge is needed in order to secure that the fly sinks right down as soon as it touches the water, and this calls for the projection of a loop of line from the hand, so that it shoots out to the far bank above the fly. A decent fisherman can catch rainbow trout in these streams, but a bad one cannot. Anyhow, the fish are there to be caught.

My first experience was unusual. It happened that some cousins of the Palairets, the noted cricketers who were school-friends of mine, have a home at Taupo. It happened also that the head of the family, who is called Bran all over the North Island, is about the best fisherman in the Antipodes. He is also about the kindliest and most knowledgeable sportsman I have ever met. It was a day's journey in the train, a night at a hotel called the Château, and then half a day in a service motor-car. I was told to get out of the car at Waitakanui bridge, eight miles before Taupo. Sure enough, at the little bridge, there was Bran in long wading-boots with his own car, and with a couple of rods ready at the slope against the wind-screen. Stepping out of the service bus, I was invited imme-diately to step into the other pair of wading-boots, and then to step into the pool below the bridge. At the second cast the reel went whizz, and a six-pound rainbow trout was dancing about in what Bran called the ditch at the end of the thirty yards of line. Nothing so sudden has ever happened to me in any stream in any part of the world. So I went on catching half a dozen whoppers a day for the next three weeks, and otherwise having perhaps the best time of my life in the superb sunshine.

How anyone who can live at Taupo ever grows old I cannot imagine. There is a cleanness and zest in the air and a fresh-ness pervading the hills and the streams and the flats in between which give one that feeling of the youth of the world which is so often talked about but seldom discovered. All the same, there is nothing new about New Zealand. The landscape gives one the impression that it has been there since the beginning of time. The mountains look like the mountains of the moon.

As for the proper natives of the country, the Maoris, brown, merry, and equally undevoted to work and to worry, and withal on the male side the best natural players of Rugby football yet discovered, they are, after Mr. Jones of Dwch-wlchy, the most curiously skilful fishermen of the world. A Maori boy of 6, or a Maori young man of 60, will walk into a patch of manuka bush, cut a six-foot limb as straight as he can find, peel it, whip on a ring at the point, and he has got his fishing-rod. He may possess an elementary brass reel, but probably he holds a skein of parcel string in his left hand, threads it through the top ring, attaches a foot of thick gut furnished with a hook disguised with a feather or two. He will then cast a perfect fly as far as he wants to, and search out every square inch of a pool where any rainbow can possibly be, with an easy accuracy that defies imitation. I was never able to surprise the secret of how the Maori persuades the fly to conduct itself like a small fish, perpetually within a few inches of the bottom. If there is a rainbow in the pool the Maori will have it out. On the other hand, quite a good fisherman from home may work out a pool blank with his ten-guinea split cane and furniture to match; then, if one who knows how, after a few minutes, will start at the head of the pool and fish it down with his fly, working near the bottom instead of from two to five feet too high in the water, he will likely enough pull out three lively fat strips of silver.

It happens that I never saw a Maori doing any work. I saw them standing about with tools by the roadside; but no doubt they do work sometimes with the inherent skill they exhibit with a manuka cane in their hands. At any rate, they are the only people in the world I have met whose fishermen by a river-bank never show the least trace of selfishness or jealousy. A Maori, with the same equanimity and a bland smile, will fish down a pool in front of you, or follow after you, will catch a fish for you, or invite you to land one of his own. It is his country, and you are perfectly certain (though you may not know it) to be paying him some modicum of rent for every square yard of water you yourself fish. That is what you buy your licence for, and not to maintain a landlord or a Fishing Association.

Indeed, this land of streams has many surprises for the man from home, at any rate in the Taupo district. The bottom of the lake is fine lava shale like little chips of oyster shell. But how this fine shale stays there is remarkable, since if a piece of lava becomes detached from a river-bank it floats down past you. Where bits of rock float down rivers one may hope for anything. One day I saw a specially round blob floating past me, so I picked it out; and after I had boiled it in water, steamed it, and soaked it in neat whisky, it proved to be the very best pipe in shape and substance I have ever come across since the days when one could buy truly good pipes for seven and sixpence in Colin Lunn's shop in the High at Oxford. But then there is no pipe tobacco ever invented at all in the same class as the Number Three Bulldog Toasted Navy Cut, which one can obtain in New Zealand, but which, owing to the annoyance of the proprietor with the Labour Government for interfering with the working hours of his employees, he refuses to export.

I would not say the same for the Labour Governments of Australia, but the Labour Government of New Zealand never caused me any inconvenience, and it has not yet devised any legislation to prevent a rainbow trout from seizing a fly with the dash of a hussar, and running away with the speed of a hare.

CHAPTER XX

HOLLYWOOD

THE approach to Hollywood by way of the South Sea Islands is as good as any other.

I do not include Australia in the South Sea Islands, because it is too large and not pacific enough. Nor do I include New Zealand, because it is too realistic. But Fiji, Samoa, Hawaii, and any other green speck in the ocean taken as worthy of approach by an American luxury liner may be regarded as a stepping-stone on the flat path in the direction of romance.

There could in theory hardly be a better way of approaching Hollywood than by a route which includes nothing except the sea that looks real. Even an American luxury liner, though doubtless a real ship, has many of the internal characteristics of a fairy-tale. You read on the wall of your cabin that you have only to press the button, ring up the central operator (always a young lady with a golden voice of cordial assent), and anything you require will happen. In due course your cabin-steward will appear, and anything you ask for will immediately be O.K.'d, but you do not necessarily live happily ever afterwards, even within the margin of that day, for none of the promises ever comes true.

Nevertheless, they let you sign a chit for anything, and there is nothing from a cine-camera to a campstool that you cannot obtain from the central store amidships on C. deck. You may never see an officer, or be sure there is a captain, but no doubt they are there; and any able seaman you chance upon is as good as a captain. Simply a matter of not being used to the way of life which drifts to sea from the mainland of America; and one lives in extreme comfort, in complete safety, on excellent food, and not a dull moment.

I happened to see a boat lowered at midnight into a placid

sea under the southern moon somewhere off Honolulu when
we were swapping captains with a sister-ship outward bound.

The band played, and after about an hour we obtained
a new captain to last us for the rest of the voyage. That
is to say, I saw him climb into the ship somewhere near the
waterline. But it was an adventure. So many different
authorities were in charge of the evolution, including a
boatswain in dungaree overalls, who had the loudest voice
and was most listened to, that the boat descended at an
obtuse angle with the horizontal, and one of the boat's crew
had omitted to hold on to his life-line. One had a feeling that
the whole manœuvre was organised as an entertainment for
the passengers. I should add that the incident ought not to
be taken as typical, because this was the first voyage of the ship
at the end of a three-months strike of nautical employees on
that side of America. There is no doubt, too, that the luxury
liner was navigated on perfect Great Circles from Auckland to
Fiji, and thence to Los Angeles via Samoa and Honolulu, nor
that the familiar strains of " Aloha " were in perfect time and
rhythm on all arrivals and departures.

These South Sea Islands are entirely up to reputation,
vividly green and blue and yellow, bathed in a perpetual sunshine of laziness. Gorgeous resorts for a month's holiday,
but not the sort of places to live a life in. In short, an ideal
route of introduction to Hollywood.

When one says Hollywood in that sort of way one means
Hollywood as it is supposed to be. There is nothing unreal
about Los Angeles, one of the biggest sea-ports of the world,
attached to the very biggest oilfield on earth; the fifth biggest
city in the United States. For an American city Los Angeles
is leisurely. The industrial neighbourhood is unexpectedly
presentable, because the oilfields at a reasonable distance look
like a forest of iron pine-trees and not at all like our own
forbidding conglomerations of slag-heap and chimney. Nor
indeed could any machination of man prevent the sunshine of
California from transmuting the industrial into the picturesque. Nor will any activity of man in California ever be
able to shed the traditions and culture left behind by ancient
Spain. You may barrage these with blocks and skyscrapers

and speedways and asphalt roads, but you will not be able to eliminate them from the general aspect of town and country.

Everyone knows now that Hollywood is a symbolic term for all the widespread suburbs and outer fringes of Los Angeles. Whether Santa Monica, on the sea, is a part of Los Angeles I have forgotten, but Culver City, where there are more film studios than in Hollywood, certainly is; and ten minutes or so in a motor-car will carry you to Beachwood and other pleasantly named centres of habitation, all of them well-stocked with studios. Not that the studios are obtrusive. They are simply, as it were, scattered Colleges of the central University of limelight.

We have been well instructed in the festivity and glamour and gorgeousness of this pervasive wonderland. We have also been well instructed in the opposite notion that Hollywood is steeped in laborious days of strenuous service to art, beginning almost at dawn, and all to bed by ten. So far as I could see, neither of these pictures is truer to life than the other. At any rate, the stars there, when they shine, shine for the most part in the daytime, and few of them have breakfast much before 9 a.m. Besides fixed and unfixed stars, there are planets whose risings and settings are irregular.

My general impression of this storied world was that everybody outside the purlieus of the city itself enjoyed themselves very much in the most delicious sunshine, took a great deal of exercise, and appeared peculiarly fit and full of life. Especially the children; and nowhere do the children of the reasonably well-to-do have a better time. No doubt I saw the best side of everything because I was there only a month, and was staying all the time with C. Aubrey Smith in his modern equivalent of a Roman villa, aptly scheduled as *The Round Corner*, up in the Beverley Hills.

If the more modern generation does not know that this erstwhile eminent actor-manager and present foremost figure of the films was in his regenerate days an England cricketer whose manner of bowling endowed him with the title of "Round-the-corner" Smith, all I can say is that this ignorance is one reason why cricket has gone to the dogs. If it has.

Roman villas were not necessarily large or palatial, but they aimed at embodying good taste with all that the Romans knew about comfort. Imagine a white Roman villa of moderate size, with a gabled roof of large, thick, red tiles, with a small apical tower surmounted by a cricket bat, ball, and wicket arranged as a weather-vane. This desirable residence on a spur-like shoulder among mountains covered with green bushes, and slit by occasional shelves of yellow stone, the house set in a steep garden on the edge of a deep valley with a little lake amid the black trees at the bottom; all of this under a perfect blue sky and caressing sunshine. Then you know how pleasant it can be to dwell in the Beverley Hills. But even then you will not know the perfection of the white bedroom in which I slept, nor the excellence of the tiled bathroom, nor will any pen be able to describe to you the marvellous effects of changing light that wash over the Beverley Hills in the hour before a reluctant sun decides he must leave the soft brilliance of California to a spell of velvet darkness.

Goodness knows what is happening in the other Roman villas dotted over the hillsides, quite far apart, or in the distant sea of electric light where lies Los Angeles, when the little wind at nightfall sends a sigh through the bushes on the mountains. But at *The Round Corner* there is the rest and quiet of an English home under a Spanish roof.

You must know that the first fortnight I was in Hollywood or within range of it, Aubrey Smith, who is certainly one of the hardest worked of the senior stars, was not working at all. The progress of the drama of " The Prisoner of Zenda " was at a stage where Colonel Sapt was not immediately concerned with the affairs of Ruritania. So, like many a new arrival in Hollywood, I did not get onto the sets at once. I did, however, get into a number of hospitable households where one met heroes and heroines leading a much more simple life than rumour allows to them.

Boris Karloff, for instance, has a home, of a size quite disproportionate to his celebrity, which is not easy to find because it is hidden in a thick patch of trees in a cleft of hills resembling one of the wooded combes of Exmoor, where the red deer hide. He is an ex-Indian Civil Servant and a noted Greek scholar; so his success as a monster is easily explained. He understands the type, from the Hindu fakir who likes sitting on nails, down to the Zeus of Olympus, who, as the protagonist of marital disturbances, may be supposed to be a main character of Hollywood. This does not prevent him from giving quite civilised parties several times a week to more people than can crowd into the maze of small rooms, a disposal of a covered staircase with many landings, on the side of a hill. There were always so many stars when I was there that you could not see the sky.

Less populous, but more approachable, was the home of Nigel Bruce. There is a boulevard leading into Los Angeles with broad strips of lawn the whole length of it, and an avenue of palm-trees. There, if you know the number of it, you can distinguish Nigel Bruce's spacious villa from the other white villas with red-tiled roofs. Otherwise you can enter by a gate at the back of the garden and be sure you are right because of the largest and deepest swimming-pool in the neighbourhood.

There one evening I sat in a cool salon and listened to Herbert Marshall, David Niven, Bruce himself, P. G. Wodehouse, three scenario writers (all engaged in writing the scenarios which P. G. had been imported at a high price to write), G. O. Allen (who is not on the films, but only escaped them by a skein of silk), and half a dozen other names that you would know if I could remember them. All were talking at once, all on different subjects, and nobody was listening to anybody else. In fact, I was the only one who was not talking. I was trying to listen to P. G. Wodehouse telling the air how he thought his own stories ought to be portrayed. But all I could hear was the silken voice of Allen trying to explain how perfectly charming was the lady.

Nigel Bruce, who is a good wicket-keeper, kept on asking questions about cricket and cricketers, but nobody paid any attention. The current captain of the England eleven appeared to have been employed lately in reviewing most of the more eminent lady stars, and would not talk about anything else.

Personally, I began with an advantage, because I saw quite a batch of the lady stars at a distance in a rather dim light in a resort called The Brown Derby, pronounced "Durby," much frequented by the *élite* for lunch and dinner. Quite informal, but very *recherché*. One felt one was seeing life. I came to the conclusion in the dim light that Constance Bennett was hard to beat. The worst of it was that there were some half-dozen other ladies who had succeeded in reproducing her appearance so successfully as to baffle distinction.

But so far as I could judge, the lady who made the best show out of doors in the searching sunshine was Mary Astor. She was the only brilliant lady I knew from the studios who came to watch the cricket matches.

The cricket matches were played on Sunday on the perfectly beautiful ground which a local urban council gave over to the enthusiastic disposal of Aubrey Smith. This park-like expanse of ideal turf has since been flooded out, but no doubt it will reappear. We had several first-rate cricket matches, in which neither Aubrey nor I altogether failed as bowlers. Indeed, I record with delight that in the first match I had to be taken off because I was getting too many wickets too quickly. This reminds me that Mary Astor was said to have said that she knew that Gubby Allen was a good bowler from the way he batted. I quite believe the story, because Mary Astor can say things and has quite enough wit to say a thing like that on purpose. It would go so well with her perfect two-piece tailor-made and her unarguable red hair. I am quite certain that everybody on both sides, except myself, thought that she had come specially to see him play. At any rate, it was worth while for anyone to sit on the grass with his back against a palm-tree and look at her.

I was not a bit surprised about a year afterwards to see Mary Astor climb off a tree-trunk after drifting three days in a storm called "Hurricane," looking as *soignée* and as fresh as from a beauty parlour in Paris.

I should add that G. O. Allen took the trouble to knock up an unexceptionable 77 not out, nearly as good as his innings in the Test Match at Brisbane. He tried even harder.

There is nothing at all fictional about the cricket in Hollywood. There are some quite good and keen players, including Ronald Colman. My nephew, Pat Somerset, looks very nice

in the field, but he did not make as many runs as I expected
of him.

Talking of cricket, I am reminded that a notable quality
of California is that one can suddenly plunge there into
strenuous exercise of a kind one has not indulged in for
years, and be delightfully surprised next morning by waking
up without a trace of stiffness. It is, I suppose, the peculiar
soft dryness of the air. Again, nowhere else does a cricket
ball look so large, so round, and so distinct; not even at the
Cape.

Ronald Colman was not playing cricket when I was there.
He was playing Rudolf Rassendyl in "The Prisoner of
Zenda." That was the film the greater part of which I saw
made in the Selznick studios.

The fascination of the big studios cannot be exaggerated.
The scale on which everything is done, the perfection of the
staff-work whereby everyone knows exactly what is wanted
every moment of every day, and the precise efficiency of the
execution remind one of a British battleship. Indeed, the way
the camera parties do their job recalls the accuracy and discipline of a gun's crew. What is more, no odd workman or
assistant is ever adrift. A whistle sounds, a voice calls for
Fred, and Fred appears in a blue overall with a hammer in
his hip pocket, runs up a ladder and drives in a nail. Another
whistle, and a call for Homer. Homer appears on the instant
with a tin contraption, and in a few seconds blows out a cloud
of incense to increase the darkness in the bushes on the edge
of the moat.

Most remarkable of all is the speed with which large castles
and city walls are built. One day I was down at Selznick's
watching Douglas Fairbanks and Ronald Colman doing the
famous scene in the dungeon in the Castle of Zenda, under
the direction of John Cornwall, with Black Michael looking
on in a chair beside me in the person of Raymond Massey.
Next day I went to see the continuation, but where I had
been sitting had now become a stone passage with a flight of
stone stairs and a castle gate at the end of it. And just across
a courtyard where the day before I had seen a huge empty
hall, rather like one of the old moulding lofts at Portsmouth

where the Nelson-time battleships were built, there was to-day a magnificent baronial hall with a huge fireplace of flaming logs, with great pillars and arches and high transomed windows. Nothing could more resemble ancient stone. The flicker of the logs under the open chimney was worthy of Glamis Castle.

That was not all. One had only to walk a dozen yards, through a forest of piled scenery, and there was the façade and the drawbridge and the moat of a veritable Austrian Schloss. The moat was very clever, because it was let into the floor only to the depth of a few inches, except for a narrow central ditch about five feet deep, into which Ronald Colman presently was to plunge in order to swim across to the castle. The bottom of the moat was painted a dark colour and autumn leaves were floating on the surface. Entirely realistic. What is more, Ronald Colman took three headers into the moat, and swam across three times in his tight-fitting black uniform in order to oblige the cameramen, who were perched on a long cantilever over the moat. Ronald Colman did not seem to mind how often he aimed his precarious plunge into the dark water; but he went away and changed into dry clothes every time. Stars must not catch cold.

One has to be careful in one's sidereal observations, because every principal has a "stand-in" who resembles him or her closely enough to be mistaken. Ronald Colman had a "stand-in" named Roosevelt, whom I pointed out to another visitor as the man himself after having watched the show for a week. The only "stand-in" I was sure about was Aubrey Smith's, because no one could quite duplicate his stature, aquiline distinction, and rugged aristocracy. His regular "stand-in" was a tall, retired English General. Nevertheless, I did see Aubrey Smith successfully duplicated. I do not think the scene was actually embodied in the film, but there was a shot in "The Prisoner of Zenda" when Colonel Sapt performed a terrific ride through the forest. For this I saw a perfect mask made of Aubrey Smith's face; first of all the cast and then the positive. This was grafted skilfully onto the face of Aubrey's other "stand-in," a tall, long-legged cowboy from Arizona. Aubrey performed up to the point of setting his left heavily spurred jack-boot in the stirrup. Then the camera picked up the cowboy at the point where he drove his spurs into the flank of his charger, and dashed off on the ride, doing several ambushes by the way. There was a similar incident when the principal actors began a duel up to the point of clashing swords, and the remainder of the fight was fought out by two mask-faced fencing masters. The illusion was complete.

Nor was illusion confined to the actors. There was a bit of a North-West frontier town which was, I think, used in "Bengal Lancer." As one entered the mud-built gate and saw the Indian railway station and the Indian train and the flat-roofed buildings, one had to pretend in order not to be in Peshawar. The train was made of wood, including the engine, but you had to tap it to find out.

Then, too, there was a street in outer New York and a section of a Chinese town which would pretty well deceive a native. Such scenery was not mere flimsiness and façade, but unexpectedly solid in real still life.

When it came to the actual shooting I do not know how many times Ronald Colman was required to dive into the moat, because when I was present he and the cameramen were merely rehearsing. But I did see Marlene Dietrich, Melvyn Douglas, and Herbert Marshall in the Paramount studios, doing one line of the film called "Angel," under the direction of Lubitsch, who for the matter of that acted all three parts himself, and played the piano too.

The setting was superb. A baronial hall, of the modern type, with every possible kind of wall decoration, pictures of ancestors, tapestries, suits of armour, and a forest of all periods of furniture. In the foreground was a piano. The husband, Herbert Marshall, stood on one side, leaning against the piano. Melvyn Douglas, the lover, stood on the other side. The two of them were trying to remember a tune by reciprocal hummings. Marlene was ready at hand to glance at a picture paper when required. When all was ready, Marlene strolled to the piano, drawling in her wonderful voice, "You two men are working too hard. You ought to relax. Let me play you something," and she sat down and played a sleepy waltz.

To me it appeared that this was quite all right the first time through. But Lubitsch thought otherwise, and the incident was repeated with intervals for about two hours. Lubitsch knew exactly what he wanted done, but what he wanted done grew under his hand.

In between each shot, after a pause for conversation and cigarettes, Marlene sat down at a dressing-table before a huge looking-glass which was wheeled in on small pneumatic tyres, and she was repaired with minute care by two specialists, even to the gold-dusting of the tips of her curls. As I was sitting next to the *prima figura*, I reckon I am one of the few living authorities who have synchronously seen her side face and front face. It occurred to me that I had never seen her side face on the films.

Marlene goes through the process of preparation, exhibition, and reparation with good-natured Nordic patience. Lubitsch concentrates on one detail at a time. For instance, the first shot had to be repeated because of a little ruffle just at the join of the left sleeve of the coat of the two-piece blue suit. After about an hour, Lubitsch was giving a lecture on the point that one of the gentlemen was the husband and the other the lover, and Marlene, would she please not look at them both with quite the same eyes when she addressed them as "you two men." Just about the time we had to tear ourselves away, Lubitsch was inculcating his conception of how she ought to sit down and play her tune. Please would she not drift straight away into her piece, but execute two or three preparatory runs up and down the keyboard. Like so. Marlene seemed to play pretty well, but Lubitsch played a great deal better. Indeed, he put as much style into his instruction as if he were on the concert platform with an audience of a thousand.

Lubitsch accepted the two gentlemen as mere pillars of the piano and of the situation. They could execute their tentative hum in search of their tune just as they liked. What they liked did not vary throughout the two hours, which was quite clever of them. It is not at all easy to hum rumpty-tumpty-tum with exactly the same tone and incidence repeatedly for two hours. What is more, they both of them worked their subsidiary glances exactly the same every time. When I saw the film afterwards in England they were still doing it.

One could not help being struck by the unvarying patience and good temper, not only of the performers, but of the four or five dozen other experts of various degrees, concerned in the operation of the simplest shot. There may be temperamental *primi signori* and *prime donne* in the film world, but I did not detect them. What is more, there seemed no grading of importance. Your Ronald Colman or Madeleine Carroll might drive up in a magnificent car, whereas Fred, the man with the hammer, arrived on his legs, but once inside they appeared to pal up as complete equals. None of the swells threw their slimness about. I noticed, however, that one and all treated Aubrey Smith with almost studied respect and deference, which treatment he always gracefully parried with paternal and friendly courtesy.

On the whole, the most interesting piece of film-making I saw was the scene in "The Prisoner of Zenda" when Rassendyl, having been crowned King of Ruritania, drives back from the Cathedral with Princess Flavia in the state coach. This went on for a whole morning. The properties were as usual superb, but the coach was supported like a sedan chair on four poles with a couple of stage hands on each side who jigged the vehicle to represent slight joltings over the cobbled pavement of Strelsau. The near side of the coach was not there. Ronald Colman in royal robes and crown and Madeleine Carroll in ermine and a coronet sat in state and repeated about ten lines of oscillating back-chat: sometimes as given in the script, otherwise in private conversation during the intervals. Through the side-window of the coach one could see Life Guards of Ruritania clattering along, but they were merely pictures on a conveniently disposed screen.

Ronald Colman kept on saying his lines wrong, but Madeleine Carroll knew hers with precision, and never once forgot to say "That's ber'er" in a perfect American accent, although, as you know, she is entirely English. If she had said "That is better" in an Oxford accent (she being a graduate of Birmingham University) Ruritania would not have gone down

in the Middle West. I know all about this because Mary
Astor explained it to me, sitting in a deck chair and looking
as attractive in black weeds as I had seen her in tweed tailor-
mades. At the time I began to feel quite sure that Mary
Astor ought to have been the Princess instead of figuring as
the lady who got Black Michael into so much trouble.

No doubt it occurs, but I was not lucky enough to see anybody engaged in overwhelmingly hard work on any of the
sets. Patience and repetition, yes; a good deal of patient waiting, too. Douglas Fairbanks, junior, employed in homely
fashion his intervals between fighting duels on drawbridges
and insulting everybody in Ruritania whom he did not like.
He used to stroll out of a side door, doff his doublet and
shirt and all else he could conveniently doff, sit down on a
baulk of timber and sunbathe his shapely torso. I thought at
the time that this would make a good shot to introduce into
the film. That is exactly what the debonair and attractive
villain, Rupert of Hentzau, would have done in real life.

Perhaps one does not obtain any proper insight into film
work by blowing in upon the sets for a casual half-hour here
and there. Nor indeed can one blow in casually, because the
big gates of the studios are carefully guarded and every
entrant checked and double-checked. I believe Sir Cedric
Hardwicke could not get into his own studio at one time. One
day I saw Sonja Henie in her silver Packard carefully inspected and cross-examined by a guard before she was
admitted.

If however one spends a privileged ten days regularly following the production of one particular picture, one does go
away with a fair comprehension of the meticulous detail and
constructive patience required in the making of these modern
marvels.

It may interest picture-goers to know that in spite of the
fabulous salaries of the actors, these salaries amount only to
ten per cent. of the total wage bill. This shows how large a
part is played by the technicians and other personnel of the
film world.

Many visitors to Hollywood have left on record their disappointment with Hollywood. The Hollywood they found

was not the Hollywood of their dreams. Perhaps it was that I had no dreams left after three months in Australia, the land which is the apotheosis of the wide-awake. But for my part, in many and extensive travels, I have never come across a more fascinating spot. Not that Hollywood is a spot. It extends itself into garden cities, garden suburbs, a vast countryside, locations in the plains, every kind of mountain with a distant backbone of the snow-capped Sierra Nevada. You can fish for trout in the hills, learn rodeo on the locations, ride in the Row before breakfast, obtain rather better lawn tennis than anywhere else, play golf and bathe to your heart content. So far as I saw, it is a world of wholesome, happy youth, middle age, and age. Artificiality may be hiding its head somewhere, but certainly it does not intrude.

The sunshine and the climate!

Even on the threshold of make-believe, life can be worth living.

INDEX

THE PAVILION LIBRARY

All books from the Pavilion Cricket Library are available through your local bookshop or can be ordered direct from Pavilion Books Ltd.

	hardback	paperback
Through the Caribbean Alan Ross	£10.95	£5.95
Hirst and Rhodes A. A. Thomson	£10.95	£5.95
Two Summers at the Tests John Arlott	£10.95	£5.95
Batter's Castle Ian Peebles	£10.95	£5.95
The Ashes Crown the Year Jack Fingleton	£10.95	£5.95
Life Worth Living C. B. Fry	£10.95	£5.95
Cricket Crisis Jack Fingleton	£9.95	£4.95
Brightly Fades the Don Jack Fingleton	£9.95	£4.95
Cricket Country Edmund Blunden	£9.95	£4.95
Odd Men In A. A. Thomson	£9.95	£4.95
Crusoe on Cricket R. C. Robertson-Glasgow	£9.95	£4.95
Benny Green's **Cricket Archive**	£9.95	£4.95

Write to Pavilion Books Ltd.
196 Shaftesbury Avenue
London WC2H 8JL

Please enclose cheque or postal order for the cover price plus postage

UK   55p for first book
       24p for each additional book to a maximum of £1.75

Overseas   £1.05 for first book
           35p for each additional book to a maximum of £2.80

Pavilion Books reserve the right to show new retail prices on covers which may differ from those previously advertised in the text or elsewhere and to increase postal rates in accordance with the Post Office.